The Sweetness of Life

This book examines the home and leisure life of planters in the antebellum American South. Based on a lifetime of research, the late Eugene Genovese (1930–2012), with an introduction and epilogue by Douglas Ambrose, presents a penetrating study of slaveholders and their families in both intimate and domestic settings – at home, attending the theater, going on vacations to spas and springs, throwing parties, hunting, gambling, drinking, entertaining guests – completing a comprehensive portrait of the slaveholders and the world they built with slaves. Genovese subtly but powerfully demonstrates how much politics, economics, and religion shaped, informed, and made possible these leisure activities. A fascinating investigation of a little-studied aspect of planter life, *The Sweetness of Life* broadens our understanding of the world the slaveholders and their slaves made, a tragic world of both "sweetness" and slavery.

Eugene D. Genovese, one of the most significant and distinguished historians of his time, spent a lifetime studying the society of the Old South. His books include *The Political Economy of Slavery*, *The World the Slaveholders Made*, *In Red and Black*, *From Rebellion to Revolution*, *The Southern Dilemma*, *A Consuming Fire*, and *Roll, Jordan, Roll*, which was awarded the Bancroft Prize. With his wife, the late Elizabeth Fox-Genovese, he wrote *Fruits of Merchant Capital*, *The Mind of the Master Class*, *Slavery in White and Black*, and *Fatal Self-Deception*. A past president of the Organization of American Historians, Genovese died in 2012.

Douglas Ambrose is the Carolyn C. and David M. Ellis Distinguished Teaching Professor of History at Hamilton College in Clinton, New York. The author of *Henry Hughes and Proslavery Thought in the Old South* and coeditor of *The Many Faces of Alexander Hamilton*, Ambrose was a student of both Eugene D. Genovese and Elizabeth Fox-Genovese.

Cambridge Studies on the American South

Series Editors

Mark M. Smith, *University of South Carolina, Columbia*
Peter Coclanis, *University of North Carolina at Chapel Hill*

Interdisciplinary in its scope and intent, this series builds upon and extends Cambridge University Press's longstanding commitment to studies on the American South. The series offers the best new work on the South's distinctive institutional, social, economic, and cultural history and also features works in a national, comparative, and transnational perspective.

Titles in the Series

The Sweetness of Life

Southern Planters at Home

EUGENE D. GENOVESE

Edited by
DOUGLAS AMBROSE

CAMBRIDGE
UNIVERSITY PRESS

CAMBRIDGE
UNIVERSITY PRESS

University Printing House, Cambridge CB2 8BS, United Kingdom

One Liberty Plaza, 20th Floor, New York, NY 10006, USA

477 Williamstown Road, Port Melbourne, VIC 3207, Australia

4843/24, 2nd Floor, Ansari Road, Daryaganj, Delhi – 110002, India

79 Anson Road, #06-04/06, Singapore 079906

Cambridge University Press is part of the University of Cambridge.

It furthers the University's mission by disseminating knowledge in the pursuit of education, learning, and research at the highest international levels of excellence.

www.cambridge.org
Information on this title: www.cambridge.org/9781316502891
DOI: 10.1017/9781316481189

First published 2017

Printed in the United States of America by Sheridan Books, Inc.

A catalogue record for this publication is available from the British Library.

ISBN 978-1-107-13805-6 Hardback
ISBN 978-1-316-50289-1 Paperback

For Anne Marie and Katie Fasulo
and
In Memory of Louis Fasulo (1951–2005)

Those who have not lived before the Revolution will never know the sweetness of life.

– Talleyrand*

* "Celui qui n'a pas vécu [au dix-huitième siècle] avant la Révolution ne connait pas la douceur de vivre."

Contents

Editor's Preface

I

Eugene Genovese died on September 26, 2012. In the five and a half years before his death and after that of his beloved wife Elizabeth Fox-Genovese on January 2, 2007, he dedicated himself to numerous projects. The first resulting publication, *Miss Betsey: A Memoir of Marriage*, appeared in early 2008.[1] The second, nicknamed "the Betsey project," resulted in five volumes. Working with his good friend David Moltke-Hansen, who served as the project's general editor, Genovese helped oversee the publication of the first four volumes, each devoted to a particular theme, of Betsey's shorter writings. The fifth volume, a reader, contained mostly selections of those essays deemed most significant from the four thematic volumes.[2] While this work was nearing completion, Genovese published in 2011 the third and final volume of his and Betsey's "master class" trilogy: *Fatal Self-Deception: Slaveholding Paternalism in the Old South*.[3] In declining health, shortly before his death, Genovese was attempting to put the finishing touches on *The Sweetness of Life*. Although not part of the "master class" series, it drew on many of the same materials to explore the way of life planters idealized, often in the face of daily experience, and committed to defend to the bitter end.

He sent out the manuscript for review by friends; he died as the reviews were coming in. Although by most measures a productive scholar,

[1] Eugene D. Genovese, *Miss Betsey: A Memoir of Marriage* (Wilmington, DE, 2008).
[2] David Moltke-Hansen, ed., *History and Women, Culture and Faith: Selected Writings of Elizabeth Fox-Genovese*, 5 vols. (Columbia, SC, 2011–2012).
[3] Eugene D. Genovese and Elizabeth Fox-Genovese, *Fatal Self-Deception: Slaveholder Paternalism in the Old South* (Cambridge, 2011).

Genovese did not publish as frequently as some, mainly because of the intensiveness of his research, but he always was able to write quickly once he had concluded that research. By late 2011, he no longer had the energy to write at his usual pace. He did incorporate some of the suggestions and edits that his friends provided, but by the summer of 2012 he simply lacked the strength to compose the introduction and conclusion to the manuscript. As Genovese told me during that summer before he died, he did not mind death, but he deeply resented his increasing incapacity to work on his unfinished final monograph.

Several months after Genovese's death, I received the computer files of *The Sweetness of Life*. The chapters themselves were in good shape; the writing was polished, most of the footnotes nearly complete. Practically every page of *The Sweetness of Life* rests on and reflects a lifetime of research. Yet, the volume has qualities that set it apart from nearly all of Genovese's other work. *The Sweetness of Life* concentrates primarily – but not exclusively – on describing rather than analyzing the Old South's master class. That descriptive focus encompasses, as does no other book he wrote as sole author, white women and children. Individual chapters indicate the lack of a tight, overarching argument; each chapter on the recreational and leisure habits of antebellum southern elites stands more or less on its own, without tight connections to chapters that precede or follow it. Thus, although the chapters have no clear ordering principle, I have decided not to alter Genovese's organization of them; they appear below as he had arranged them. The decision to present them as he had left them demonstrates my general editorial approach to the text; I have added some minor corrections and edits, but the chapters that follow closely resemble the manuscript Genovese left behind when he died.

Some of the chapters may strike the reader as incomplete, appearing more as catalogs than as tightly focused arguments. This is especially true of Chapters 4 and 5, whose titles, "Vignettes: Sundry Pleasures" and "Vignettes: Charms of High Life," capture the snapshot-like character of their content. Some chapters end abruptly. Some do not draw on some relevant scholarship, and this is not surprising, as much of it appeared after Genovese wrote. And some readers may find it curious that Genovese ends this volume by focusing on "matters not so sweet" even as he suggests that the overall "sweetness" of planter life helped lead the slaveholders into a death struggle to defend it. But these qualifying judgments in no way vitiate the book's value. The chapters, and the book as a whole, seek not to advance a particular interpretation, but rather to depict details of life: the joys of eating oysters or attending a concert by

Jenny Lind; the burdens and rewards of entertaining visitors; the rituals and social negotiations of courtship and marriage. Each chapter reveals Genovese's profound intimacy with his sources and his subjects. All of his scholarship has displayed this mastery of the material, but *The Sweetness of Life* does so in a distinct manner.

One senses that Genovese had been accumulating for decades the bits and pieces of evidence that fill the chapters in this book, storing them away like gems until he could mount them appropriately. His primary lifelong scholarly objective – establishing the distinctive character of southern slave society and the hegemonic leadership of the master class – led him to concentrate on the evidence that most effectively supported that goal. The preference of many mistresses for a dish of syllabub after dinner or the penchant of young men in the 1850s for double-breasted reefing jackets was not the sort of evidence that advanced that purpose. But when Genovese encountered accounts of planters' eating habits or fashion tastes or musical interests he knew that these matters, no less than the slaveholders' religious beliefs or political convictions, were parts of who they were, parts of the world they made and lived in relation to others.

Much of Genovese's scholarly work speaks to "big" historical themes – "the world the slaves made," "the mind of the master class," "slavery and bourgeois property in the rise and expansion of capitalism," "the political economy of slavery." Yet he knew that one needed to have a wide and deep knowledge of the people engaged in those big themes to understand and write convincingly about them. Although he ran the risk, especially in his earlier work such as *The Political Economy of Slavery*, of depicting the masters as a class and paying little attention to the particular constituent elements of it, he knew that however much classes acted as units within broad historical processes, they consisted of living human beings struggling to make sense of the meaning of life. And it is those human beings, whom he encountered in the sources in which he immersed himself during more than fifty years of research, who live again in the pages of the present book. No aspects of their lives, however apparently trivial to modern eyes, escaped his notice.

In *The Sweetness of Life* Genovese continued the pursuit of his "lifelong ambition of writing a comprehensive book on the slaveholders."[4] He ended up writing not one book, but several, and he knew that the

---

[4] "Eugene D. Genovese and History: An Interview," in Robert Louis Paquette and Louis A. Ferleger, eds., *Slavery, Secession, and Southern History* (Charlottesville, VA, 2000), 207.

larger project would not be "comprehensive" without a detailed account of the slaveholders' leisure. Genovese once wrote, "No subject is too small to treat. But a good historian writes well on a small subject while taking account (if only implicitly and without a single direct reference) of the whole."[5] *The Sweetness of Life* treats what many might see as a "small" subject, and Genovese certainly makes few direct references in the book to his "comprehensive" argument regarding the slaveholders and their place in history. Nor does he devote much attention to scholarly debates, as he did in much of his other work on southern history. But *The Sweetness of Life* adds immeasurably to that argument, revealing to us, as all of Genovese's work sought to do, that "the history of every people," including that of antebellum southern masters, "exhibits glory and shame, heroism and cowardice, wisdom and foolishness, certainty and doubt, and more often than not these antagonistic qualities appear at the same moment and in the same men."[6]

Although discrete chapters may lack sharpness in argument, taken together they vividly depict the wide variety of leisure activities in which southern slaveholders participated. These chapters required only a light editorial hand. The introduction and conclusion are, however, another matter. Genovese had composed a brief introduction, and I have included a version of it following the preface. In a private conversation a few months before he died, Genovese told me he knew that he would have to provide a more formal introduction, but, as mentioned earlier, he lacked the strength to write it. My edited preface seeks to fill that void, discussing *The Sweetness of Life* within the context of Genovese's *oeuvre*. Since the original manuscript lacks a conclusion, and Genovese left no rough or partial draft of one, I have added a brief epilogue. It evaluates the contributions of *Sweetness of Life* to an understanding of antebellum southern history and discusses in what direction Genovese's scholarship may have been headed had he not died.

II

"I have come," Genovese states in his brief introduction, "neither to praise nor bury the slaveholders but to limn some of the features of their

---

[5] Eugene D. Genovese, "American Slaves and Their History," in Eugene D. Genovese, ed., *In Red and Black: Marxian Explorations in Southern and Afro-American History* (Knoxville, TN, 1984 [1970]), 103.

[6] Eugene D. Genovese, "William Styron Before the People's Court," in Genovese, *In Red and Black*, 216.

lives, which may help us to understand them better, however harsh the ultimate judgment rendered." Here, the "features of their lives" concern neither ideology, nor religious belief and practice, nor the politics of the sectional conflict, although all these are present in explicit and implicit ways. Instead, Genovese focuses on how the slaveholders spent their down time: how they entertained guests, what they ate, where they vacationed, and what cultural activities – music, theater, hunting, dancing, opera, circuses – they partook of. The book thus differs in a fundamental way from nearly all of Genovese's other scholarly works. From its opening chapter, *The Sweetness of Life* immerses the reader in the world of leisure that the slaveholders made, but Genovese does so in an almost disarming manner, setting a leisurely tone to describe the leisurely life. Although he makes clear that this world was inseparable from and made possible by the world of master–slave relations that his other work so carefully delineates, he is not primarily interested in analyzing the connections between leisure and the other dimensions of the slaveholders' world. One gets the sense from reading Genovese's rich descriptions of the various aspects of planter leisure life that he wants "us to understand them better" by seeing them as more than actors in the great drama that tore the nation apart. Although the "harsh ultimate judgment" – a judgment that Genovese always emphatically maintained they deserved – must be "rendered," his depiction of the slaveholders at home allows us to see them in their fullness and to better comprehend them and the world they made. But by looking at leisure – at the seemingly nonpolitical, nonideological dimension of life – *The Sweetness of Life* enhances our understanding of the masters' political, ideological, and psychological commitment to that world and, thus, their willingness to sacrifice so much to preserve it.

However much, therefore, *The Sweetness of Life* may depart from Genovese's other work in terms of content and tone, it must be understood as an extension of a number of Genovese's central concerns regarding the history of the Old South. What strikes the reader when considering all of Genovese's work is the consistency of his interpretation over time. Although he, like most academics, modified, qualified, refined, and in numerous ways tweaked his arguments, his work as a whole maintains its overall unity. Genovese was more fortunate than many scholars in that he had several opportunities to publish reflections on his own writings decades after they first appeared. In introductions to the second edition of *The Political Economy of Slavery*, first published in 1965 and republished in 1989, *The World the Slaveholders Made* (1969; 1988), and *In Red and Black: Marxian Explorations in Southern and Afro-American*

History (1971; 1984), and in interviews and other forms of recollection, Genovese acknowledged how new evidence and other scholars' work had led him to reevaluate certain aspects of his understanding of the slave South. But those reevaluations never altered the foundation or the basic contours of the interpretive edifice he constructed over the course of his fifty-year career. Even his transformation from Marxist atheist to Roman Catholic in the 1990s did not substantively change his argument regarding the character of southern society and the nature of the sectional conflict. As he stated in an interview from the late 1990s, after he had returned to the Catholicism of his youth, "I developed my interpretation of the slave South from a self-consciously Marxist point of view, and I have found no reason to discard the essentials of that interpretation, which, if anything, I have strengthened over time."[7]

That interpretation, from first to last, understood the Old South as a modern slave society, in but not of the bourgeois, capitalist world that gave it life and, eventually, destroyed it in a great war between incompatible social systems driven by both ideological and material imperatives that those systems generated. The master–slave relation – an unequal but nonetheless contested struggle – provided the foundation of the southern social order and "permeated the lives and thought of all who lived in the society it dominated."[8] The slaveholders ruled southern society, albeit through constant negotiation with both their slaves and nonslaveholding whites. The hegemony the slaveholders exercised, like all hegemony, was never absolute or unchallenged, but it did allow them to protect the property basis of their power and their overall leadership of the Old South's economy, politics, and culture.

The Sweetness of Life reinforces and extends most if not all of these pillars of Genovese's interpretation of the slave South. Although one can read and enjoy it on its own terms – like all of Genovese's work, it displays his graceful prose, sly wit, sharp storytelling skills, and remarkable ability to evoke a time and place – it assumes even greater power when read as an integral if distinct part of Genovese's scholarly corpus. In a relaxed, gentle manner, Genovese demonstrates how much planter leisure life reveals his larger concerns with, among other topics, political and social negotiations among various white southerners; interactions – both friendly and not-so-friendly – between northerners and southerners; the

---

[7] "Genovese and History: An Interview," in Paquette and Ferleger, eds., *Slavery, Secession, and Southern History*, 206.
[8] Elizabeth Fox-Genovese and Eugene D. Genovese, *The Mind of the Master Class: History and Faith in the Southern Slaveholders' Worldview* (Cambridge, 2005), 1.

slaveholders' position within a transatlantic cultural world; and the slaveholders' complex cultivation and exercise of cultural hegemony. Uniting
and transcending all of these particular concerns looms Genovese's
understanding of both the master–slave relation as "the determining factor within southern civilization" and the tragic nature of the slaveholders
and their world.[9]

Genovese always understood classes as essentially relational. No class
existed in isolation from others, and the classes that constituted a social
order shaped one another through their various relations. Although, with
the enslaved, the master class was his main focus and the master–slave relation the most critical element in determining that class's character, he did
not neglect the role of nonslaveholding whites in shaping the slaveholders
and southern society. Some of his work highlighted the extensive and often
intense negotiations into which slaveholders had to engage with nonslaveholders.[10] In *The Sweetness of Life* those negotiations are not narrowly
political. They instead lie implicit in an aggregation of untaught feelings,
impressed into mind by customs, practices, and activities that, while having serious political consequences, primarily concerned cultural and social
relations. Some leisure activities, Genovese demonstrates, such as public
dances, cockfights, and hunting and fishing parties, promoted intermingling across class lines. Other episodes, such as masters making their private libraries available to poorer neighbors and encouraging – or at least
not forbidding – their daughters to marry nonelite men, helped facilitate
the social mobility that allowed talented and ambitious nonslaveholders to
rise in status. Both of these sets of activities minimized or blurred difference, and thus the potential conflict, among the white classes.

Some practices did reflect the tension within the South between the
aristocratic tendencies of the masters and the nonslaveholders' more
democratic, egalitarian displays. Although planters may have assumed
an attitude of noblesse oblige in certain circumstances, by offering,
for example, their carriages to "poorer neighbors off to a wedding or
other special occasion"[11] or entertaining the surrounding community
with a barbeque or similar feast, they had to avoid putting on airs that

---

[9] Drew Gilpin Faust, "The Peculiar South Revisited," in John B. Boles and Edward T.
Nolen, eds., *Interpreting Southern History: Historiographical Essays in Honor of
Sanford W. Higginbotham* (Baton Rouge, 1987), 79.

[10] See, for example, Eugene D. Genovese, "Yeoman Farmers in a Slaveholders' Democracy,"
Agricultural History, 49, 2 (April 1975), 331–342; Genovese and Fox-Genovese, *Fatal
Self-Deception*, 40–59.

[11] Eugene D. Genovese, *The Sweetness of Life: Southern Planters at Home* (Cambridge,
2017), 85.

might alienate nonslaveholders who jealously guarded their civil and
political equality and were sensitive to aristocratic pretensions. So too,
as much as masters followed the latest transatlantic fashions in dress,
they "had to be careful to dress in a manner congenial to local taste."
Genovese tells the story of aspiring Democratic politician Powhattan
Ellis of Mississippi, whose tastes for silk stockings and perfume,
mocked by rivals, "ruined his [political] career." And Genovese also
points to instances in which the cultural and social expectations that
accompanied slaveholder status helped solidify the slaveholders' class
hegemony but also posed serious threats to individual masters. Those
with political aspirations, Genovese notes, "needed a reputation for
generosity and willingness to help those in distress. They had to spend
freely on entertaining supporters and could not easily refuse to endorse
their notes." More than a few masters paid a high price for such "generosity," and, as Genovese makes clear, it was often the slaves of the
generous master who paid that price as financially strapped slaveholders sold off their human assets. By simply describing these aspects of
the masters' leisure life, Genovese reminds us of how class relations –
among slaveholders, nonslaveholders, and slaves – were inextricably
bound together and informed apparently nonpolitical leisure activities
in southern slave society.

Genovese's interest in the Old South, he once said, flowed from his
recognition that the Civil War – or War for Southern Independence, as
he preferred to call it – was the defining event in American history. Like
many Americans fascinated by that war's scale and significance, Genovese
sought to understand what could have produced such a long and bloody
conflict. As he memorably put it in his first book, "I begin with the
hypothesis that so intense a struggle of moral values implies a struggle of
world views and that so intense a struggle of world views implies a struggle of worlds – or rival social classes or of societies dominated by rival
social classes."[12] The political context in which the slaveholders operated placed them side-by-side and often face-to-face with Northerners
whose political power and ideological convictions increasingly threatened the slaveholders' welfare. Yet this process of ruling class conflict,
which Genovese believed became irrepressible, not only took time but
also required that many of the ties that had bound Southerners and
Northerners together had to weaken so that each side could ultimately

---

[12] Eugene D. Genovese, *The Political Economy of Slavery: Studies in the Economy and Society of the Slave South* (Middletown, CT 1989 [1965]), 7.

see the other as antithetical to its survival and flourishing. *The Sweetness of Life* details many of the ways in which leisure united North and South through common interests and activities – and how those interests and activities, like the political union itself, became gradually marked by suspicion and antagonism.

Although many of the chapters in this book describe instances in which Northerners and Southerners shared certain tastes or enjoyed some common activities – say, a love of oysters or a passion for pianos – Chapter 7, which focuses primarily on vacationing at the various spas and springs in antebellum America, contains the most sustained discussion of relations between Northerners and Southerners. These fashionable vacation spots welcomed patrons from all sections of the country, allowing slaveholders to mingle with Yankees at Saratoga in New York or at White Sulphur Springs in Virginia. This chapter also, and not surprisingly, devotes the most attention one finds in the book to both intrasouthern and intersectional political matters. The resort communities had an unwritten rule that "political proselytizing fell into the category of things just not done," but, Genovese immediately adds, "politics was everywhere." "The significance of the springs for southern politics can hardly be exaggerated, however much it proceeded *sotto voce*."[13] Southern political leaders informally caucused among themselves, cementing alliances and planning strategy. In addition to this internal southern political maneuvering, the springs also revealed the deepening sectional conflict. Between the 1830s and 1850s, "increasing numbers of Southerners received hostile receptions at northern springs" and "increasingly, Northerners and Southerners kept to themselves and interacted with cold formality." Some southern voices "cried out against summer treks to the North," objecting to everything from the draining of southern wealth to the "resentment, insults, and South-baiting" that slaveholders received from white and black Northerners. Yet, notwithstanding these objections, the sectional intermingling persisted. "Northern springs remained attractive," Genovese notes, and "possibly half of the Southerners who traveled to summer vacation spots in the 1850s still went north."[14] The description of relations between Northerners and Southerners, like most of the discussions in *The Sweetness of Life*, depicts an uneasily, even brittle, shared world of both conflict and coexistence, of "rival social classes" – here one of leisure and relaxation rather than of political union – that has not yet proved incapable of accommodating both of them.

[13] Genovese, *Sweetness of Life*, 210.
[14] ibid., 203–205.

III

In opening *Roll, Jordan, Roll,* Genovese's tour de force on "The World the Slaves Made," he wrote that slavery, although "cruel, unjust, exploitative, [and] oppressive," "bound two peoples together in bitter antagonism while creating an organic relationship so complex and ambivalent that neither could express the simplest human feelings without reference to the other."[15] In all his work on the Old South, Genovese insisted that the worlds of masters and slaves were made together. Such ties did not preclude the existence of spaces in which both had degrees of autonomy, but the classes developed in relation to rather than in isolation from one another. Although *The Sweetness of Life* focuses on slaveholders and their leisure, Genovese makes clear throughout the book that much of that leisure world reveals the ubiquitous presence and inescapable influence of slaves. Whether noting the presence of slaves providing service at dinner parties and other social functions, the contributions of African cooks to the South's distinct cuisine, or the enlistment of slaves in young slaveholders' romantic maneuvers, Genovese depicts how interwoven blacks and whites were in the southern social and cultural fabric. In this volume, Genovese refrains from analyzing slavery as a system of production and instead concentrates on illuminating the organically grown folkways that slavery generated even as he regularly reminds us that how masters and slaves understood shared activities could vary dramatically.

In noting these different understandings, Genovese echoes implicitly arguments from *Roll, Jordan, Roll* and *Fatal Self-Deception,* especially that being bound together in an organic relation hardly implied harmony between classes. In Chapter 4, for example, Genovese discusses the elaborate holiday parties many masters provided for their slaves. These masters, he notes, "doubtless gave their slaves an elaborate holiday with a view toward reconciling them to their lot and improving their productivity and discipline but also to reassure themselves of their own kindness and sense of Christian responsibility." That need for reassurance led these "self-serving exploiters" to see slave singing and dancing as "testimony to the slaves' contentment under kind masters." But the masters and mistresses failed to "grasp the satirical treatment of whites in songs and dances." What a slaveholder saw as affirmation of his benevolence towards "my negroes," the slaves themselves understood as an occasion not only for carnavalesque mockery of the master class, but also for

---

[15] Eugene D. Genovese, *Roll, Jordan, Roll: The World the Slaves Made* (New York, 1974), 3.

"enjoying each others' company and finding pleasurable moments in a grim world" (Chapter 4, 49, 48).[16]

Although some aspects of the relations between masters and slaves in *The Sweetness of Life* support Genovese's argument regarding the different meanings each class often derived from shared experiences, he does not focus on those relations to convey that argument. Interested as he is in capturing the fullness of his subjects' lives, Genovese often discusses slaves not because doing so advances a specific scholarly interpretation, but because they lived within the world he wishes to describe. Slaves accompany masters on hunting and fishing parties; they travel with them to summer destinations; they help accommodate guests who take advantage of their masters' hospitality; they sleep in their owners' bedrooms. What emerges most clearly from *The Sweetness of Life* is not the profundity of an argument about the master–slave relation, but, instead, the presumption of slave presence in nearly all aspects of the slaveholders' lives. One sees this especially in those episodes in which Genovese notes how foreign and Northern visitors to the South expressed shock at both the ubiquity of slaves and the intimacy with which masters and mistresses interacted with them. In his section on bedrooms in Chapter 2, for example, Genovese discusses how when "Catherine Hopley arrived from England to teach on a plantation, a slave girl offered to sleep on the floor of her bedroom," a practice common to many plantations, especially those in the low country. "Startled rather than charmed, Hopley declined." Similarly, "Frances Trollope raised her eyebrows when a Virginia gentleman told her that, since his marriage, he and his wife had grown accustomed to having a black girl sleep in their bedroom."[17] However much such accounts reveal the slaveholders' callousness toward those whom they subjected to such indignities, the casualness with which they acted vis-à-vis their slaves speaks volumes to the depth of their unconscious acceptance of the basic legitimacy of their world. In the decades leading up to the Civil War, abolitionists challenged slaveholders to examine the premises and assumptions on which their social order rested. *The Sweetness of Life* indirectly but powerfully reminds us that many Southerners either failed to accept that challenge or did so and found those premises and assumptions valid. The slaveholders who inhabit the pages of this book bespeak the confidence and the "fatal self-deception" with which they lived their lives – and with which they marched their society into a long and cataclysmic war to protect the social basis of those lives.

[16] Genovese, *Sweetness of Life*, 160, 152–153.
[17] ibid., 79.

Genovese alternates between casually describing a world of habit and custom in which masters assume the existence and legitimacy of slavery and interjecting sudden reminders of the brutal realities of slaveholding. By doing so, he captures both the all-too-human character of the masters – their aspirations to gentility, their love for their spouses and children – and the inhuman system that made possible those aspirations and, to a large extent, provided the means to express that love. Ice houses often permitted planters to keep food and beverages chilled throughout the summer, and southern publications advised slaveholders on how best to build and maintain these vital elements of gracious living. "On one matter" related to ice houses, Genovese notes, "the press remained silent: Ice houses also served as places to whip slaves severely out of the sight of squeamish whites."[18] In his detailed examination of the place of pianos and piano playing in slaveholder homes in Chapter 2, Genovese touchingly portrays loving husbands and doting fathers who "took unabashed delight in having wives and daughters play on good instruments" and who "swelled with pride at the musical accomplishments" displayed.[19] A master who "delighted to present a piano to his devoted wife and to accommodate a charming daughter's pleading and teasing" produced scenes of domestic refinement and familial love. Genovese then suddenly shifts the thrust of the discussion. "Yankee troops," he notes, apparently "sensed the pleasure pianos brought the young ladies, for they relished chopping them up. The more cultured shipped the pianos home to their own women." Although he recognizes that "meanness and greed" probably motivated most of these actions, he gently but devastatingly suggests that "perhaps the soldiers sensed that even some planters could only satisfy the passion of their sweet young things by selling a slave to pay for the piano that brought so much pleasure to family and friends."[20]

In that one seemingly modest sentence, Genovese conveys a powerful sense of the evil of slavery. And, as he did in all his work, he establishes the intimate, inseparable connection between the planters' physical comforts and their slaves' labor and, especially, their slaves' physical bodies. Passages such as this make *The Sweetness of Life* a study that both gently immerses the reader into the graceful life of slaveholders and simultaneously assaults him or her with the human costs of that life. This necessary tension between Genovese's admiration for the masters as "decent men and women" who sought to build a worthy civilization and his horror at the

[18] ibid., 58.
[19] ibid., 71.
[20] ibid., 73.

enormity on which it rested may well be the most distinguishing character-
istic of all his work, including, perhaps especially, *The Sweetness of Life.*
Consider thus his discussion of holiday celebrations in Chapter 4.
Genovese moves seamlessly from noting the joy experienced by slaves
during Christmas week to their "grim" mood at New Year's. Slaveholders
celebrated the ushering in of a new year, but slaves knew that it meant that
masters had to settle their business accounts. The harsh realities of business – of being entangled in and subject to the vicissitudes of local, national,
and global markets – meant that some slaves "faced sale to cover heavy
debts" or risked being hired out and thus being forced "to leave families
and friends for a year's work elsewhere." Like pianos and icehouses, "the
wonderfully festive spirit" of the Christmas holiday "had a dark side."
January 1, for many slaves, became known as "heartbreak day."[21]

IV

The Sweetness of Life thus represents another chapter in what Genovese
repeatedly called his "life's work." "I began my studies of the Old South
as an undergraduate," he wrote in 1988, "with the idea of writing a history of the slaveholders."[22] A recurring theme in that history, one that
The Sweetness of Life emphasizes from its very title to its last page, is
the tragic nature of the slaveholding class. Although some have criticized
Genovese for being overly sympathetic to the masters, he never permitted that sympathy for his subjects to excuse them from moral judgment.
Indeed, for Genovese, the tragic character of the slaveholders resided
precisely in their simultaneous holding of noble and ignoble qualities,
of being both admirable and reprehensible at the same time. Even as an
undergraduate "with a fierce and ... dogmatic Marxist bias," he came to
see the slaveholders as "surprisingly strong and attractive men ... who
stood for some values worthy of the highest respect and who contributed
much more to modern civilization than they have been credited with."
But he "also viewed them as objectively retrograde and as responsible for
the greatest enormity of the age – black slavery itself." As he continued

---

[21] ibid., 161–162.

[22] Eugene D. Genovese, *The World the Slaveholders Made: Two Essays in Interpretation*
(Middletown CT, 1988 [1969]), xxi. For other references to his history of the slave-
holders being his "life's work," see Eugene D. Genovese, "Hans Rosenberg at Brooklyn
College: A Communist Student's Recollections of the Classroom as War Zone," in
Genovese, *The Southern Front: History and Politics in the Culture War* (Columbia, MO,
1995), 22; Genovese, *Political Economy of Slavery*, xv; "Genovese and History: An
Interview," in Paquette and Ferleger, eds., *Slavery, Secession, and Southern History*, 202.

through the decades to study the masters, his "respect and admiration for the best members of that class" rose markedly. "But so," he wrote in 1989, did "my sense of horror at what, despite the best of intentions, they wrought. For the way white folks done black folks, as a former slave woman put it, they won't ever pray it away. The juxtaposition of these two aspects of the slaveholders' life and legacy defines the genuine historical tragedy to which they succumbed."[23]

Genovese drew a sharp distinction between the historical judgment of the slaveholders – a judgment that demanded that they assume "collective and personal responsibility for their crimes against black people" – and our need to recognize that "the Old South produced great men who, at their best, stood for some lasting values and for a way of life in many ways admirable."[24] Although he suggested that those values and admirable aspects of their way of life exposed some of the shortcomings and erroneous assumptions underlying the individualism and atomization of modernity, his primary motive for devoting his life to the study of the slaveholders was to understand what he always called "our greatest national tragedy": the Civil War. The slaveholders – like all ruling classes – often proved guilty of "ideological posturing, gaping contradictions, and a dose of hypocrisy," but they nonetheless fashioned a world that they sincerely believed preserved and promoted the best of Western civilization.[25] They destroyed their world in a great "counterrevolution against secular rationalism, radical egalitarianism, and majoritarian democracy," and their defeat, Genovese always insisted, we must accept as just.[26] But the study of history, he also insisted, is about much more than seeing the just cause triumph and the evil side defeated. It is, as *The Sweetness of Life* so beautifully but subtly demonstrates, to be reminded of "that melancholy wisdom so trenchantly offered us by Santayana, 'The necessity of rejecting and destroying some things that are beautiful is the deepest curse of existence.' "[27]

* * *

[23] Genovese, *Political Economy of Slavery*, xxiv. See also Eugene D. Genovese, *The World the Slaveholders Made: Two Essays in Interpretation* (Middletown, CT 1988 [1969]), xxii; Eugene D. Genovese, *The Southern Tradition: The Achievement and Limitations of an American Conservatism* (Cambridge, MA, 1994), xiii.

[24] Fox-Genovese and Genovese, *Mind of the Master Class*, 5; Genovese, *World the Slaveholders Made*, xxii.

[25] Genovese and Fox-Genovese, *Fatal Self-Deception*, 5.

[26] ibid., 3.

[27] Eugene D. Genovese, "Ulrich Bonnell Phillips: Two Studies," in Genovese, *In Red and Black*, 295.

Genovese left only a rough outline of an acknowledgments page. In it he thanks Barbara Orlsolits who "checked notes and quotations, collected materials, and offered encouragement and incisive comments on the text." He also thanks Hale Sheffield who "made available the letters on N. W. E. Long and related materials in his possession."

* * *

Preparing a great scholar's manuscript for publication proved a formidable intellectual and emotional challenge, especially since my relation with Genovese extended well beyond the mentor–student association. Humbled by the task, I leaned heavily on others to help me complete it. David Moltke-Hansen provided constant counsel and support. His friendship with Genovese and his immense respect for and understanding of Genovese's work made his comments and suggestions especially valuable. In the preface to *Fatal Self-Deception*, Genovese remarked that Karen E. Fields's "often biting criticism reinforced her reputation as one not to trifle with." Her extensive and incisive – and "often biting" – comments on a draft of *The Sweetness of Life* have improved it immensely. The manuscript also benefited from Fay Yarborough, who carefully read and critiqued an early draft. Genovese often remarked that a friend who is not a critic is no friend at all; Robert L. Paquette remains a most faithful friend and a superb critic. Mark E. Smith offered his characteristically thoughtful comments on the preface and epilogue. Joseph Capizzi offered valuable support and insights. William J. Hungeling, Genovese's friend and the executor of his estate, helped enormously, not least by shipping Genovese's hard drive and other important materials to me after his death. Robin Vanderwall provided indispensable assistance with the challenging task of turning multiple and non-uniform computer files into a coherent whole. Several Hamilton College students helped track down sources and polish up the footnotes; special thanks to Michael Adamo and Philip Parkes. At Cambridge University Press, Lewis Bateman demonstrated, yet again, why he is one of the most important figures in academic publishing. His professionalism, patience, and commitment to the project inspired and sustained me. Upon Lew's retirement, Deborah Gershenowitz and Kristina Deusch supplied encouragements and expert guidance. I am also grateful to Fred Goykhman for copyediting and to Bob Ellis for indexing the book. Sheila O'Connor-Ambrose read countless drafts, offered valuable comments, and kept me keeping on. Above all, she knows better than anyone how much this project constituted a labor of love to a man to whom we both owe more than we can ever calculate.

Editor's Note on Prices

Throughout *The Sweetnss of Life* Genovese cites amounts that masters and others spent on various items. In order to provide modern readers with some sense of what those amounts mean in terms of modern prices, I have compiled this basic guide. Economists and economic historians who measure the relative value of historic to modern prices warn that such calculations are complicated, and these figures are meant to suggest rough equivalences, not precise comparisons. I have provided commodity real price equivalents based on the calculations provided by MeasuringWorth, a website founded and supervised by Samuel H. Williamson of the University of Illinois, Chicago.[1] I have provided base-ten dollar amount equivalents from $1 to $1,000 for 1830, 1840, 1850, and 1860. All the modern amounts reflect 2014 dollars.

1830:

$1 = $26.50
$10 = $265
$100 = $2,650
$1,000 = $26,500

1840:

$1 = $28.30
$10 = $283
$100 = $2,830
$1,000 = $28,300

[1] www.measuringworth.com/

1850:

$1 = $31.30
$10 = 313
$100 = 3,130
$1,000 = 31,300

1860:

$1 = $29.40
$10 = $294
$100 = $2,940
$1,000 = $29,400

Abbreviations

AHR   *American Historical Review*

AS   *George Rawick, ed., The American Slave: A Composite Autobiography, 19 vols. (Westport, CT, 1972)*

DBR   *De Bow's Review*

DD   *Robert Lewis Dabney, Discussions: Evangelical and Theological, ed., 3 vols. C. R.Vaughan (Carlisle, PA, 1982) DD* indicates material from vol. 4, also based on Vaughan's editing (Harrisonburg, VA, 1994)*

DGB   *Dictionary of Georgia Biography, 2 vols., eds, Kenneth Coleman and Charles S. Gruff (Athens, GA, 1983)*

DHUNC   *Documentary History of the University of North Carolina, ed. R. D. W. Connor, et al., 2 vols. (Chapel Hill, NC, 1953)*

DNCB   *Dictionary of North Carolina Biography, ed. William S. Powell, 6 vols. Chapel Hill, NC, 1979–1994)*

EE   *Electronic edition*

ERD   *The Diary of Edmund Ruffin, ed. William Kaufman Scarborough, 3 vols. (Baton Rouge, LA, 1972–1989)*

HLW   *Writings of Hugh Swinton Legare [ed. Mary S. Legare], 2 vols. (Charleston, SC, 1846)*

HT   *The Handbook of Texas, ed., Walter Prescott Webb, ed., 3 vols. (Austin, TX, 1952–1976)*

JCCP   *The Papers of John C. Calhoun, ed. successively Robert Lee Meriwether, Edwin Hemphill, and Clyde N. Wilson, 26 vols. (Columbia, SC, 1959–2003)*

JSH   *Journal of Southern History*

LCL   *Loeb Classical Library*

QRMECS *Quarterly Review of the Methodist Episcopal Church, South*
SA   *Southern Agriculturalist*
SBN   *The South in the Building of the Nation, ed. J. A. Chandler,*
        12 vols. (Richmond, VA, 1909)
SLM   *Southern Literary Messenger*
SPR   *Southern Presbyterian Review*
SQR   *Southern Quarterly Review*
TCWVQ   *The Tennessee Civil War Veterans Questionnaires, ed. Coleen*
        Morse Elliott and Louise Armstrong Moxley, 5 vols. (Easley,
        SC, 1985)
TRP   *The Papers of Thomas Ruffin, ed. J. G. deRoulhac Hamilton,*
        4 vols. (Raleigh, NC, 1918),
TSW   *Complete Works of the Reverend Thomas Smyth, D. D., ed.*
        J. William Flinn, 10 vols. (Columbia, SC, 1908)
WMQ   *William and Mary Quarterly*

Manuscript Collections

* Southern Historical Collection at the University of North Carolina

Samuel Agnew Diary*
James W. Albright Diary and Reminiscences*
Harrod C. Anderson Papers, at LSU
Ashmore Plantation Journal*
Everard Green Baker Diary*
Barbour Papers, at University of Virginia
Barnsley Papers*
Mary Eliza Battle Letters, at North Carolina State Archives (Raleigh)
Thomas L. Bayne Autobiographical Sketch*
Taylor Beatty Diary *
Mary Jeffreys Bethell Diary*
John Houston Bills Papers*
Priscilla Bond Diary, at LSU
Esther G. Wright Boyd Notes and Recollections, at Tennessee State
   Library and Archives (Nashville)
Brashear and Lawrence Family Papers *
Gustave A. Breaux Diaries, at Tulane University
Keziah Brevard Diary, at USC
Annie Laurie Broidrick, "A Recollection of Thirty Years Ago," at LSU
Catherine Barbara Broun Diary *
William Phineas Browne Papers, at State of Alabama Department of
   Archives and History (Montgomery)
Lucy Wood Butler Diary*
Cabell-Ellet Papers, at University of Virginia

Campbell Family Papers, at Duke University
Franc M. Carmack Diary*
Eliza Ann Carmichael*
Kate Carney Diary*
Carson Family Papers, at Tennessee State Library and Archives (Nashville)
Alexander Chesney Journal, at Library of Congress
Mary Jane Chester Papers*
Langdon Cheves III Collection, at South Carolina Historical Society (Charleston)
Eliza Clitherall Autobiography*
John Fletcher Comer Farm Journal*
Concordia Parish (La.) Inquest File, at LSU
John Hamilton Cornish Diary*
Thomas Edward Cox Account Books*
Edward Cross Papers, at University of Arkansas (Fayetteville)
Anne Tuberville (Beale) Davis Diary and Meditations*
Louis M. De Saussure Plantation Record Book
Dromgoole and Robinson Papers, at Duke University
Marcus B. De Witt Papers *
B. Franklin Doswell Papers, at Washington and Lee University
Durnford Letters, at Tulane University
John Early Diary*
William Ethelbert Ervin Journal*
Holden Garthur Evans Diary, at Mississippi Department of Archives and History (Jackson)
Alexander K. Farrar Papers, at LSU
Lucy Muse Walton Fletcher "Autobiography," Summer, 1844, at Duke University
Mary G. Franklin Papers, at Duke University
Lucy Virginia French Smith Diaries, at Tennessee State Library and Archives
Thomas Miles Garrett Diary*
Gayle Family Papers, at State of Alabama Department of Archives and History
Sarah Gayle Diary*
Julia A. Gilmer Diary *
Graham Philosophic Society Minute Books, at Washington and Lee University.
Iveson L. Graves Papers*

James H. Greenlee Diary*
John Berkeley Grimball Diary*
Meta Morris Grimball Journal*
William Hooper Haigh Diary and Letters*
Herndon Haralson Papers *
Henderson Papers*
Gustavus A. Henry Papers*
Carolyn Lee Hentz Papers*
William P. Hill Diary*
Mrs. Isaac Hilliard's Diary*
William H. Holcombe Papers*
Robert Philip Howell Memoirs*
Franklin A. Hudson Diaries*
Hughes Family Papers*
Fannie Page Hume Diary*
Susan Nye Hutchinson Papers*
Andrew Hynes Papers, at Historic New Orleans Collection
Meredith Flournoy Ingersoll, comp., "Excerpts from the History of the
    Flournoy Family" (typescript), at LSU
Jackson–Prince Papers*
Joseph Jones Collection, at Tulane University
Mitchell King Papers*
Thomas Butler King Papers*
Carl Kohn Letter Book, at Historic New Orleans Collection
Dewitt Langston, Jr., "Memories of My Family" [typescript in private
    possession of Caroline Langston] at LSU
Lea Family Papers*
Francis Terry Leak Diary *
Ledoux and Company Record Book, at LSU
George Lester Collection, at LSU
N. W. E. Long, C. S. A., Letters, 1862–1864, in Private Possession
Louisiana: West Feliciana Parish Police Jury Minutes, 1850
Eliza L. Magruder Diary, at LSU
Basil Manly Sr. Papers*
Basil Manly Jr. Papers*
Eliza Ann Marsh Diary*
Massenburg Farm Journal*
McBryde Family Papers*
Duncan G. McCall Plantation Journal and Diary, at Duke University
William McKean Letterbook, National Archives

Lucilla Agnes (Gamble) McCorkle Diary*

Mayes-Dimitri-Stuart Papers, at Mississippi Department of Archives and History (Jackson)

John McLaren McBryde Papers*

Dr. McGuire Diary, at Tulane University

McIntosh Papers*

James Wistar Metcalfe Papers and Diary*

William Porcher Miles Papers*

Minis Collection*

Mitchell Account Book, at North Carolina State Archives (Raleigh)

Columbus Morrison Journal*

John Nevitt Plantation Papers*

Newstead Plantation Diary*

Flavellus G. Nicholson Journal, at Mississippi Department of Archives and History (Jackson)

Dr. James Norcom Papers, at North Carolina State Archives (Raleigh)

Norton-Chilton-Demeron Papers *

Haller Nutt Papers, at Duke University

James H. Otey Papers*

Outlaw Papers*

Louise Taylor Pharr Book*

Physician's Fee Book*

Philip Henry Pitts Diary and Account Book*

Planters' Club Letters: Hancock County, Ga.. (ms), at Georgia, Department of Archives and History (Atlanta)

Abram D. Pollock Papers *

William Campbell Preston Papers, at USC

Prudhomme Papers*

Quince-Watters Papers*

John A. Quitman Papers*

David A. and Malinda B. Ray Papers*

Renwick Papers, at Duke University

David Rice Plantation Journal, at LSU

Alfred Landon Rives Papers, at Duke University

Roach-Eggleston Papers*

Benjamin and B. W. Robinson Papers*

Nancy McDougall Robinson Collection, at Mississippi Department of Archives and History (Jackson)

Edmund Ruffin Papers*

Elizabeth Ruffin Diary*

George Washington Sargent Papers
H. M. Seale Diary, Jan. 10, 1857, at LSU
Senior Speeches North Carolina Collection*
Leah and Rebecca Simpson Papers *
Singleton Family Papers*
Alonzo Snyder Papers, at LSU
Southall and Bowen Papers*
Leonidas Pendleton Spyker Diary, at LSU
Henri de St. Geme Papers, at Historic New Orleans Collection
Ferdinand Lawrence Steel Papers *
Frank F. Steel Papers *
Stirling Papers, at LSU
Sturdivant Plantation Records*
Francis Taylor Diary*
Ella Gertrude Clanton Thomas Diary, at Duke University
Thornwell Papers, at USC
William F. Tucker Papers*
Tureaud Papers, at LSU
Dr. H. M. Turner Account Book*
Tyler Family Papers, at College of William and Mary
Isaac Barton Ulmer Papers*
William D. Valentine Diaries*
Sarah Lois Wadley Private Journal
John Walker Diary*
Samuel Walker Diary, at Tulane University
Walker-Reid Memoranda*
Henry Clay Warmoth Magnolia Plantation Journal*
West Manuscripts, at South Carolina Historical Society (Charleston)
James William White Papers*
Robert and Newton Woody Papers, at Duke University
B. C. Yancey Papers*

Introduction

A land without ruins is a land without memories – a land without memories is a land without history.

        – *Fr. Abram Joseph Ryan, "A Land Without Ruins"*[1]

The South, bitterly lamenting its defeat, dwelt neither on class privileges, nor on racial arrogance, nor on the exploitation and oppression of blacks. Rather, as expressed by Father Abram Joseph Ryan, "the poet of the Lost Cause," it bore witness to a lost world experienced by its ruling class as one of republican virtue, manly courage, and a Christian life. Since I know how the lament sounds these days, let me recall two anecdotes.

Sometime in the 1960s, shortly after I had published my first book, *The Political Economy of Slavery*, I had the pleasure of attending a small dinner party in Charlottesville, Virginia, hosted by Willie Lee Rose – that great southern lady – and her husband. The conversation turned to my book, which Willie Lee was praising, when William Abbott, editor of the *Journal of Southern History*, remarked – with greater perspicacity than most of my reviewers showed – that, although the book was impressive and all that, he nonetheless gagged on it. Why so, asked Willie Lee. "Because the underlining theme of the book is that the slaveholders were honorable, courageous, and admirable people, who could not be intimidated or bought off and who would fight to the death for their principles. Gene was saying that since slavery was an enormity not to be borne, our slaveholding grand pappies had to be killed." I remarked, "Nothing

---

[1] Abram Joseph Ryan, *Father Ryan's Poems* (Mobile, AL, 1879), 54.

personal, Bill." He gave me a southern "Uh-huh," and retorted, "I know, Gene, but, still, it goes down mighty hard in these parts."

For some twenty years, my friend, the late Professor Charles Crowe of the University of Georgia, and I sparred over our respective attitudes toward the Old South and the slaveholders. Charles was a rough polemicist who did not spare his adversaries, whether friends or not. On more than one occasion I felt his lash. One day I gave a paper at a conference at the University of Georgia, after which he confronted me: "Gene, listening to you, I finally figured out why you are so soft on the slaveholders. You actually like those people." I could not tell a lie: "Yes, Charles, I do."

A point of explication: In 1968, I wrote: "In irreconcilable confrontations ... it is precisely the most admirable, manly, principled, and by their lights moral opponents who have to be killed; the others can be frightened or bought."[2]

When I began my study of the Old South as a senior at Brooklyn College, I received a shock. I grew up in Brooklyn in a working-class Sicilian-American family. At age fifteen, to the distress of my parents, I joined the young Communist movement. Knowing nothing of the Old South, I had imbibed the stereotypes and prejudices that continue to lead Northeasterners – and guilt-ridden Southerners – into a Manichean view of the slaveholders. I worked on an Honor's Paper on agricultural reform in the Old South and plunged into primary sources. I could not believe what I was finding. The slaveholders – or a great many of them – whom I had been taught were blood-sucking sadists, interested solely in economic gain, turned up as thoughtful, educated critics of the nineteenth-century society and moral order. The best of them courageously defended their "way of life" and a social system they believed immeasurably more humane than the emergent world capitalist system. And that "way of life," resting as it did on slavery – on the oppression and exploitation of black people – had many admirable qualities and quotidian moments that prepared the slaveholders to stake their lives on it.

I have come neither to praise nor bury the slaveholders, but to limn some of the features of their lives, which may help us understand them better, however harsh the ultimate judgment rendered. Yes, I do "like them" – and I see as genuine tragedy the equanimity with which they allowed their finest qualities to proceed *pari passu* with their worst in defense of a historical enormity.

---

[2] Eugene D. Genovese, "To the Editor," *American Historical Review* 73 (1968): 995.

I

A Gracious People

High living and hospitality were universal. Well-bred gentlemen set the key-note for good manners; horse-racing; fox-hunting; fish-fries; bird-suppers; and whist parties brought the people together and promoted good fellowship. The old Virginia gentleman was the beau ideal in the mind of every aspiring youth of that day.

– *The Reverend Dr. William S. White of Virginia*[1]

HOSPITALITY

Life in southern slave society centered in the countryside – in plantations, farms, and villages. Charleston, Richmond, and New Orleans aside, most southern cities looked like small towns to visiting Europeans and Northerners. Towns with a thousand or so people anchored slave society culturally, socially, and politically. They did not threaten to dominate the countryside, as did the cities and commercial towns during the transition from seigneurial to bourgeois society in Europe and from rural-freehold to bourgeois society in the North. In the heartland, many miles often separated farms and plantations. Frederick Law Olmsted, traveling through northern Mississippi in the 1850s, remarked that rarely did a plantation have a dozen "intelligent families" within a day's ride: "Any society that a planter enjoys on his estate must, therefore, consist in a great degree of permanent guests." To overcome isolation, churches and county court-houses provided meeting places for social and educational events. In the

---

[1] *"Stonewall" Jackson's Pastor: Rev. William S. White, D. D., and His Times (1800–1873): An Autobiography* (Harrisonburg, VA, 2005 [1891]), 17.

larger communities, political barbecues, dinners, and rallies supplemented them. Brief and extended visits from friends and kin enhanced social life.[2]

"In those days," wrote the well-respected scientist Joseph LeConte of Georgia, "literally everybody was glad to see everybody else and to have a visitor stay as long as possible, and no one had the least hesitation in doing so." LeConte recalled that his northern uncle spent winters at his father's rice plantation, and that Alfred Nisbet, who supported a wife and five children on $2,000 a year, entertained no thought of limiting his guests' stay. A story may be apocryphal, but folks in the low country accepted it as paradigmatic: A couple came to spend their honeymoon on John Couper's plantation on St. Simons and stayed until the birth of their second child.[3]

"Virginia hospitality" – a commonplace in the eighteenth century – metamorphosed into "southern hospitality" in the nineteenth. Northern states, notably Massachusetts, promoted rural inns to discourage individuals from turning their homes into stopping places for travelers. Virginia did the opposite. Early in the nineteenth century, American inns, especially in the South, were generally of poor quality. Travelers preferred to stay with families that supplemented their incomes and had much better facilities. Generally, travelers had pleasant experiences, but some hosts resented having to take them in. The Marquis de Chastellux, Louis-Philippe, and James Stuart found some women who boarded strangers surly, peevish, and resentful. In the absence of local taverns, the inflow of visitors, including passers-by, compelled some of the well-to-do to charge for food and lodgings they might have provided without cost under other circumstances. Travel in Texas replicated travel in the East. In 1858, Louise Wigfall and her father found lodgings at a farmhouse, "whose owners were accustomed, in a country where there were no inns, to receive occasional travelers."[4]

---

[2] Frederick Law Olmsted, *A Journey in the Back Country* (New York, 1970 [1860]), 120.
[3] William Dallam Armes, ed., *The Autobiography of Joseph LeConte* (New York, 1903), 60, quote at 105; [Joseph LeConte], *LeConte's Report on East Florida*, ed. Richard Adicks (Orlando, FL, 1978), 6, 8; on Couper see Barbara Hull, *St. Simons Enchanted Island: A History of the Most Historic of Georgia's Fabled Golden Isles* (Atlanta, GA, 1980), 60.
[4] Seymour Dunbar, *A History of Travel in America*, 4 vols., (New York, 1968 [1915]), 1:221–222; Gaillard Hunt, *As We Were: Life in America, 1814* (Stockbridge, MA, 1993), 53–54; Louis-Philippe, King of France, *Diary of My Travels in America*, tr. Stephen Becker (New York, 1976), Apr. 26, 29, 1797; James Stuart in William Brownlow Posey, ed., *Alabama in the 1830's, As Recorded by Travelers* (Birmingham, AL, 1938), 6; William M. Mathew, ed., *Agriculture, Geology, and Society in Antebellum South Carolina: The Private Diary of Edmund Ruffin* (Athens, GA, 1992), Mar. 15–18 (141), Apr. 20–22, 1843

Southerners counted hospitality among the Christian virtues, which included forbearance. And many Christians needed all the forbearance they could muster. Anna Matilda King of the St. Simon's, Georgia, wrote to her son that Miss Margaret Cuyler had concluded a three-week visit: "She is on the whole more bearable – than on her former visits." Aunt Yates, a friend rather than kin of Mississippi's David Holt and family, arrived for weeks or months at a time. Unfortunately, she was forever rebuking the children for boisterousness, albeit to little avail.[5]

Yet, Richard Beale Davis, in *Intellectual Life in Jefferson's Virginia*, suggests that the manners of Virginia gentlemen may have owed as much to such ancients as Aristotle and Horace as to Christianity. Southerners seem to have accepted Jonathan Swift's Ciceronian description of good manners as "the art of making those people easy with whom we converse." Thomas Jefferson spoke of "our practice of placing our guests at their ease and showing them we are so ourselves." In that spirit, Thomas Roderick Dew praised the "unbounded" hospitality of the ancient Greeks, the medieval Europeans, the Arabs, and the Tartars. Abolitionists acknowledged southern hospitality but with a nasty twist. James Birney hurled a grenade at Senator F. H. Elmore of South Carolina, charging that the vaunted southern hospitality rested on "unpaid wages of the laborer – the robbery of the poor."[6]

(209–210); Mrs. D. Giraud Wright [Louise Wigfall], *A Southern Girl in '61: The War-Time Memories of a Confederate Senator's Daughter* (New York, 1905), 4–5.

[5] A. M. King to Lord King, May 15, 1849, in Anna Matilda King, *Anna: The Letters of a St. Simons Plantation Mistress*, ed. Melanie Pavich-Lindsay (Athens, GA, 2002), 57; Thomas D. Cockrell and Michael B. Ballard, eds., *A Mississippi Rebel in the Army of Northern Virginia: The Civil War Memoirs of Private David Holt* (Baton Rouge, LA, 1995), 4, 22–24; Thomas D. Cockrell and Michael B. Ballard, eds., *A Mississippi Rebel in the Army of Northern Virginia: The Civil War Memoirs of Private David Holt* (Baton Rouge, LA, 1995), 4, 22–24;

[6] Cynthia A. Kierner, "Hospitality, Sociability, and Gender in the Southern Colonies, *JSH* (1996), 455; Richard Beale Davis, *Intellectual Life in Jefferson's Virginia, 1790–1830* (Chapel Hill, NC, 1964), 6; Swift quoted in Caroline Moore, "Being a Gentleman: Manners, Independence and Integrity," in Digby Anderson, ed., *Gentility Recalled: "Mere" Manners and the Making of the Social Order* (London, 1996), 57; Jefferson quoted in William Howard Adams, *The Paris Years of Thomas Jefferson* (New Haven, CT, 1997), 16; Thomas Roderick Dew, *Digest of the Laws, Customs, Manners, and Institutions of the Ancient and Modern Nations* (New York, 1884 [1852]), 47; James G. Birney, "Correspondence," *Anti-Slavery Examiner*, May 1, 1838, p. 28. For "unpaid labor," see Elizabeth Fox-Genovese and Eugene D. Genovese, *Slavery in White and Black: Class and Race in the Southern Slaveholders' New World Order* (New York, 2008), 158–163.

Brushing off carping abolitionists, young ladies held gentlemen to high standards of deportment and did not take kindly to undue familiarity. The young Maria Bryan explained her unfavorable reaction to a Mr. Bailey, who arrived from the North to teach at Mount Zion Academy in Georgia in 1826: "I am very much disappointed with him indeed. He is very good looking in face and person, really handsome at times, but he is so much a coxcomb in his manners that it does away with all the agreeable impression he makes." More particularly, the ladies carefully monitored the manner in which men addressed them. Emma Holmes of Charleston resented men who addressed ladies they hardly knew by their Christian names, and Dr. Strother much irritated the young Sarah Lois Wadley when he called her "Miss Sarah": "Tabitha and I exchanged glances. I had said that evening that I liked to be called 'Miss Wadley' by new acquaintances. She had said that evening that she expected to be called 'Miss Wadley' by new acquaintances."[7]

Chastellux declared Virginians deserving of their reputation "for living nobly in their homes and of being hospitable. They receive strangers both willingly and well." More than a half-century later in Lexington, Margaret Junkin paralleled "fox-hunting English," "smoking Germans," and "opium-eating Chinese" with "visiting Virginians." Without large cities, Virginians created society in their rural neighborhoods and had slaves prepare and serve food and look after guests. As a much-appreciated bonus, gentlemen who stayed overnight at the plantation could expect brandy or wine for a nightcap and an "eye-opener" when they awoke the next morning or at the breakfast table. From the seventeenth century, many Virginians routinely had a mint julep before breakfast. In eighteenth-century Virginia even children had an eye-opener of peach brandy with mint and crushed ice. William Wells Brown's master, mistress, and young son loved their pitcher of mint julep before morning prayers and breakfast. Brown, allowing, "I loved the julep as well as any of them," maneuvered to get a share. Even in the low country and on the Sea Islands, passers-by of various kinds received a warm welcome from whites and blacks. Blacks acquired a reputation for sharing food with anyone who stopped by – gifts, not sales. For reasons whites could not fathom, most slaves had plenty of eggs. In the lonely and monotonous

---

[7] Maria Bryan to Julia Ann Bryan Cumming, Dec. 11, 1826, in Carol Bleser, ed., *Tokens of Affection: The Letters of a Planter's Daughter in the Old South* (Athens, GA, 1996), 15; Emma Holmes, Feb. 26, 1861, in John F. Marszalek, ed., *The Diary of Miss Emma Holmes* (Baton Rouge, LA, 1979), 9; Wadley Private Journal, Mar. 23, 1863.

upcountry, numerous relatives and friends were welcome to stay for weeks. Junius Hillyer remarked, "Our house was scarcely ever free from company." Upcountry warmth extended even to Yankee peddlers whom Hillyer acknowledged as "educated and gentlemen in their manners and men of fine sense."[8]

D. W. Mitchell, an Englishman who spent a decade in America, primarily in Virginia, embraced Southerners as a sociable people who exchanged unceremonious visits. Younger family members spent days and weeks together with neighbors and relations: "They are also fond of a rural life; more so, I think, than the English. In this respect it is very different in the North, where rural life seems to be a life of repulsive drudgery, and the towns are looked to for pleasure, ambition, refinement, and social intercourse." British travelers, whether pro- or antislavery, extolled the rough Southwest.[9]

Like planters across the South, Alexander Stephens of Georgia gave guests the run of the place to do pretty much as they pleased. Leonidas Polk of Tennessee and Louisiana rarely had two consecutive days without company for breakfast, dinner, or supper or without overnight guests, but the family routine proceeded as usual. Between meals guests entertained themselves. Yet their wants were looked after and frequently anticipated by the slaves who would often seem invisible. "G. M.," a Northerner, wrote of the typical South Carolinian: "He has in his carriage and feelings, something of the Don; yet he is republican and would not exact from another what he would be unwilling to render in return. Be generous and confiding, and he will out-do you in generosity and confidence." A Canadian recalled from his visit to the McCords and Hamptons in

---

[8] Marquis de Chastellux, *Travels in North America in the Years 1780,1781, and 1782*, 2 vols., rev. tr. H. C. Rice, Jr. (Chapel Hill, NC, 1963), 2:441; Margaret Junkin Preston to [?], Nov. 25, 1850, in Elizabeth Preston Allan, *The Life and Letters of Margaret Junkin Preston* (Boston, MA, 1923), 49; Mrs. Pryor [Sara Agnes Rice Pryor], *Mother of Washington and Her Times* (New York, 1903), 198; William W. Brown, *Narrative of William W. Brown, An American Slave, Written by Himself* (London, 1849), 13; T. Reed Ferguson, *The John Couper Family at Cannon's Point* (Macon, GA, 1994), 77–82; Henry William Ravenel, "Recollections of Southern Plantation Life," ed. Marjorie Stratford Mendenhall, *Yale Review*, 25 (1936), 757; *The Life and Times of Judge Junius Hillyer: From His Memoirs* (Tignall, GA, 1989), 45.

[9] D. W. Mitchell, *Ten Years in the United States: Being an Englishman's Views of Men and Things in the North and South* (London, 1862), 30. Travelers' comments in Posey, ed., *Alabama in the 1830's*, 4. For nightcaps and eye-openers, see Curtis B. Pye, "Letters from the South," in Eugene L. Schwaab and Jacqueline Bull, eds., *Travels in the South: Selected from Periodicals of the Time*, 2 vols. (Lexington, KY, 1973), 2:531–532; Olmsted, *Back Country*, 150.

South Carolina, "To accept the hospitality of the Southerner meant that he would do all he could for you."[10]

Reuben Davis, a prominent black-belt politician, wrote proudly of Monroe County, Mississippi: "Owing to the great fertility of the soil, the people were generally prosperous. I suppose there was never a community more frank and genial in their hospitality, or more liberal in their dealings with both friend and stranger. It is not too much to say that every house was opened to the traveler – every hand outstretched to aid and welcome him." In the 1840s, a Presbyterian minister, his wife, and four children visited the family of Dr. David Holt of Wilkinson County, Mississippi, and stayed more than a year, somehow surviving the dancing, card-playing, fun-loving ways of their Episcopalian hosts. Relatives and friends came for a week, a month, a year. In the wealthy sugar parishes of Louisiana hardly a month passed without overnight guests on the plantations, and few families sat down to dinner without guests. In a burst of graciousness toward despised Yankees, A. B. Meek of Alabama credited them with contributing to the Southwest's reputation.[11]

The necessity for mutual adjustment made hospitality – "the chief of social virtues" – an imperative. To function as society's leading element, especially in difficult times, the well-to-do needed to know their peers. And in bad times, they needed informal networks of reciprocity.

The frequent trips that husbands took for business, political meetings, church conferences, and other purposes placed severe burdens on their families. The women undertook to combat the loneliness by seeking female neighbors and kin, cooperating in church groups, and sometimes making their own trips to see families. One benefit: Many felt compelled to learn something of the plantation management.[12]

[10] Alexander H. Stephens, *A Constitutional View of the Late War Between the States* (2 vols. (New York, 1970 [1868, 1870]), 1:115; William M. Polk, *Leonidas Polk, Bishop and General*, 2 vols. (New York, 1915), 1:188; G. M., "South-Carolina," in *New England Magazine*, 1 (1831), 247; the Canadian's recollections in Louisa M. Smythe, ed., *For Old Lang Syne: Collected for My Children* (Charleston, SC, 1900), 4; George Cary Eggleston, *A Rebel's Recollections* (Baton Rouge, LA, 1996 [1871]), 44.

[11] Reuben Davis, *Recollections of Mississippi and Mississippians* (Oxford, MS, 1972 [1879], 8; Cockrell and Ballard, eds., *Mississippi Rebel in the Army of Northern Virginia*, 22–24; J. Carlyle Sitterson, "The McCollams: A Planter Family of the Old and New South," *JSH*, 6 (1940), 347–367; Meredith Flournoy Ingersoll, comp., "Excerpts from the History of the Flournoy Family" (typescript); A. B. Meek, *Romantic Passages in Southwestern History* (Mobile, AL, 1857), 51.

[12] Philip Hamilton, "Gentry Women and the Transformation of Daily Life in Jeffersonian and Antebellum Virginia," Angela Boswell and Judith N. McArthur, eds., *Women Shaping the South: Creating and Confronting Change* (Colombia, MO, 2006), 22–23; Anne Sinkler Whaley LeClerq, ed., *Between North and South: The Letters of Emily*

Friendly scientists in Charleston provided letters of introduction to Sir Charles Lyell, the distinguished geologist, but they issued a caveat. They told him to move about rapidly if he expected to get any work done, or local hospitality would eat up all his time at dinners and social events. "Much has been said in praise of the hospitality of the southern planter," Lyell told his fellow Britons, "but they alone who have traveled in the southern states, can appreciate the perfect ease and politeness with which a stranger is made to feel himself at home." The liberality of the big planters charmed Alexander MacKay, an antislavery British traveler, who reported having a slave to attend to him constantly. Lyell and Mackay reiterated what British travelers had reported from the early days of the Republic.[13]

In the aftermath of the abolitionist eruption in the 1830s, J. S. Buckingham arrived in Charleston with letters of introduction from friends in Washington and the North: "By all parties I was received with a great deal of cordiality and kindness, and nearly all of them took the earliest opportunity to wait on us at the hotel." After similar receptions in Savannah and Augusta, he praised the "graceful ease and quiet elegance" of well-bred southern ladies and gentlemen. In contrast, Northerners betrayed "doubts and ambiguity" about their relative rank and position. Overstrained efforts to be thought genteel made strangers feel themselves to be in the presence of persons anxious about the opinion of others and new to polished society. Alexander Wilson, Philadelphia's acerbic ornithologist, confessed to finding the hospitality of Southerners, especially Charlestonians, impressively gracious. Aaron Burr, repairing to John Couper's place on St. Simons after his duel with Alexander Hamilton, could hardly believe the attentions rendered by the numerous servants.

Ralph Waldo Emerson experienced similar graciousness, which he gratuitously associated with masters' duplicity toward slaves. Bishop

Wharton Sinkler, 1842–1865 (Columbia, SC, 2001), 145; Carmichael Diary, Oct. 9, 10, 1837, Sept. 6, 1840; Davis Diary, Dec. 8, 1839; Fletcher "Autobiography" (ms), Winter, 1841–1842; Bethell Diary, Sept. 4, 1857, Aug. 13, 1860; Carney Diary, May 16, 1859, Jan. 1, 1861; Bills Diary, April 1, June 25, Oct. 10, 1853, July 13 1860, Jan. 5, 1865; Mrs. H. G. Lewis to Mrs. J. M. Hunt, July 29, 1837, in Hughes Family Papers.

[13] Charles Lyell, *Travels in North America, Canada, and Nova Scotia, with Geological Observations*, 2nd ed., 2 vols. (London, 1855 [1845]), 1:155; Lyell, *A Second Visit to the United States of North America*, 2 vols., (London, 1849), 1:245; Alexander MacKay, *The Western World; Or, Travels in the United States in 1846–1847*, 3 vols. (New York, 1968 [1849]), 2:81. Also, Jane Louise Mesick, *The English Traveller in America, 1785–1835* (Westport, CT, 1970), 61–62; Allan Nevins, ed., *American Social History as Recorded by British Travellers* (New York, 1923), 7.

William Meade of Virginia probably did not know of Emerson's slur, but he had an answer of sorts. Meade made much of an incident in South Carolina that he thought typical of the South. He and his family visited a plantation to find the white family absent. House servants, one of whom read Meade's letter of introduction, entertained the Meades courteously and lavishly for two days.[14]

For Harriett Martineau, who opposed slavery, Southerners were the best mannered of Americans, despite a touch of arrogance, and New Englanders the least. She added that Southerners received travelers wonderfully – except for abolitionists. In Virginia twenty years later, Olmsted commented, "Between man and man, more ceremony and form is sustained, in familiar conversation, than well-bred people commonly use at the North." In the Southwest, Matilda Charlotte Houstoun, the British novelist, applauded the "courtesy and civility of Texans." The combination of hospitality with fierceness toward abolitionists extended beyond the master–slave relation. Dr. Rush Nutt, a Virginian on a visit to western Mississippi, complimented the Chickasaws: "No people express hospitality more than the Indians, or with a better will, & live as if all things were in common." Indians and Southerners shared some traits. Nutt added, "To their enemies [the Indians] are implacable." A common saying: A Southerner would remain polite until angry enough to kill.[15]

In the 1850s, the popular novelist G. P. R. James settled in Virginia as British consul. Virginia-reared Lieutenant-Governor Thomas Caute Reynolds of Missouri told James to expect unsurpassed hospitality. James observed that in the cities only the well-to-do could afford hospitality, whereas in the country almost everyone practiced it whether they could afford it or not. He considered Southerners in a class by themselves – open and frank, unostentatious and unpretentious. A stranger – at least if

---

[14] J. S. Buckingham, *The Slave States of America*, 2 vols. (New York, 1968 [1842]),8, 91, 123, 163; Alexander Wilson to Daniel H. Miller, Feb. 22, 1809, Clark Hunter, ed., *The Life and Letters of Alexander Wilson* (Philadelphia, PA, 1983), 301; Linda T. Prior, "Ralph Waldo Emerson and South Carolina," *South Carolina Historical Magazine*, 79 (1978), 256; Hull, *St. Simon's Enchanted Island*, 59 (Burr); William Meade, *Sketches of Old Virginia Family Servants* (Philadelphia, 1847), 7.

[15] Harriet Martineau, *Retrospect of Western Travel*, 2 vols. (London, 1838), 1:145, 210, 225; Frederick Law Olmsted, *A Journey in the Seaboard Slave States* (New York, 1968 [1856]), 51; Mrs. [Matilda Charlotte.] Houstoun, *Texas and the Gulf of Mexico; or, Yachting in the Gulf of Mexico* (Austin, TX, 1968 [1845]), 127; C. P. Roland, "The South of the Agrarians," in William C. Havard and Walter Sullivan, eds., *A Band of Prophets: The Vanderbilt Agrarians after Fifty Years* (Baton Rouge, LA, 1982), 26; Rush Nutt Diary, 1805 (11), in Haller Nutt Papers; also, Dunbar, *Travel in America*, 2: 502–503.

with a proper letter of introduction – was expected to stay for dinner and, indeed, spend the night. A dinner planned for five or six would expand without ado to accommodate thirty or so. The wealthiest planters often entertained twenty, thirty, fifty, or more people at a time. Ferry Hill, a small plantation in western Maryland with twenty-five slaves, had up to ten callers arrive each day: Two to five stayed for dinner, and two to four stayed the night, some for from three days to more than three weeks. Hence the diary entry for January 7, 1838: "There has been no company tonight to interrupt the quiet of the family."[16]

To accommodate many guests at one time, the wealthier built large plantation houses with separate quarters, unattached or attached with private entrances. Yet even they had to improvise. John C. and Floride Calhoun had eight bedrooms at Fort Hill, but they were hardly enough when, as often happened, relatives and friends poured in. Children had to squeeze, and guests doubled or tripled up. Anna Matilda King had no idea how to put up twenty Harringtons in her modest home. She managed. Her boys shared a room; she slept with her daughter; she consigned the white servants to the living room; and she gave her own room to her guests. Maria Broadus squeezed seven guests into her small house in Charlottesville: "I had a bedstead and trundle-bed for the ladies. A bedstead and a bed on the floor for the gentlemen, a lounge in a small room for another gentleman, and a pallet in Mr. Broadus' study for us. The children I put in their mammy's room." On the more affluent lowcountry plantations, a guest expected a full house and settled for a crude mattress in any space available.[17]

[16] T. C. Reynolds to G. P. R. James, June 20, 1853, in "Glimpses of the Past: Letters of Thomas Caute Reynolds, 1847–1885," *Missouri Historical Society*, 19 (1943), 27; G. P. R. James, "Virginia Country Life" (1858) in Schwaab and Bull, eds., *Travels in the Old South*, 2:519–520; Kinloch Bull, Jr., *The Oligarchs in Colonial and Revolutionary Charleston: Lieutenant Governor William Bull II and His Family* (Columbia, SC, 1991), 43; Carmichael Diary, April 23–25, 1838; Harvey Toliver Cook, *The Life and Legacy of David Rogerson Williams* (New York, 1916), 211; Mary D. Robertson, ed., *Lucy Breckinridge of Grove Hill: The Journal of a Virginia Girl, 1826–1864* (Kent, OH, 1979), 3; Henry Edmund Ravenel, *Ravenel Records* (Atlanta, GA, 1898), 108; Clement Eaton, *Henry Clay and the Art of America Politics* (Boston, MA, 1957), 77; Fletcher M. Green, ed., *Ferry Hill Plantation Journal* (Chapel Hill, NC, 1961), Jan. 7, 1838 (5, Green's calculations).

[17] Franklin L. Riley, ed., "Diary of a Mississippi Planter," in *Publications of the Mississippi Historical Society*, 10 (1909), 305; John Niven, *John C. Calhoun and the Price of Union: A Biography* (Baton Rouge, LA, 1988), 155; Anna Matilda King to Thomas Butler King, June 2, 1842, in T. B. King Papers; Maria C. Broadus to Mrs. Bickers, June 11, 1855, in Archibald Thomas Robertson, *Life and Letters of John Albert Broadus* (Philadelphia, 1909), 128; John B. Irving, *A Day on Cooper River*, 2nd ed. enl. and ed.

Northerners received the same treatment as Southerners – unless suspected of hostility to the South. In the wealthy Florida parishes of Louisiana in the 1820s, Timothy Flint observed: "The opulent planters have many amiable traits of character ... high-minded and hospitable, in an eminent degree ... frank, dignified." In the 1850s, the Methodist Reverend W. H. Milburn, a Northerner, depicted the South as "full of generous, noble people, independent in thought and speech, tolerant of the opinions of others, as they are bold in the avowal of their own .... No questions were ever asked me as to my views of the 'peculiar institution,' no pledges in regard to my conduct were either desired or given." Milburn had been taken "at once into the homes and the hearts of the people, and during the six years of my sojourn in that land, I experienced nothing but kindness." Years later in the North, "My feelings instinctively turn toward Alabama as a home, and toward the Southern people as my kindred." [18]

Solon Robinson, the northern agricultural journalist and reformer, declared the planters of western Mississippi wonderfully cordial. Even unfriendly Northerners usually escaped rebuke from well-mannered hosts. Bennet H. Barrow of Louisiana complained that Northerners did not know how to behave or know when they were being disagreeable. A traveling salesman from the North explained his preference for the South: "Up North people say, 'What do you know?' Out West they say, 'What can you do?' Down South here they say, 'Come in.'" In the 1850s, deepening suspicion of Northerners took a toll, but Southerners tried to remember their manners. In 1860, Frank Steel visited relatives in Washington County, Mississippi, and wrote to his Republican family in Ohio to recommend that Mrs. Whitney go south. A traveler will be in no more danger in the South than in the North, provided only that he "has learned the important art of holding his tongue":

If you were to visit a neighbor's house and interfere with his domestic arrangements, it is probable he would not welcome you again, if he did not drive you away at the time. So it is here .... Northerners who have not common prudence

by Louisa Cheves Stoney (Columbia, SC, 1842 [1932]), 173; Also, Chastellux, *Travels*, 2:441; Elizabeth Silverthorne, *Plantation Life in Texas* (College Station, TX, 1986), 182; Edgar Jones Cheatham, "Washington County, Mississippi: Its Antebellum Generation" (M. A. thesis; Tulane University, 1950), 100–101.

[18] Flint quoted in Edwin Adams Davis, ed., *Plantation Life in the Florida Parishes of Louisiana, 1836–1846, as Reflected in the Diary of Bennet H. Barrow* (New York, 1943), 9–10; William Henry Milburn, *Ten Years of Preacher-Life: Chapters from an Autobiography* (New York, 1859), 278, also 325, 334.

enough to keep them from meddling with what they have nothing to do, are sent off in a hurry – and very rightly too. To be sure, at a time like this, some Southerners act hastily and don't distinguish between friends and enemies. This is to be regretted, but it is the legitimate fruit of Northern nullification.[19]

Catherine Cooper Hopley, an English governess in Virginia, explained that the common expression "come by" meant "do drop in." In town, people were always passing by and were welcome to stop and visit. Southerners displayed "unsuspicious confidence towards people once introduced by a mutual friend; while towards an entire stranger perhaps no people on earth are more distant and reserved than those same confiding Southerners." Strangers on legitimate business or in trouble or recognizably respectable found a kind welcome. According to the ex-slave Solomon Northup, even slaves, traveling with passes, could stop at any plantation and receive food and shelter from master or overseer. "The planters are real gentleman," a peddler from New Jersey told Henry Yates Thompson of England. "When he knew I was come, a planter would send down his carriage to ask me to church. No one would do that in the North or Canada." Moses Drury Hoge admired the serious tone of life he found in Ohio but preferred the warmth of his native Virginia.[20]

The South welcomed peddlers – many of them Jews – much more warmly than the North did. Planters extended customary hospitality, putting them up for the night. With a low population density, rural Southerners appreciated their services and acceptance of southern racial mores. Jews often combined their efforts as peddlers to facilitate business operations and, when successful, became partners in store ownership. Many of the Jewish storekeepers of the Southwest, having begun as peddlers, established a reputation for honesty and settled in without incident. The most successful, like Julius Weiss of New Orleans and Fayetteville, Mississippi, became prosperous merchants. Jews did well in Richmond's dry goods business and cheap clothing trade, much as Italians did well

[19] Herbert Anthony Kellar, ed., *Solon Robinson: Pioneer and Agriculturalist: Selected Writings*, 2 vols. (Indianapolis, IN, 1936 [1848]; B. H. Barrow Diary, April 26, 1843, Feb. 26, 1844, in Davis, ed., *Florida Parishes*, 286, 317; traveling salesman quoted in Wilma Dykeman, *The French Broad* (New York, 1955), 146; F. F. Steel Diary, Dec. 8, 1860.

[20] Catherine Cooper Hopley, *Life in the South from the Commencement of the War*, 2 vols. (New York, 1971 [1863]),1:58–59; 2:227. H. Y. Thompson, Aug, 29, 1963, in Christopher Chancellor, ed., *An Englishman in the Civil War: The Diaries of Henry Yates Thompson* (New York, 1971), 59; Solomon Northup, *Twelve Years a Slave* (New York, 1970 [1854]), 158–159; Peyton Harrison Hoge, *Moses Drury Hoge: Life and Letters* (Richmond, VA, 1899), 49.

in the fruit and confectionary trades. Jews who became planters or merchants moved in elite circles.[21]

Doctors and dentists who traveled long distances to see patients on plantations often stayed the night. Jeremiah Harris, a schoolteacher in Virginia, who more than once found himself in a downpour when going about his duties, always found the nearest home open to him. Francis Terry Leak of Mississippi put up "quite a poor man" and his family on their way to Memphis. The South adopted colonial Virginia's practice of opening homes to respectable lower-class passers-by. In time, even South Carolinians, who in colonial times had overseers entertain poor strangers, gave way to a considerable extent.[22]

COSTS AND INCONVENIENCES

The legendary hospitality of Virginia's eighteenth-century gentry came at a price not easily borne. The affluent William Byrd put up an endless array of visitors for weeks at a time but worried about his ability to make ends meet. Thomas Jefferson tartly wrote to his daughter, "The character of those we recieve [sic] is very different from the loungers who infest the houses of the wealthy in general." Loungers notwithstanding, Jefferson hoped for a reformation that relegated hospitality to daytime visits and left the family alone in the evening. Benjamin Henry Latrobe appreciated the warmth, splendor, and hospitality of the Virginians but thought them financially irresponsible.[23]

[21] Jacob Rader Marcus, ed., *Memoirs of American Jews*, 3 vols. (Philadelphia, 1955), 1:7, 9–30, 47–57, 353–367, 2:21–46; Bertram Wallace Korn, *Jews and Negro Slavery in the Old South 1789–1865* (Philadelphia, 1861), 37–38; A. H. Arrington to Kate Arrington, Feb. 17, 1857; Mitchell, *Ten Years in the United States*, 58–59; Olmsted, *Seaboard Slave States*, 27–28; Franklin M. Garrett, *Atlanta and Environs: A Chronicle of Its People and Events*: vol 1: Athens, GA, 1954), 1:214–215; Olga Reed Pruitt, *It Happened Here: True Stories of Holly Springs* (Holly Springs, MS, 1950), 87. On storekeepers, see Elliott Ashkenazi, *The Business of Jews in Louisiana, 1840–1875* (Tuscaloosa, AL, 1988), 40.

[22] Hopley, *Life in the South*, 1:231–232; Charles W. Turner, ed., *An Old Field School Teacher's Diary (Life and Times of Jeremiah C. Harris)* (Verona, VA, 1975), Jan. 22, 1851, March 25, 1852, April 13, 1852 (21–24); Leak Diary, Sept. 10, 1858; Edmund S. Morgan, *Virginians at Home: Family Life in the Eighteenth Century* (Williamsburg, VA, 1952), 42; Rhys Isaac, *The Transformation of Virginia, 1740–1790* (Chapel Hill, NC, 1982), 34; Bull, *Oligarchs in Charleston* 43.

[23] Richmond Croom Beatty, *William Byrd of Westover* (New York, 1970), 181, 194; Thomas Jefferson to Martha Jefferson, Feb. 5, 1801, in Edwin Morris Betts and James Adam Bear, Jr., eds., *The Family Letters of Thomas Jefferson* (Columbia, MO, 1966), 195–196; Edward C. Carter, III, et al., eds., *The Virginia Journals of Benjamin Henry Latrobe, 1795–1798*, 2 vols. (New Haven, CT, 1977), 1:xxxi, 2:330–331 (Nov. 12, 1797).

John Hartwell Cocke expressed the Virginia ideal as "hospitality without ostentation." Yet Cocke knew that the costs of endless entertaining
devoured the profits of the best of managers. In the 1830s, George Tucker
observed that since eighteenth-century Virginia planters could neither
transport nor sell much produce locally, expending it on guests made
sense. Tucker added that rural isolation made possible a level of hospitality that proved irksome and economically difficult in the cities. David
Hunter Strother ("Porte Crayon"), a Virginia Unionist who considered
slavery an economic liability, espied deterioration in hospitality as gentlemen's finances became straitened. Yet Strother's fiction registered the
complaint of innkeepers about competition from "squires" who opened
homes to travelers, providing free service to potential paying customers.
In 1850, John Hill Wheeler attributed the decline of certain lowcountry North Carolina families to recklessness: "Hospitality carried to an
extreme, and an excessive fondness for conviviality, were the charac-
teristics of those days." Augustus Chapman Allen and John K. Allen of
Houston would not have Texans outdone. They spent some $3,000 a
year to provide lodgings for strangers. Yet, all these gentlemen probably
had read Petronius' scathing portrait of *arrivistes* who spent money they
did not have on lavish dinner parties.[24]

The costs of hospitality, Edmund Ruffin of Virginia charged, were
ruining agriculture: "Spongers posed greater danger than cholera," and
farmers faced condemnation as misers if they refused to indulge idlers.
Ruffin knew whereof he spoke. A man and woman, arriving in a carriage, asked to spend the night at Leonidas Pendleton Spyker's plantation
in Louisiana. Spyker, master of 114 slaves, refused. To his chagrin, they
camped at his gate. "I have lost 5 or 6 thousand dollars already this
year by accommodating travellers, got the measles and lost 4 negroes,
besides a doctor's bill of fully $500 to say nothing of loss of time." While
in Confederate service, Felix Pierre Poché – from a planter family in
Louisiana – "had the mortification of being refused hospitality for dinner
by an old Lady ... Mrs. Walker of Bayou Boeuf." He had never in his life
been so treated.[25]

[24] Cocke quoted in Carly Johnston, *Stewards of History: The Covenant of Generations in
a Southern Family* (Internet ed., 1999 [1818]), 7; George Tucker, *The Life of Thomas
Jefferson*, 2 vols. (London, 1837), 1:73–74; Cecil D. Eby, Jr., *"Porte Crayon": The Life
of David Hunter Strother* (Chapel Hill, NC, 1960), 60, 83; John Hill Wheeler, *Historical
Sketches of North Carolina from 1584 to 1851*, 2 vols. in 1 (Baltimore, 1964 [1851]),
2:284; *HT*, 1:29; Petronius, *The Satyricon*, tr. P. G. Walsh (Oxford, 1996), ch. 6.
[25] Edmund Ruffin, "Causes of the Depressed Condition of Virginia," *Farmers' Register*, 2
(1835), 95–96; Feb. 16, 1857, *ERD*, 1:35; Spyker Diary, Aug. 11, 1857; Edwin C. Bears,

In South Carolina, upcountry as well as lowcountry planters entertained lavishly and frequently in their townhouses. The upcountry elite, wrote Lucius Verus Bierce, had a "kind of reserve, at first unpleasant to a person from the North as it borders, in appearance, on haughtiness. This, however, is owing more to habit than feeling, and the most disinterested Kindness is often cloaked under the appearance of haughty disdain." Among affluent upcountry politicians, James L. Orr, Wade Hampton, and James H. Hammond won the plaudits of Benjamin F. Perry. Not everyone could afford their generosity. In the low country William Gilmore Simms had his own system of accounting and failed to run a plantation profitably: "My position entails upon me a good deal of company, and this involves an expenditure quite inconsistent with the resources of a Cotton plantation which has been too frequently mismanaged, and where an undue indulgence of the slaves is permitted." Simms apologized to William Hawkins Ferris for not having done something or other: "A continued flow of company, which, on a southern plantation, does not imply fashionable call, and a pressure of domestic duties, could not be set aside, have thitherto conspired to defeat my purpose." To the poet and novelist John Esten Cooke of Virginia, Simms moaned over the "scores" of visits from friends and whole families who descended every week. Of the "perpetual flow of visitors," Simms wrote to Hammond: "And they came at a season when we are all nigh starving. I can neither get fowls nor meats of any kind. It is a spring famine here, always a season of scarcity & especially at this period." Fortunately, a neighbor had sent him a wild turkey, and he succeeded in buying another as well as a quarter of venison. But he remained in distress: "My pigs are poor in the swamp ranges; and I have no muttons: You may judge how I must have been compelled to use my wits to supply my larder. Add to this that I am reduced to Western Whiskey as my chief almost sole beverage."[26]

ed., *A Louisiana Confederate: Diary of Felix Pierre Poché*, tr. Eugenia Watson Somdal (Natchitoches, LA, 1972), Oct. 22, 1863, 43.

[26] Lucius Verus Bierce, "The Piedmont Frontier, 1822–23," in Thomas D. Clark, ed., *South Carolina: The Grand Tour, 1780–1865* (Columbia, SC, 1973), 65; Stephen Meats and Edwin T. Arnold, eds., *The Writings of Benjamin F. Perry*, 3 vols. (Spartanburg, SC, 1980), 2:141, 326, 336. In Mary C. Oliphant et al., eds., *The Letters of William Gilmore Simms*, 6 vols. (Columbia, SC, 1952–1982), see Simms to N. B. Tucker, Jan. 30, 1850 (3:10–11); to William Hawkins Ferris (4:138–139); to John Esten Cooke, April 14, 1860 (4:216); to J. H. Hammond, April 9, 1859 (4:140). On the distinction between fashionable, formal, and other calls, see Elizabeth Fox-Genovese, *Within the Plantation Household: Black and White Women of the Old South* (Chapel Hill, NC, 1988), 225–226.

Olmsted and other antislavery Northerners at times dismissed southern hospitality as a myth, insisting that even big planters charged strangers from a half dollar to a dollar and a quarter. James Redpath, an acerbic abolitionist, called the richest planters the least hospitable and – surprise! – called their slaves the most so. Redpath's objectivity may be judged from his pronouncement: "I had so often seen anti-slavery travellers accused of abusing hospitality, that, when I went South, I resolved to partake of none. I never even took a cigar from a slaveholder without seizing the earliest opportunity of returning it, or giving him an equivalent in some form." The evidence for his charge remains obscure, in contrast to abundant evidence that, apart from occasional *parvenus* and misanthropes, planters welcomed strangers and, if anything, took offense at offers to pay. But hosts had complaints of their own, including extraordinary Yankee presumption and bad manners. An incident may stand for countless others. In Raleigh, North Carolina, Old "Greenpea Williams," a Yankee who made periodic trips through the South, ate fifteen peaches at the Mordecai's place, commenting, "These are very indifferent peaches." The "very indignant" Mordecai women, being southern ladies, said nothing.[27]

An astonished James Kirke Paulding of New York gushed over Virginia hospitality. People, not merely kin and close friends, came to a plantation in families and stayed six months: "A stranger here is just as much at home as a child in his cradle." Paulding insisted that the common people were especially hospitable. But nonslaveholders and small slaveholders frequently needed compensation. They gave a warm reception to friends and kin but expected fifty cents or a dollar for the bed and board. Northern travelers lavishly praised the friendliness of backcountry farm folks, even those whose sleeping and sanitary facilities left much to be desired. If many yeomen required a half dollar or so for payment, they usually did so out of necessity. Strapped for cash and largely self-sufficient, they could hardly afford the costs of putting up strangers, no matter how generous they were inclined to be. A county official or a lawyer who went to the home of a small slaveholder or yeoman to take depositions expected to pay if he stayed for dinner. And in a society in which many men rose into the planter class, old habits persisted at least among the first generation of the well-to-do.[28]

[27] Olmsted, *Seaboard Slave States*, 242–245; Olmsted, *Back Country*, 408–410; James Redpath, *The Roving Editor: Or, Talks with Slaves in the Southern States* (New York, 1859), 139 n.; Ellen Mordecai, *Gleanings from Long Ago* (Raleigh, NC, 1974), 2.

[28] [James Kirk Paulding], *Letters from the South*, 2 vols. (New York, 1819), 1:22; Floyd C. Watkins, "James Kirke Paulding and the South," *American Quarterly*, 5 (1953), 223; Mrs.

From the Valley of Virginia, Chastellux reported that farmers expected strangers to pay for lodgings but charged much less than innkeepers, who passed heavy taxes along in exorbitant charges. At the home of a small slaveholder near Charlottesville he had a moderately priced "excellent dinner" of eggs, ham, chicken, and whiskey. There and elsewhere, then and later, farmers sought to cover costs they could not easily bear. At that, farmers, from the early days on, often refused to take money. George Gilmer, former governor of Georgia, and his lady stopped at the homes of yeomen in Carrol, County in 1837 and, finding them terribly over-crowded, offered to sleep in their wagon. Horrified, the family squeezed them into their primitive dwelling, straining every muscle to make them comfortable. The most distinguished visitors would be lucky to get a bed to themselves and made do with crude provisions, albeit courteously offered.[29]

Southern hospitality carried some painful social tensions. William Wirt complained in 1799 of "a troop of visiting cousins here, who have come from afar, and whom we cannot, you know, decently invite to leave our house." In particular, cousins often went to school together and remained close thereafter. And in general, visitors helped with household chores, children studied together, and older children helped to raise younger. However much Southerners welcomed guests, the burden weighed heavily. John Randolph of Roanoke complained about having too many visitors: "Indeed, I have once more regretted that not at home was inadmissible in the country [Virginia]." In Charleston the Episcopalian Reverend Jasper Adams, citing Abraham and Lot, traced southern hospitality to respect for biblical injunction. He condemned the practice of having servants lie to unwelcome visitors that their mistresses were not at home.[30]

James Hine (of New York), Dec. 20, 1833, and Charles Lanman (of Michigan), 1840s, in Edward J. Cashin, ed., *A Wilderness Still the Cradle of Nature* (Savannah, GA, 1994), 161, 163, 182; Joe Gray Taylor, *Eating, Drinking, and Visiting in the South: An Informal History* (Baton Rouge, LA, 1982), 47; James C. Bonner, *Georgia's Last Frontier: The Development of Carroll County* (Athens, GA, 1971); Lyell, *Second Visit*, 2:62–63; John Walker Diary, Mar. 2, 1837.

[29] Chastellux, *Travels*, 2:397–398, 414; Clement Eaton, *The Mind of the Old South* (Baton Rouge, LA, 1964), 224–225.

[30] Wirt quoted in John P. Kennedy, *Memoirs of the Life of William Wirt, Attorney-General of the United States*, 2 vols. (Philadelphia, 1850), 1:72; Sept. 4, 1827, in Kenneth Shorey, ed., *Collected Letters of John Randolph of Roanoke to Dr. John Brockenbrough, 1812–1833* (New Brunswick, NJ, 1988), 96; Jasper Adams, *Elements of Moral Philosophy* (Philadelphia, 1837), 188–189.

The constant arrival of unannounced guests relieved boredom and often proved a joy, but it irritated those who had things to do or wished to read a book or found visitors tedious. Peter Randolph advised the young Thomas Jefferson to go away to college since, if he lived at home, visitors would eat up a quarter of his time. Circumstances did not change much. In 1840, Maria Bryan Harford complained of constant visits by neighbors: "They come and sit and have nothing to say." She racked her brain in attempts to converse and resented having to interrupt her work to entertain them. In later years, Linton Stephens visited Judge J. A. Lumpkin and family only to have their pleasant evening ruined by two "bores" who arrived unannounced and did not take hints to leave. It is not likely that either Stephens or Lumpkin read Søren Kierkegaard, but both would have applauded his observation in "Either/Or": "All men are bores. Surely no one will prove himself so great a bore as to contradict me." Pauline DeCaradeuc Heyward complained of unwanted visitors whose presence kept her family from having the house guests they preferred.[31]

Travelers needed to know something about local mores and notions of respectability. Carolinians may have been, as Susan Nye Hutchinson suggested, the "most attentive and hospitable people in the world." But they expected travelers to play by the rules. When the Episcopalian Reverend John Hamilton, Cornish, a Northerner, moved to Edisto Island in 1840, he got a jolt when he paid an unannounced call on Dr. Dill and his family. Mrs. Dill, entertaining some ladies, failed to recognize him. Dr. Dill did not arrive to greet him for some twenty minutes, during which he found himself in a room with ladies who spoke not a word to him. Never had he experienced such discourtesy: "If this is a true specimen of Southern hospitality – of Southern refinement – of Southern politeness – Deliver me from it." Cornish received apologies in due time, but he had received a hard introduction to the fastidiousness with which southern ladies, perhaps perceiving Yankee presumption, enforced do's and don'ts.

---

[31] Sarah N. Randolph, *The Domestic Life of Jefferson, Compiled from Letters and Reminiscences* (New York, 1871), 26–27; Joan E. Cashin, ed., *Our Common Affairs: Texts from Women in the Old South* (Baltimore, 1996), 55, 59, 64; Maria Bryan Harford to Julia Ann Bryan Cumming, Aug. 7, 1834, in Bleser, ed., *Tokens of Affection*, 172, 317–318; Linton Stephens to A. H. Stephens, July 15, 1860, in James D. Waddell, *Biographical Sketch of Linton Stephens, Containing a Selection of His Letters, Speeches, State Papers, Etc.* (Atlanta, GA, 1877), 229–230; Robert Bretall, ed., "Either/Or," *A Kierkegaard Anthology*, ed. (New York, 1946), 21; Mary D. Robertson, ed., *A Confederate Lady Comes of Age: The Journal of Pauline DeCaradeuc Heyward, 1863–1888* (Columbia, SC, 1992), Oct. 15, 1864 (59).

In 1849, George White, the statistician, lauded the citizens of Forsyth County, Georgia, as nowhere excelled for sociability: "The houses of all are open to all worthy strangers." His readers understood what he meant by "worthy." J. S. Wise recounted the typical sweet Presbyterian girl of Lexington, Virginia, who mastered the art of receiving an uninvited and presumptuous gentlemen caller. She would stall interminably until he left: "Her father would immolate her for taking such a liberty – as asking you to stay for dinner." To get to know one of those Presbyterian girls, you had to invite her to join you at church.[32]

Prolonged visits with relatives and friends sometimes came at a high psychic cost. With reference to kinsman Thomas Ruffin – North Carolina's great jurist whose daughter had married Edmund's son – Edmund Ruffin explained that his intimacy with and high regard for Judge Ruffin "makes me both levy and pay a burdensome tax, as to most others of his numerous family & their connections by marriage." In kindness, they "seem to think that they owe to my family attentions because of their kinship, however remote ... Thus they tax me, & compel me to tax them." He fretted that he would have offended these kind people if he had passed without calling on them. Only Mrs. Roulhac and John Kirkland, acquaintances, seemed to derive any pleasure from his visits; his kinsmen merely accepted the necessity to return visits. "Yet this is much better than most of the visiting & receiving visits, & social intercourse, which takes up so much of our time & life." If southern hospitality included the opening of homes to countless visitors, gestures had to be returned. Dr. William Henry Holcombe of Natchez, working on a long article on Scarlet Fever for a homeopathic journal, moaned that he and his wife had an annoying task to perform. Poor Becky "has to call on all the super-aristocracy, aristocracy proper, semi-aristocracy, sub-aristocracy, and pseudo-aristocracy of Natchez."[33]

Occupying Union troops poured contempt on southern claims to chivalry, but many grudgingly acknowledged that they experienced admirable hospitality, courtesy, elegance, refinement, and cultivation. Many bitterly anti-Yankee Confederate women did not forget their manners and showed remarkable generosity toward hungry Union stragglers. Catherine Barbara Brown of Virginia had trouble with the soldiers'

---

[32] Hutchinson Journal, July 2, 1815; Cornish Diary, June 29, 1840; George White, *Statistics of the State of Georgia* (Savannah, GA, 1849), 254; J. S. John S. Wise, *The End of an Era* (Boston, MA, 1900), 241–242.

[33] *ERD*, Sept. 23, 1857 (1:108); Holcombe Diary, June 4, 1855.

inability to understand the southern attitude: "Every one offered to pay and said every man in their country would have to pay for meals, did scarcely seem to understand the generosity of the south feeding their enemies."[34]

THE LIBRARIES OF GENEROUS NEIGHBORS

Planters and professionals opened their private libraries to friends and neighbors, compensating for weak institutional lending libraries. Francis Lightfoot Lee of Virginia educated himself by devouring many of the three hundred books on Richard Lee's plantation. Philip Fithian of New Jersey found a library of more than a thousand volumes at Nomini Hall in Virginia. In the early nineteenth century, the Presbyterian Reverend Samuel Eusebius McCorkle's church in Salisbury, North Carolina, had "a well-stocked lending library" that included Rollin, Mosheim, Gibbon, Hume, Burke, and Addison. Isaac Harby of Charleston made his annotated books available to students in his excellent academy. Alexander Stephens constantly lent neighbors books from the large library he had accumulated over thirty years. In Arkansas, friends and neighbors drew freely on the extensive library of the Massachusetts-born, Harvard-educated Albert Pike.[35]

A good many men who rose to prominence in the South had that early advantage. S. S. Prentiss began his career in Mississippi as a tutor for the five children of William B. Shields, who placed his large and excellent law library at Prentiss's disposal. In Georgia, Governor Wilson J. Lumpkin and his brother, Chief Justice Joseph Lumpkin of the state Supreme Court, had the benefit of their father's extensive library. Langdon Cheves, leading member of the Charleston, South Carolina bar and later president of the Bank of the United States, began life as a storekeeper's apprentice

---

34 Randall C. Jimerson, *The Private Civil War: Popular Thought during the Sectional Conflict* (Baton Rouge, LA, 1988), 132; Broun Diary, Nov. 7, 1862.
35 Alonzo Thomas Dill, *Francis Lightfoot Lee: The Incomparable Signer, 1734–1797* (Williamsburg, VA, 1977), 3; John Fea, "The Way of Improvement Leads Home: Philip Vicker Fithian's Rural Enlightenment," *Journal of American History*, 90 (2003), 472; James F. Hurley and Julia Goode Eagan, *The Prophet of Zion-Parnassus: Samuel Eusebius McCorkle* (Richmond, VA, 1934), 92; Henry Cleveland, *Alexander H. Stephens in Public and Private. With Letters and Speeches Before, During, and Since the War* (Philadelphia, 1866), 23; Gary Philip Zola, *Isaac Harby of Charleston, 1788–1828: Jewish Reformer and Intellectual* (Tuscaloosa, AL, 1994), 53; John Gould Fletcher, *Arkansas* (Fayetteville, AR, 1989), 98, 265; also Daniel W. Crofts, *Old Southampton: Politics and Society in a Virginia County, 1834–1869* (Charlottesville, VA, 1992), 46–47.

and educated himself out of his employer's fine library. Benjamin Perry, the leader of South Carolina's upcountry unionists, used the library of Pendleton's postmaster, John Lee, and then of Lee's sister, Mrs. Dench. Perry carried one great extravagance through life – the purchase of books. He spent $200 at a sale of Thomas Cooper's library and $300–500 on each of a number of other occasions. By 1849, his law library had cost him close to $3,000, and the rest of his library another $3,000. As a young man, Joel Chandler Harris worked for J. A. Turner, publisher of the *Countryman*, and benefited handsomely from having the use of the library at Turner's plantation near Eatonton, Georgia. Dennis Redmond, another agricultural editor, made his "admirable" and "fine"" library available to the young Paul Hamilton Hayne, thereby helping launch a distinguished literary career.[36]

A good library ensured a supply of books to young relatives. Jefferson Davis immersed himself in the library on the plantation of his brother Joseph, which included the *Federalist*, Elliott's debates on the Constitution, Adam Smith's *Wealth of Nations*, the novels of Goldsmith and Scott, and the poetry of Byron and Burns. As a schoolboy in Virginia, Moncure Conway, later a radical abolitionist, made heavy use of the library of his uncle, Richard Conway. Men improved their lot in life by a self-education that depended on access to books provided by the wealthy and members of the learned professions. Columbus Morrison regularly borrowed books from a Professor Bumbry. Ferdinand Lawrence Steel, a small farmer in Carroll County, Mississippi, working to improve himself, was indebted to his Methodist minister for opening his private library to him. A nonslaveholder in Tennessee recalled that the local slaveholders encouraged poor boys to get an education, and lent him books. Upcountry small farmers as well as plantation and town ladies shared books, notably history and biography, with neighbors and friends.[37]

In 1860, Dr. James Henderson Dickson and George Davis organized the first public library in Wilmington, North Carolina, purchasing many

---

[36] Dunbar Rowland, ed. *Mississippi: Comprising Sketches of Counties, Towns, Events, Institutions, and Persons, Arranged in Cyclopedic Form*, 4 vols. (Spartanburg, SC, 1976 [1907]), 2:468 (Prentiss); *DGB*, 2:642 (Lumpkin); Vernon Huff, Jr., *Langdon Cheves of South Carolina* (Columbia, SC, 1977), 22; Lillian Kibler, *Benjamin F. Perry, Unionist* (Durham, NC, 1946), 30, 38, 202–203; Bertram Holland Flanders, *Early Georgia Magazines* (Athens, GA, 1944), 168.

[37] Clement Eaton, *Jefferson Davis* (New York, 1977), 35–36; Mary Elizabeth Burtis, *Moncure Conway, 1832–1907* (New Brunswick, NJ, 1952), 7; Columbus Morrison Journal, various entries for 1845, esp., Dec. 5, 16; F. L. Steel Diaries, Feb. 12, 1865; *TCWVQ*, 4:1555, 1559; Paul D. Escott, ed., *North Carolina Yeoman: The Diary of Basil Armstrong Thomason, 1853–1862* (Athens, GA, 1996), Diary, Jan. 18, 1859 (127).

books from New York for it, and generating a local library association. Unfortunately, the South had few such philanthropists. Still, in the prosperous days of the eighteenth century, the planters of down east North Carolina prided themselves on their private libraries, which, if not necessarily large, contained the best that English letters had to offer. At Cape Fear and some other communities, gentlemen combined to establish a public library as part of their effort to stimulate community discussion of the arts and sciences. Especially during the nineteenth century, the public library became a place for gentlemen to meet and discuss the issues of the day. While the willingness of individuals to open their libraries to neighbors, especially young men from middle-class or poor families, eased class antagonisms, it did not solve educational difficulties.[38]

Gentlemen strove to choose their books carefully. Books available to young women included religion, history, classical literature, and much else, but not many trendy novels or anything likely to encourage rebelliousness. Few presumed to tell young ladies or gentlemen what to read, but almost everyone took pains to control their access to books. The elite foreshadowed George Santayana's remark to Ezra Pound that it did not much matter what books students read, so long as they read the same books. Basil Armstrong Thomasson, who taught the children of poor farmers in western North Carolina, atypically remarked that his scholars had enough books. Amelia Akehurst Lines, a northern-born teacher, had a more typical experience: She had twenty-one students, each of whom had to use a different book.[39]

Educated Southerners relied primarily on their own resources and especially their books at home. Early nineteenth-century Charlestonians possessed many books, most published in England. Colonial planters, despite a slide into Deism, bought religious books and pamphlets in large numbers. The theological library of William Byrd ranked with that of Cotton Mather, and the theological libraries of other Virginians matched those in Massachusetts. Inventories of eighteenth-century Virginia show numerous large private libraries, which featured books on law, theology, medicine, the classics, and English literature. John Mercer had one of

---

[38] *DNCB*, 2:67; John H. Wheeler, *Sketches of North Carolina, 1584–1851*, 2 vols. (Philadelphia, 1854), 2:284; George Gilman Smith, *The Story of Georgia and the Georgia People*, 2 vols. in 1 (Macon, GA, 1900), 545.

[39] Escott, ed., *North Carolina Yeoman*, Diary, Aug. 20, 1857 (207); Amelia Akehurst Lines Diary, June, 21, 1858, in Thomas Dyer, ed., *To Raise Myself a Little: The Diaries and Letters of a Georgia Teacher, 1851–1886* (Athens, GA, 1982), 86; Noel Stock, *The Life of Ezra Pound* (New York, 1970), 374.

Virginia's largest libraries, which included 284 law books, many unavailable elsewhere in the state. In eighteenth-century Edenton, a center of elite culture in eastern North Carolina, Samuel Johnston, a Yale graduate, probably had the largest private library in the province, with books on law, science, agriculture, theology, history, biography, and classical and modern literature.[40]

Private libraries of more than a thousand volumes dotted the nineteenth-century South. The Reverend Thomas Smyth of Charleston had one of the largest in the United States with 20,000 volumes. His theological collection was reputedly magnificent. He said that he "felt a special call to collect a large library, not for myself, but for my brethren's sake, and for posterity." Charles Carroll of Carrolton had upwards of a thousand volumes; Ebenezer Pettigrew of North Carolina, 3,000; James Cathcart Johnson, a rich planter, may have had as many or more. Elisha Hammond of South Carolina, a great if unsung teacher, prepared his son James Henry and such luminaries as Chancellor James J. Caldwell of South Carolina and Governor John Gayle of Alabama for college. His influence extended well beyond those he taught directly, for he made himself accessible to bright young men like John Belton O'Neall, liberally lending them books. John D. Ashmore of Anderson District had almost 1,500 volumes and William Gilmore Simms about 12,000. Hugh Legaré had a large collection in ancient and modern European languages. The mother of Senator Charles Izard of South Carolina built a library of some 2,500 volumes.[41]

William C. Preston, raised in Virginia in a planter family, credited his father's library for his intellectual progress as a boy. Hugh Blair Grigsby had 6,000 volumes, many of which had come from John Randolph's choice collection. In Georgia, James Hamilton Cooper, who had command of five languages, had 5,000 volumes, and Joseph Addison Turner, agricultural editor and planter, had 1,300, some 300 of them on the law. George Wimberly Jones DeRenne moved his library of more than 1,000

[40] Davis, *Intellectual Life in Jefferson's Virginia*, 11; D. S. Freeman, "Aristocracy of the Northern Neck," *SBN*, 10:73–74; William Hamilton Bryson, *Census of Law Books in Colonial Virginia* (Charlottesville, VA, 1978), xii, xviii (Mercer); Don Higginbotham, *The Papers of John Iredell*, 3 vols. (Raleigh, NC, 1976), 1:xlvii (Johnson).

[41] Smyth quoted in G. R. Brackett, "Christian Warrior Crowned," in *TSW*, 10:783; Clyde N. Wilson, *Carolina Cavalier: The Life and Mind of James Johnston Pettigrew* (Athens, GA, 1990), 4, 25; Oliphant, et al., eds., *Letters of Simms*, 4:399, n. 20; Linda Rhea, *Hugh Swinton Legaré: A Charleston Intellectual* (Chapel Hill, NC, 1934), 203–204; William Dusinberre, *Them Dark Days: Slavery in the American Rice Swamps* (New York, 1996), 36 (Izard).

volumes to Savannah in hopes of saving it from Sherman's army, which, however, burned it, as it burned John Bachman's outstanding library. In Florida, a German traveler visited a Mr. Myers of Pensacola and reported on his large and well selected library and large collection of newspapers. In East Tennessee, J. G. M. Ramsey had a library of some 4,000 volumes.[42]

Southwestern planters bought a considerable if uncounted number of books on religion, political theory, and medicine, as well as English classics. Elisha Washington, with plantations in Mississippi and Arkansas, had 5,000 volumes. M. W. Philips of Mississippi, planter and agricultural reformer, probably had as many books as Hugh Davis of Alabama, a planter who had 631. In the early days of the Republic of Texas, Ashbel Smith of Houston had a library of notable quality and size, and even in an outpost like Nacogdoches, a few men, notably lawyers, had several hundred volumes. Anson Jones, president of the Republic of Texas, physician and owner of only five slaves, had 1,000 – medicine and science, history and philosophy – with which his sister Mary tutored his children. Most books were in English, but some in French and Latin and two in Greek. Stephen Austin and Louis T. Wigfall, among other wealthy Texans, acquired ample libraries. The Ingram brothers on the San Bernardo River, both avid readers, had from 300 to 400 volumes and a collection of maps and atlases.[43]

[42] *The Reminiscences of William C. Preston*, ed., Minnie Clare Yarbrough, (Chapel Hill, NC, 1933), 4; Kate Mason Rowland, *The Life of Charles Carroll of Carrollton, 1737–1832, with His Speeches Public Papers, and Correspondence*, 2 vols. (Whitefish, MT,), 1:66; Frank J. Klingberg and Frank W. Klingberg, eds., *The Correspondence between Henry Stephens Randall and Hugh Blair Grigsby, 1856–1861* (Berkeley, CA, 1952), 136, ed. n. 71; Mills Lane, ed., *Neither More nor Less than Men: Slavery in Georgia* (Savannah, GA, 1993), 59 (Couper); Grady McWhiney, *Cracker Culture: Celtic Ways in the Old South* (Tuscaloosa, AL, 1988), 206; *DGB*, 1:252, 2:1010; Carol Bleser, ed., *Secret and Sacred: The Diaries of James Henry Hammond, a Southern Slaveholder* (New York, 1988), 3–4, 7, 93, and Carol Bleser, ed., *The Hammonds of Redcliffe* (New York, 1981), 3–4; Fletcher M. Green, *The Role of the Yankee in the Old South* (Athens, GA, 1972), 104; William B. Hesseltine, ed., *Dr. J. G. M. Ramsey, Autobiography and Letters* (Knoxville, TN, 2002), viii; John Rudolph Niernsee to Miss L. R. Simpson, Sept. 20, 1838, in Simpson Papers.

[43] John Hebron Moore, *The Emergence of the Cotton Kingdom in Old Southwest: Mississippi, 1770–1860* (Baton Rouge, LA, 1988), 137; Clement Eaton, *The Freedom-of-Thought Struggle in the Old South* (New York, 1964), 59 (Philips); William R. Hogan, *The Texas Republic: A Social and Economic History* (Austin, TX, 1969), 186–187, 252; *HT*, 1:856; Herbert Gambrell, *Anson Jones: The Last President of Texas* (Garden City, NY, 1948), 420–421; Silverthorne, *Plantation Life in Texas*, 181; Alvy L. King, *Louis T. Wigfall: Southern Fire-Eater* (Baton Rouge, LA, 1970), 10.

Presumably, the many private libraries judged "large" or "fine" included a few hundred carefully selected books. Local reputations attached to such forgotten men as Joel Abbot, a prominent planter, politician, and nationally respected physician in Wilkes County, Georgia, and A. A. Smuts of Savannah, a merchant whose library included rare illuminated medieval manuscripts.[44]

Since estate appraisers often undervalued libraries, their estimates may be taken as minimal. The wealthy Plowden Weston's library had an estimated value of $15,000. William Terrell of Sparta, Georgia, congressman, owner of 200 slaves, who endowed the chair in agricultural science at the state university, had a library appraised at $1,500. In the heavily slave-holding region in the Broad River Valley of South Carolina substantial libraries abounded, with emphasis on history, biography, and religious works. Marshall's *Life of Washington* rivaled religious books in popularity, and Martha Harris's collection ran from Clarendon's six-volume history to James Foster's sermons. James Barrow, famous for his hospitality at "Beulah," had the finest collection to be found between Savannah and Athens. Thomas Holly Chivers, the well-known poet, preferred the fast life of the Northeast but sought consolation in the large library on his plantation. In Greensboro, Alabama, Sophia Pearson lamented the loss of her academy school's teacher's library, appraised at $2,000.[45]

Among the leading divines, James Warley Miles (Episcopalian) had a magnificent library of 1,600 volumes. Moses Waddel (Presbyterian) administered a large circulating library that included history and philosophy as well as religious subjects. The young John C. Calhoun and William H. Crawford retained fond memories of the fourteen weeks they spent immersed in Waddel's library. James Henley Thornwell (Presbyterian), not a man given to boasting, claimed America's largest private collection of works on logic. Bishop Stephen Elliott (Episcopalian) had an exceptionally large library in Savannah, richly complemented by an art

---

[44] *DGB*, 1:1 (Abbot); Eaton, Freedom-of-Thought, 60 (Smuts); John Q. Anderson, ed. *Brokenburn: The Journal of Kate Stone, 1861–1868* (Baton Rouge, LA, 1955), Dec. 25, 1863 (270).

[45] G. C. Rogers, Jr., *The History of Georgetown County, South Carolina* (Columbia, SC, 1970), 259 (Weston); E. Merton Coulter, *Daniel Lee, Agriculturalist: His Life North and South* (Athens, GA, 1972), ch. 10; E. Merton Coulter, *Old Petersburg and the Broad River Valley of Georgia: Their Rise and Decline* (Athens, GA, 1965), 27, 157; James C. Bonner, ed., *The Journal of a Milledgeville Girl, 1861–1867*, ed. (Athens, GA, 1964), 38 (on Barrow); Charles Henry Watts, II., *Thomas Holley Chivers: His Literary Career and His Poetry* (Athens, GA, 1956), 5; Sophia E. Pearson to John W. Ellis, June 14, 1846, in Noble J. Tolbert, ed., *The Papers of John Willis Ellis*, 2 vols. (Raleigh, NC, 1964), 1:19.

collection. Father Guillou of Natchez (Catholic) left some 400 volumes at his death in 1863. Speaking in Belfast, Ireland in the 1840s, Frederick Douglass had some sport. He held up a notice of the sale of a southern clergyman's estate, which included land "together with twenty-seven negroes – some of them very fine – a library chiefly theological – two mules and an old waggon." To the laughter of his audience, Douglass remarked, "We should be sadly weeping that such a man ever lived."[46]

TOWNHOUSES

The lavishness of planter hospitality and the scale of planter libraries often contrasted with the modesty of their country homes. The rarity of impressive plantation mansions puzzled travelers. Many wealthy planters, worth perhaps $40,000–50,000, lived in double log cabins or modest extensions of them. A "Gentleman on a Tour of Business in the Southern Country" noted in 1817, as others did decades later, that wealthy planters on the Georgia coast spent their summers elsewhere. The plantation "dwelling house," he wrote, was no family mansion, but "perhaps a mere shell, destitute of those improvements necessary for a comfortable residence." In the up country, Judge Junius Hillyer recalled fashionably, expensively dressed masters and mistresses who lived in rude plantation houses, while they maintained residences in places like Madison Springs. In the 1850s, ex-Governor John Forsyth described the typical planter's house as a rude log structure "with rail fences and rickety gates."[47]

From colonial days, coastal planters had both a country home and a more costly and handsome townhouse. For every planter who built an imposing mansion and furnished it extravagantly, numerous others settled for a comfortable, inexpensive, unpretentious dwelling that hardly met the model of what slaves called the Big House. Louis Hughes, who

[46] Ralph Luker, *A Southern Tradition in Theology and Social Criticism, 1830–1930: The Religious Liberalism and Social Conservatism of James Warley Miles, William Porcher DuBose and Edgar Gardner Murphy* (New York, 1984), 85 (Miles); Charles M. Wiltse, *John C. Calhoun*, 3 vols. (Indianapolis, IN, 1944–1951), 1:26; *JHTW*, 4:232; V. S. Davis, "Stephen Elliott," 56–57; William Henry Elder, *Civil War Diary, 1862–1865* (Natchez, MS, n.d.), July 4, 1863 (51); J. E. D. Shipp, *Giant Days; or, The Life and Times of William H. Crawford*, (Americus, GA, 1909), 30; William S. McFeely, *Frederick Douglass* (New York, 1991), 128.

[47] "Tour of Georgia," in Schwaab and Bull, eds., *Travels in the South*, 1:144–145; *The Life and Times of Judge Junius Hillyer: From His Memoirs* (Tignall, GA, 1989), 75–77; James C. Bonner, *A History of Georgia Agriculture, 1732–1860* (Athens, GA, 1964), 68 (Forsyth).

had been a slave in Tennessee, described his wealthy master's plantation home as log-built and comfortable but hardly palatial; he described the townhouse in Memphis as impressive, with mahogany furniture and imported trimmings.[48]

With capital invested in slaves and land, most planters found that the costs of building a genuine mansion ran too high. Critics declared the slave economy backward, southern wealth fictitious, and planters' claims to affluence fraudulent. The criticisms had more than a few grains of truth, as did the apologetics that paid tribute to plain republican values, rustic simplicity, and lack of pretension. Some planters engaged in speculative plunging, but not many rushed into the extraordinary expenditures required to build a mansion, especially if they intended to furnish it with the best Europe had to offer. The mansion remained an ideal to be realized late in life, primarily as a legacy to generations that would carry on the family name. Planters who sought to live luxuriously and entertain lavishly preferred to live in town for at least part of the year. When in the country, they spent most of their time outdoors and provided simple, comfortable houses to accommodate guests. Those who flaunted their wealth did so where it would more be widely noticed – in Charleston, Savannah, Natchez, or another accessible town.[49]

Styles varied, but townhouses generally had two levels, some three, each with several rooms. The larger, well-appointed ones in Athens, Georgia, for example, had porticos, piazzas, and spacious gardens, which became more elaborate as time went on. In Holly Springs, Mississippi, wealthy planters entertained elegantly in townhouses that featured up-to-date watering systems as well as costly furniture. In the 1830s, Joseph Holt Ingraham of Natchez, among others, complained about the dearth of flowers in plantation yards. Yet, Southerners had a passion for flowers, and by the 1840s, practice satisfied passion. Charleston became renowned for lovely gardens well before the fashion spread to lowcountry plantations. Savannah boasted camellia japonicas, which grew to

---

[48] Louis Hughes, *Thirty Years a Slave: From Bondage to Freedom* (New York, 1969 [1857]), 16–17, 59–63; Daniel R. Hundley, *Social Relations in Our Southern States* (Baton Rouge, LA, 1979 [1860]), 57; Richard Beale Davis, *Intellectual Life in the Colonial South, 1515–1763*, 3 vols. (Knoxville, TN, 1978), 3:1166; Joe Gray Taylor, *Eating, Drinking, and Visiting in the South: An Informal History* (Baton Rouge, LA, 1982), 54.

[49] Some planters, accustomed to luxurious town living, tried to upgrade their plantation homes. See, Burnette Vanstory, *Georgia's Land of the Golden Isles* (Athens, GA, 1956), 79; Samuel Gaillard Stoney, *Plantations of the South Carolina Low Country* (Charleston, SC, 1938), E. Merton Coulter, *Wormsloe: Two Centuries of a Georgia Family* (Athens, GA, 1955), 213–214.

great heights. A horticultural revival marked the 1850s, as planters took great pride in their flowers, trees, and approach to the Big House. Valcour Aime of Louisiana, a wealthy sugar planter, beautified his plantation with famous gardens, trees, and vines from Korea, Japan, Siam, Madagascar, and Central America. Live oaks – or magnolias, crepe myrtles, and Pride of India cedars – lined drives or shaded yards. Front yards sported zinnias, dahlias, hollyhocks, and especially roses.[50]

Town elites had discrete, historically grounded styles. In Natchez, colonial Spanish and French tastes blended with Anglo-American to create a specific style or, better, styles: wide roofs and windows, balconies, paved patios and courtyards, impressive pillars, deep chimneys, spacious rooms with high ceilings. Foreign architects, craftsmen, and plantation slaves skilled in brickmaking and ironwork, designed and built elaborate homes with dazzling gardens. Planters imported well-seasoned timber, materials, and furniture from England, France, and Italy: ironwork from Philadelphia; silver fittings for doors, bronze chandeliers, Brussels carpets, elegant wallpaper, elaborately carved mahogany and rosewood furniture, exquisite curtains and draperies, handsome silver tableware and china, paintings, and sculpture. The planters of the Delta thereby demonstrated how sweet life could be for wealthy planters. Precious few less wealthy slaveholders could keep up with these Joneses.[51]

---

[50] Ernest C. Hynds, *Antebellum Athens and Clarke County, Georgia* (Athens, GA, 1974), 123; Pruitt, *It Happened Here*, 27, 60, 65; [Joseph Holt Ingraham], *The South-West. By a Yankee*, 2 vols. (n.p., 1966 [1835]), 2:98, 100–103, 115; James C. Bonner, *A History of Georgia Agriculture, 1732–1860* (Athens, GA, 1964), 172–173; Ulrich Bonnell Phillips, *Life and Labor in the Old South* (Boston, MA, 1948[1929]), 335–337; Franklin L. Riley, ed., "Diary of a Mississippi Planter," in *Publications of the Mississippi Historical Society*, 10 (1909), 306–307; Jean Bradley Anderson, *Piedmont Plantation: The Bennehan-Cameron Family and Lands in North Carolina* (Durham, NC, 1985), 52–53; Glyndon G. Van Deusen, *The Life of Henry Clay* (Boston, MA, 1937), 151; Rembert W. Patrick, *Aristocrat in Uniform: General Duncan L. Clinch* (Gainesville, FL, 1963), 158; Walter J. Fraser, Jr., *Charleston! Charleston!: The History of a Southern City* (Columbia, SC, 1989), 177–178; Caroline Couper Lovell, *The Light of Other Days* (Macon, GA, 1995), 20; Alicia Hopton Middleton, "A Family Record," in Middleton et al., *Life in Carolina and New England During the Nineteenth Century* (Bristol, RI, 1929), 61;. On Aime, see Harnett T. Kane, *Plantation Parade: The Grand Manner in Louisiana* (New York, 1955), 31, 33; for chinaberry trees, see Camilla Davis Trammell, *Seven Pines: Its Occupants and Their Letters, 1825–1872* (Houston, TX, 1986), 83.

[51] See esp. Theodora Britton Marshall and Gladys Crail Evans, *They Found It in Natchez* (New Orleans, La., 1939), 179 ff – the language of which I have freely appropriated here. Also, Pierce Butler, *The Unhurried Years: Memories of the Old Natchez Region* (Baton Rouge, La., 1948), 3–5, 15.

2

Dining Room, Parlor, and Lawn

Une cuisine et une politesse! Oui, les
deux signes de vieille civilisation.[1]

The Big House, as slaves customarily called their master's home, varied
in style and size over time across the South and even within a small
geographical area. Arriving from the Northeast in 1839, the urbane
Priscilla Cooper Tyler limned the essentials of President John Tyler's
home in Williamsburg, Virginia: "The home is very airy and pleasant,
fronting on a large lawn and surrounded by a most beautiful garden.
The parlor is comfortably furnished, and has that homelike and occupied look which is so nice." She considered the dining room opposite to
the parlor across a broad passage "too bright and shiny almost to step
upon, and ... also a very spacious room, with a great deal of old family
silver adorning the sideboard, and some good pictures on the walls."
Two rooms, one a sitting room, lay behind the parlor and the dining-
room. And there was "a large double house flanked by offices in the
yard in which the library is kept, and one of which is used for law and
business purposes by Mr. Tyler's father and himself." She added, "The
room in the main dwelling furthest removed and most retired is the
'chamber,' as the bedroom of the mistress is always called in Virginia.
This last, to say nothing of others, or of the kitchen, storerooms and

[1] Gilberto Freyre, the great Brazilian historical sociologist, quoted this *bon mot* but could
not recall its origin. No matter: It speaks for itself. Here, we shall primarily discuss the
dining of the elite. For fine accounts of the dining among the non-elite, see especially, Joe
Gray Taylor, *Eating, Drinking, and Visiting in the South: An Informal History* (Baton
Rouge, LA, 1982), 21.

pantries, is a most comfortable retreat, with an air of repose and sanctity about it."[2]

Ladies and gentlemen took dining seriously as a ritual that marked a way of life. Mary Randolph of Virginia observed, "The government of the family bears a Lilliputian resemblance to the government of the nation." She insisted, if implausibly, that mistresses rose early and prepared the table while the servants were eating. For Martha McCulloch-Williams of Tennessee, "Proper dinners mean so much – good blood, good judgment, good conduct." In the early 1830s, Frances Trollope, the English novelist, read southern cookbooks, which reinforced her impression that Southerners considered cuisine the most important ingredient in being southern. Yet during Reconstruction, Edward King, in his sympathetic portrait of the "Great South," observed that probably no Northerner went south without raging against the poor quality of food outside well-to-do homes and the best hotels. In the mountains King found "hot and indigestible corn bread, fried and greasy ham or bacon, as it is universally called in the South." The occasional beefsteak came "remorsefully fried until not a particle of juice remained." No wonder Southerners drank whiskey at table: They needed it. King nonetheless concluded that wherever "culture and refinement" prevailed, so did "the best of cookery, an educated taste in wines, and a thorough appreciation of good things."[3]

The kitchens stood well removed from the Big House not only to protect from fire, but also to shut out odors, music, and the chattering voices of the black children who usually gathered there. Some dining rooms were even across from the porch, semi-detached from the main part of the house. In the more affluent townhouses the kitchen would be in the basement, along with the pantry; a dumbwaiter carried food up to the dining room. The southern penchant for detached buildings bemused Harriet Beecher Stowe, who settled in Florida after the War: "In the South, where building-material is cheap, and building is a slight matter,

---

[2] From Mrs. Tyler's letters to her sisters, in Oliver Perry Chitwood, *John Tyler: Champion of the Old South* (New York, 1939), 198–199; see also, Elizabeth Tyler Coleman, *Priscilla Cooper Tyler and the American Scene, 1816–1889* (University, AL, 1955), 72–75.

[3] Mary Randolph, *The Virginia Housewife; or, Methodological Cook* (Philadelphia, 1860 [1831]), iii; Martha McCulloch-Williams, *Dishes and Beverages of the Old South* (Knoxville, TN, 1988 [1913], 9; Frances Trollope, *Domestic Manners of the Americans* (Gloucester, MA, 1974 [1832]), 154; Edward King, *The Great South: A Record of Journeys*, 2 vols. (New York, 1969 [1875]) 2: 791. References to beef may be misleading. We may wonder how much of it was veal, which became a favorite, as the beef was usually tough and did not keep well: Taylor, *Eating, Drinking, and Visiting*, 54; Sam Hilliard, *Hog Meat and Hoecake: Food Supply in the Old South* (Carbondale, IL, 1972), 81.

there is a separate little building for every thing; and the back part of the estate looks an eruption of little houses .... There is a milk-house, a corn-house, a tool-house, a bake-house, besides a house for each of the leading servants, making quite a village."[4]

Not every traveler and sojourner found the setting charming. No few recoiled from the appearance and demeanor of the black dining room servants. Mrs. Hall complained, as did travelers long after, that "the nasty, black creatures whom they have for servants" marred southern parties, which lacked "any appearance of style." Dressed in coarse, ill-made cloth, "They all look so dirty. You can't imagine how disagreeable it is to have so many of the creatures about." Thirty years later at a neat and attractive farmhouse, Frederick Law Olmsted could not abide the two "dirty, slovenly dressed, negro girls" who waited on table. In contrast, when Benjamin Perry of South Carolina dined with Martin Van Buren at Kinderhook, New York – "a sumptuous dinner" for seven or eight – he noted only one waiter, a young white woman: "All the guests were well attended to. At a Southern table there would have been three or four negroes in each other's way, and the table not so well waited on." Catherine Cooper Hopley of England, teaching in Virginia, grumbled that the slaves served at their own pleasure, often delaying from one to three hours. Yet, in private homes from tidewater to Texas, guests appreciated being fanned during hot summer dinners. Clara von Gerstner of Germany welcomed slaves who carried long-handled fans of peacock feathers to keep flies off food. Plantations and townhouses in Louisiana featured a "punkah" – a large ceiling fan propelled by servants. By 1830 or so, complaints about raucous stag dinners faded, although college students and single young men carried on the obnoxious tradition, replete with vulgar jokes and coarse language.[5]

In eighteenth-century Charleston, the rural styles of buildings and town houses suggested nothing so much as the prestige and influence of the planters. Well into the nineteenth century, slaves served at extravagant dinner parties in specially colored livery that identified the elite family. Yet, even for the wealthiest of planters, unanticipated kitchen crises

[4] Harriet Beecher Stowe, *Palmetto Leaves* (Gainesville, FL, 1968 [1873]), 239; Herschel Gower and Jack Allan, *Pen and Sword: The Life and Journals of Randal W. McGavock* (Nashville, Tenn., 1959), 28.

[5] Henry St. John Dixon Diary, July 6, 1860, in Stephen Berry, ed., *Princes of Cotton: Four Diaries of Young Men in the South, 1848–1860* (Athens, GA, 2007), 136–137. For the prevalence of too many servants at dinner and other functions, see Lorri Glover, *Southern Sons: Becoming Men in the New Nation* (Baltimore, 2007), 33, 174.

spoiled the best of plans. The Coupers of St. Simon's, Georgia, presided over elegant dinner parties, replete with fine wines. Yet, on some occasions the meat spoiled, and the fishermen brought in little. Hosts and guests had to make do with bacon and eggs or whatever poor fare could be put together.[6]

AT TABLE

Especially before Victoria's crowning as Queen of England, gentlemen often dined without their ladies, reveling in abominable language, rowdiness, and competition to consume the most liquor. Thomas Jefferson contrasted the good table manners in Paris with the drunken behavior in Virginia. A mortified William Campbell Preston recollected the "habitual smut" of William Branch Giles of Virginia, William H. Crawford of Georgia, and other men of standing: "All the gentlemen of that generation had fallen into this sort of talk, a practice that was said to have come to us from the higher circles of England where a foulness of conversation had been propagated by Mr. [Charles James] Fox and his boon companions." A check on miserable behavior: Educated Southerners read Horace and Petronius, who pilloried vulgarity and pretension at the dinner parties of arrivistes.[7]

Table etiquette improved steadily by the 1830s. Still, in the 1850s, to the dismay of Rosalie Roos, a Swedish teacher in Charleston, respected gentlemen spit in presence of ladies and put their feet up on chairs. Governor Joseph Brown of Georgia mentioned prominent men who indulged in "profane swearing in public and private, a mode of parlance and emphasis that, like that of drinking in high life, has to be tolerated on account of the respectability and number of men of wealth and social power who follow it; but which lowers the dignity and weakens the influence of many of the able men of the state." "W. J. G." wrote frankly of boorish behavior at upper-class dinners and welcomed its passing.

---

[6] Maurie D. McInnis, *The Politics of Taste in Antebellum Charleston* (Chapel Hill, NC, 2005), 48–49, 255; Walter J. Fraser, Jr., *Charleston! Charleston!: The History of a Southern City* (Columbia, SC, 1989), 129–130; T. Reed Ferguson, *The John Couper Family at Cannon's Point* (Macon, GA, 1994), 77, 81–82.

[7] David Moltke-Hansen, "Expansion of intellectual Life," in Michael O'Brien and David Moltke-Hansen, eds., *Intellectual Life in Antebellum Charleston* (Knoxville, TN, 1986), 32; on Jefferson, see Charles Downer Hazen, *Contemporary American Opinion of the French Revolution* (Gloucester, MA, 1964), 9–10; Minnie Clare Yarbrough, ed., *The Reminiscences of William C. Preston* (Chapel Hill, NC, 1933), 7. See "Dinner at Trimalchio's" in Petronius, *The Satyricon*, tr. P. G. Walsh (Oxford, 1996), ch. 6.

In contrast, Frances Trollope reported from Washington, southern congressmen, unlike northern, sat politely at table, removing their hats and refraining from spitting. In 1844 the northern-born Episcopalian Reverend John Hamilton Cornish described a dinner with fifteen gentlemen at the local club on Edisto Island "as decorous & orderly as though they were a Clergymen's table, instead of the Club-House. I think not more than three bottles of wine were drunk & the other liquors remained untasted." Arthur Middleton's locally famous stag parties displayed fine wines and the superb service provided by John, the ever-attentive butler.[8]

As etiquette improved, so did cuisine. American cuisine, including southern, absorbed European fine tastes slowly and unevenly. But then, continentals, particularly the French, grew impatient with British practices. At least as early as the reign of Queen Anne, the French ambassador complained that England possessed some twenty-four religious sects but only two fish sauces. R. F. W. Allston reported on Preston's dinner in Columbia in honor of Governor Manning. Allston endured bad soup, albeit served in a silver terrine, but dinner recouped quickly: "A magnificent feast it was ... We had salmon trout from the lake, bass and whiting from the sea, a saddle of mutton from England (butcher'd there) capons from N. Y., Pheasants from N. W. Canvass back from the Chesapeake and such beautiful dessert & creams as you might imagine." In 1867, Harriet Beecher Stowe got a taste of plantation dining in Florida: "Our dinner was a beautiful display of the luxuries of a Southern farm – finely-flavored fowl, choicely cooked fish from the river, soft-shell turtle soup, with such a tempting variety of early vegetables as seemed to make it impossible to do justice to all." She judged the home-made wine reminiscent of good sherry and savored the assorted "dainties" for dessert.[9]

---

[8] Rosalie Roos to Ulrika Roos, July 30, 1852, in Rosalie Roos, *Travels in America, 1851–1855*, tr. Carl L. Anderson (Carbondale, IL, 1982), 60; Herbert Fielder, *A Sketch of the Life and Times and Speeches of Joseph E. Brown* (Springfield, MA, 1883), 56; Trollope, *Domestic Manners*, 154; W. J. G., "The Character of the Gentleman," *SQR*, 7 (1853), 75–77; Cornish Diary, March 28, 1844; Alicia Hopton Middleton et al., *Life in Carolina and New England During the Nineteenth Century* (Bristol, RI, 1929), 63; Rene Ravenel Diary, May 6, 1800, May 9, 1801, Sept. 12, 1811, in Henry Edmund Ravenel, *Ravenel Records* (Atlanta, GA, 1898).

[9] "Conservative Cookery," *SLM*, 16 (1850), 470; R. F. W. Allston to Adele Petigru Allston, Dec. 8, 1854, in J. H. Easterby, ed., *The South Carolina Rice Plantation, as Revealed in the Papers of Robert F. W. Allston* (Chicago, IL, 1945), 122; Harriet Beecher Stowe, *Palmetto Leaves* (Gainesville, FL, 1968 [1873]), 239–240. Lowcountry planters also had a taste for she-crab soup. Turnips, sweet potatoes, and catsup were popular with all classes. See John Martin Taylor, *Hoppin' John's Charleston, Beaufort, and Savannah: Dining at Home in the Lowcountry* (New York, 1997), 46, 48; Taylor, *Eating, Drinking, and Visiting*, 37–38.

In all parts of the South, the well-to-do consumed great quantities of champagne, the quality of which invites conjecture. The *Southern Planter* of Richmond claimed in 1859 that Americans bought more champagne than the rest of the world put together. However hyperbolic this assertion, Southerners consumed a great deal, and knowledgeable contemporaries judged some of it good. Still, we may doubt the quality of the large quantities served at political and other events – as when upcountry unionist John S. Preston, running for the South Carolina legislature in 1854, provided supporters with three wagonloads of champagne. In Mississippi in 1841, during the struggle over repudiation of the state debt, the Democratic newspapers assailed anti-repudiation Whigs who "drink champagne as the ordinary beverage of the day." Margaux and other Clarets, which traveled better than most good wines, appeared on the tables of the well-to-do. Madeira, sherry, and port were served with main courses as well as with dessert. Wealthy Virginians favored fine old Madeira as an aperitif before light suppers, and the ladies enjoyed it in desserts by mixing it with ice cream or ice, sugar, and nutmeg.[10]

Jefferson, a connoisseur, considered wine "a necessary of Life" and promoted the French and Italian, as well as the production of American as healthful substitutes for hard liquor and the heavily alcoholic Madeira and port. Dr. William Michel, speaking at the Medical Society of South Carolina, agreed, recommending wine in moderation as healthful. John C. Calhoun proved exceptional in drinking claret at dinner and Madeira afterwards. Called "East India," Madeira became a favorite dinner wine with the more aristocratic Carolinians and Virginians. Among foreign travelers, John Melish commented on its frequent use for holiday toasts in Georgia, and Charles Augustus Murray rated the Madeira served in Virginia as excellent. Planters served milk to the ladies and whiskey, which cost half as much as Madeira, to the men. But many Virginia planters, while generous in making liquor available to guests, did not serve it at table.[11]

---

[10] "Champagne Wine – Some Curious Facts about It," *Southern Planter*, 19 (1859), 168; Dallas C. Dickey, *Seargent S. Prentiss: Whig Orator of the Old South* (Baton, Rouge, LA, 1945), 209–210; Cornish Diary, March 28, 1857 (visiting Hammond).

[11] James M. Gabler, "Jefferson and Wine" in Damon Lee Fowler, ed., *Dining at Monticello: In Good Taste and Abundance* (Charlottesville, VA, 2005), quote at 86; Lisa King, "America's First Wine Connoisseur," *Wine Spectator*, 15 (1991), 24–33; Dr. William Michel, "Essay on Wine," *Carolina Journal of Medicine, Science, and Agriculture*, 1 (1825), 28; John Niven, *John C. Calhoun and the Price of Union: A Biography* (Baton Rouge, LA, 1988), 155; Frederick Law Olmsted, *A Journey in the Seaboard Slave States* (New York, 1968 [1856]), 92 and 326–327 (North Carolina); John Melish, *Travels in*

Farmers, unlike planters, usually could not afford wine at table, preferring water, whiskey, or homemade beer. Jefferson produced beer principally for his slaves and hired white workers. In the 1790s Louis-Philippe tasted good beer only in the homes and inns of German immigrants. In Alabama, farmers and planters made their own beer, much of it intended for their slaves. Virginia planters and hill country whites in Arkansas held persimmon beer parties for their slaves and enjoyed persimmon wines and liquors themselves. In North Carolina young women especially enjoyed sweet beer made from locust tree bark. Whatever beer was made of, it was likely raw. In Beaufort District, South Carolina, L. M. De Saussure, a planter-physician with eighty-seven slaves, fermented ginger beer in twenty-four hours and served it three days after bottling. Homemade brandies and cordials sold cheaply by the glass, since almost every farmer made his own. The rapidity with which farmers produced them suggests that imbibers required strong stomachs. Everard Green Baker of Mississippi, a planter, recommended Miss Leslie's recipe for blackberry cordials: mash ripe blackberries, place in a linen bag, squeeze out the juice, and add a pound of beaten loaf sugar for every quart. Boil the concoction into a thin jelly; when cold, add a quart of brandy per quart of juice. For teetotalers, substitute vinegar for brandy.[12]

the United States of America, 2 vols. (Philadelphia, 1812), 1:42; Sir Charles Augustus Murray, *Travels in North America during the Years, 1834, 1835 and 1836* (London, 1839), 2:282; D. W. Mitchell, *Ten Years in the United States: Being an Englishman's Views of Men and Things in the North and South* (London, 1862), 86; Mrs. [Sara Agnes Rice] Roger Pryor, *My Day: Reminiscences of a Long Life* (EE: 1997 [1909]), 60, 119. Jefferson enjoyed Italian wines, praising Chianti Classico but awarding the palm to Montepulciano: John Hallman, *Thomas Jefferson on Wine* (Jackson, MS, 2006), 3, 303–304.

[12] Taylor, *Eating, Drinking, and Visiting*, 44; for Preston, see Ethel Trenholm Seabrook Nepveux, *Sarah Henry Bryce, 1825–1901: A Glimpse at a Remarkable Woman in the Turbulent Civil War Era* (Charleston, SC, 1994), 28; Edwin Morris Betts, ed., Thomas Jefferson's Farm Book: With Commentary and Relevant Extracts from His Writings (Charlottesville, VA, 1987), 414; Louis-Philippe, King of France, *Diary of My Travels in America*, tr. Stephen Becker (New York, 1976), Apr. 13, 1797 (41); Weymouth T. Jordan, *Ante-Bellum Alabama: Town and Country* (Tallahassee, FL, 1957), 75; Rosena H. Lassiter to Susan E. Southall, Apr. 12, 1864, in Brashear and Lawrence Family Papers (locust beer); Hugh Jones, *The Present State of Virginia: From Whence Is Inferred a Short View of Maryland and North Carolina*, ed. Richard L. Morton (Chapel Hill, NC, 1956), 86; Taylor Diary, March 20, 1748; *Farmers' Register*, 6 (1838), 58–61; Nellie Lloyd, in *AS*: S. C., 3 (pt. 3), 128; John Gould Fletcher, *Arkansas* (Fayetteville, AR, 1989), 20; Lyle Saxon et al., *Gumbo Ya-Ya: A Collection of Louisiana Folk Tales* (New York, 1945), 239; De Saussure Plantation Record Book, 1857; Baker Diary, undated entry, probably 1848. In Virginia and Kentucky, metheglin (spiced mead) was a great favorite: J. Winston Coleman, Jr., *Stage-Coach Days in the Bluegrass: Being an Account of Stage-Coach*

South Carolina had no few "two-bottle a day" gentlemen and delighted in showing visitors their orchards and wine cellars. In the 1830s Charles Augustus Murray praised the wines served in Charleston and New Orleans as better than those usually served at suppers in Britain. Southerners, he said, served good wine at all meals, not merely – as abroad – at extravagant dinner parties. Even Francis Lieber, who complained about almost everything southern, agreed with Murray.[13]

The ladies did not qualify as teetotalers or even as abstemious. Most eschewed whiskey and did not drink wine, except champagne, in substantial quantities. In Tennessee and westward they enjoyed apple toddies made with whiskey and "Grandmother's Cherry Bounce" from corn liquor. Generally, the ladies preferred apricots, cherries, and peaches soaked in brandy; peach and raspberry cordials; and peach, strawberry, and blackberry wines. The low country favored several kinds of blancmange, including a popular version that combined milk with substantial amounts of wine and brandy and an alternative with isinglass, cream, sugar, blanched almonds, vanilla, and wine. Syllabub, ostensibly a ladylike substitute for serious imbibing, was a drink or dessert made from sweetened milk or cream, eggs and powdered sugar lemon, curdled with white wine, or Madeira. It was then whipped until stiff and chilled. Punch sounds innocent enough but – especially as "Roman punch" – it came heavily spiked with rum and home-made peach brandy, a widespread favorite. The ubiquitous Christmas eggnog combined a pint of brandy and rum or whiskey with a quart of milk.[14]

In the low country good taste prevailed and ostentation provoked scorn. Jonathan Everts, a northern traveler in Georgia in 1822, dined

Travel and Taverns in Lexington and Central Kentucky, 1800–1890 (Lexington, KY, 1995), 61–62.

[13] Richard Barry, *Mr. Rutledge of South Carolina* (New York, 1942), 75; Sir Charles Augustus Murray, *Travels in North America during the Years, 1834, 1835 and 1836* (London, 1839), 2:280; Lieber Diary, April 2, 1835, in Thomas Sergeant Perry, ed., *The Life and Letters of Francis Lieber* (Boston, MA, 1882), 105; for low country ladies see J. S. Buckingham, *The Slave States of America* (New York, 1968 [1842]), 1:125. For Champagne and wine bottles in the archeological digs at low country plantations, see James L. Michie, *Richmond Hill Plantation, 1810–1868* (Spartanburg, SC, 1990), 119.

[14] [Sarah Rutledge], *The Carolina Housewife*, ed. Anna Wells Rutledge (Columbia, SC, 1979 [1847]), 142–143, 149–150, 155, 171; Randolph, *Virginia Housewife*, 147, 150–151, 160–161, 172–173; McCulloch-Williams, Dishes and Beverages of the Old South, 72-76-77, 82–83, 233; Lettice Bryan, *The Kentucky Housewife* (Bedford, MA, n.d. [1839]), 408; Marion Cabell Tyree, ed., *Housekeeping in Old Virginia* (Louisville, KY, 1884), 422; Harriet Ross Colquitt, *The Savannah Cookbook: A Collection of Old Fashioned Receipts from Colonial Kitchens* (Atlanta, GA, 1960), 113.

with Connecticut-born Dr. Lemuel Kollock in Savannah. Mrs. Bratton, Kollock's niece, set "the most elegant table in the city." The fare: duck, bacon, oysters (cooked two ways), onions, bread, and boiled rice, followed by cherry pie, cranberry pie, quince oranges and other preserves, salad, cheese, butter and a "very delicious" pineapple-flavored whipped cream. Everts dined in other homes, concluding, "The luxury of this city, as exhibited at dinners, is very great." At the plantation of a drunken Mr. Mongin and his miserable slaves, he was pleasantly surprised by the breakfast of ten to twelve hot dishes and many cold ones. But he wondered: How did the slaves manage to prepare such a feast in a kitchen with so few utensils? In contrast, Mrs. David Hillhouse of Washington, Georgia, dined at Mr. C.'s in Savannah and did not enjoy being told the price of the chicken pie, ham, and wine, although she much enjoyed them along with the fish, oysters, shrimp, crab, apple dumplings, and cheese. She exploded in a letter to her son: "What a waste of money in a man that will not or cannot pay a debt of one dollar, and what a waste of paper and time in noticing such nonsense."[15]

"The chief magnificence of the Virginians," the Marquis de Chastellux remarked in the 1780s, "consists in furniture, linen, and silver plate." In colonial times and long afterwards, the gentry of Virginia's Northern Neck anxiously awaited the arrival of the ships laden with large quantities of imported fine furniture, porcelain, silk and cotton drapery, silver and plate flatware, and delicate glassware, calf-bound books, jewelry, musical instruments, tools, and toys. As late as 1802, when George Tucker married and settled in eastern Virginia, he ordered furniture from London and New York, judging it better and cheaper than anything in Richmond. Wealthy planters in Mississippi and Louisiana ordered custom-made furniture through New Orleans.[16]

Life in the big house became hectic during the summer, when servants took up carpets and rugs and polished the wooden floors daily, scouring them with dry pine needles. Sarah Gayle, wife of the governor of Alabama, annoyed at having her comfort disturbed by the scouring of

---

[15] Everts in Edward J. Cashin, ed., *A Wilderness Still the Cradle of Nature* (Savannah, GA, 1994), 63–64; Mrs. David Hillhouse to David Hillhouse, April 25, 1808, in Marion Alexander Boggs, ed. *The Alexander Letters, 1787–1900* (Athens, GA, 1980), 50–51.

[16] Marquis de Chastellux, *Travels in North America in the Years 1780, 1781, and 1782*, 2 vols., rev. tr. H. C. Rice, Jr. (Chapel Hill, NC, 1963), 2:441; Robert Allen Rutland, *George Mason: Reluctant Statesman* (Baton Rouge, LA, 1961), 21 (Northern Neck); "Autobiography of George Tucker," *Bermuda Historical Quarterly*, 18 (1961), 110; William C. Davis, *Jefferson Davis: The Man and His Hour* (New York, 1991), 184.

her dining room, rationalized: "[It] endangers the health of the servant." Mahogany became the rage among the wealthy. Slaves polished it daily by rubbing with cloth moistened with cork and a mixture of beeswax and turpentine. Robert Stafford, a planter on Cumberland Island, produced 600 pounds of beeswax and honey. Servants had to rub hard to keep brass handles shiny. Throughout the South, slaves recognized mahogany sofas, desks, and tables as a mark of their masters' status and affluence. Early in the nineteenth century, the Coupers of St. Simon's, Georgia, spent $50 to $150 for mahogany sideboards, bureaus, and armoires. Bedsteads cost up to $80, dining room tables up to $100, breakfast tables between $10 and $20. The Duncan Clinches of Georgia, when married in the 1840s, spent more than $300 – an overseer's yearly salary – for mahogany bedsteads and a buffet and table for their dining room. Many well-to-do planters settled for artificial mahogany, which they made by planing a surface until smooth, rubbing it with a solution of wine, spirits, and carbonate of soda, followed by a coat of linseed oil. In Texas, from its republic onward, a mahogany sofa marked status.[17]

Only the most affluent planters and merchants could afford fine china and silver utensils. About 1815 in Petersburg, Georgia, fashionable blue dining sets cost $30 or more, silver spoons forty dollars a dozen. Cut-glass goblets, at $12 dollars, were used sparingly. Cicely Cawthon, an ex-slave in Georgia, recalled "Mistis had a set of fine glass she hardly ever used except got for mighty special company." John Berkley Grimball paid $110 for a set of China in 1833. In England, crude cutlery became common among the lower classes with the rise of factory production during the late eighteenth century, but forks did not come into general use in Milledgeville, the capital of Georgia, until the mid-1830s. Commonly, yeomen ate from wooden dishes and bowls, with a wooden spoon often the only utensil. Pewter spoons, bowls, and dishes slowly came into general use. Emily Burke reported from Georgia that the principal difference between yeomen kitchens and planters' lay with the utensils. Most yeomen, especially on the rough frontier, settled for

[17] Sarah Gayle Diary, Nov. 22, 1832; George Cary Eggleston, *A Rebel's Recollections* (Baton Rouge, LA, 1996 [1871]), 45; *Plantation Life: The Narratives of Mrs. Henry Schoolcraft* (New York, 1969 [1860]), 182-183n; Jordan, *Ante-Bellum Alabama*, 67; Mary R. Bullard, *Robert Stafford of Cumberland Island: Growth of a Planter* (Athens, GA, 1995), 5–6; Caroline Couper Lovell, *The Light of Other Days* (Macon, GA, 1995), 12; Ferguson, *The John Couper Family*, 75; Rembert W. Patrick, *Aristocrat in Uniform: General Duncan L. Clinch* (Gainesville, FL, 1963), 160; William R. Hogan, *The Texas Republic: A Social and Economic History* (Austin, TX, 1969), ch. 2.

pots, ovens, and skillets, maybe a kettle. Kitchens on the better-stocked plantations had Dutch ovens, spider pans (frying pans with legs), toasters, waffle irons, mortar and pestles, butter-making churns, and other instruments, as well as sugar, flour, and preserves. Slave cooks honed their skills in the quarters with much praised one-pot meals, including coosh-coosh – a fried cornmeal cereal popular in Louisiana – and ash cakes. The slave cooks who were so highly valued for their skills, produced the greatest delicacies of southern cuisine, but, as Elizabeth Fox-Genovese remarks, they did so in the master's kitchen and for his family and guests. Plantation cooks had trivets of various heights that they placed at just the right distance from the coals, long-handled forks, a spit for roasts, and an assortment of ladles, waffle-irons, and chafing dishes. Burke wondered that so small a room accommodated all this and more.[18]

Even small and middling slaveholders had a black woman cook. On large plantations the cook had one or more assistants. Cooks ran the kitchens with an iron hand, quick to inflict corporal punishment on slackers and incompetents. While Mum Jenny cooked for the whites, the three cooks under her supervision provided for the adult slaves, nurses, and the sick. Amelia Thompson Watts noted that she kept "a stout hickory stick. There was order in her department." In the Carolina low country Black Louisa supervised a large household and gardening staff of men and women. Ellen Betts of Louisiana recalled the mammy who doubled as cook "had to stoop to Aunt Rachel jes like dey curtsy to Missy." Women staffed the pastry department. Southerners loved desserts and considered first-rate pastry cooks priceless. In Charleston, masters sent slave girls to Sallie Seymour, a free woman of color described by Alicia Middleton as "the oracle for all the good things

---

[18] E. Merton Coulter, *Old Petersburg and the Broad River Valley of Georgia: Their Rise and Decline* (Athens, GA, 1965), 135; Christopher Hill, *Reformation to Industrial Revolution* (London, 1967), 9; James C. Bonner, *Milledgeville: Georgia's Antebellum Capital* (Athens, GA, 1978), 70; 19; Cicely Cawthon, in Ronald Killion and Charles Waller, eds., *Slavery Time When I was Chillun Down on Marster's Plantation* (Savannah, GA, 1973), 35; J. B. Grimball Diary, May 7, 1833; Emily P. Burke, *Reminiscences of Georgia* (Oberlin, OH, 1850), 178–179; Jennifer L. Eichstedt and Stephen Small, *Representations of Slavery: Race and Ideology in Southern Plantation Museums* (Washington, DC, 2002), 83; Elizabeth Fox-Genovese, *Within the Plantation Household: Black and White Women of the Old South* (Chapel Hill, NC, 1988), 161. For southern kitchens, see Taylor, *Eating, Drinking, and Visiting*. In the rural and small-town Northwest, the knife rather than fork fed the mouth: see R. Carlyle Buley, *The Old Northwest: Pioneer Period, 1815–1840*, 2 vols. (Bloomington, IN, 1950), 1:484.

of life which supplied the hospitable board at Pappoosequaw for two generations." [19]

The aristocratic Margaret Hunter (Mrs. Basil) Hall of England, visiting the United States in 1827, left descriptions of lavish dinner parties in the homes of the wealthy. Frances Trollope described the dinners of rich Northerners as "extremely dull" occasions meant to show off wealth, with ladies determined to wear half their income. The splendor of the dinner parties in Newport, Rhode Island, with its complement of aristocratic Southerners, impressed John and Caroline Preston of South Carolina as surpassing anything they had ever seen. Diamonds and lace worth $6,000 adorned one woman.

Mrs. Hall did not favor her readers with details until astonished by Governor John Taylor's home in Columbia, South Carolina. Dinner began at 4:30 P.M. Most southern families dined at 2 P.M. or 3 P.M. or a bit later, although in the low country the Westons and a few others carried on the English tradition of high tea and a main meal later in the day. The Taylors served turkey, duck, fish, roasted and boiled chicken, corned beef, and ham, which Mrs. Taylor carved. Sweet and Irish potatoes, cabbage, rice, and other vegetables were piled up, with eight pies for dessert. "Dinner was queer." In Charleston, Mrs. Hall dined with Stephen Elliott, James Louis Petigru, and other dignitaries: "A family dinner in Charleston is a very plain affair, if we are to judge by this [Elliott's] specimen ... No second course or pie or pudding." She objected to gentlemen's leaving their wives home, although she witnessed that offense throughout the Union. At a dinner in Charleston she remarked on the prettiness of the young women but protested their being "dressed so ill that they would mar even real beauty." Offsetting her disappointment with Charleston, she raved about dinner, and especially breakfast, at Mr. Skirving's plantation on the Combahee. But then, Mrs. Skirving was English. [20]

[19] Elisabeth Muhlenfeld, *Mary Boykin Chesnut: A Biography* (Baton Rouge, LA, 1981), 45; "A Family Record," in Middleton et al, *Life in Carolina and New England*, 5; T. Watts, "A Summer on a Louisiana Cotton Plantation in 1832," in Pharr Book (ms.); *AS:La.*, 4 (Pt. 1), 75.

[20] Una Pope-Hennessey, ed., [Margaret Hall], *Aristocratic Journey: Letters of Mrs. Basil Hall Written During a Fourteen Months' Sojourn in the United States* (New York, 1931), 28, 129–130, 139, 208–209, 211, 223; Fredrika Bremer, *Homes of the New World: Impressions of America*, 2 vols. (New York, 1853), 1:100; Trollope, *Domestic Manners*, 299; William Campbell Preston to Waddy Thompson, Aug. 28, 1853, in Preston Papers. The upper crust of New York and New England dined between 2 P.M. and 4 P.M. in adherence to the English model, but by 1868 Henry Adams complained that no one in Boston dined at 2 P.M. any longer: *The Education of Henry Adams* (Boston, MA, 1872), 241. Cf. Josephine Pinckney, *Three O'Clock Dinner* (New York, 1945).

The low country's sporting clubs held lavish stag dinners. On St. Simon, the St. Clair Club met for dinner once a month. A dozen or so gentlemen rotated in providing food and service in a convivial atmosphere. Deeming carriages effeminate, they arrived on horseback and dined at 5 P.M. before a roaring fire. A dinner presided over by John Couper featured blue East India china and was prepared by Sans Foix, a renowned free-black chef, who, according to Anna Matilda King, could debone a turkey and yet maintain its shape. The menu: clam broth and chicken mulligatawny soup, followed by a spread of crab-in-shell, roasts, vegetables, and shrimp or oyster pies, usually flavored with wine. Simple desserts: small tarts of orange marmalade, dried fruits, and nuts. After-dinner drinks: rum, brandy, and punch. Throughout the South, stag dinners persisted among planters. When James H. Hammond dined with gentlemen, Mrs. Hammond dined with the Reverend Mr. Cornish. Gentlemen attended public dinners without their ladies, ate at private clubs in town and village, and hosted stag dinner parties. Usually, their wives prepared the dinners, supervising their slaves and retiring to eat alone. Children rarely had dinner with parents, never when guests were present. Southwestern ladies occasionally had "women's dinners" to which a man or two might be invited to share gumbo, turkey, chicken, beef tongue, vegetables, plum pudding, and syllabub.[21]

At dinner everything except soup and dessert arrived at once, with meat and fish kept hot under polished silver covers. "Nobody ever heard of dinners being served in courses," Mary Clifford Hull wrote of early Wilkes County, Georgia. The more affluent set tables with two tablecloths. After removal of the top cloth, a fresh bottom cloth featured desserts. Households had a good supply of tablecloths, for tables required protection against the dripping food. Even less affluent planters tried to provide fine china and pewter dishes and silverware – status symbols all. In serving most of dinner at once, Southerners carried on a practice

---

[21] Cornish Diary, Oct. 21, 1863; Mary A. Steel to Elijah Steel, July 5, 1839, in F. L. Steel Papers; [Rutledge], *Carolina Housewife*, 55; also, Trollope, *Domestic Manners*, 25; Anna Matilda King, *Anna: The Letters of a St. Simons Plantation Mistress*, ed. Melanie Pavich-Lindsay (Athens, GA, 2002), 13, n. 4; Jennifer L. Eichstedt and Stephen Small, *Representations of Slavery: Race and Ideology in Southern Plantation Museums* (Washington, DC, 2002), 85. For "women's dinners" see Eliza Ann Marsh Robinson Diary, Jan. 13, 1855, in Joan E. Cashin, ed., *Our Common Affairs: Texts from Women of the Old South* (Baltimore, 1996), 116; Hilliard Diary, Mar. 29, 1850. For syllabub, see Tyree, ed., *Housekeeping in Old Virginia*, 427–428; Archie K. Davis, *Boy Colonel of the Confederacy: The Life and Times of Henry King Burgwyn, Jr.* (Chapel Hill, NC, 1985),13.

that steadily receded in England after about 1820, replaced by dinner à la Russe – one course after another in a much more expensive routine that required more servants. But the English late afternoon dinner hour, which was waning in the North, continued to flourish in the South. The temptations to gentility affected even some farm folk in western Virginia, who had white table cloths for dinners of bacon with corn bread or with cabbage soup. They fed themselves and their guests heartily rather than elegantly. The frontiersmen developed a taste for venison, which they passed on to subsequent generations, although among the elite, roasted and fried venison earlier replaced the frontiersmen's rough stews. During the early nineteenth century, southern cooks generally shifted from roasting to frying. The elite served venison with generous quantities of claret.[22]

Mr. Vanderhorst of Charleston impressed the thirty-two-year-old John Berkeley Grimball when he held a stag dinner for eight in 1832, attended by two Manigaults, a Rutledge, and other elite citizens. Grimball, who drank too much wine, commented on the food: "It was indeed a most hospitable entertainment, but half as much on the table would have been in better taste." Grimball, with little self-confidence in his abilities as a host, carefully studied gentlemen's practices, recording menus and studying procedures: "I put down these dinners [menus] because they are given by men of acknowledged Taste – and will afford hints, should I undertake to give one myself." Grimball's language recalls the scene in "Dinner at Trimalchio's" in Petronius' Satyricon, which Grimball doubtless had read: "I cursed my stupidity, and did not ask a single question thereafter, in case I should give the impression of never having dined in respectable company." No small matter. In Rome, writes Patrick Faas, table manners had been an indicator of social status. Grimball became an exemplary host – with a good deal of guidance from his wife Meta.[23]

---

[22] Mary Clifford Hull, "Old Days in Wilkes County," in Boggs, ed., *Alexander Letters*, 124–125; Paul Johnson, *The Birth of the Modern: World Society, 1815–1830* (New York, 1991), 758–759; Damon L. Fowler, "Historical Commentary" to Annabella P. Hill, *Mrs. Hill's Southern Practical Cookery and Receipt Book* (Columbia, SC, 1995 [1867, 1872]), vi. On dinner form and tablecloths, see Mrs. Roger Pryor [Sara Agnes Rice Pryor], *My Day: Reminiscences of a Long Life* (New York, 1909), 55. For yeomen, see Henry Howe, *Historical Collections of Virginia* (Charleston, SC, 1845), 153; and Hilliard, *Hog Meat and Hoecake*, 53. On wine in cooking, see [Rutledge], *Carolina Housewife*, 61–63. Opinion on the claret varied widely. Anthony Trollope, for one, complained that claret imported into to the United States was of inferior quality: *North America*, ed., Donald Smalley and Bradford Allen Booth (New York, 1951 [1862]), 39.
[23] J. B. Grimball Diaries, July 7, Sept. 16, 1832; June 13, 1832; Petronius, *Satyricon*, §41; Patrick Faas, *Around the Roman Table*, tr. Shaun Whiteside (Chicago, 1994), 48.

In November, 1832, Grimball gave a small dinner at 4 P.M. – to last three hours or so – for "Mssrs. Rose, Vanderhorst, Arthur Middleton, Manigault, Ogelby [the British consul], Laffan & Wilkins." Elated, he could not "recollect a dinner with which I have been more content in every respect – It cost without including wines – $27." Presumably, he did not charge himself for the cost of the items raised on his own plantation. Some of the expenditure went to a local coffee house for the turtle soup, since Grimball's cook had not made it for some time. Meta did not dine with the gentlemen but arranged everything. Courses were served in the Charleston manner, rather than all at once country style:

First course: turtle soup, ham, four vegetables;
Second course: (ham and vegetables still on the table), boiled mutton, three "very fine boiled trout," scalloped oysters;
Third course: roast turkey, venison, turtle steaks and fins;
Fourth course: macaroni pie.
Dessert: plum pudding and apple pie, floating island, jelly, blancmange, English cheese, butter, fruit, cakes, Malaga grapes.

In place of or in addition to trout, turkey, mutton, and venison, Grimball might have served – as his friends often did – bass or whiting, wild duck, roast veal, and roast chicken. Ice cream was an especially popular dessert in the low country. As a substitute for ice cream, ladies valued syllabub. The fare did not much change during the next thirty years or at such semi-public affairs as at the annual dinners of Charleston's New England Society or the militia dinners in honor of the governor. Menus included some French sauces.[24]

Those who hosted dinner parties considered twelve to a table ideal – an ideal often ignored. Among the Coupers and other wealthy planters of the low country and Sea Islands, the number of guests at dinner was more often than not twenty-four or so. In January 1847, Meta entertained about twenty-five people at a supper party that John thought a success. Meta and daughter Elizabeth played the piano, and the company danced a cotillion. Supper at 10 P.M. included roast turkey and duck, boiled ham, and scalloped oysters, as well as jellies, blancmange, apples, oranges, and syllabub: "After the ladies retired the Gentlemen

[24] See e.g., J. G. Grimball Diaries, Oct. 19, 1855, Oct. 29, 1857; and the menus in William Way, *History of the New England Society of Charleston, South Carolina for One Hundred Years, 1819–1919* (Charleston, SC, 1920), 273–274, and Jean Martin Flynn, *The Militia in Antebellum South Carolina Society* (Spartanburg, SC, 1991 [1917]), 6–7. For ice cream, see Lovell, *Light of Other Days*, 18.

sat down – Three other hot ducks were brought in and took the place of the first three – and when the Turkey was sufficiently eaten, it gave place to a hot oyster pie – We had Champagne – using two bottles – and four Decanter of Madeira."[25]

In November 1859, John A. Selden of Virginia, proprietor of the Westover long associated with the Byrds, had a dinner party for thirty men and women, including his twelve children. He followed in December with "the most magnificent dinner I ever saw" for some fifty-two people, and had "a large dinner party of my neighbors at Christmas." John Houston Bills of Tennessee attended a fine dinner at Judge Miller's with about thirty ladies and gentlemen and a stag party with "a very foolish set" at Mr. Williams's. Stag dinners, rather than being foolish, frequently provided occasions for caucusing on important church, college, or business matters. Dinners designed to promote political objectives were tricky. Although many Charlestonians admired and supported Hammond, they did not visit him because they were not rich enough to match his hospitality: "This, in a city like Charleston," William Gilmore Simms wrote to Hammond, "where people live by appearances, is one of the most vital matters ... There are hundreds of this class whom social incapacity alone kept aloof."[26]

Aristocratic manners blended with democratic. Jefferson upset fastidious diplomats at White House dinners by having guests seat themselves at table. Anthony Merry, the British minister, became so angry that a contretemps ensued. Traveling in South and North, J. S. Buckingham commented on "the disagreeable peculiarities" by which middle-class manners in America differed from those in England: "Gentlemen waited till the ladies were seated at dinner but then rose and left the table without them." The seating arrangement in Columbia, South Carolina, amused Bernhard, Duke of Saxe-Weimar Eisenach. At Professor Robert Henry's, "I observed a singular manner which is practised; the ladies sit

---

[25] McCulloch-Williams, *Dishes and Beverages of the Old South*, 287; Ferguson, *Couper Family*, 78; J. B. Grimball Diaries, Jan. 29, 1847. Meta Morris Grimball's diary did not record her reactions.

[26] John Spencer Bassett and Sidney Bradshaw Fay, eds., "The Westover Journal of John A. Selden, Esqr., 1858–1862," in *Smith College Studies in History*, 6 (Northampton, MA, 1921), Nov. 7, Dec. 1, 25, 1859 (31, 302, 318); Bills Diary, Aug. 17, 1843, Jan. 19, 1847; Simms to Hammond, Aug. 18, 1852, in Mary C. Oliphant et al., eds., *The Letters of William Gilmore Simms*, 6 vols. (Columbia, SC, 1952–1982), 3:195–196; also, Taylor Diary, Oct. 29, Nov. 6, 1791, Feb. 18, May 31, Sept. 11, Oct. 6, 1792; Baker Diary, Nov. 7, 1855, Dec. 30, 1855, March 1, 1849; James S. Guinard to Dr. S. Percival, July 4, 1837, in Childs, ed., *Planters and Businessmen*, 24–25; M. King Diary, Feb. 13, March 4, 1852.

down by themselves at one of the corners of the table. But I broke the old custom, and glided between them: and no one's appetite was injured thereby."[27]

South Carolina had Charleston; Virginia had Richmond. Richmond grew into a sophisticated city but had less impact than did Charleston on its state's elite culture. Dr. James Waddell Alexander complained in 1826 that in Virginia, "No farmer would think of sitting down to dinner with less than four dishes of meat or to breakfast without several different kinds of warm bread." Impressed by the lavish dinners, and many attendant slaves, he lamented, "The old Virginians never count the cost of dinners even when they give little to the support of the gospel."[28]

Mrs. Merry, wife of the snobbish British ambassador, sneered at Dolly Madison's White House dinners as in "the old bountiful Virginia fashion." John Tyler had a different complaint about dinner with the Madisons at the White House. He much enjoyed the champagne, but could not abide the newly adopted French style of cooking: "I had much rather dine at home in our plain way ... What with their sauces and flum-flummaries, the victuals are inedible." George Ticknor of Harvard, visiting Montpelier, Madison's plantation, wrote more favorably to William H. Prescott: "The table is very ample and elegant, and somewhat luxurious; it is evidently a serious item in the account of Mr. M's happiness, and it seems to be his habit to pass about an hour, after the cloth is removed, with a variety of wines of no mean quality."[29]

Customarily, gentlemen remained at table after dinner for at least an hour or so of conversation. In the late 1830s, George W. Featherstonhaugh, the geologist, attended a dinner in Charleston and commented on the after-dinner conversation with Thomas Pinckney and Langdon Cheves,

---

[27] Dumas Malone, Jefferson and His Time, 6 vols. (Boston, 1962–1981), 4:385–386; Buckingham, *Slave States*, 1:466–467; Bernhard, Duke of Saxe-Weimar Eisenach, *Travels Through North America during the Years 1825 and 1826*, 2 vols. (Philadelphia, 1818), 1:212.

[28] William Cabell Bruce, *John Randolph of Roanoke, 1773–1833: A Biography Based Largely on New Material*, 2 vols. (New York, 1970 [1922]), 2:120, 150, 153, 437; Edmund S. Morgan, *Virginians at Home: Family Life in the Eighteenth Century* (Williamsburg, VA, 1952), 77–78; Taylor Diary, June 4, 1787, Mar. 31, 1789.

[29] Maud Wilder Goodwin, *Dolly Madison* (New York, 1901), 91; John Tyler to Letitia Tyler, Feb. 1, 1817, in Lyon Gardiner Tyler, *The Letters and Times of the Tylers*, 3 vols. (Williamsburg, VA, 1884–1896), 1:288–289; Ticknor to Prescott, Dec. 16, 1824, in *Life, Letters, and Journals of George Ticknor* (Boston, Mass., 1876), 347. Louisiana planters favored French chefs and reveled in elegant dinner parties.

who considered money and commercial ventures topics worthy of Yankees. At luxurious dinners with fine wines, Featherstonhaugh felt at home with well-informed discussions of British politics and literature. Repartee and free-wheeling exchanges marked the rhetorical polish for which Carolinians became famous. The dinner table brought together, in the words of Mitchell King, the wealthy and influential merchant, "Our own friends – our own peculiar set ... Pringle, Petigru, Poinsett, Drayton!"[30]

In 1804, Representative David Bard of Pennsylvania taunted his southern colleagues: "The negroes are in every family; they are waiting on every table; they are present on numerous occasions when the conversation turns on political subjects, and cannot fail to catch ideas that will excite discontentment with their condition." Frances Trollope subsequently expressed astonishment at the indifference to the presence of slaves: "They talk of them, of their condition, exactly as if they were incapable of hearing." Political remarks strained nerves, and gentlemen tried to change the subject. During and after the nullification crisis, dinner became touchy, but most unionists and nullifiers seem to have given old friends the benefit of the doubt, expecting to stand together against outside aggression.[31]

After dinner, card-playing and other games cheered the more affluent homes despite clerical disapproval. In Virginia, Episcopalians put away their cards when the bishop visited, for he would leave if he saw card-playing. The Episcopalian ladies and gentlemen of Charleston, along with Jews and some other Christians, freely played whist, old maid, and keno. The Swedes – and probably many others – played cards after dinner but behind shut blinds, lest they offend neighbors. Early in the nineteenth century the ladies of Richmond played loo with gusto. Despite the modesty of wins and losses, a competitive atmosphere plunged them

---

[30] John Davis, *Travels of Four and a Half Years in the United States of America*, ed. A. J. Morrison (New York, 1909 [1803]), 82; George William Featherstonhaugh, *A Canoe Voyage up the Minay Sotor*, 2 vols. (St. Paul, MN, 1970 [1847]), 2:311; Archie Vernon Huff, Jr., *Langdon Cheves of South Carolina* (Columbia, SC, 1977), 185; Merrill G. Christopherson, "Anti-Nullifiers," in Waldo W. Braden, ed., *Oratory in the South, 1828–1860* (Baton Rouge, LA, 1970), ch 3, King quoted at 76.

[31] Bard quoted in Winthrop D. Jordan, *White over Black: American Attitudes toward the Negro*, (Baltimore, 1968), 388; Trollope, *Domestic Manners*, 249. For restraint of political exchanges at dinner see, e.g., J. B. Grimball Diary, May 17, 1832; Hammond Diary, Feb. 7, 1841, in Carol Bleser, ed., *Secret and Sacred: The Diaries of James Henry Hammond, a Southern Slaveholder* (New York, 1988), 27.

into unladylike outbursts that shocked the gentlemen who occasionally observed them. We hear little of such doings in later years.[32]

Chess had special significance for participating ladies. When Jefferson declared Anna Payne "the chess heroine," he hit a sensitive chord, for chess gave women a chance to best their men in a game in which intelligence counted for everything. Fifty years later, Mary Howard Schoolcraft of South Carolina remarked that southern women accepted chess as an intellectual challenge. Catherine Ann Devereux Edmondston of North Carolina thought nothing of playing chess all day. Schoolcraft and Edmondston taught their children, girls as well as boys, to play. The young people of Charleston had a Morphy's Chess Club and published a chess monthly.[33]

Caveat: Henry Charles Lea, writing in the mid-1840s, reminded Southerners that the ancient Greeks serve as a model for dining and drinking. A decade later, "S. A. L." fired a salvo at the gentry's elaborate dinner parties by recalling the course of Greek and Roman eating habits. From a warrior people's roughness, the Greeks slipped into a decadence that led to humiliation at the hands of Philip of Macedon at Chaeronea. The Romans, including their great legions, became "effeminate and despicable." "S. A. L." brought the lesson home: "In our own day, luxurious dining and modes of living are beginning to obtain to an extent dangerous to the manly virtues and patriotic devotion to our country, when it may be required of us to sacrifice our comforts and enjoyments, and endure privation, suffering, and even death itself, in its defence and glory."[34]

---

[32] Susan Dabney Smedes, *Memorials of a Southern Planter*, ed. Fletcher M. Green (New York, 1965 [1887]), 21–22; Emma Holmes, Apr. 22, May 1, 1862, in John F. Marszalek, ed., *The Diary of Miss Emma Holmes* (Baton Rouge, LA, 1979), 149, 157; Elliott Ashkenazi, ed., *The War Diary of Clara Solomon: Growing Up in New Orleans, La., 1861–1862* (Baton Rouge, LA, 1995), entries for 1861; Daniel E. Sutherland, ed., *The Civil War Diary of Ellen Renshaw House* (Knoxville, TN, 1996), 14; Rosalie Roos to Ulrika Roos, July 30, 1852, in Rosalie Roos, *Travels in America, 1851–1855*, tr. Carl L. Anderson (Carbondale, IL, 1982), 60; Samuel Mordecai, *Richmond in By-Gone Days* (Richmond, VA, 1946 [1860]), 264–266.

[33] Jefferson to Madison, Aug. 13, 1801, in James Morton Smith, ed., *The Republic of Letters: The Correspondence between Thomas Jefferson and James Madison, 1776–1826*, 3 vols. (New York, 1995), 2:42. *Plantation Life: Schoolcraft Narratives*, 365–366; Edmondston Diary, Apr. 26, 1861, in Beth G. Crabtree and James Welch Patton, eds., *"Journal of a Secesh Lady": The Diary of Catherine Ann Devereux Edmondston, 1860–1866* (Raleigh, NC, 1979), 57; May 30, June 16, 1859. For Morphy's Club, see Thornwell Jacobs, ed., *Diary of William Plumer Jacobs, 1842–1917* (Atlanta, GA, 1937), May 30, June 16, 1859 (43).

[34] Henry Charles Lea, "The Greek Symposium," *SLM*, 11 (1845), 625–630; S. A. L., "Good Eating among the Greeks and Romans" *SLM*, 21 (1855), 713–726, quote at 726.

BREAKFAST, SUPPER, AND OUTDOOR DINING

Europeans, then and since, have generally contrasted hearty American breakfasts, northern and southern alike, favorably with their own. Southern inns served eggs, ham, veal with oysters, grilled birds, among other items, and hard liquor for those who spurned the coffee. In Louisa County, Virginia, the Marquis de Chastellux preferred bad local whiskey to the coffee. Despite the earlier presence of coffee houses, coffee drinking only became the rage after 1815 or so in America as well as Europe, but only Louisiana offered palatable coffee. Olmsted might have spoken out of Yankee prejudice when he referred to "the abominable preparation which passes for coffee," but the Methodist Bishop George Foster Pierce of Georgia rendered a similar judgment. As an itinerant, he traveled from the low country to Texas, speaking from rich experience about the "execrable stuff." More delicately, Methodist Bishop James O. Andrew of Georgia referred to the availability of good coffee as Texans' measure of a good life.[35]

The breakfast hour varied according to social class or, rather, occupation. Farmers, tradesmen, overseers, and slaves had breakfast early, but many planters waited to eat leisurely in mid-morning. Just about every available food crowded Virginia's breakfast tables. At the Virginia Springs, experienced proprietors, knowing guests' expectations, served twelve to fifteen kinds of wheat, bran, buckwheat, rice, and other grains made into hot and cold cakes, mutton, venison chops, fried chicken, cold corned beef, ham, eggs, and cheese. Philip Holbrook Nicklin ("Pelegrine Prolix") advised every Northerner "to eat fried chickens wherever he meets with them in Virginia." The same spread did for supper. Breakfast in town and in the countryside varied in accordance with the meats available. In season – from November through February, breakfast among the elite of Charleston might include pan-fried quail with grits, country ham and gravy, as well as ham biscuits and scrambled eggs. Humbler inns and farms served ham, bacon, sausages, and fried pork instead of, say, venison. With luck, the food did not swim in grease. Rice left uneaten at dinner might be served fried for breakfast. At southeastern Methodist

35 Chastellux, *Travels*, 2:388; Frederick Law Olmsted, *A Journey in the Back Country* (New York, 1970 [1861]), 162; George Foster Pierce, *Incidents of Western Travel: In a Series of Letters* (Nashville, TN, 1857), 60; J. O. Andrew, "Travels in the West," *Miscellanies: Comprising Letters, Essays, and Addresses* (Louisville, KY, 1854), 102. From 1815 to 1830, coffee drinking in the United States increased by 500%: Johnson, *Birth of the Modern*, 756.

conferences, breakfast included meats, boiled partridges, boiled eggs, hominy, waffles, rice cakes, and fritters.[36]

On Louisiana's large plantations, known for fine dining, breakfast included prawns, New England salmon, local fish, claret, and coffee. Clara Solomon reported on Jewish practice in New Orleans: "Breakfast aristocratic. Trout and cream cheeses." And shrimp, too, despite Jewish law. Simms described breakfast hominy to Scots-born James Lawson of New York: "The corn coarsely ground and boiled to a tolerable consistency – say that of mush – makes our hominy, and is the standing breakfast dish with us. It should be seasoned with salt while boiling, and eaten with butter. The children eat molasses with it, as they do with mush." Southerners loved good butter but had difficulty getting it. Since plantations and farms did not produce enough butter, planters paid exorbitant prices to get the quality they craved. Simms also described shrimp, served with rice or bread and tomatoes, as a lowcountry favorite for dinner: "Our shrimp may remind you of your lobster, but is considered of far greater delicacy." Lobster and lobster sauces recurred in southern cookbooks, but from where they came is not clear. One hypothesis suggests that southern cooks referred to crayfish. Potato-pone pies served as dessert. Small birds abounded from the low country to Texas, and quail, snipe, partridges, and plover filled pies when not roasted.[37]

A light supper came about 9 P.M., usually of cold leftovers, perhaps with freshly baked bread, or, as at the Porchers in Greenville, South Carolina, with sweets and salad. Virginia's ladies and gentlemen dressed for suppers of biscuits, sandwiches, and light cakes, served on trays in

[36] Eggleston, *Rebel's Recollections*, lvii–lviii; Philip Holbrook Nicklin ["Pelegrine Prolix"], *Letters Descriptive of Virginia Springs. The Roads Leading Thereon and the Doings Thereat, 1834 and 1836*, 2nd ed. (Austin, TX, 1978), 27, quote at 8; John Martin Taylor, *Hoppin' John's Charleston, Beaufort, and Savannah: Dining at Home in the Lowcountry* (New York, 1997), 28–32; Taylor, *Eating, Drinking, and Visiting*, 54; Oct. 7, 1854, in Suzanne L. Bunkers, *The Diary of Caroline Seabury, 1854–1863* (Madison, WI, 1991), 31; Greenlee Diary, Jan. 1837; David S. Shields, "When the Flavors Return: Notes toward the Resuscitation of a Southern Cuisine" (unpubl.), 49; John Donald Wade, *Augustus Baldwin Longstreet: A Study of the Development of Culture in the South* (New York, 1924), 225.

[37] Caroline Couper Lovell, *The Golden Isles of Georgia* (Boston, MA, 1933), 121–126, 136; Easterby, ed., *South Carolina Rice Plantation*, 16; Ferguson, *Couper Family*, 167; William H. Russell, *My Diary North and South* (Boston, MA, 1863), 150; Oct. 3, 6, 1861, Ashkenazi, ed., *Diary of Clara Solomon*, 168, 174; *SP*, 3 (1843), 177; Simms to James Lawson, July 7, 1839 (1:149–150), Oct. 1, 1846 (2:187) in Oliphant. ed., *Letters of Simms; Farmer and Planter*, 8 (1857), 36; Hilliard's Diary, Jan. 19, 1850; McCall Account Book, Oct.–Dec., 1851; Graves Papers, 1857–1858. For controversies over lobsters, see especially Hill, *Southern Practical Cookery*, 43–44.

drawing rooms or outdoors. In Florida supper, often referred to as "tea," included cakes or bread and honey. Maine-reared Joseph Holt Ingraham, of Natchez, described supper in the Southwest as a sort of high tea not served at table. Supper was usually heavier – say, fried ham and eggs with biscuits. In Montgomery at the Confederacy's founding convention, Thomas Cobb of Georgia noticed a great uniformity in suppers. Fish salad and fried oysters followed oyster soup. Then came ham or beef, sardines with waffles, cakes, jellies, and charlotte russe, topped off with Ambrosia, a local favorite of sliced oranges and grated coconut. In Virginia, luscious blackberries often replaced oranges. Afterwards, the gentlemen retired for champagne and cigars, returning to end the evening with their ladies, who had been singing and conversing. Large quantities of watermelon – a great favorite among all classes of whites as well as blacks – sometimes substituted for supper. The letters between Mary and Charles Jones over the terrible disappointment of a failed watermelon crop had the ring of funeral orations. The taste for watermelon never died. Everywhere, enthusiasm greeted the arrival of the first crop. Confederate émigrés introduced watermelon to Brazil after the War, turning production and distribution into a big business.[38]

Picnics, a social preference, usually featured "a cold collation," as Cornish called it. Especially popular among belles and beaux, they entranced elders as well. Frank F. Steel of Ohio, visiting Kentucky, was not alone in attending two picnics in one week. The popularity of picnics increased steadily, especially when big planters assumed the costs. Politics occasioned mammoth barbecues. Reports usually were enthusiastic, but occasionally we read, as in Baker's diary: "Attended a sorry barbecue."

[38] John S. Wise, *The End of an Era* (Boston, MA, 1900), 68; Mrs. William Smith to Isabella Middleton Smith, Jan. [?], 1863, in Daniel E. Huger Smith et al., eds., *Mason-Smith Family Letters, 1860–1868* (Columbia, SC, 1950), 29; Octavia Bryant to Winston Stephens, Sept. 2, 1858, Octavia Bryant Journal, Oct. 21, 1859 in Arch Frederic Blakely et al., eds., *Rose Cottage Chronicles: Civil War Letters of the Bryant-Stephens Families of North Florida* (Gainesville, FL, 1998), 33–34, 48; J. H. Ingraham, *Sunny South; Or, The Southerner at Home* (New York, 1968 [1860], 54; Josephine Bacon Martin, ed., *Life on a Liberty County Plantation: The Journal of Cornelia Jones Pond* (Darien, GA, 1974), 38; T. R. R. Cobb to Marion Cobb, Feb. 8, 1861, in A. L. Hull, ed., "The Correspondence of Thomas Reade Roots Cobb, 1860–1862," *Publications of the Southern Historical Association*, 11 1907), 2:119–120. On watermelons, see the correspondence between Mary Jones and C. C. Jones, Jr., in Robert Manson Myers, ed., *The Children of Pride: A True Story of the Children of the Civil War* (New Haven, CT, 1972), 226–227; Eugene C. Harton, *Lost Colony of the Confederacy* (Jackson, MS, 1985), 82–83; also, Taylor Diary, Aug. 25, 1787, Aug. 28, 1794; Cornish Diary, July 18, 1840; Leak Diaries, July 18, 1856; Albright Diary, Aug. 13, 1864.

Frontier barbecues might be stag, held in tandem with a local horse race, featuring wine as well as corn whiskey. A hint on costs: In 1827 eighteen South Carolina gentlemen went off to a picnic ("frolic"). Thirty-seven bottles of claret, port, and brandy cost $35 or about a dollar per bottle.[39]

The "fishing party," as described in a letter to Elijah Steel of Washington, Mississippi, had a hundred people assembled early in the morning at "Beauty's Bower, a very appropriate name; it is a beautiful and romantic spot at the junction of two creeks." The hosts erected an arbor, sparing no pains to provide fresh fish, drinks, and ice cream. A fishing party picnic might include ham, cold chicken, cold broiled pigeon, sandwiches and pickles, champagne, claret, and ale. Participants liberally downed the fish "with sufficiency of grog, agreeably."[40]

"THE PRIDE OF OUR TABLES"

In ancient Rome oysters represented a sign of wealth and status. Pliny the Elder described them as "The pride of our tables." With no few other Southerners, John Archibald Campbell of Alabama, Associate Justice of the U.S. Supreme Court, recalled with disgust the testimony of Seneca and Pliny that Vedius Pollio had a careless slave thrown to his lampreys and oysters. "Who," Seneca asked, "did not hate Vedius Pollio for feeding slaves to his lampreys?" In the South, too, oysters reigned supreme among sea foods, livening parties and roasts. Maryland held pride of place as a source of oysters, but the entire coast from Virginia to Texas produced abundant numbers. The York, Rappahannock, and other rivers teemed with oysters too large to be eaten raw, and Virginians became skilled in cooking them. John Walker of Virginia paid his slaves fifty cents per bushel to dig oysters.[41]

[39] Cornish Diary, Sept. 25, Oct. 29, 1846, May 29, 1858; Frank F. Steel to Anna Steel, Aug. 19, 1861; Nicholson Journal, Sept. 7, 1860; F. Garvin Davenport, *Cultural Life in Nashville on the Eve of the Civil War* (Chapel Hill, NC, 1941), 28; Baker Diary, Aug. 27, 1859; Rutledge, *Carolina Housewife*, viii–ix.

[40] Unsigned letter to Elijah Steel, June 14, 1838, in F. L. Steel Papers; Ingraham, *Sunny South*, 167; Taylor Diary, July 1, 1786.

[41] Mark Kurlansky, *The Big Oyster: History on the Half Shell* (New York, 2006), 115; Pliny the Elder, *Natural History: A Selection*, ed. John F. Healy (London, 1991), Bk. 32:59; also, Seneca, "On Mercy," in Moral Essays, 3 vols., tr. John W. Basore (LCL), 1:1.18.2; [John Archibald Campbell], "Slavery among the Romans," *SQR*, 28 (1848), 404; Hilliard, *Hog Meat and Hoecake*, 84; Claudia L. Bushman, *In Old Virginia: Slavery, Farming, and Society in the Journal of John Walker* (Baltimore, 2002), 66; *SLM*, 1 (1835), 244.

Oysters were also the rage in the Northeast. New York, the North's center for the collection and distribution of oysters, throve on sales to upstate and to New England and sold about six million dollars worth annually in Manhattan. New York did not send significant amounts of oysters to the South. Southerners considered northern oysters small and harsh; Northerners considered southern oysters bland.[42]

Southern mistresses and cooks prepared the ubiquitous oysters in a wide assortment of ways. They pickled them in large quantities, but then, they pickled any number of items: shrimp, beef, pork, onions, tomatoes, cucumber, mangoes, cabbages, and artichokes. And they enjoyed pickled brains as well as hog brains mixed with eggs at breakfast. Marylanders, Virginians, and Carolinians sent oysters pickled in Madeira to kinsmen and friends in the interior. Oysters were not the only such gifts. In the low country Mrs. Langdon Cheves told her aunt that she had just received a basket of turnips from one friend and a dish of sausages from another: "This is the custom here."[43]

Southerners loved oyster soup, which could be made simply with water, but, with minor variations, they preferred it rich enough to serve as a meal in itself. They loaded the soup with butter, heavy cream, flour, and eggs spiced with cloves, mace, and pepper. Rebecca Maxwell Couper's famous oyster soup called for six quarts of oysters and the yolks of eighteen hard-boiled eggs. At dinner and at oyster parties and picnics, hosts served oysters fried, scalloped, as fritters, and in stews, often with turkey and sweets and accompanied by eggnog and apple toddy. Virginians loved oyster pies, some baked. Turkey and pheasant were roasted with oyster stuffing, notably in the Mississippi Valley. Oyster salad included hardboiled egg yolks, butter, vinegar, mustard, and pickled cucumbers; desserts in pies baked with sweetbreads.[44]

[42] Kurlansky, *Big Oyster*, 47–48, 102–103, 173.

[43] Hill, *Southern Practical Cookery*, 45, 49, 345, 435, and see infra, n. 42; Taylor, *Hoppin' John's Charleston, Beaufort, and Savannah*, 37; Taylor, *Eating, Drinking, and Visiting*, 24; Mrs. Cheves, quoted in Huff, Jr., *Langdon Cheves*, 184.

[44] T. Reed Ferguson, *The John Couper Family at Cannon's Point* (Macon, GA, 1994), 78. The various preparations of oysters have been culled from Tyree, ed., *Housekeeping in Old Virginia*; Bryan, *Kentucky Housewife*; Randolph, Virginia Housewife; Mary L. Edgeworth, *The Southern Gardener and Receipt Book*, 3rd ed., Philadelphia, 1859); McCulloch-Williams, *Dishes and Beverages of the Old South*. See also, W. Emerson Wilson, ed., *Plantation Life at Rose Hill: The Diaries of Martha Ogle Forman, 1814–1845* (Wilmington, DE, 1976), 55 (Dec. 8, 1817); Catherine Cooper Hopley, *Life in the South from the Commencement of the War*, 2 vols. (New York, 1971 [1863]), 1:78, 164; Thomas Old to Ebenezer Pettigrew, March 17, 1825, in Sarah McCulloh Lemmon, ed., *The Pettigrew Papers*, 2 vols. (Raleigh, NC, 1971,1988), 2:59; W. Emerson Wilson,

Supply and consumption of oysters seemed endless. That is why in 1839 the touring Clara von Gerstner found Charleston streets covered with powdery dust processed by blacks from plentiful oyster shells that yielded excellent lime. Yet Charlestonians were no more avid for oysters than other coastal inhabitants and even people in the interior. Louisianans often enjoyed oysters at supper with turkey, and Texans applied Mexican techniques. Before railroads improved importation of foodstuffs, the small inns ("supper rooms") that accommodated travelers in upcountry Georgia included small, salty oysters along with partridge and squirrel as basic fare. In the 1830s, Cave Burton, Esq., a fictional character in James Glover Baldwin's *Flush Times of Alabama and Mississippi*, boasted that he and his friend D. L. "never failed to break an oyster cellar in Tuscaloosa whenever they made a run at it" – that is, eat all the oysters in the inn. At the founding Confederate convention in Montgomery, Cobb happily informed his wife, "They have splendid oysters here and I intend to send you some by express."[45]

John Rutledge's mother became insolvent, and the indigo plantation of 200 slaves heavily encumbered. Rutledge, his family dangerously in debt, hosted a gala oyster roast to reassure the community that he remained solvent and able to entertain in high style. Rutledge was running for office, and custom forbade the imprisonment for debt of sitting members of the Commons. He invited voters from Christ Church parish, whom

---

ed., *Plantation Life at Rose Hill: The Diaries of Martha Ogle Forman, 1814–1845* (Wilmington, DE, 1976), 55 (Dec. 8, 1817); Thomas Old to Ebenezer Pettigrew, March 17, 1825, in Sarah McCulloh Lemmon, ed., *The Pettigrew Papers*, 2 vols. (Raleigh, NC, 1971, 1988), 2:59. On the Atlantic coast skilled slaves collected and sold oysters and other shellfish. Oyster loaves supplemented the oyster sauce that flavored fish. The Grimballs and other lowcountry families favored scalloped oysters, but frequently included oysters fried or in pies or soup: J. B. Grimball Diaries, Nov. 1, 1832. For charming descriptions of the preparation of oysters – soup, stewed, in cream, fried, and scalloped, as well as combined meat and oyster sausages, turkey hash, and chicken fricassee – see, [Rutledge], *Carolina Housewife*, 42, 57–59, 64, 77, 79; also, Hill, *Southern Practical Cookery*, 20–21.

[45] Frederic Trautman, ed., "South Carolina through a German's Eyes: The Travels of Clara von Gerstner, 1839," *South Carolina Historical Magazine*, 85 (1984), 221.; Bills Diary, Feb. 12, 1844, Dec. 26, 1867; Hogan, *Texas Republic*, 37; James Holmes, *"Dr. Bullie's" Notes: Reminiscences of Early Georgia and of Philadelphia and New Haven in the 1800s*, ed. Delma Eugene Presley (Atlanta, GA, 1976), 94; Joseph G. Baldwin, *The Flush Times of Alabama and Mississippi* (New York, 1957 [1853]), 119; T. R. R. Cobb to Marion Cobb, Feb. 10, 1861, in A. L. Hull, ed., "The Correspondence of Thomas Reade Roots Cobb, 1860–1862," *Publications of the Southern Historical Association*, 11 (1907), 170. Also, Thomas Frederick Davis, *History of Early Jacksonville, Florida* (Jacksonville, FL, 1911), 150–152.

he then visited individually for some six weeks prior to the election. He won. Rutledge hired Yemassee Indians to hunt game and assigned slaves to fish. An enormous quantity of oysters came from the sea at the far end of Bull's Bay. Rutledge sent woodcutters to get "palmetto cabbage" – the heart of the palmetto tree, which had to be extracted with great skill, lest the excision kill the tree. Palmetto cabbage, roasted over a slow fire, tasted like a mixture of cauliflower, asparagus, and artichokes, with a tang of its own. Guests came from long distances to an outdoor dinner scheduled for 1 P.M. Long cypress tables held the family's best china, silverware, and linen. Everyone showed up on time, since oysters had to be served promptly. Gentlemen drank hot whiskey punch, ladies eggnog spiced with rum. A trained young black girl ("pickaninny") served every two guests sizzling oysters. The guests reassembled at 3 P.M. for the rest of dinner: crawfish in aspic, shrimp, and watercress salad; baked whole red snapper in a Bordeaux sauce; terrapin stew; venison patty, pudding of palmetto hearts; and yams. Ladies in long skirts carefully navigated around the benches. The gentlemen left first in order to spare them the embarrassment of exposing their toes.[46]

Through subsequent decades, especially during Christmas season, the low country bristled with elaborate oyster roasts, which the young ladies favored as occasions to frolic with beaux or prospective beaux. Slaves, there and elsewhere, made their presence felt as essential to proper hospitality. Eliza Pinckney's father invited local ladies and gentlemen to assemble at 2 P.M. to watch well-trained slaves roast oysters over a roaring outdoor fire. Serving maids passed among the throng with salvers laden with oysters, small roasted marsh birds, ham, hare, and hot rolls, as well as vegetables and homemade pickles. The gentlemen drank toddy, the ladies tea and hot chocolate. The low country had another oyster party season in late August and early September. Here and there a dissident voice: A small cotton planter in northern Alabama amused Olmsted with an account of an oyster party in town, at which he tried to eat "the nasty things" without appearing disconcerted before the ladies.[47]

Cornish attended his first oyster roast unaware of the need for strict punctuality. He arrived too late to savor the oysters but noted the arrangement at table: "The Gents were in one group & the Ladies in another on the Green, & terribly at a loss how to get together again for want of a

[46] Barry, *Mr. Rutledge*, 35, 41–45.
[47] Frances Leigh Williams, *Plantation Patriot: A Biography of Eliza Lucas Pinckney* (New York, 1967), 38; Olmsted, *Back Country*, 213.

house to dance in. They found one at last." Cornish learned his lesson. A week later he arrived on time, noticing tables that featured waffles, johnny-cakes, crackers, and tea:

At length the oysters were brought on plates from the fires & placed on a long table. The ladies arranged themselves along one side, & the Gentlemen who had till now been talking and smoking by themselves gradually drew around to the other. Presently, a young Gentlemen takes up a cluster of Oysters in his hand, & with a knife opens one, loosens him from his moorings & then presents it across the table in the shell still holding it in his – to a young Lady, who with her delicate fingers, which drop like pearls from her mitts, take up the delicious morsel & with a smile of great satisfaction, causes the unconscious victim to disappear within her ruby lips.

At first, Cornish thought he witnessed a joke, but, seeing the procedure repeated along the table, he recognized a rite. Guests devoured the oysters in fifteen minutes, after which scouts reported that they had found a house to dance in. A week later Cornish attended an oyster roast at Whitemarsh Seabrook's, approving the table arrangement, "which tended to break up the stiffness."[48]

Reuben Allen Pierson, with the Confederate army in Virginia, wrote to his sister Mary in Louisiana that the troops were all "passionately fond" of oysters. The Gulf Coast teemed with them, a source of local pride. Ebenezer Davies of Britain found those at New Orleans "gigantic," although not as well cooked as in the North. Mobile's many "oyster saloons" served oyster pâté as well as the oysters that became a rage among all classes. The vast quantities off the Florida coast stunned William Cullen Bryant, who thought that oysters provided an important part of the diet of the local poor. And in Charleston the dinner parties of the free colored elite, like those of the whites, featured champagne and oysters.[49]

---

[48] Cornish Diary, Aug. 21, Sept. 3, 14, 1841.

[49] Reuben Allen Pierson to Mary Catherine Pierson, Apr. 5, 1863, in Thomas W. Cutrer and T. Michael Parrish, eds., *Brothers in Gray: The Civil War Letters of the Pierson Family* (Baton Rouge, LA, 1997), 176; Edmund Ruffin, "Farming the Great Dismal Swamp," in *Nature's Management: Writings on Landscape and Reform, 1822–1859*, ed., Jack Temple Kirby (Athens, GA, 2000), 187; James B. Avirett, *The Old Plantation: How We Lived in Great House and Cabin Before the War* (New York, 1901), 22; Ebenezer Davies, *American Scenes, and Christian Slavery: A Recent Tour* (London, 1849), 7; Harriet Elizabeth Amos, "Social Life in an Antebellum Cotton Port: Mobile, Alabama, 1820–1860" (Ph.D. diss., University of Alabama, 1976), 167, 181; William Cullen Bryant, *Letters of a Traveller; Or, Notes of Things Seen in Europe and America* (New York, 1850), 121–122; James Marsh Johnson to Henry Ellison, Dec. 23, 1859, in Michael P. Johnson and James L. Roark, eds., *No Chariot Let Down: Charleston's Free People of Color on the Eve of the Civil War* (Chapel Hill, NC, 1984), 41. For the popularity

A SMALL MATTER OF REFRIGERATION

Ice was not *sine qua non* for gracious dining, but it helped. Europeans viewed ice as an aristocratic pleasure; Americans viewed it as a luxury within the grasp of the middle classes. A contributor to the *Southern Quarterly Review* in the 1840s described ice as a desirable luxury in warm climates, the cost of which made it accessible to all classes. Yet, interior towns and plantations dependent on local sources for ice had great difficulty. No southern city or town could afford to buy and distribute an amount of ice adequate for more than its well-to-do. Virginia's rivers froze to a record two inches in 1780 and thereafter often enough to provide ice for local needs. But George Washington fretted over its preservation. Robert Morris of Pennsylvania advised Washington to build a subterranean ice vault. Virginians learned to pack ice in grass or sawdust and to draw off the water from the melting. Thomas Jefferson studied the ice houses of Italy before he built his own. The cost of transporting ice to plantations ran high, and planters had to hire wagons and feed the wagoners. By the 1820s, Henry Cogswell Knight of Massachusetts, a poet, observed, "Most planters have an ice house, and contrive to keep the ice cool all summer."[50]

In 1857 John Walker paid workers fifteen or more dollars to fill his ice house. The ice cut from his ponds ranged from two to four inches thick, sometimes from five to eight. Workers layered it with sawdust or pine needles. Despite Walker's hope, the supply rarely lasted until late September. In 1859, a Selden of Westover hauled seven wagon loads and two ox carts of ice, one and a half inches thick, from Mr. Rowland's pond.

of oysters in northern cities, see Francis J. Grund, *Aristocracy in America: From the Sketchbook of a German Nobleman* (Gloucester, MA, 1968 [1839]), 72, 118–119. For variations on the cooking of oysters, see Mrs. to Mr. David Hillhouse, April 25, 1808, in Boggs, ed., *Alexander Letters*, 50–51; Everts in Cashin, ed., *Wilderness*, 63–64; T. R. R. Cobb to Marion Cobb, Feb. 8, 1861, in Hull, ed., "Correspondence of Thomas Reade Roots Cobb," 167; Ferguson, *Couper Family*, 167.

50 "Ice," *DBR*, 19 (1855), 709–710; John Michael Vlach, *Back of the Big House: The Architecture of Plantation Slavery* (Chapel Hill, NC, 1993), 80–82; William S. Forrest, *Historical and Descriptive Sketches of Norfolk and Vicinity* (Philadelphia, 1853), 90–91; "Refrigeration and Ventilation of Cities," *SQR*, 1 (1842), 423–425; Donald Jackson and Dorothy Twohig, eds, *The Diaries of George Washington* (Charlottesville, VA, 1978), Jan. 8, 1785 (4:74), also June 5, 1785 (4:148–149); Fowler, ed., *Dining at Monticello*, 175; Arthur Singleton [Henry Cogswell Knight], *Letters from the South and West* (Boston, MA, 1824), 7; Edmund Ruffin, Jr. Plantation Diary, Jan. 31, 1851, March 21, 1861, and entries for Dec.–Jan. during the 1850s; Augustus Longstreet Hull, *Annals of Athens, Georgia, 1801–1901* (Danieldsville, GA, 1906), 147.

About ten days later he spent a day and a half hauling more. Apparently, he had a good ice house. During December and January, slaves cut ice from frozen rivers and ponds and packed them into plantation ice houses. Had the ice business been well organized, much of Virginia might have been self-sufficient, but rarely was enough ice cut and stored during the cold months to meet the demands of summer, much less build an inventory against the possibility of a warm next winter. Problems mounted the farther south one went. Athens, Georgia, had an ice house early in its history, but the local ponds that supplied it froze only once in five years. In the Southeast, ice houses were usually sunk deep, whereas in Louisiana the soft soil and the danger of flooding required that they be built over ground.[51]

Mary L. Edgeworth of Georgia, in her *The Southern Gardener and Receipt Book*, suggested that an underground ice house be eighteen-by-twelve feet with ceilings ten to twelve feet high, encased by one foot of dry tan or powdered charcoal. A contributor to the *Tennessee Farmer* argued that underground ice houses defeated their purpose by conducting heat. He recommended above-ground ice houses, with one house built inside another, walls eighteen to twenty inches apart, spaces filled with charcoal or tan bark. The floor, filled with sand, should absorb moisture and keep the air dry. Meanwhile, southern journals republished articles from northern sources on the construction of ice houses. On one matter the press remained silent: Ice houses also served as places to whip slaves severely out of the sight of squeamish whites.[52]

For many decades, Northerners shipped ice to southern ports, but by the 1840s inland towns were beginning to enjoy ice, much of it shipped down the Mississippi from the Old Northwest. With the coming of railroads, the supply of ice began to catch up with the demand. Ice cream and other delicacies came into favor. The upper South fared better than the lower. The Ohio River froze over often enough to ease the problem for towns and plantations to the south. The arrival of

---

[51] For the cutting and storing of ice in Virginia, see Bushman, *In Old Virginia*, 191–192; Bassett and Fay, eds., "Westover Journal of John A. Selden," Jan. 11–12, 25, 1859 (282–283).

[52] Edgeworth, *Southern Gardener and Receipt Book*, 401; "Construction of Ice Houses," *Tennessee Farmer*, (1837), 190, 362; "Ice Houses," *SA*, 1 (March, 1841), 142; *Life of William Grimes, the Runaway Slave. Written by Himself* (New York, 1825), 9; Jennifer L. Eichstedt and Stephen Small, *Representations of Slavery: Race and Ideology in Southern Plantation Museums* (Washington, DC, 2002), 88.

a supply of ice provoked squeals of delight from Charleston to the Mississippi.[53]

Tryphena Fox, a plantation tutor near Vicksburg in the 1850s, complained about the high cost of ice, but it still had eager buyers. Supplying many were some twenty cutting and exporting companies in and around Boston. Machines sawed the ice into blocks, which were then wrapped in sawdust or hay. Most of the ice went to Europe, the East Indies, West Indies, and South America, but from the 1830s southern cities and towns imported considerable amounts. Ice became a necessity for New Orleans, which, according to the *Daily Picayune*, consumed 40,000 tons per year, trailing only New York, Philadelphia, Boston, and Baltimore. Tallahassee, the backwater capital of Florida, imported ice from New York from 1835 on. Large blocks were cut out of the lakes of New York and New England, stored in sawdust and wood shavings, repackaged during spring and summer, and sent south in packets. Ox and mule teams carried the ice overland to Tallahassee and other towns. To get a share, Southerners had to have access to a town with northern shippers.[54]

CREDIT WHERE DUE

Southerners, proud of their cuisine, sometimes gave credit where due. Ridiculing the Irish cooks favored in the North, Mary Howard Schoolcraft, a South Carolina planter's daughter, boasted, "The negroes are born cooks." She insisted, however improbably, that when a cook fell ill, the master could call in any field hand, male or female, confident of a good result. In reality, consternation gripped farms and plantations when a cook got sick without an adequate replacement. In St. Mary's parish, Louisiana, a guest remembered the plantation "feast" as opening with

---

[53] Elizabeth Catherine Palmer to Esther Simons Palmer, Sept. 3, 1847, Louis P. Towles, ed., *A World Turned Upside Down: The Palmers of South Santee, 1818–1881* (Columbia, SC, 1996), 124; Hilliard, *Hog Meat and Hoecake*, 53

[54] Wilma King, ed., *A Northern Woman in the Plantation South: Letters of Tryphena Blanche Holder Fox, 1856–1876* (Columbia, SC, 1993), 11; "Refrigeration and Ventilation of Cities," *SQR*, 1 (1842), 423; "Ice Trade of the United States," *American Quarterly Register and Magazine* (Philadelphia), 1 (1848), 132–133; Thomas Ewing Dabney, *One Hundred Great Years: The Story of the Times-Picayune from Its Founding to 1940* (Baton Rouge, LA, 1940), 101; Bertram H. Groene, *Ante-Bellum Tallahassee* (Tallahassee, FL, 1971), 37; E. Merton Coulter, *The South During Reconstruction, 1865–1877* (Baton Rouge, LA, 1947), 269–270. New England's ice trade to New Orleans and the Orient led Henry David Thoreau and others to literary musings: see F. O. Matthiessen, *American Renaissance: Art and Expression in the Age of Emerson and Whitman* (New York, 1968), 117–119.

"Gumbo, of African descent ... I do not know that one of those old, long practiced creole darky cooks under the inspiration of Madame, could beat the old serpent himself with tempting viands." Less flamboyantly, Dr. Joseph Jones reported from the Confederate army that some units ate much better than others. The advantage went to slaveholders with experienced body servants. Soldiers of all classes, barely knowing how to cook, ate a great deal of their own burned bread and grease-ladened fried food. Doctors had to treat diarrhea, dysentery, and assorted abdominal ailments.[55]

Joseph Holt Ingraham, visiting the markets of New Orleans, saw few white faces: "Servants do all the marketing, and the gentlemen and ladies do not, as in Boston, Philadelphia, and elsewhere, visit the market-places themselves, and select their own provision for their tables." Olmsted reported from North Carolina and Mississippi that small farmers as well as planters sent slaves to choose and buy food for them, and that many slaves planned meals for their mistresses. Masters routinely congratulated their wives for successful dinner parties, but both, when pressed, acknowledged – even proclaimed proudly – that their cooks deserved credit. In Natchez, John Wistar Metcalfe casually noted, "My cook Cuilty gave them a very fashionable dinner about three o'clock." Whites depended on blacks for more than the cooking. Charlestonians held up dinner until the free black fishermen on whom they relied for fresh fish brought in their catch. As Huger Smith explained, "For only the fish that entered your kitchen alive was worthy of the regard of a gourmet."[56]

Indians taught whites and blacks to catch and prepare the wild animals that figured prominently in southern diet, and to cultivate and prepare vegetables: Irish potatoes, squash, most beans, and maize ("Indian corn"). But settlers did not throw small game on the coals without

[55] *Plantation Life: Schoolcraft Narratives*, 234, 506; Jewell Lynne De Grummond, "Social History of St. Mary's Parish, 1845–1860" *Louisiana Historical Quarterly*, 32 (1949), 33; Charles W. Turner, ed., *An Old Field School Teacher's Diary (Life and Times of Jeremiah C. Harris)* (Verona, VA, 1975), May 11, 1855 (39); James O. Breeden, *Joseph Jones, M. D.: Scientist of the Old South* (Lexington, KY, 1975), 108; H. M. Schiller, "Health and Medicine," in *Encyclopedia of the Confederacy*, ed., Richard N. Current, 4 vols. (New York, 1993), 2:754; Ingraham, *Sunny South*, 53–54. For the African influence on the Virginia version of Gumbo, see Fowler, ed., *Dining at Monticello*, 107.

[56] [Joseph Holt Ingraham], *The South-West. By a Yankee*, 2 vols. (Ann Arbor, MI, 1966 [1835]), 1:102–103; Olmsted, *Seaboard Slave States*, 359; Olmsted, *Back Country*, 153; Virginia Writers Program, *The Negro in Virginia* (Winston Salem, NC, 1991), 38; James Wistar Metcalfe Diary, March 6, 1843; D. E. Huger Smith, *A Charlestonian's Recollections, 1846–1913* (Charleston, SC, 1950), 64.

removing hide, hair, and guts. Bear, an early favorite, declined rapidly in availability. In much of the South, venison remained popular and plentiful. Wild turkey continued as a staple; only the more substantial planters raised their own turkeys. Where the supply of wild turkey shrank, farmers and planters raised chickens. As game became scarce in long-settled areas, domestically raised pork gained in popularity. Wealthy planters also served mutton. Guests at John Rutledge's oyster roast raved about the venison patties and wanted to know what had gone into the making. Rutledge summoned his proud, dignified, male game cook, who replied, in the manner of all great chefs: a little of this, a little of that. How long had they been cooked? Just long enough. Asked where the recipe came from, he explained that his pappy had gotten it from the Chickasaws.[57]

Although opossum, raccoon, rabbit, squirrel, and "chittlins" eventually came to be viewed as food for the lower classes, even the most fastidious ladies and gentlemen enjoyed them without embarrassment. Opossum and squirrel had provided much of the frontiersmen's diet. Subsequently, much of the diet of lower-class whites and slaves retained its charms for much of the elite. Francis Taylor, a planter in Orange County, Virginia, recorded, "Went to squirrel barbecue." Squirrel, "excellent eating," turned up at the table of no few planters, including the governor of Florida. In Georgia, as in Kentucky, cooks fried and broiled squirrels and made squirrel soup.[58]

Black women usually served as cooks on the plantations, but men served on some of the larger plantations and in townhouses. Male or female, cooks held pride of place among servants. Most of the reputedly great ones were men – or perhaps the men were more readily celebrated. The Chesnuts' Mulberry Plantation owed its reputation as the culinary capital of the upcountry South Carolina to Romeo, their Charleston-trained cook. Except in and about New Orleans, few planters could afford to send slaves to study cooking in Paris; slaves so favored were generally male. Prosper Ernest Fournier, an African, was the most famous of the local Paris-trained black cooks. In Washington, slaveholders placed

[57] Taylor, *Eating, Drinking, and Visiting*, 3–8, 22, 24, 28, 31; Silverthorne, *Plantation Life in Texas*, 86; Barry, *Mr. Rutledge*, 44. On Indian contributions see John B. Boles, *Black Southerners, 1619–1869* (Lexington, KY, 1984), 93–94; Sam Hilliard, "Hog Meat and Cornpone: Food Habits in the Ante-Bellum South," *Proceedings of the American Philosophical Society*, 113 (1969), 5–6; Taylor Diary, April 21, 1787.

[58] Hopley, *Life in the South*, 1:278 (Florida); Lettice Bryan, *The Kentucky Housewife* (Bedford, MA, n.d. [1839]), 13–14, 137, 413. Opossum was a favorite dish among college students: Lisa Tolbert et al., eds., *Two Hundred Years of Student Life at Chapel Hill: Selected Letters and Diaries* (Chapel Hill, NC, 1993), 32.

slaves as apprentices to the French cooks who reigned in the foreign embassies.[59]

Cooks had a reputation for violent temperaments. After all, they considered themselves artists. If Arturo Toscanini could throw his baton at erring musicians in his orchestra, why should not Alcey have had that privilege on the Dabney plantation in Mississippi? Here and there, mistresses as well as slaves feared cook's wrath and stayed out of her or his way. The stories became less charming when unhappy cooks poisoned the white family. And cooks, unhappy or no, opened kitchens and the plantation larder to runaways. William McKean, an overseer in Chesterfield County, Virginia, wrote to James Dunlop, his employer: "You seem astonished that we were beset with thieves in the shape of runaway negroes. I can assure you that it is nothing uncommon in this Country, in fact it is the very manner in which they are supported, if they did not steal from the neighboring plantations & receive support from the servants around, they could not live." McKean knew runaways "to lodge in the kitchens of gentlemen in Town for a month at a time without ever being discovered & supported entirely by his own servants; there is scarcely a runaway in any neighborhood but a great portion of the servants about know of it & assist in supporting him."[60]

Whites did not downplay African and Indian influences in southern cooking before nearly as much as after the War. African-born slaves, few and far between after 1830, appeared disproportionately among cooks. Here and there, slaveholders frankly acknowledged preference for the culinary skills of Africans in the kitchen. The recipes in Sarah Rutledge's *The Carolina Housewife* (1847) drew on French cuisine but also Indian, English, Italian, and German, skillfully blending African techniques, herbs, and spices to produce gumbos, jambalayas, and other famous popular dishes, as well as dishes thought of in the low country as French. The

---

[59] Charles Lyell, *A Second Visit to the United States of North America*, 2 vols. (London, 1855), 2:126; Bremer, *Homes*, 1:292; Weymouth T. Jordan, *Hugh Davis and His Alabama Plantation* (University, AL, 1948), 7; Muhlenfeld, *Mary Boykin Chesnut*, 45. Also see D. E. Huger Smith on Renty, the chief cook on a rice plantation, in Smith, *Carolina Rice Plantation*, 82; for male plantation cooks in the low country, see also William Dusinberre, *Them Dark Days: Slavery in the American Rice Swamps* (New York, 1996), 113. On French cooks, see Saxon et al., *Gumbo Ya-Ya*, 145–147; Constance McLauglin Green, *Washington: Village and Capital, 1800–1878* (Princeton, NJ, 1962), 43.

[60] Smedes, *Memorials of a Southern Planter*, 150–151; Edward T. Tayloe to B. O. Tayloe, July 16, 1855; K. John Q. Anderson, ed. *Brokenburn: The Journal of Kate Stone, 1861–1868* (Baton Rouge, LA, 1955), 171; William McKean to James Dunlop, Dec. 11, 1816, in McKean Letterbook.

contributions of inventive black cooks, including okra, peanuts, sesame seeds, and yams were unmistakable, as Southerners freely acknowledged. The Indians contributed corn, squash, pumpkins, pepper, cowpeas, and sweet potatoes (sometimes also called yams).[61]

UPCOUNTRY DINING

Upcountry South Carolina had a planter elite of its own. Dinners were plainer but no less hearty than in the low country. Calhoun served beef, ham, poultry, and mutton, with corn and wheat bread, vegetables and fruit. The gentry at Society Hill, which included some of the state's leading families, served pretty much the same fare at dinner: gumbo, steak, fried chicken, rice, fruit preserves, wines and liquor. Henry Junius Nott, writing from his professorial chair in Columbia in 1831, teased his low-country friend Hugh Legaré: "After all, it is not a bad country where one can, on an average twice a week throughout the year, eat Scotch salmon, pâté de foie gras and tranches de chavreuil [venison] moistened with Champagne, Chateaux Margaux, Johannisberger, not to mention such common things as Amontillado & Sercial [Madeira]." Nott reviewed the last three months: "Not less than some forty or fifty dinners en régle; & during the legislature, the service is still more active." Virginians and Carolinians, struggling with semi-frontier conditions, carried their taste westward.[62]

Although the word "elegant" appears in contemporary descriptions of southern dinners, few Europeans invoked it. Dinners could indeed meet European standards of elegance on a significant scale in New Orleans, with its French and Spanish traditions, but only here and there in Charleston, Savannah, Natchez, or at the table of a Jefferson or Madison. Spanish influence on upper class Southerners appeared in ollo, ropa vieja, gazpacho, and fritters. Traveling westward, even urban sophisticates dined, as it were, country style. The world-traveling James Johnston Pettigrew

---

[61] Frances Robotti and Peter Robotti, *French Cooking of the New World: Louisiana Creole and French Canadian Cuisine* (New York, 1967), 5; *AS: La.*, 5 (Pt. 3), 17; [Rutledge], *Carolina Housewife*, 55; Damon L. Fowler, "Historical Commentary" to Hill, *Southern Practical Cookery*, xliii; Taylor, *Eating, Drinking, and Visiting*, 4. The notion that African cuisine contributed significantly to southern remains in dispute. For the negative, see Taylor, *Eating, Drinking, and Visiting*, 88–89.

[62] Niven, *Calhoun*, 156; Harvey Toliver Cook, *The Life and Legacy of David Rogerson Williams* (New York, 1916), 211–212; also, Douglas Summers, *A City without Cobwebs: A History of Rock Hill, South Carolina* (Columbia, SC, 1953), 69; Michael O'Brien, *A Character of Hugh Legaré* (Knoxville, TN, 1985), 5, 40.

of North and South Carolina described the dinner party hosted in New Orleans by Judah Benjamin and Chief Justice George Eustis as the most elegant he had ever attended. A typical dinner at the home of Louisiana's leading planters and bankers usually included turtle soup, venison steaks with truffles, boiled trout, and seafood.[63]

Dr. James Holmes of the Georgia low country wrote of some peculiarities of upcountry dining: "Often when we were invited out to dinner, we were received into a splendidly furnished drawing room with lace curtains, Brussels carpets, mirrors, and all the rest. The ladies were in full and appropriate dinner costume, and everything was calculated to put upon his best behavior." Then the trouble started. "So far so good. But when dinner was announced, we expected to see the folding doors thrown open. Each gentleman with a lady upon his arm took up the line of march. With our hostess in front accompanied by some favored gallant, we were led down into the basement or what low-country people call the cellar." Holmes chafed at the ladies' odd practice of sending a plate of collards or other greens with a strip of bacon. Although the table had "turkey and ham and every imaginable good dish," guests got none until they had eaten the greens. Peculiarities aside, much of the upcountry Georgia gentry ate well. Thomas Cobb announced that he had never had a better cooked or tastier dinner than he had at Mr. Flinn's home in Milledgeville. Yet, dining might be crude even among wealthy and prominent planters, who seemed to survive primarily on corn bread and bacon, much like their slaves and the yeomen. Turkey, venison, and roast beef abounded. An appreciative tourist declared Mrs. Beale's venison second to none.[64]

Southerners, high and low, then and now, have taken justifiable pride in their barbecued pork. The most fastidious French or Italian connoisseur of veal might envy its leanness and succulence. Alas, when a Southerner did not hit the mark, the results were awful. Featherstonehaugh reported

[63] Clyde N. Wilson, *Carolina Cavalier: The Life and Mind of James Johnston Pettigrew* (Athens, GA, 1990), ch. 9; Vincent H. Cassidy and Amos E. Simpson, *Henry Watkins Allen of Louisiana* (Baton Rouge, LA, 1964), 33; also, De Grummond, "Social History of St. Mary's Parish," 33–34; Edgeworth, *Southern Gardener and Receipt Book*, 59, 212.

[64] Holmes, *"Dr. Bullie's" Notes*, 100–101; T. R. R. Cobb to Marion Cobb, Jan. 25, 1861, in Hull, ed., "Correspondence of T. R. R. Cobb," 158; "Interior Georgia Life and Scenery," in Eugene L. Schwaab and Jacqueline Bull, eds., *Travels in the Old South: Selected from Periodicals of the Time*, 2 vols. (Lexington, KY, 1973), 2:413; C. G. Parsons, *An Inside View of Slavery: A Tour among the Planters* (Savannah, GA, 1974 [1855]), 113–115; Richard D. Arnold to wife, Dec. 6, 1837, in Richard H. Shryock, ed., *Letters of Richard D. Arnold, M.D., 1808–1876* (Durham, NC, 1929), 16.

greasy bacon, pork, and venison at southern inns from Virginia to Arkansas. He wondered how Southerners, who ate well at home, calmly accepted the foisting of such misery on them. On circuit, Judge Sparks protested against meat horribly fried in what seemed a ton of lard, fatty cold meats, poorly cooked potatoes and collards, inferior corn bread, and smelly, inedible hash of pig liver and lungs. In short, better to avoid the inns and maneuver an invitation to a private home.[65]

Gentlemen enjoyed coarse dishes now often dismissed as slave food. Black-eyed peas were a great favorite, and "hog and hominy" (meal mixed with water or buttermilk) had numerous devotees. Simms extolled "Hop-in-John" to northern friends: "The peas boiled with bacon makes [sic] a favorite dish with us. Boiled with rice, equal parts, and a piece of bacon, seasoned with all-spice & pepper, they make a dish vulgarly called Hop-in-John among us – a dish of which our children are all very fond." Ladies and gentlemen enjoyed the hoe-cakes often associated with slaves and poor whites. An ex-slave woman explained: "You mix a cup of meal wid water an' pat it into small cakes. Grease it, if you got grease – dat keep it from stickin'. Den you rake out de ashes an' stick it on de hoe into de bottom of de fire an' cover it up. Let it cook 'bout five minutes, den take it out, rub de ashes off an' pick out de splinters. Wash it off wid warm water an' eat it fo' it cools. Don't taste like nothin' if you let it get cold." Sometimes, the hoe was held above the fire to prevent burning, but Fannie Nicholson, another ex-slave, protested, "'Twaren't no hoe-cake lessen de ashes burned it." Among masters, hoe cakes ceased to be baked on hoes, but critics grumbled that they never tasted as good.[66]

Americans had a bad reputation among foreign travelers for eating with incredible rapidity. Dining in Macon, Georgia, an annoyed Fredrika Bremer could not relax and converse at dinner. She was constantly asked if she wanted another helping. Eating seemed the only thing on anyone's mind. Yet most travelers thought that Southerners – the planters at least – did better than Northerners, taking time to enjoy their food, at least when dining in private homes rather than at inns. Hugh Legaré snapped back

[65] George W. Featherstonehaugh, *Excursion through the Slave States* (New York, 1968 [1844]), 16–17, 27, 100; for Sparks see Wade, *Augustus Baldwin Longstreet*, 79.
[66] W. G. Simms to James Lawson, July 7, 1839, in Oliphant et al., eds., *Letters of Simms*, 1:149; Virginia Writers Program, The Negro in Virginia (Winston Salem, N. C., 1994 [1940]), 70; Daniel R. Hundley, *Social Relations in Our Southern States* (Baton Rouge, LA, 1979 [1860]), 85–86. The use of red pepper and vinegar in the pig barbecue struck a cotton planter's northern bride: Lavinia Ervin to Her Parents, Dec. 10, 1853, in James C. Bonner, ed., "Plantation Experience of a New York Woman," *North Carolina Historical Review*, 33 (1956), 397.

at Mrs. Hall's contention that Americans, including Southerners, fixated on eating, accusing her and other Europeans of envy: "We never, in all our experience, heard so much about eating, except in a passage across the Atlantic, with a company of French gourmands." Yet a good many planters ate as rapidly as yeomen did. Buckingham saw gentlemen in the Alabama River Valley wolf down dinner in ten minutes. Dr. M. W. Philips of Mississippi gravely instructed fellow planters to give slaves thirty to forty-five minutes to eat comfortably. Philips himself needed ten to fifteen.[67]

Much country dining took place outdoors. Throughout the South, picnics and barbecues punctuated the landscape. In good weather a barbecue or picnic often substituted for after-church dining. During the summer at about 7:30 P.M., Virginians dressed for light outdoor suppers. In the early eighteenth century, the suppers tended to be community affairs, often held at the courthouse, with each family bringing its own food. As the century wore on, individual planters hosted them to welcome neighbors. Virginia Springs held especially fashionable picnics that often included favorite foods, champagne, poetry readings, and dancing and provided an occasion for the ladies, vying for attention, to dress colorfully.[68]

PIANOS

English and continental bourgeois who counted themselves lords of their households saw "ladylike accomplishments," notably piano-playing, as an antidote to the indolence of wives and mothers and as confirmation of the family's gentility. During the eighteenth century the South bought the larger share of European pianos and harpsichords shipped to America. Subsequently, Philadelphia, Boston, and New York housed most of the piano manufactories, supplemented primarily by

---

[67] Bremer, *Homes*, 1:334–335. Also, Jane Louise Mesick, *The English Traveller in America, 1785–1835* (Westport, CT, 1970), 300–301; Trollope, *Domestic Manners*, 47; Charles Dickens, *American Notes for General Circulation* (Harmondsworth, 1972 [1841]), 292; Rhys Isaac, *The Transformation of Virginia, 1740–1790* (Chapel Hill, NC, 1982), 44; *HLW* (1829), 2:260; Buckingham, *Slave States*, 1:467; Philips in *Southern Cultivator*, 4 (1846), 127.

[68] Hume Diary, June 20, 1860; Wise, *End of an Era*, 68; Morgan, *Virginians at Home*, 82–83; Taylor Diary, Sept. 4, 1790; Mary M. Hagner [Mark Pencil], *The White Sulphur Papers, or Life at the Springs of Western Virginia* (New York, 1839), 102–103. Across the Ohio River in Cincinnati, picnics were less popular, and ladies and gentlemen did not sit on the grass together: Trollope, *Domestic Manners*, 138, 299.

Baltimore, Charleston, Albany, NY, and a few other places. In 1829 they accounted for 2,500 pianos valued at $750,000; probably, most were sold in the North.[69]

By 1815 the piano became a symbol of respectability and culture in southern towns and countryside, as it had in Europe and the North. By 1860 the piano industry produced 22,000 per year – a piano for every 1,500 people in the United States. Americans claimed that their towns had ten times as many pianos as did the English. During the eighteenth century, the gentry of Virginia's Northern Neck equipped their homes with harpsichords and other instruments, which pianos gradually replaced. By 1800 a small recently founded town like Sparta, Georgia, had eleven pianos. In Mount Meigs, Alabama, Dr. J. Marion Sims paid a professional call on a Mr. Baldwin, a parvenu cotton planter: "Everything was so rough and uncouth on the outside that I did not expect to find anything on the inside to contradict the impression." But he did: "I didn't expect to find a piano in this wilderness; who would have dreamed of it?" Even small planters in remote areas bought a piano for wives and daughters as soon as affordable. In South Carolina, Cornish arrived at the home of William Johnson: "very unpromising ... but within was an elegant piano and other things to match, & we sat down to a very sumptuous repast." The larger homes had a music room with piano and other instruments and space to dance. Young people danced at every opportunity; usually to piano music.[70]

A trip to New York or Philadelphia offered an irresistible temptation to buy a piano. Honeymoon couples like Thomas Clemson and Anna Maria Calhoun could not resist. Henry E. Steinway personally selected a

[69] Arthur Loesser, *Men, Women, and Pianos: A Social History* (New York, 1954), 267–268; Daniel Spillane, *History of the Pianoforte: Its Development and the Trade* (New York, 1969 [1890]), 84, 125. For the significance of pianos in the economy of Boston, see Chaim M. Rosenberg, *Goods for Sale: Products and Advertising in the Massachusetts Industrial Age* (Amherst, MA, 2007), 72–73. Jane Austen, William Makepeace Thackeray, Hannah More, and Maria Edgeworth – writers popular in the South – were among the critics of bourgeois pretensions to gentility.

[70] Johnson, *Birth of the Modern*, 129, 131; Russell Blaine Nye, *Society and Culture in America, 1830–1860* (New York, 1974), 132; Arthur C. Cole, *The Irrepressible Conflict, 1850–1865* (New York, 1934), 230–231; D. S. Freeman, "Aristocracy of the Northern Neck," *SBN*, 10: 70; John Rozier, ed., *The Granite Farm Letters: The Civil War Correspondence of Edgeworth and Sallie Bird* (Athens, GA, 1988), xxi; J. Marion Sims, *The Story of My Life* (New York, 1884), 152; Green, ed, *Ferry Hill Plantation Journal*, 62, 69 (June 25, July 15, 1838); Janet Sharp Hermann, *Joseph E. Davis: Pioneer Patriarch* (Jackson, MS, 1990), 51; Cornish Diary, Nov. 14, 1855; Huger Smith, *Recollections*, 62–63.

piano, purportedly the most expensive in northern Mississippi, for Maria Bodie Mason of Holly Springs. Some wealthier planters – as well as female academies, all of which taught music – bought pianos, other musical instruments, and sheet music in New York, Philadelphia, and Boston. Northern firms also sold indirectly through southern agents. Politicians and journalistic critics like J. D. B. De Bow railed against the large sums that Southerners spent in the North, but even De Bow lavishly praised the fine pianos of Mssrs. Chickering & Sons in Philadelphia. The expensive pianos of old lowcountry planters like the Balls might be inlaid and ornamental.[71]

Music teachers supplemented their incomes as piano tuners for plantation homes and townhouses. Repairmen were available in the towns, but how well tuned Southerners kept their pianos remains hard to gauge. Barbara Leigh Smith Bodichon of Great Britain, who thought the ladies of Washington disagreeable, exclaimed: "Good Lord defend us, how they all play on pianos ... Too much like the railway rattle and smash." Maggie Howell, Varina Davis's sister, described a popular song banged out on an out-of-tune piano by every girl in a hoopskirt or calico frock between Richmond and the Mississippi.[72]

Independent dealers in towns did good business. Atlanta had a piano dealer in residence in 1860. In Marietta, Georgia, a druggist sold pianos on the side for $300. Dealers sold on credit, usually short-term. A prominent piano dealer in Vicksburg said that he had not lost one percent on his accounts before the War, but he could not collect afterwards. The Wetumpka Argus complained in 1845 that planters plunged into debt by giving their daughters $600 pianos they could not afford. In 1860, the father of fifteen year-old Sarah Lois Wadley's bought a piano for her;

[71] Ernest McPherson Lander, Jr., *The Calhoun Family and Thomas Green Clemson: The Decline of Southern Patriarchy* (Columbia, SC, 1983), 11; Olga Reed Pruitt, *It Happened Here: True Stories of Holly Springs* (Holly Springs, MS, 1950), 52–53 (Mason); E. Grey Dimond and Herman Hattaway, eds., *Letters from Forest Place: A Plantation Family's Correspondence* (Jackson, MS, 1993), 36, 60; Anna Matilda King to Thomas Butler King, Feb. 21, 1850; Basil Manly Letterbook for Richmond Female Academy, 1853–1854; Fletcher "Autobiography" (ms.), 1841; C. C. Jones to C. C. Jones, Jr., Feb. 21, 1851, in Jones Collection; De Bow, "Editorial Miscellany," *DBR*, 28 (1860), 614; Anne Simons Deas, *Recollections of the Ball Family of South Carolina and The Comingtee Plantation* (Charleston, SC, 1978 [1909]), 158.

[72] Albert Stoutamire, *Music of the South: Colony to Confederacy* (Rutherford, NJ, 1973), 98, 100; March 17, 1858, in Barbara Leigh Smith Bodichon, *An American Diary, 1857–8*, ed., Joseph W. Reed, Jr. (London, 1972), 132; Barrow Diary, Sept. 17, 1840, in Davis, ed., *Florida Parishes of Louisiana*, 211; Clement Eaton, Introduction to Olmsted, *Back Country*, xvi.

soon after, she learned that they could not afford to live in Vicksburg and had to move to Lyndhurst, Louisiana.[73]

Prices varied widely. Early in the nineteenth century Mrs. Hay thought Sarah Gilbert of Washington, Georgia, could get her a good piano for as little as $200. In 1858, Cornish was pleased: "The new piano arrived. Cost $75 – expenses $12.65 – $87.65 – a small sum for a rich Tones Grand Piano." The costs to Mrs. Hay and Mr. Cornish may have been for secondhand pianos, which sold for $150 or as low as $75. But the five pianos sold by Grovesteen and Truslow of New York to the Baptist Female School in Richmond in the 1850s for $196.50 to $265 probably were not. Planters paid $300–600 in the 1850s for pianos deemed "good." In 1857 J. H. Bills paid $325 plus $5.00 shipping costs in Tennessee. In 1850 Anna Matilda King bought her impatient children a piano for $453 on credit. In Mississippi, the Associate Presbyterian Reverend Samuel Agnew thought his sister Mary should have been delighted with the piano her father bought her at $550 in 1861: "It is splendid but ought to be for cost." The well-to-do took special pride in expensive rosewood pianos. Occasionally, a protest: "The money is my own," snapped Varina Davis to her mother, Margaret Howell, in 1847. "I have refused a piano because I wanted to apply the $450 to a better use." In the 1840s, $450 seemed about right for a good piano. Robert Martin of North Carolina, Stephen Douglas's father-in-law who doted on his daughters, outdid others when he paid $700. Harpsichords still graced some southern parlors.[74]

Rosalie Roos associated piano-playing with women and complained that gentlemen seemed more interested in their hands and prettiness than in their talent. To her disgust, some gentlemen fell asleep. William Battle

[73] Franklin M. Garrett, *Atlanta and Environs: A Chronicle of Its People and Events*, 2 vols. (Athens, GA, 1954), 1:491; Morrison Journal, April 29, 1860; William C. Harris, *Presidential Reconstruction in Mississippi* (Baton Rouge, LA, 1967), 33; Charles S. Davis, *The Cotton Kingdom in Alabama*, (Montgomery, AL, 1939), 182; *Wadley Journal*, Jan. 24, May, 14, 1860.

[74] Sarah Gilbert to Felix Gilbert, May 17, 1806, in Boggs, ed., *Alexander Letters*, 34; Cornish Diary, Jan. 16, 1858; A. J. McElveen to Z. B. Oakes, Oct. 4, 1854, in Edmund L. Drago, ed., *Broke by the War: Letters of a Slave Trader* (Columbia, SC, 1991), 99; Francis M. Manning and W. H. Booker, *Religion and Education in Martin County, 1774–1974* (Wilmington, NC, 1974), 198; Manley Letterbook, 1854; Anna Matilda King to Thomas Butler King, Feb. 21, 1850; Bills Diary, June 26, 1857; Agnew Diary, Oct. 31, 1861; Varina Davis to Margaret Howell, Jan. 3, 1847, in Hudson Strode, ed., *Jefferson Davis: Private Letters, 1823–1889* (New York, 1966), 45. On rosewoods, see C. C. Jones to his sons, Aug. 19, 1851, in Joseph Jones Collection; Pruitt, *It Happened Here*, 52–53; Fletcher "Autobiography" (ms.), 1841; George Fort Milton, *The Eve of Conflict: Stephen A. Douglas and the Needless War* (Cambridge, MA, 1934), 32 n.

of Alabama made clear to his cousin, Virginia Tunstall (Clay-Clopton), that he considered piano-playing by a man a quasi-criminal act. Yet more gentlemen played the piano than Roos and Battle suggested. Calhoun was one and would not have appreciated the insult. B. Franklin Doswell, a student at Washington College, muttered about the paucity of pianos in Lexington, a Presbyterian stronghold. Unable to practice, he thought his piano-playing skills were deteriorating.[75]

The young ladies' music brightened interminable visits to each other's homes. Cornish passed a "pleasant" evening at the home of Col. J.: "One of the young ladies being at home, we had music." Foreigners admired the pianos and the organization of evenings around them. Buckingham reported that Mr. Deere of Tennessee, a wealthy planter, had imported an "excellent" piano from London for his daughter. Bremer especially enjoyed evenings around the piano in Charleston: "The domestic life, the dancing, the music, and the evening games are altogether in the Swedish style." Adam Hodgson thought he was at home when he heard English tunes played on the piano or harp in plantation homes at Natchez. The Unitarian Reverend Abiel Abbot, President of Bowdoin College testified that the young ladies of Charleston played the piano, guitar, and harp well. Hopley, a discerning Englishwoman, recounted a visit to the governor of Florida during the winter of 1861–1862: "Great doings were going on in the parlour beneath. The piano was giving forth the liveliest airs, while merry steps kept time to the music, and scarcely a day passed, that some other cousin did not arrive to add to the group. The girls were all excellent musicians, and there were two good pianos in the house, often both in use at the same time."[76]

Fathers doted on their daughters: "We are all very anxious to hear you once more at your old Piano," Gustavus Henry wrote to Miss Susan, his fourteen year-old away at a female academy. It "stands in the Corner, ready for you when you get home." Young ladies also entertained family

[75] Rosalie Roos to Alex Roos, Aug. 13, 1854, in Roos, *Travels in America*, 122; Virginia Clay-Clopton, *A Belle of the Fifties: Memoirs of Mrs. Clay of Alabama* (New York, 1905), 7; *JCCP*, 26:534; Harry St. John Dixon Diary, in March 16, 1860, in Berry, ed., *Princes of Cotton*, 50; B. F. Doswell to Emma Doswell, Mar. 1, 1847.

[76] Cornish Diary, Oct. 11, 1840; Buckingham, *Slave States*, 2:263; Bremer, *Homes*, 1:303;; John Henry Hammond, ed., "The Abiel Abbot Journals: A Yankee Preacher in Charleston Society, 1818–1827," *South Carolina Historical Magazine*, 68 (1967), 115–139; Adam Hodgson, *Letters from North America, Written During a Tour in the United States and Canada*, 2 vols. (London, 1824), 1:185; Hopley, *Life in the South*, 2:260. For male piano players, see, e.g., Oct. 9, 1861, Ashkenazi, ed., *Diary of Clara Solomon*, 181; Edwin J. Scott, *Random Recollections of a Long Life, 1806 to 1876* (Columbia, SC, 1884), 91.

and friends by playing the guitar or, less frequently, the violin or flute. However well they played, and whatever others thought, planters and farmers took unabashed delight in having wives and daughters play on good instruments. "Mrs. Halsey in Scuppernong has a piano," Mary Blount Pettigrew wrote to James Johnston Pettigrew, "& it would be hard to describe how delighted Mr. H. is with it."[77]

Gentlemen swelled with pride at the musical accomplishments of their wives and daughters, but not every lady pleased her guests. Philip Fithian, enthralled by the playing, singing, and dancing of the seventeen-year-old Miss Jenny Washington in 1774, contrasted her performance with that of most Virginia belles he knew. Young ladies did not study the principles of music and "think it a labour quite sufficient to thump the Keys of a harpsichord into the air of a tune mechanically, & think it would be Slavery to submit to the Drudgery of acquiring Vocal Music." Ebenezer Pettigrew, a young planter in eastern North Carolina, quietly suffered when entertained by the lady of the family he stopped by to see: "But mercy defend me! The contrast, the person, with her great hand hammering down on the keys, by which a rattling sound was produced more like an empty cart in quick motion with all the boards loose, than that delightful music which I had been hearing all the week from the fair hand of the lovely Nancy." Poor Pettigrew thought to himself: "What mortifications must we endure. I sought for my bed as soon as good manners would permit." Some years later Ann, his wife, reported a more pleasant evening, when "Mama had a splendid tea party," with a great assemblage of finely dressed belles and "especially the music on the Piano by Miss Betsy Graham & Miss Susan Gaston." The Reverend Robert Lewis Dabney of Virginia took a strong interest in female education but not in piano-playing. Perhaps he was revealing himself as just another dour Calvinist, but perhaps he was rendering an accurate aesthetic judgment. Dabney thought only one young lady among his acquaintances played well.[78]

---

[77] G. A. Henry to Susan Henry, [?], 1848; Mary Blount Pettigrew to James Johnston Pettigrew, in Lemmon, ed., *Pettigrew Papers*, 2:560. The guitar figured among the accomplishments of the renowned Octavia Le Vert of Mobile: Frances Gibson Satterfield, *Madame Le Vert: A Biography of Octavia Walton Le Vert* (Edisto Island, SC, 1987), 17. Also, Eleanor P. Cross and Charles B. Cross, Jr., eds., *Glencoe Diary: The War-Time Journal of Elizabeth Curtis Wallace* (Chesapeake, VA, 1968), 79.

[78] June 24, 1774, Farish, ed., *Journal and Letters of Philip Fithian*, 123–125; Ebenezer Pettigrew to Frederick Blount, May 26, 1814, Ann Blount Pettigrew to Ebenezer Pettigrew, Jan. 10, 1825, in Lemmon, ed., *Pettigrew Papers*, 1:463, 2:55; Thomas Cary Johnson, ed. *Life and Letters of Robert Lewis Dabney* (Carlisle, PA, 1977), 40.

A lady who played poorly distressed gentlemen, who could not avoid asking her to play when visiting her or vice versa. Ladies who played the piano were expected to sing. Charles Edward Leverett of South Carolina sympathized with poor Mary Augusta Secunda Grimké, whose inability to sing rendered her lovely piano playing almost pointless. Joseph Cumming of Georgia, stationed in Pensacola during the War, explained to his wife that he had visited two young French women only to find that they did not play the piano: "I don't think I will prosecute the acquaintance." In contrast, the single, twenty-three year-old Baker called on Miss Mabella: "quite an accomplished Lady – talks well – performed sweetly on the Piano Forte – & altogether is an agreeable companion." Mary Jones Chester pushed her schoolgirl daughters to play well and make her proud by performing when they returned home. Mothers without pianos arranged to have daughters practice in the homes of their ministers or wealthier neighbors.[79]

As daughters of the moderately well-to-do joined those of the wealthy at private schools, more and more learned to play well. At home, young women taught their younger sisters. Played well or badly, the piano became a social center at which ladies, young and old, could shine. Young ladies fretted about keeping in practice, and the more conscientious practiced before breakfast. After the War, Martha Steagall of Gonzales, Texas, fleeing to Brazil never to return, took her piano with her.[80]

Margaret Junkin Preston of Lexington, Virginia, an accomplished writer, designed the furnishings for the home of Robert E. Lee when he became president of Washington College. A one-armed Confederate veteran made all the furniture, and Lee's son said, "a handsomely carved piano, presented by Stieff, the famous maker of Baltimore, stood alone in the parlour." Jeff Hamilton, Sam Houston's body servant, insisted that Mrs. Houston had the first if not the only grand piano in Texas and that men, women, and children came from miles around to hear her and her daughter play. Songs varied as favorites, but a few like "Drink to Me

[79] Kemp P. Battle, *History of the University of North Carolina*, 2 vols. (Spartanburg, SC, 1974 [1907]), 1:595; Charles Edward Leverett to Milton Leverett, Apr. 12, 1859, in Frances Wallace Taylor et al., eds., *The Leverett Letters: Correspondence of a South Carolina Family, 1851–1868* (Columbia, SC, 2000), 84; Joseph B. Cumming to Katherine H. Cumming, Nov. 16, 1861, in W. Kirk Wood, ed., *A Northern Daughter and Southern Wife: The Civil War Reminiscences and Letters of Katherine H. Cumming, 1860–1865* (Augusta, GA, 1976), 49–50; mother-daughter correspondence for Dec. 27, 1840, May 15, 1841, in Chester Papers; Cornish Diary, Aug. 23, 1844; Baker Diary, March 24, 1849.
[80] Wadley Private Journal, Feb. 6, 1861; S. R. Jackson, Jan. 15, 1835, in Jackson-Prince Papers; Ingraham, *Sunny South*, 219; Harton, *Lost Colony of the Confederacy*, 21, 78.

Only with Thine Eyes" and "Coming through the Rye" remained popular. Across the South, young ladies played and sang operatic arias by Rossini, Donizetti, Gluck, Beethoven, and Handel. Rossini, Bellini, and Donizetti wrote operas well adapted to the piano. Homes in the low country had piano transcriptions of complete operas.[81]

A father delighted to present a piano to his devoted wife and to accommodate a charming daughter's pleading and teasing. Apparently, Yankee troops sensed the pleasure that pianos brought the young ladies, for they relished chopping them up. The more cultured shipped the pianos home to their own women. Meanness and greed aside, perhaps the soldiers sensed that even some planters could only satisfy the passion of their sweet young things by selling a slave to pay for the piano that brought so much pleasure to family and friends.[82]

THE READING CIRCLE

The Bible and published sermons held pride of place in the family reading circles of planters and yeomen, low-country gentry and mountain folks. Husband and wife had favorite passages that served as texts for informal sermons. Political speeches circulated as pamphlets or published in newspapers claimed wide attention. The ladies also read a good deal of poetry and novels. Discussion followed reading aloud. Mothers and daughters read to each other and to the family from books of various types. Commonly, illiterates sent for local schoolboys to read newspapers and political speeches to them.[83]

---

[81] Capt. Robert Edward Lee, *The Recollections and Letters of General Robert E. Lee, by His Son* (New York, 1904), 203; Jeff Hamilton, *My Master: The Inside Story of Sam Houston and His Times, as Told to Lenoir Hunt* (Austin TX, 1992), 28; Ingraham, *Sunny South*, 219; Sallie Bird to Edgeworth Bird, June 21, 1863, in Rozier, ed., *Granite Farm Letters*, 113; Huger W. Jervey, "The South's Contribution to Music," *SBN*, 7:385–386; Battle, *University of North Carolina*, 1:596; Arthur Loesser, *Men, Women, and Pianos: A Social History* (New York, 1954), 361. In Louisa County, Virginia, young ladies sang together from "Norma" for wounded Confederate troops: Patterson Journal, Sept. 14, 1862, in John G. Barrett, ed., *Yankee Rebel: The Civil War Journal of Edmund DeWitt Patterson* (Chapel Hill, NC, 1966), 63.

[82] Annie Clark Jacobs in James W. Silver, ed., *Mississippi in the Confederacy: As Seen in Retrospect* (Baton Rouge, LA, 1961), 171; Wilson, *Carolina Cavalier*, ch. 19; Charles E. Beveridge et al., eds., *The Papers of Frederick Law Olmsted*, 2 vols. (Baltimore, 1977, 1981), 2:251; Olmsted, *Back Country*, 284–285.

[83] Wadley Private Journal, Mar. 4, 1863; Mary E. Moragné in Delle Mullen Craven, ed., *The Neglected Thread: A Journal of the Calhoun Community* (Columbia, SC, 1951), xxxv. Columbus Morrison read *Lady of the Lake* to his wife: Morrison Journal, July

The celebrated Baptist Reverend A. J. Broadus of Virginia read religious poetry to his wife and children. Some memorable evenings included sight translations of Plato, but his family often had to proceed without him. On Sundays the U. S. Secretary of the Treasury William H. Crawford of Georgia, like modest farm folks, drilled his children in the Bible, reading Psalms aloud to them. Families in town and country read together, especially on Sundays. Those who skipped church read the Bible or printed sermons or selections from favorites such as John Bunyan or Richard Baxter. The head of household offered an exegesis and led the discussion. Sometimes, a visitor led the night's reading. Since James Greenlee had weak eyes, his wife usually read to him, but they sometimes reversed roles or read together. He read aloud two sermons on "the great supper," commenting, "Oh Lord impress more forcibly divine truth on our hearts and minds & enable us to give a reason for the hope that is in us." Sundays also featured religious readings to servants.[84]

Husbands and wives sometimes read the same book separately and exchanged views. The Jefferson Davises and James Chesnuts, like other couples, negotiated. The ladies deferred to their husbands' preference for history but contributed classics, poetry, and novels. Reading together started early in many a courtship: the Bible, Shakespeare, Milton, Hannah Moore, various novels, or the surprisingly popular Lord Byron. Books read aloud in the cotton heartland included Margaret Oliphant Wilson's *Zaidee*, Washington Irving's *Sketchbook*, Jane Austen's *Pride and Prejudice*, and Thackeray's *Vanity Fair*. Susan Dabney Smedes of Mississippi described the reading of poetry, especially aloud in groups, as the rage among the children of the plantation elite. Young men like William Hooper Haigh, a lawyer in Fayetteville, North Carolina, enjoyed reading aloud to groups of women.[85]

2, 1846. Northerners, too, read to the family, esp. the Bible: David D. Hall, *Cultures of Print: Essays in the History of the Book* (Amherst, MA, 1996), 31, 56–61.

[84] Archibald Thomas Robertson, *Life and Letters of John Albert Broadus* (Philadelphia, 1909), 331; Chase Mooney, *William H. Crawford, 1772–1834* (Lexington, KY, 1974), 16; Hume Diary, June 22, 1860; Hutchinson Journal, Oct. 1, 1826; Greenlee Diary, Feb. 27, 1853, also April 3, 1849, March 17, 1850.

[85] William C. Davis, *Jefferson Davis: The Man and His Hour* (New York, 1991), 188; Muhlenfeld, *Mary Boykin Chesnut*, 54; M. King Diary, Sept. 18, 1853; Hutchinson Journal, Dec. 9, 1832; A. F. Dickson, *Plantation Sermons* (Philadelphia, 1856 [2011]). On courtship reading see Stowe, *Intimacy and Power*, 117; James C. Bonner, ed., *The Journal of a Milledgeville Girl, 1861–1867*, ed. (Athens, GA, 1964), Anna Maria Green Diary, June 27, 1862 (17); Richard L. Troutman, ed., *The Heavens are Weeping: The Diaries of Richard Browder, 1852–1856* (Grand Rapids, 1987), Jan. 1, 185 91; Jean V. Berlin, *Diary of a Southern Refugee During the War, by a Lady of Virginia* (Lincoln,

When father was away, mother or oldest child led the family reading, and daughters read to mothers, as well as vice versa. Sarah Eve Adams had the pleasure of evenings in which her daughter read religious tracts particularly for her. Nineteen-year-old Louisa Quitman and her siblings suffered dull evenings when their father was fighting in Mexico and no visitors appeared. She then read to the family until 10 or 11 P.M. – newspapers, Mungo Park's *Travels*, a life of Napoleon, Sir Walter Scott. Mahala Roach took special pleasure from these sessions, finding Susan Warner's *The Wide, Wide World* to her taste since "I can sew so much better when I hear a pleasant book."[86]

The family reading circle provided boys with their first lessons in the oratory requisite for careers in politics, law, or the ministry. They listened to their fathers read political speeches and sermons and read aloud themselves. Their experience often began with poetry as well as light fare, and they expected gentle criticism by parents and older siblings.[87]

Young ladies away at school and women of the household, joined by friends, had their own reading circles. The women of the Thomas Butler King household in the Georgia low country met regularly in the mornings to read an inspirational work like Anne Manning's *The Household of Sir Thomas More*, along with King's latest report on politics or the railroad promotion in which he was caught up. Occasionally, a favored gentleman read to an informal ladies' gathering. When the ladies read alone, they often included political literature. Fannie Page Hume of Virginia may serve as an example. She enjoyed reading aloud James Barbour's "fine speech at the inauguration of the Clay statue – it was a noble tribute" – and Representative D. W. Vorhees's speech on "'The American Citizen' at the University of Virginia – it is fully worthy of its reputation –eloquently written." She also read an antislavery speech "violent in its tendency" but with some "prettily written" parts.[88]

NE, 1995 [1867], Mar. 20, 1863 (201); Saida Bird to Edgeworth Bird, June 21, 1863, in Rozier, ed., *Granite Farm Letters*, 113; Smedes, *Memorials of a Southern Planter*, 168–169; Haigh Diary, July 16, 1843, May 15, 1844.

[86] Adams Diary, Dec. 3, 1813; Louisa Quitman to John A. Quitman, Feb. 1847; Mahala Roach Diary, Feb. 3, 1853, in Roach-Eggleston Papers.

[87] Introduction, Waldo W. Braden, ed., *Oratory in the South, 1828–1860* (Baton Rouge, LA), 74.

[88] Edward M. Steel, Jr., *T. Butler King of Georgia* (Athens, GA, 1964), 125; also, Carmichael Diary, Sept. 29, 1837; Ray Diary, 1860–1861; Hume Diary, April 10, 14, 1860; Jan. 5, 1861 (Vorhees, a pro-southern Democrat of Indiana); Haigh Diary, 1844.

HOME SCHOOLING

Rich and poor benefited from home schooling by dedicated parents. The mothers of John C. Breckenridge and J. E. B. Stuart taught them to read. Parents pondered the education of daughters as well as sons. A proud Charlotte Beatty reported that her "dear little Sara," was "reading beautifully" at age four and "finished the New Testament this day, having read it thro." Some planters preferred to educate their daughters at home, fearing that even the best schools did not teach them thoroughly. No few fathers required that their daughters put their minds to serious and difficult subjects.[89]

Home schooling strengthened the family reading circle. Most of the burden fell on parents but much on older children. A bright, well-schooled son or daughter supplemented or even replaced parents as teacher of the younger children. President Anson Jones of the Republic of Texas and his siblings in a small slaveholding family were well taught by their older sister Mary. Among prominent clergymen in Virginia, the Baptist Reverend Broadus paid tribute to his sister Martha, who laid the foundation of his education. The Presbyterian Reverend John H. Bocock's career began at home, where older sons taught younger siblings. R. L. Dabney, an accomplished theologian, considered an older brother his first real teacher and credited his sister with encouraging his Latin studies. The mother and older brothers of Professor John Barbee Minor of the University of Virginia tutored him until he was sixteen. In upcountry South Carolina, Louisa McCord taught her brother and sister English and French, writing, and arithmetic. Countless aunts and some uncles drilled nieces and nephews in the Bible.[90]

Fathers read to sons and daughters and heard recitations in subjects from history and natural philosophy to Latin and French. Alexander Stephens and Joseph LeConte credited their fathers with critical

---

[89] Beatty Diary, Feb. 23, Dec. 30, 1843; Thomas Palmer Jerman to Harriet R. Palmer, Sept. 25, 1858, in Towles, ed., *World Turned Upside Down*, 224.

[90] Herbert Gambrel, *Anson Jones: The Last President of Texas* (Garden City, NY, 1948), 420; Robertson, *John Albert Broadus*, 26; J. H. Bocock, *Selections from His Writings* (Richmond, VA, 1891), ix; Thomas Cary Johnson, ed. *Life and Letters of Robert Lewis Dabney* (Carlisle, PA, 1977), 26–27; E. C. Trope, Jr., "John Barbee Minor," in W. Hamilton Bryson, ed., *Legal Education in Virginia, 1779–1979: A Biographical Approach* (Charlottesville, VA, 1982), 417; on McCord, see Sophia Dulles to John Heatley Dulles, May 8, 1834, in Cheves Family Papers, and Huff, Jr., *Langdon Cheves*, 187; A. B. Van Zandt, *"The Elect Lady": A Memoir of Mrs. Susan Catherine Bott, of Petersburg, Va.* (Philadelphia, 1857), 26–27, 84.

contributions to their education directly through instruction and indirectly through loving concern. General John B. Earle of Revolutionary War fame taught his daughter well. She, in turn, prepared her son, James T. Harrison, to enter college at thirteen, graduate with honors at seventeen, study law with J. L. Petigru, and have the satisfaction of twice refusing appointment to the Supreme Court of Mississippi.[91]

More often, Southerners credited their mothers, although a discount should be applied for The Chivalry's romantic nostalgia. "The very best teacher, who had twenty or more pupils to instruct," Edgeworth Bird of Georgia wrote his daughter Saida in 1862, "could never have taken the same pains or been near so thorough as your dear Mama has been, and you both owe her double duty and love during life." Widows took on a heavy burden in the education of their children. The widowed mothers of George Mason, Governor John Willis Ellis, Justice William Gaston, and Governor Richard Keith Call, among others, prepared them well for their distinguished careers.[92]

With the Episcopal Church in ruins after the Revolution, mothers and grandmothers kept the faith alive through religious instruction of children. And for diverse reasons, in early nineteenth-century Europe and America, mothers wanted to teach their children themselves rather than expose them to bad influences. The education of Cornelius Walker, John Girardeau, and other prominent clergymen began with their mothers' instruction. Girardeau learned to read at age five, taught by a mother who used the Bible as her textbook. She probably invoked the same textbook when she "corrected" him soundly" for swearing for the first and last time in his life.[93]

[91] Rudolph R. von Abele, *Alexander H. Stephens: A Biography* (New York, 1946), 18; William Dallam Armes, ed., *The Autobiography of Joseph LeConte* (New York, 1903), 21–22; Morrison Journal, Sept. 20, 23, 1846; Cornish Diary, Jan. 24, 1859; J. A. Orr, "James T. Harrison," *Publications of the Mississippi Historical Society*, 8 (1904), 187–192; Martha R. Jackson Journal, 1833–1835, in Jackson-Prince Papers.

[92] Edgeworth Bird to Sallie (Saida) Bird, Jan. 12, 1862, in Rozier, ed., *Granite Farm Letters*, 57; Rutland, *George Mason*, 6–7; Noble J. Tolbert, ed., *The Papers of John Willis Ellis*, 2 vols. (Raleigh, NC, 1964), 1:xli; R. D. W. Connor, "William Gaston: A Southern Federalist of the Old School and His Yankee Friends, 1778–1844," *Proceedings of the American Antiquarian Society*, n. s., 43 (1933), 386; Elizabeth F. Ellet, *The Women of the American Revolution*, 2 vols. (New York, 1848), 2:139; Herbert J. Dougherty, *Richard Keith Call, Southern Unionist* (Gainesville, FL, 1961), 4–5.

[93] W. A. R. Goodwin, "Northern Influences" and C. E. Grammer, "The Rev. Dr. Cornelius Walker," in W. A. R. Goodwin, ed., *History of the Theological Seminary in Virginia and Its Historical Background*, 2 vols. (New York, 1923), 1:439 1:620; George A. Blackburn, ed., *The Life Work of John L. Girardeau* (Columbia, SC, 1916), 10, 13; Johnson, *Birth of the Modern*, 728–729.

For most southern families home schooling may have meant no more than inculcation of basic literacy, but for many it provided a solid educational foundation. Clergymen did much of the tutoring in the homes of wealthy planters in Virginia. During colonial times and immediately thereafter, Scotland, especially Edinburgh, supplied well-educated clergymen to Virginia to tutor boys like John Marshall, Thomas Jefferson, James Monroe, and the Lees. In consequence, as John Melish reported at the beginning of the nineteenth century, the children of the wealthy were well educated, "But the system seems to be defective so far as the mass of the people are concerned." In later years the Baptist Reverend Richard Furman attended school briefly, but, taught at home by his parents, he became proficient in Latin, Greek, and Hebrew, mathematics, physics, classical literature – and marksmanship. Floride Clemson, Calhoun's granddaughter, went to school for only two years but her correspondence reveals a woman of fine education. Drilling at home prepared William Porcher Miles for Moses Waddel's rigorous Willington Academy.[94]

Prominent men credited parents with preparing them to move in upper or respectable middle-class society. George Henry Calvert did not learn much at his village school but did learn a great deal from his mother, including "the finer properties in the intercourse of the drawing-room and dining-room" as well as the "culture of the graces, and amenities of social commerce." She taught him "the movements and demeanor involved in what is termed good breeding." Anna Waties, complaining of the failure of a Sabbath school, remarked, that the well-off felt qualified to teach their children at home. That was 1803 in Stateburg, South Carolina. It might just as well have been said in 1860 in Mississippi.[95]

CHAMBERS AND MASTER BEDROOMS

Especially in the low country, house slaves slept in the master bedroom, although many planters preferred to have a female slave arrive early to

---

[94] Richard Beale Davis, *Intellectual Life in Jefferson's Virginia* (Chapel Hill, NC, 1964), 47; Beveridge, *Marshall*, 1:53; Malone, *Jefferson and His Time*, 1:40–46; Alonzo Thomas Dill, *Francis Lightfoot Lee: The Incomparable Signer, 1734–1797* (Williamsburg, VA, 1977), 5; John Melish, *Travels in the United States of America in the Years 1806 and 1807, and 1810 and 1811*, 2 vols. (Philadelphia, 1812), 1:241–242; Carolyn L. Harrell, *Kith and Kin* (Macon, GA, 1984), 13; Charles M. McGee and Ernest M. Lander, Jr., *A Rebel Came Home: The Diary and Letters of Floride Clemson, 1863–1866* (Columbia, SC, 1989), xi; sketch in Miles Papers.

[95] Calvert quoted in Ida Gertrude Everson, *George Henry Calvert: American Literary Pioneer* (New York, 1974), 36–37; Waties quoted in Johnson and Roark, *Black Masters*, 19.

kindle a fire. Elizabeth and Della Allston required slaves to sleep in separate quarters, for they feared the consequences of being alone in the house with slaves who might drink too much or prove ungovernable. In contrast, Jessie Wilson wrote to her father that she did not fear to be alone because three servants – a man and two women – slept in the house. And Lindsey Faucet's mother slept in the same bed as her mistress when the master, a lawyer, went off on business. On the larger plantations masters preferred the convenience of one or two slave children with them at night. Slave boys as well as girls described how, as children and adolescents, they slept in mistress' room, usually at the foot of the bed. In hot, humid southern summers, slaves fanned mistresses to sleep. Masters and mistresses, when sick or dying, had the comfort of a slave to care for them.[96]

When Catherine Hopley arrived from England to teach on a plantation, a slave girl offered to sleep on the floor of her bedroom. Startled rather than charmed, Hopley declined. Frances Trollope raised her eyebrows when a Virginia gentleman told her that, since his marriage, he and his wife had grown accustomed to having a black girl sleep in their bedroom. Why? "Good heaven, if I wanted a glass of water during the night, what would become of me." It is not clear that Trollope recognized a put-on. Still, how the whites protected the privacy of their lovemaking remains a mystery – if in fact they bothered to.[97]

Frances Kemble said that planters' wives and daughters had a "black pet" or two asleep at the foot of their beds, rather like puppies. A woman told James Redpath, "They made me sleep in their bedroom, on a mattress on the floor but paid no regard to my feelings, any more than if I was a cat." Yet, black children who played in the Big House provided special pleasures for the white ladies. Julia Barnsley was entranced: "Two little

---

[96] Barry, *Mr. Rutledge*, 23; Cornish Diary, Dec. 31, 1861; Magruder Diary, Apr. 19, 1857; James Benson Sellers, *Slavery in Alabama* (University, AL, 1964), 88. Jesse Sanford of Milledgeville, Georgia, who owned six plantations and several hundred slaves, had twenty-five domestic servants. James C. Bonner, *Milledgeville: Georgia's Antebellum Capital* (Athens, GA, 1978), 36. As many as two or three maids waited on the white girls. For references to sleeping in masters' bedrooms, see Austin Steward in *Twenty-Two Years a Slave and Forty Years a Freeman* (Reading, MA, 1969 [1857]), 18–19 and Benjamin Drew, *A North-Side View of Slavery: The Refugee, or, the Narrative of Fugitive Slaves in Canada* (New York, 1968 [1857]), 223. For a death-bed scene, see Cornish Diary, Oct. 2, 1859.

[97] Hopley, *Life in the South*, 1:41; Trollope, *Domestic Manners*, 250. For women who witnessed the sexual activity of masters and mistresses, see Thavolia Glymph, *Out of the House of Bondage: The Transformation of the Plantation Household* (New York, 2008), 43.

colored girls are enjoying the evening by looking at pictures of which they are very fond, as every night nearly they are begging for books to look at pictures, a looker on would suppose they were connoisseurs in the art of engraving." With Nancy McDougall Robinson's children away at school, she was lonely, but three "of the sable children of Africa," were playing on the carpet before the fire, "and their merriment drives all cares away."[98]

Charles Joseph Latrobe of England pitied masters rather than slaves, whom he called "pet and spoilt children." Josiah Henson testified about his old master, "As the first negro child ever born to him, I was his especial pet." But did Justice Peter V. Daniel of Virginia view one of his few slaves as a pet when he took him to the seashore to recuperate from a serious illness? William Green of Maryland depicted his master as a veritable monster who nonetheless favored and freed his father. Green judged the manumission of his father as probably the master's only good deed. John S. C. Abbott, a northern historian on tour, reasoned that many masters loved their slaves as they loved their pets, and that many slaves responded with servile cringing. But in the late 1840s the antislavery Matilda Charlotte Houstoun, appalled by racial prejudice in the North, charged that New Yorkers considered blacks "creatures decidedly inferior to a domestic animal" and treated them "with less respect than the pet dogs." Houstoun observed slave children at play in Louisiana: "The owners seem often really fond of these odd little animals, independently of their selfish interest in them, as representatives of so many dollars." She thought blacks better off in Kentucky than in Ohio.[99]

In the absence of the master a slave girl might share her mistress' bed. One did not appreciate the honor. Feigning sleep, she kicked her and was thereupon dispatched to the floor. Europeans and Northerners

---

[98] Frances Kemble, *Journal of a Residence on a Georgia Plantation in 1838–1839* (New York, 1863), 23; James Redpath, *The Roving Editor: Or, Talks with Slaves in the Southern States* (New York., 1859), 322; Julia Barnsley to George S. and Lucien Barnsley, Sept. 9, 1853; N. M. Robinson Diary, Dec. 4, 1853.

[99] Charles Joseph Latrobe, *The Rambler in North America*, 2nd ed., 2 vols. (London, 1836), 2:15; Josiah Henson, *Father Henson's Story of His Own Life* (New York, 1962 [1858]), 8; John P. Frank, *Justice Daniel Dissenting: A Biography of Peter V. Daniel, 1784–1860* (Cambridge, MA, 1964), 60; *Narrative of Events in the Life of William Green (Formerly a Slave), Written by Himself* (EE: 2000), 1853), 7; John S. C. Abbott, *South and North; or, Impressions Received during a Trip to Cuba and the South* (New York, 1969 [1860]), 90–91, 169–170; Mrs. [Matilda Charlotte] Houstoun, *Hesperos: Or, Travels in the West*, 2 vols. (London, 1850), 1:291, quotes at 1:195, 2:157.

had mixed reactions to the comings-and-goings of servants in bedrooms. Olmsted and Featherstonehaugh howled that ever-present black servants never closed a door behind them. Harriet Martineau fumed about slaves "perpetually at one's heels, lolling against the bed-posts before one rises in the morning." They were forever "spoiling everything that one had rather do for one's-self." The more audacious women slaves in the Big House tried on their mistresses' dresses and finery. When caught, they were whipped, perhaps as much for fancying themselves lovely as for impertinence.[100]

A postscript to bedroom tittle-tattle: Travelers carried change for black servants, who expected tips. Consequences followed from a refusal to meet expectations. The Reverend Alexander Taggart McGill of Princeton, a friend of the Reverends James Henley Thornwell and Benjamin Morgan Palmer, spent the winter of 1852–1853 as a professor of ecclesiastical history at the Columbia Theological Seminary in South Carolina. He stayed with the Reverend George Howe, whose servants – "lazy, lying and deceitful rascals" – did not tend his fire properly: "They know I don't whip, neither do I pay; and they don't care whether I freeze or not."[101]

A PECULIARITY

Ladies and gentlemen of eighteenth-century Virginia frowned on mixed bathing and occupied separate sections at beaches. Yet they accepted nudity among blacks to a degree that upset even such worldly travelers as the Marquis de Chastellux and Johann David Schoepf. At dinner, the younger servants brought food and cleared the dishes almost nude. Boys

[100] Ophelia Settle Egypt et al., eds., *Unwritten History of Slavery: Autobiographical Accounts of Negro Slaves* (Washington, DC, 1968), 93, also, 101, 126, 185; Featherstonehaugh, *Excursion through the Slave States*, 100; Olmsted, *Seaboard Slave States*, 410; Harriet Martineau, *Society in America*, 2 vols. (New York, 1837), 2:104, 3:309; Trollope, *Domestic Manners*, 250; also, Charles Lyell, *A Second Visit to the United United States of North America*, 2 vols., (London, 1849), 1:263; Duncan Clinch Heyward, *Seed from Madagascar* (Chapel Hill, NC, 1937), 71; Tera W. Hunter, *To "Joy My Freedom": Southern Black Women's Lives and Labor after the Civil War* (London, 1997), 4–5. For expectations of tips, see John Lambert, *Travels through Canada and the United States of North America in the Years 1806, 1807, and 1808*, 2 vols., 2nd ed. (London, 1814), 2:238; John Finch, *Travels in the United States of America and Canada* (London, 1833), 242.

[101] Alexander Taggart McGill to Mary Taggart, Dec. 28, 1852, in Margaret DesChamps Moore, ed., "A Northern Professor Winters in Columbia, 1852–1853," *South Carolina Historical Magazine*, 60 (1959), 185.

wore shirts that barely covered their private parts, while others helped in the dining room in the buff. Neither ladies nor gentlemen took notice. Tyrone Power, the celebrated Irish actor, touring coastal South Carolina in the early 1830s, remarked without disapprobation on the black youngsters "quite naked perhaps, rolling on the kitchen floor." Benjamin Henry Latrobe, fresh from England, gasped at the sight of naked boys and girls on every plantation and young women with uncovered breasts. Thereafter the abolitionists ever more stridently expressed horror at the thought of white girls and women in the company of naked and semi-naked black boys.[102]

W. H. Wills, riding from North Carolina to Alabama in 1837 and Charles Dickens in Virginia in 1842, recoiled from the sight of naked black children at play – a reaction shared by Jenny Porter, who had been a slave in Alabama. Had Willis, Dickens, and Porter proceeded to the sugar parishes of Louisiana, they would have seen the same, although the sight flourished most openly in the Sea Islands and the low country, where the children might be as old as twelve. John S. Wilson, among other physicians, did not think it a good idea, especially since some of the children ran around clad barely or not at all in winter as well as summer. Some masters may have skimped on clothes for their slaves, but black and poor white children, being children, preferred to be unencumbered. So did many of the adult black oarsmen, who, however, would likely be out on the water only with white men.[103]

---

[102] Jordan, *White over Black*, 161–162; Johann David Schoepf, *Travels in the Confederation, 1783–1784*, tr. Alfred J. Morrison (New York, 1968 [1788]), 2:47; Tyrone Power, *Impressions of America, during the Years 1833, 1834, and 1835*, 2 vols. (London, 1836), 2:63; Edward C. Carter, III et al., eds., *The Virginia Journals of Benjamin Henry Latrobe, 1795–1798*, 2 vols. (New Haven, CT, 1977), May 22, 1797 (1:225); Ronald G. Walters, *The Antislavery Appeal: American Abolitionism after 1830* (Baltimore, 1976), ch. 5.

[103] Clement Eaton, *The Freedom-of-Thought Struggle in the Old South* (New York, 1964), 39 Charles Dickens, *American Notes for General Circulation* (Harmondsworth, 1972 [1841]), 182; V. Alton Moody, *Slavery on Louisiana Sugar Plantations* (Baton Rouge, LA, 1941), 80; [Ingraham], *South-West*, 1:236; "Sketches of South Carolina" (1843), in Schwaab and Bull, eds., *Travels in the Old South*, 2:329–330; Guion Griffis Johnson, *A Social History of the Sea Islands, with Special Reference to St. Helena Island, South Carolina* (Westport, CT, 1969), 139; J. S. Wilson, "Peculiarities and Diseases of Negroes" (1860), as reprinted from *American Cotton Planter and Soil of the South* in James O. Breeden, ed., *Advice among Masters: The Ideal in Slave Management in the Old South* (Westport, CT, 1980), 287–288; I. Jenkins Mikell, *Rumbling of the Chariot Wheels: Doings and Misdoings in the Barefoot Period of a Boy's Life on a Southern Plantation*, (Columbia, SC, 1923), 250.

The ladies saw nothing. Were they pretending or did they have trouble seeing blacks, at any age and however naked, as men? Frances Trollope, aghast at the familiarity of southern mistresses with their house servants, wondered, "I once saw a young lady, who, when seated at table between a male and a female, was induced by her modesty to intrude on the chair of her female neighbor to avoid the indelicacy of touching the elbow of a man. I once saw this very young lady lacing her stays with the most perfect composure before a negro footman."[104]

---

[104] Trollope, *Domestic Manners*, 249–250. Only occasionally did a southern lady express disgust at seeing black children naked: See, e.g., Hutchinson Diary, July 29, 1815.

3

Horses and Hounds

I charge the young not to despise hunting or any other schooling. For these are the means by which men become good in war and in all things out of which must come excellence in thought and word and deed.

— *Xenophon*

The beardless youth, freed at last from his tutor, finds joy in horses and hounds.

— *Horace*[1]

UNDER SCRUTINY

In 1774, John Budd of New Jersey described northern settlers in South Carolina as so oppressed by heat that they spent their time riding, hunting, fishing, visiting neighbors, and drinking: "They live at their ease and wallow in luxury; till death, out of pity to their families and acquaintances, removes the nuisance." This northern stereotype did not recede significantly before the War. Caroline Seabury, a northern teacher in Mississippi, found plantation life "dead-level monotony," punctuated by an occasional murder or duel. Southerners visited the North because "[t]he stagnant waters of social life are seldom rippled by any excitement." The abolitionist C. G. Parsons wrote in the 1850s, "Young men and young women have nothing to do – and the theater, the billiard table, the drinking saloon, the horse race, the cock fight, are but so many ways derived

---

[1] "On Hunting," in Xenophon, *Scripta Minora*, trans. E. C. Marchant (LCL), 1:§18; Horace, *Ars Poetica*, tr. H. Rushton Faircloth (LCL), §160.

to banish ennui, and prevent life from being a burden." Southerners, although allowing a kernel of truth, saw their lives differently.[2]

CARRIAGES

Southern counterpoints began with a love of horses and penchant for carriages. The spirit of noblesse oblige required gentlemen to transport guests who had none. They provided for clergymen and teachers but also for poorer neighbors off to a wedding or other special occasion. From colonial days, possession of a two-wheeled riding chair, chaise, gig, or sulky marked elite status. John Lambert, an early nineteenth-century British traveler, found the carriages of wealthy Charlestonians inferior to those of wealthy Northeasterners. Decades later, Osgood Mussey replied angrily to the claim that Virginia had more carriages than comparable northern states did by asserting the greater comfort and elegance of northern carriages. It did seem to J. S. Buckingham that every well-to-do family in Savannah had its own carriage, and that Charleston boasted more carriages than any other city in the United States. William Howard Russell reported in 1861 that styles were changing in the North, but slowly if at all in the South. Carriages figured in the first challenge of an act of Congress before the Supreme Court. Congress levied a $16 tax on carriages, and Virginians, who relied on carriages much more than Northerners, charged discrimination. The Kentucky Bluegrass became famous for its elegant carriages, and Lexington claimed twice as many as any American town of comparable size. Lexington suffered a relative decline but retained a reputation for splendid carriages.[3]

[2] John Budd, "Short History of South Carolina," in Eugene L. Schwaab and Jacqueline Bull, eds., *Travels in the South: Selected from Periodicals of the Time*, 2 vols. (Lexington, KY, 1973), 1:23; Suzanne L. Bunkers, *The Diary of Caroline Seabury, 1854–1863* (Madison, WI, 1991), Jan. 10, 1857 (46); C. G. Parsons, *An Inside View of Slavery: A Tour among the Planters* (Savannah, GA, 1974 [1855]), 135.

[3] Taylor Diary, Aug. 25, 1794; Cornish Diary, Aug. 20, 1842, April 7, 1845; Beatty Diary, Jan. 3, 1843; Mahala Roach Diary, July 17, 1853, in Roach-Eggleston Papers; Alan D. Watson, "Luxury Vehicles and Elitism in Colonial North Carolina," *Southern Studies*, 19 (1980), 147–156; John Lambert, *Travels through Canada and the United States of North America in the Years 1806, 1807, and 1808*, 2 vols., 2nd ed. (London, 1814), 2:151; Osgood Mussey, *Review of Ellwood Fisher's Lecture on the North and the South* (Cincinnati, OH, 1849), 38–40; J. S. Buckingham *The Slave States of America* (New York, 1968 [1842]), 1:124, 559–560; Martin Crawford, ed., *William Howard Russell's Civil War: Private Diary and Letters, 1861–1862* (Athens, GA, 1992), 22 (Aug. 24, 1861); on the carriage tax, see Forrest McDonald, with the assistance of Ellen S. McDonald, *A Constitutional History of the United States* (Malbar, FL, 1986), 51; J. Winston Coleman,

Various carriages included the four-wheeled Barouche, with a half-cover that could be raised or lowered. A favorite in Mississippi, it accommodated four passengers. The four-wheeled Rockaway, open at the sides, had two or three seats. Other kinds of carriages abounded – or seemed to, since the New Yorkers, who controlled much of the trade, renamed every slight variation of standard models. Julia Gardiner Tyler of New York and Virginia compared the Barouche and the Rockaway: "I still think the Barouche carriage would be the best establishment for me – I like the conspicuousness of the coachman's seat, and you know a Rockaway is considered a family concern instead of an article of luxury, and I assure you I would be tempted to ride in the Barouche fifty times to where I would once in a Rockaway." The Reverend J. Lynn Bachman described the carriage of the Presbyterian Reverend Frederick A. Ross, son of a wealthy Virginia planter, as "Napoleonic." Bachman suggested that Ross had his daughter Rowena in mind when he furnished it: "The upholstery was of the handsomest gray silk, the furnished trappings were silver, even to the clasp that opened the door, the steps were portable." Yet, some carriages were ungainly, unpainted, and graceless.[4]

The carriages that Southerners bought from firms like Rogers of Philadelphia and Brewster of New York did not come cheap, and elegant carriages ran into big money. Thomas Jefferson shipped some home from Paris, one of which, bought during his presidency, cost $1,200. In later years Virginia Clay of Alabama bought a Landau for $1,600 in Philadelphia. Considered gorgeous, it took Huntsville by storm. James L. Bryan of North Carolina bought a carriage in New York for $163.62; Franklin Hudson of Louisiana for $500; Thomas Green Clemson of South Carolina for $350 in Philadelphia. The price of most carriages fell somewhere in between – with $600–700 common – and the cost of carriage horses added to the burden. (A comparison: A cotton gin cost $125.) Charles Manigault, who wanted the best, announced, "Damn the Expense." He spent $540 for two horses in 1841 – roughly his expenditure for five two-room cabins to house forty slaves.[5]

Jr., *Stage-Coach Days in the Bluegrass: Being an Account of Stage-Coach Travel and Taverns in Lexington and Central Kentucky, 1800–1890* (Lexington, KY, 1995), 41, 91–93.

[4] Julia Gardiner Tyler to Aleck Gardiner, Oct. 23, 1845, in Tyler Papers; Charles C. Ross, ed., *The Story of Rothwood, from the Autobiography of Rev. Frederick A. Ross, D. D.* (Knoxville, TN, 1923), 24. Also, Elizabeth Silverthorne, *Plantation Life in Texas* (College Station, TX, 1986), 180; Margaret Stevens Correspondence, 1841, in Browne Papers.

[5] Edwin Morris Betts, ed., *Thomas Jefferson's Farm Book* (Charlottesville, VA, 1987), 461; Virginia Clay-Clopton, *A Belle of the Fifties: Memoirs of Mrs. Clay of Alabama*

Most gentlemen rode horses, reserving carriages for the ladies. Hugh Blair Grigsby of Virginia, historian and editor, and the northern-born J. H. Ingraham of Natchez agreed that southern men considered the northern custom of riding in carriages "effeminate." Hugh Legaré of Charleston, who suffered a physical deformity, raised eyebrows by riding in a carriage like a woman rather than on horseback. Returning from church, young gentlemen rode alongside a lady's carriage, chatting with her; she directed the carriage driver's pace in accordance with her response to the gentleman. Yankee visitors to New Orleans were startled to see gentlemen alongside their ladies' carriages. In Virginia, Frederick Law Olmsted saw men everywhere on horseback, but mores were softening. Everything depended on local custom and particular circumstances, for in certain situations a carriage established a gentleman's status. In the Bluegrass, fancy carriages appealed to wealthy gentlemen who found stagecoaches uncomfortable and a bit too democratic. Around Nashville, the fashion capital of Tennessee in the 1850s, families traveled to church together in their own carriage.[6]

HORSES AND THEIR RIDERS

The most elegant and expensive carriages yielded to horses in southern esteem. Horses and mules had names, as befit members of the family household. Horses became the center of endless conversations among gentlemen, who identified closely with them. A common saying was: "A man is only as good as his horse." Some planters flamboyantly declared their horses more valuable than their slaves. The "manly education of boys," as Ingraham called it, absorbed the attention of southwestern planters, who taught sons of eleven or so to shoot and ride fearlessly. George Washington was said to have had his horses' hoofs polished

(New York, 1905), 116, n; Hudson Diary, Feb. 1, 185; James L. Bryan to Ebenezer Pettigrew, Nov. 13, 1843, in Sarah McCulloh Lemmon, ed., *The Pettigrew Papers*, 2 vols. (Raleigh, NC, 1971, 1988), 2:607–608; T. G. Clemson to J. C. Calhoun, Sept. 1845, in *JCCP*, 22, 109; Anson De Puy Van Buren, *Jottings of a Year's Sojourn in the South* (Battle Creek, MI, 1859), 32. For Manigault, see William Dusinberre, *Them Dark Days: Slavery in the American Rice Swamps* (New York, 1996), 46.

6 Hugh Blair Grigsby, *Discourse on the Life and Character of the Hon. Littleton Waller Tazewell* (Norfolk, VA, 1860), 16; [J. H. Ingraham], *The South-West. By a Yankee*, 2 vols. (n.p., 1966 [1835]), 2:35; J. H. Ingraham, *Sunny South; Or, The Southerner at Home* (New York, 1968 [1860], 71 ("effeminate"), 224; Michael O'Brien, *A Character of Hugh Legaré* (Knoxville, TN, 1985), 7; L. C. Capehart, *Reminiscences of Isaac and Sukey, Slaves of B. F. Moore, of Raleigh, N.C.* (EE: 2000 [1907]), 10; Charles Capen McLaughlin et al., eds., *The Papers of Frederick Law Olmsted*, 2 vols. (Baltimore, 1977, 1981), 2:90.

with a blackening brush, and the Reverend Frederick Ross spoke of him as "fully representative of the aristocracy of his day, derived from old England." Ross's father, who had more than five hundred slaves, rode a fine horse, equipped with an expensive bridle, saddle, and collar. James Wilson, the groom and "the handsomest man of the household," rode as fine a horse as his master did. Wilson kept the horses spotlessly clean and well groomed.[7]

To be a Virginian meant to be a superior horseman. Thus did Susan Dabney Smedes open her *Memorials of a Southern Planter*, which traced her father's move to Mississippi. Thomas De Leon of South Carolina declared the Virginian "a great horseman" who "rode to hounds as a matter of religion and was knight and courtier under gleam of my lady's eyes." At home in the ballroom, the Virginian was even more so in the saddle. A gentleman had to handle a horse and a gun; indeed, horsemanship and marksmanship were essential to the very definition of a man. Hence, Southerners held themselves as much superior to Northerners, who, presumably, no longer matched their skills. Ridiculing the inferior horsemanship of Northerners became a sport at West Point. As a cadet, poor Thomas J. (later "Stonewall") Jackson suffered among his fellow Southerners, for he cut an awkward figure on horseback, notwithstanding his having worked as a jockey in his youth. No one ever saw Jackson, the Confederacy's great military hero, fall from a horse, but to the day he died, he looked ill at ease. Francis Simkins Holmes, a lowcountry scientist, did not doubt a Confederate victory, in part because "our young men are the best horsemen on this continent." Confederate General Richard Taylor proved more acute: "Living on horseback, fearless and dashing, the men of the South afforded the best possible material for cavalry." One problem: "They had every quality but discipline."[8]

[7] Rhys Isaac, *The Transformation of Virginia, 1740–1790* (Chapel Hill, NC, 1982), 99; I. E. Lowery, *Life on the Old Plantation, in Ante-Bellum Days; Or, A Story Based on Facts* (Columbia, SC, 1911), 33–34; Ross, ed., *Story of Rothwood*, quotes at 8, 9. John Michael Vlach, *Back of the Big House: The Architecture of Plantation Slavery* (Chapel Hill, NC, 1993), 111–112, with an account of elaborate stables.

[8] Susan Dabney Smedes, *Memorials of a Southern Planter*, ed. Fletcher M. Green (New York, 1965 [1887]), 8; Thomas De Leon, *Belles, Beaux, and Brains of the 60s*, (New York, 1974 [1907]), 11; R. Gerald Alvey, *Kentucky Bluegrass Country* (Jackson, MS, 1992), xxii; Emory M. Thomas, *Bold Dragoon: The Life of J. E. B. Stuart* (New York, 1968), 26; James I. Robertson, Jr., *Stonewall Jackson: The Man, the Soldier, the Legend* (New York, 1997), 14, 41; Lester D. Stephens, *Science, Race, and Religion in the American South: John Bachman and the Charleston Naturalists, 1845–1895* (Chapel Hill, NC, 2000), 144; Richard Taylor, *Destruction and Reconstruction* (New York, 1992 [1889]), 62.

Those who needed help in choosing a good horse did well to consult a Methodist circuit rider. In common parlance, a desirable horse was "just as fine as a circuit-rider's horse." Traveling hundreds, even thousands of miles, circuit riders won an uncontested reputation for riding excellent horses. Their lives often depended on their horses, and Methodist Bishop William McKendree, among others, refused to ride other than a first-rate horse.[9]

In Natchez in the 1850s, Olmsted remarked: "I never saw such a large number of fine horses as there is here, in any other town of the size." The style had been set in colonial Virginia and the Carolinas. Jefferson, like other boys, learned to ride at a tender age. How else could he go anywhere in a society of spread-out settlements? Alicia Hopton Middleton of the South Carolina low country said that her father considered a pony indispensable to a boy's education "and almost equally so for girls." Nathaniel Russell Middleton began to ride at age three or four, and Raphael Jacob Moses, a leader of Charleston's Jewish community, when younger than he could recall. Daniel R. Hundley of Alabama claimed that southern boys rode well at age five, others more plausibly suggested seven or eight. "The boys are centaurs," said James Waddell Alexander of Virginia, "and I wonder at the coolness which Mrs. C., a very cautious mother, sees her son, 9 year old, galloping like the wind through woods, and over fences and ditches on a colt or a mule, or anything else that has legs."[10]

According to legend, planters, especially the Carolina Chivalry, rode much too well to suffer accidents. Riding frequently over rough terrain, men, women, and children learned to ride well, and serious accidents befell experienced riders only sporadically. Yet, every community had a disquieting story. Jefferson commiserated with Joseph Allston of South Carolina, who fell from his horse. A horse threw the wealthy young Vardrey McBee of Greenville, South Carolina, crippling him for life. Thomas L. Clingman of western North Carolina had a serious fall. Here

[9] Lollie Belle Wylie, ed., *Memoirs of Judge Richard H. Clark* (Atlanta, GA, 1898), 189; E. E. Hoss, *William McKendree: A Biographical Study* (Nashville, TN, 1916), 38.

[10] Frederick Law Olmsted, *A Journey in the Back Country* (New York, 1970 [1860]), 36–37; Dumas Malone, Jefferson and His Time, 6 vols. (Boston, MA, 1962–1981), 1:46; A. H. Middleton, "Family Record," and N. R. Middleton, "Reminiscences," in Alicia Hopton Middleton, et al., *Life in Carolina and New England During the Nineteenth Century* (Bristol, RI, 1929), 98, 185; Jacob Rader Marcus, ed., *Memoirs of American Jews*, 3 vols. (Philadelphia, 1955), 1:152; Daniel R. Hundley, *Social Relations in Our Southern States* (Baton Rouge, LA, 1979 [1860]), 31; Bayne Autobiographical Sketch (typescript), 4; Alexander quoted in William Cabell Bruce, *John Randolph of Roanoke, 1773–1833*, 2 vols. (New York, 1970 [1922]), 2:155.

and there, even Methodist circuit riders lost their lives. David McIntosh of Mississippi, a skilled horseman, demonstrated that the passion for riding did not mix well with the passion for imbibing. McIntosh died riding under the influence.[11]

Southern women rode horses enthusiastically and skillfully. In 1803, Rosalie Calvert reported from the Chesapeake to her parents in Belgium that it was once again "stylish for married ladies to ride horseback." W. H. Sparks effusively praised the women of the Southwest, giving the palm to those of Natchez, trained from girlhood "to sit fearlessly and control absolutely the most fiery steed." But Southerners considered riding astride unbecoming a lady. Philip Rice, slave of Russel Emmitt in South Carolina, recalled that Miss Ann Emmitt rode in a long side-saddle dress that hung to the ground: "Somebody allus had to help her on and off Beauty, but n'ary one of her brothers could outride Miss Ann." Varina Howells Davis rode a good deal every day but, like most women, always side-saddle. In Nashville schoolgirls as well as ladies rode side-saddle, dressed in costume à cheval. So did the strong-willed women of Texas, famous for doing things their own way.[12]

A tourist in South Carolina in 1825 dubbed the ladies and gentlemen he saw riding to church "expert equestrians." In the novels of William Gilmore Simms everyone, male and female, rides. Plantation mistresses and their daughters rode for pleasure and to church or town. Their everyday responsibilities included rides across their plantations, observing crops and visiting the slave quarters day or night. George Washington's mother, a bold and expert rider, had her own horse at thirteen. Ida

---

[11] Margaret Hayne Harrison, *A Charleston Album* (Ringe, NH, 1953), 58–59; Archie Vernon Huff, Jr., *Greenville: The History of the City and County in the South Carolina Piedmont* (Columbia, SC, 1995), 82; Anson West, *A History of Methodism in Alabama* (Spartanburg, SC, 1983 [1893]), 220; T. Terry Alford, *Prince among Slaves* (New York, 1977), 93 (McIntosh); Frederick A. Porcher, "Upper Beat of St. John's Berkeley: A Memoir," *Transactions of the Huguenot Society of South Carolina*, No. 13 (Charleston, SC, 1906), 41; Thomas E. Jeffrey, *Thomas Lanier Clingman: Fire Eater from the Carolina Mountains* (Athens, GA, 1998), 167. For ladies' carriage accidents, see Nancy Wooten Walker, *Out of a Clear Blue Sky: Tennessee's First Ladies and Their Husbands* (Cleveland, TN, 1971), 27.

[12] R. S. Calvert to M. and Mme. H. Stier, Aug. 12, 1803, in Margaret Law Callcott, ed., *The Mistress of Riversdale: The Plantation Letters of Rosalie Stier Calvert, 1795–1821* (Baltimore, 1991), 55; W. H. Sparks, *The Memories of Fifty Years* (Philadelphia, 1872), 329; Clement Eaton, *Jefferson Davis* (New York, 1977), 25; Mary Hübner Walker, *Charles W. Hübner: Poet Laureate of the South* (Atlanta, GA, 1976), 22; Eleanor Parke Custis to Elizabeth Bordley Gibson, Sept. 8, 1794, in Patricia Brady, ed., *George Washington's Beautiful Nelly: The Letters of Eleanor Parke Custis Lewis to Elizabeth Bordley Gibson, 1794–1851* (Columbia, SC, 1991), 18.

Ann Southworth doubtless won her reputation as the leading belle of Fayetteville, Tennessee, by her grace, charm, beauty, and intellect, but her first-rate horsemanship and marksmanship with a rifle added to her luster. Florence King of Georgia, having overcome a fear of horses, rode every evening with her sister.[13]

Philip Fithian wrote of Virginia in the 1770s, but his remarks applied to any part of the South in the 1850s: "Every evening, for the Benefit of exercise I ride out and commonly carry with me one of the small Girls, who partaking of the prevailing Spirit, are passionately fond of Riding." Girls rode difficult horses, in the words of Ellen Mordecai of Raleigh, "without fear" and mounted "the plough horses, when they were not working." Southern women took pride in their competence and raised their eyebrows when an occasional Julia Gardiner turned up from New York or a Fanny Kemble from England to match their ability and fervor. In the 1820s, Bernhard, Duke of Saxe-Weimar Eisenach, found well-dressed women on horseback in remote western Virginia. In the 1840s, the seventy-three-year-old mother of John Houston Bills of Tennessee rode "on horseback with ease and confidence." Louisa Susanna McCord of upcountry South Carolina rode a Canadian mustang no one else mastered. Elizabeth Allston Pringle's father reared his daughters to ride, and she described her sister as a "fearless horsewoman." Among the better-known southern women, Mary Howard Schoolcraft, Sara Agnes Rice Pryor, Elizabeth Allston Pringle, and Sarah Morgan boasted about women's riding skills.[14]

Fathers, however proud of their daughters, kept a worried eye on them. "I am glad you are to learn to ride," Jefferson wrote his daughter Mary, "but hope your horse is very gentle, and that you will never become venturesome. A lady should never ride a horse which she might not safely ride without a bridle." Sixty years later Dr. R. D. Arnold of

---

[13] Florence King to Lord King, Sept. 18, 1848, in T. B. King Papers; *AS:SC.*, III (Part 4), 18; also, Sheila R. Phipps, *Genteel Rebel: The Life of Mary Greenhow Lee* (Baton Rouge, LA, 1994), 62.

[14] Oct. 11, 1774, in Hunter Dickinson Farish, ed., *Journal and Letters of Philip Fithian: A Plantation Tutor of the Old Dominion, 1773–1774* (Charlottesville, VA, 1957), 203; Ellen Mordecai, *Gleanings from Long Ago* (Raleigh, NC, 1974), 10–11; Bernhard, Duke of Saxe-Weimar Eisenach, *Travels Through North America during the Years 1825 and 1826*, 2 vols. (Philadelphia, 1818), 1:193; Bills Diary, Oct. 4, 1846; *Plantation Life: The Narratives of Mrs. Henry Schoolcraft* (New York, 1969 [1860]), 19–20; Louisa M. Smythe, ed., *For Old Lang Syne: Collected for My Children* (Charleston, SC, 1900), 4; Elizabeth W. Allston Pringle, *Chronicles of Chicora Wood* (New York, 1976), 119.

Savannah expressed horror when his daughter attempted to ride her horse downhill: It was much too dangerous for a lady. Girls and young ladies had their own ideas, and the more spirited welcomed the challenges their fathers insisted they avoid. Notwithstanding anxieties, fathers encouraged their daughters. Calhoun wrote to Anna Maria, his wonderful daughter: "I hope you will ride often." She did – so skillfully that no horse ever threw her. And she married Thomas Clemson, who kept blooded horses on their plantation. Willie P. Mangum, concerned about his daughter's health, urged her to ride every day, and sternly told Orange, their servant, that he had better keep the horses in good shape if he knew what was good for him.[15]

Slaves rode despite limited access to horses. Here and there, they, rather than parents, taught white children to ride, and older slaves served as mentors to white boys who were learning to hunt. Favored slaves like Old Harry, Governor Henry A. Wise's coachman, or a revered plantation mammy accompanied the family on horseback rides. Jeff Hamilton, Sam Houston's man, shared his master's love of horses, "which always proved a strong tie between us." William Sinkler, planter and sportsman of South Carolina, had a superb horse trainer, whose reputation extended to Virginia. Slaves, like masters, identified riding prowess with manliness. A tutor who arrived on a plantation in Mississippi drew contempt from an old family retainer: "Lord, what sort of a man is this master is got to teach the children! He don't even know how to ride a horse!" Body servants often matched their young masters as daring riders and hunters. Masters boasted of their slaves' ability to ride but worried as well. Advertisements for runaway slaves mentioned some offenders as experienced horsemen.[16]

---

[15] Thomas to Mary Jefferson, May 8, 1791, in Edwin Morris Betts and James Adam Bear, Jr., eds., *The Family Letters of Thomas Jefferson* (Columbia, Mo., 1966), 82; R. D. to Ellen Arnold, 1851 (?), in Richard H. Shryock, ed., *Letters of Richard D. Arnold, M. D., 1808–1876* (Durham, NC, 1929), 59; Ernest McPherson Lander, Jr., *The Calhoun Family and Thomas Green Clemson: The Decline of Southern Patriarchy* (Columbia, SC, 1983), 211; J. C. to Anna Maria Calhoun, Jan. 25, 1838, in *JCCP*, 14:109; Alester G. Holmes and George R. Sherrill, *Thomas Green Clemson: His Life and Work* (Richmond, VA, 1937), 37; W. P. to Sally A. Mangum, July 4, 1842, in Henry Thomas Shanks, ed., *The Papers of Willie P. Mangum*, 5 vols. (Raleigh, NC, 1955–1956), 3:365.

[16] Nicolas W. Proctor, *Bathed in Blood: Hunting and Mastery in the Old South* (Charlottesville, VA, 2002), 42; John S. Wise, *The End of an Era* (Boston, MA, 1900), 71; James Harris Rogers, "The Model Farm of Missouri and Its Owner," *Missouri Historical Review*, 18 (1924), 153; Jeff Hamilton, *My Master: The Inside Story of Sam Houston and His Times, as Told to Lenoir Hunt* (Austin, TX, 1992), 25; Porcher, "Upper Beat of

Planters chafed and overseers screamed to no avail. Slaves slipped out at night and "borrowed" the plantation horses and mules to court or gamble. If a slave took a plow horse, he might escape with a passing rebuke, but if he played the gentleman and chose a family horse, he tempted his master's serious ire. The sight of blacks on horseback, riding well, impressed Harriet Martineau. After the War, Sidney Andrews observed the gentry's pain at seeing former slaves riding rather than walking. But after all, gentlemen had brought it on themselves by teaching favored slaves to ride and by taking pride in their horsemanship.[17]

The rage for blooded horses did not prevent wealthy Southwesterners from having carriages drawn by mules or even from riding mules in place of horses. Ingraham described the scene around Nashville, Tennessee, in the 1850s:

You might ride all over the state of Connecticut or Massachusetts without seeing the like. There they drive about in chaises, or buggies, or carry-alls. Where at the North would we meet elegant coaches with plaited harness, and all the appointments rich and complete, drawn by a pair of mules? Yet here, it is an everyday occurrence to see them, for mules here are highly esteemed. Where in the North would fashionable ladies ride mules? Yet here it is by no means uncommon.[18]

HUNTING AND FISHING

Historians continue to debate the significance of hunting as food gathering in ancient and modern times, as a badge of status and power, as an accessory to military action, and as human competition with animals. From ancient times, hunting emerged as a sport among aristocrats, who alone had the leisure. As such, it became intimately associated with aristocratic values in the training of youth for war and athletic competition – an

St. John's Berkeley," 55–57; Anne Simons Deas, *Recollections of the Ball Family of South Carolina and the Comingtee Plantation* (Charleston, SC, 1978 [1909]), 165.

[17] John Spencer Bassett, *The Southern Plantation Overseer, as Revealed in His Letters* (Northampton, MA, 1925), 12; *The Diary of Colonel Landon Carter of Sabine Hall*, 2 vols., ed., Jack P. Greene (Charlottesville, VA, 1965), July 8, 1771 (2:588, also 2:442); Byrd, Feb. 25, 1711, in Louis B. Wright and Marion Tinling, eds., *The Great American Gentleman: William Byrd of Westover, His Secret Diary for the Years 1709–1712* (New York, 1963), 131; Harriet Martineau, *Society in America*, 2 vols. (New York, 1837), 1:296–297; Sidney Andrews, *The South Since the War* (Boston, MA, 1866), 187.

[18] Ingraham, *Sunny South*, 224. Whether the Bible-reading Southerners saw a reference to Jesus' entrance into Jerusalem remains a matter for speculation. He eschewed a horse, the warrior's choice, for a donkey, which symbolized peace.

association continued by southern planters. The southern elite, too, became attracted to hunting as sport rather than as a source of food. Yet, hunting remained an important source of food even for the elite, which, however, attributed its utilitarianism to yeomen and poor whites. And the elite, as well as the middling and lower classes, needed animal fat for shortening, candles, and lye.[19]

Varro believed that the ancients ranked shepherds the most illustrious of classes. The Episcopalian Thomas Roderick Dew, who argued from secular assumptions, and the devoutly Calvinist Presbyterian Reverend Benjamin Morgan Palmer, among others, distrusted nomads. Although Dew celebrated David as a herdsman, he attributed theocracy to nomads, hinting at southern ambivalence toward the relation of herdsmen and farmers. Judge Strong of Tennessee associated hunting and herding with savages and agriculture with progress and civilization. A contributor to *Quarterly Review of the Methodist Episcopal Church, South* commented that the ancient Hebrews were nomads whom Egyptian slavery turned into productive agriculturalists. Frederick A. Porcher of South Carolina dismissed nomads as barbarians incapable of creating nations.[20]

Dissenting voices: "Moses," the Baptist Reverend Basil Manly pointedly remarked, "was a shepherd and a herdsman." R. Q. Mallard depicted Abraham as a nomad who never settled into a life of farming. The Cain who murdered his brother, the Esau who sold his birthright, the Saul who ruled unjustly, all were farmers, whereas God's favorites – Abel, Jacob, and David – were shepherds. John Fletcher of New Orleans, a principal proslavery theorist, stressed Cain as a tiller, translated as a "slave of the ground." Southerners honored great hunters. Sometimes they slipped into comic utterances or bitter irony. Recalling Nimrod as "a mighty hunter before the Lord," Hardin Taliaferro of

---

[19] José Ortega y Gasset, *Meditations on Hunting*, tr. Howard B. Wescott (New York, 1972), 31; Judith M. Barringer, *The Hunt in Ancient Greece* (Baltimore, 2001), 6–9, 42; Proctor, *Bathed in Blood*, 1, 4, 6, 37, 73; also, Emma Griffin, *Blood Sport: Hunting in Britain Since 1066* (New Haven, CT, 2007).

[20] Varro, "On Agriculture," in *Cato and Varro* (LCL), tr. William Davis Hooper, rev. Boyd Ash, Bk. 2:Intro. (p. 313). Thomas Roderick Dew, *Digest of the Laws, Customs, Manners, and Institutions of the Ancient and Modern Nations* (New York, 1884 [1852]), 14; [Benjamin Morgan Palmer], "Import of Hebrew History," *SPR*, 9 (1856), 589–591, 595–596; "The American Factory System," *QRMECS*, 2 (1848), 486; Judge Strong, "Agriculture and Civilization," *Tennessee Farmer*, 1 (1834), 11; F. A. P. [Frederick A. Porcher], "False Views of History," *SQR*, 6 (1852), 27. On David as shepherd and king, see Letter 14 in *Select Letters of St. Jerome*, trans. F. A. Wright (LCL), 4.

North Carolina and Alabama thought Uncle Davy, a notable hunter, a veritable second Nimrod. Catholic Bishop Patrick N. Lynch of Charleston made passing but implicitly positive remarks on Nimrod the hunter in the *Southern Quarterly Review*. According to one strain of proslavery thought, God cursed the black race, ostensibly identified with Noah's son Ham. Yet Nimrod "began to be a mighty one in the earth" (Genesis, 9:8–9; also, 1 Chronicles, 1:10). Genesis (10:8–11) credits Nimrod with the founding of an ancient monarchy as well as the creation of the Tower of Babel.[21]

As Southerners knew, hounds and hunting brought the Spartans ages-long fame. The ancient Greeks believed that the gods gave the art of hunting as a gift to the centaur Chiron and, through him, to favored human heroes. Lycurgus encouraged older men to hunt instead of prolonging military service. Hunting, wrote Xenophon, had become "the noblest occupation" and "makes sober and upright men ... good soldiers and good generals." Pliny recommended hunting and fishing; Cato praised hunting for preparing youth for a military life; and Cicero urged it as an enjoyable pursuit for the elderly. Edward Gibbon recounted later Roman emperors who referred to their great military expeditions as "hunting parties."[22]

The roots of personal violence in the South, write Robert E. Nisbett and Dov Cohen, lay in the culture of the settlers from the fringes of

[21] Basil Manly, "An Address on Agriculture," in *Proceedings of the Agricultural Convention of the State of Alabama* (Tuscaloosa, AL, 1842), 13; R. Q. Mallard, *Plantation Life before Emancipation* (EE: 1998 [1892]), 38; John Fletcher, *Studies on Slavery, in Easy Lessons* (Natchez, MS, 1852), 435. For Nimrod: [Hardin E. Taliaferro], *Fisher's River (North Carolina) Scenes and Characters by "Skitt," "Who Was Thar"* (New York, 1859), 62, and for hunting in northwestern North Carolina, see 62–78; [Patrick N. Lynch], "Nineveh and Its Remains," *SQR*, 16 (1849), 2. See also, Edwin J. Van Kley, "Europe's 'Discovery' of China and the Writing of World History," *AHR*, 76 (1971), 358–386; Benjamin Braude, "The Sons of Noah and the Construction of Ethnic and Geographical Identities in the Medieval and Early Modern Periods," *WMQ*, 3rd ser., 54 (1997), 114. For characterizations of Nimrod as the agent of Satan and as a black man whose rebellion against God culminated in the Tower of Babel, see Stephen R. Haynes, *Noah's Curse: The Biblical Justification of American Slavery* (New York, 2002), 10, 43, 107, 111, and, chs. 3, 6.

[22] Elizabeth Rawson, *The Spartan Tradition in European Thought* (Oxford, 1991), l2. In "Constitution of the Lacedaemonians," in Xenophon, *Scripta Minora*, see 4§7; "on Hunting," 12:§7–8; "On The Art of Horsemanship," pp. 295–363; Edward Gibbon, *The History of the Decline and Fall of the Roman Empire*, 3 vols., ed. David Womersley (London, 1994), 1:84. The author of "On Hunting" remains in question, but Marchant (vii) thinks that Xenophon wrote the main portion. For selections from aristocratic Greek and Roman sources on hunting and fishing, see K. D. White, ed., *Country Life in Classical Times* (Ithaca, NY, 1977), ch. 10. Polybius filed a rare dissent.

Britain, who, like herdsmen worldwide, have produced tough soldiers ready to maintain honor through violence. In 1839, Sir Charles August Murray remarked that American agriculturalists, northern and southern, took pride in their states but had "little local attachment." In the 1850s, Thomas R. R. Cobb of Georgia suggested that the South combined horizontal mobility with extraordinary attachment to neighborly relations of rooted place, but he scoffed at the notion that slaveholders could be a settled people: "The planter himself, having no local attachments, his children inherit none." Necessarily, the southern slaveholder "is almost nomadic." "E. A. B." of Georgia saw westward migration compelled by population pressure in the North but by soil exhaustion in the South. Whatever the cause, migration gravely weakened the rootedness that southern slave society valued and that marked the gentleman. Simms pleaded for the stability of homesteads, charging that grazing and hunting retarded civilization life. "Xy," writing in the *Virginia Literary Museum and Journal of Belles Lettres, Arts, Sciences, Etc.*, curiously identified the spirit of chivalry with roaming adventurers rather than the settlers and builders of stable communities. In his view, feudalism obliterated the chivalric public spirit by encouraging vassals to focus entirely on local affairs.[23]

Foreign and northern travelers, friendly and unfriendly, agreed on Southerners' extraordinary love of hunting. John Lambert of England commented early in the nineteenth century that hunting, fishing, shooting, and riding were the primary diversions of South Carolinians. But they were much more than diversions and sport. In 1846, J. W. Monette, in his *History of the Valley of the Mississippi*, stressed hunting as necessary for the survival of settlers who bequeathed their skills to subsequent generations. Yet, wild animals destroyed crops and humans long past frontier days. In the seventeenth century, settlers in Virginia contended with all sorts of predatory animals and destructive birds, some of which provided much of the colonists' food. Throughout the

---

[23] Robert E. Nisbett and Dov Cohen, *The Culture of Honor: The Psychology of Violence in the South* (Boulder, CO, 1996), xv, 5 (quote), 89; Charles August Murray, *Travels in North America during the Years, 1834, 1835 and 1836* (London, 1839), 1:148; T. R. R. Cobb, "An Historical Sketch of Slavery," in *An Inquiry into the Law of Negro Slavery in the United States* (New York, 1968 [1858]), ccxv; "E. A. B.," "Essay on American Society as Seen Through Southern Spectacles," *SQR*, 10 (1854), 380; William Gilmore Simms, *The Social Principle* (Tuscaloosa, AL, 1843); "Xy," "Blondel and Richard Lionheart," *Virginia Literary Museum and Journal of Belles Lettres, Arts, Sciences, Etc.*, 1 (1829)], 170–174.

eighteenth century and well into the nineteenth, bears, wild boars, wolves, and crows ravaged crops.[24]

Fox hunting in Virginia began in the eastern counties, eventually centered in the piedmont, and moved west as the planters did. Francis Taylor of Orange County rode on fox hunts three times during February–March 1786, and hunted snipes, hares, and partridges with local gentlemen. Dearth followed intense fox hunting. In North Carolina, William Garrett complained in 1805, "All the foxes near here are destroyed. The amusement of hunting I am therefore obliged to forebear until they become more plentiful." One commentator recalled that in the early days, "It was an affair of considerable preparation, some pomp, and great jollification.[25]

In 1808, John Palmer wrote to the historian David Ramsay that South Carolina's piney woods' people eked out a wretched living principally by hunting. Palmer's remarks applied to people in the backcountry across the South for decades. Small farmers, to feed their families, hunted and trapped squirrels, quail, and rabbits. They nonetheless distinguished between "critters," an honorable term bestowed upon cattle and other respected animals, and "varmints," a term of contempt applied to opossum, raccoons, squirrels, and the like. In Louisiana and Georgia, planters killed large numbers of alligators. In the early part of the nineteenth century, buffalo, long gone from the low country, still roamed the Mississippi Valley.[26]

In the 1850s, farmers in northern Alabama killed numerous ravaging bears, wolves, panthers, and wildcats, as lowcountry planters had in earlier years. Planters still had their hands full with subspecies of black

[24] John Lambert, *Travels through Canada and the United States of North America in the Years 1806, 1807, and 1808*, 2 vols., 2nd ed. (London, 1814), 2:154; John W. Monette, *History of the Discovery and Settlement of the Valley of the Mississippi*, 2 vols. in 1 (New York, 1971 [1846]), 2:11–12; Kenneth R. Wesson, "Travelers' Accounts of the Southern Character: Antebellum and Early Postbellum Period," *Southern Studies*, 17 (1978), 316.

[25] Taylor, Diary, 1786; William Garrett to Thomas Ruffin, Dec. 21, 1805, in *TRP*, 1:67; S. L. C., "A Hunting Article," *SLM*, 17 (1851), 45; Hawkeye, "Fox Hunt," in Clarence Gohdes, ed., *Hunting in the Old South: Original Narratives of the Hunters* (Baton Rouge, LA, 1967), 139–140.

[26] Philip Alexander Bruce, *Social Life in Virginia in the Seventeenth Century*, 2 vols. (New York, 1907), 1:167–217; John Palmer to David Ramsay, Dec. 3, 1808, in John Rogers Commons et al., eds., *A Documentary History of American Industrial Society* 10 vols. (Cleveland, OH, 1910), 2:166; Allan Kulikoff, *Tobacco and Slaves: The Development of Southern Cultures in the Chesapeake, 1680–1800* (Chapel Hill, NC, 1986), 219–220; G. Melvin Herndon, "Elliott L. Story: A Small Farmer's Struggle for Economic Survival in Antebellum Virginia," *Agricultural History*, 56 (1982), 521; Chesney Journal, 7–8.

bears. The killing of one became a badge of courage and skill. Still, bears killed in hunts got off lightly. Bear-baiting, an especially vicious blood sport, was common in towns like Winchester, Virginia, in the 1840s and persisted in South Carolina. A bear was declawed and blinded, and tied to a post to suffer attacks by dogs. Panthers and wolves roamed the Florida swamps into the twentieth century. In the mid-1830s, the Mississippi legislature offered a bounty for killing wolves, and Davy Crockett reported large-scale killings in West Tennessee. Another nuisance: Wildcats, flourishing in lowcountry swamps, killed rabbits, lambs, and the wild turkeys and partridges that young gentlemen hunted in considerable numbers. Wildcats posed a danger to the dogs sent to run them down and to the slaves who directed the chase. A tough, fully grown wildcat could fight off half-a-dozen dogs. Southerners reputedly considered partridge shooting as "the sport for all ages," although wild turkeys commanded a special fascination described by one gentleman as "the most respectable game bird I know." Hunters had a chance with the young ones but maximum difficulty with the fully grown.[27]

Hunting provided an important source of income in southwestern Georgia's wiregrass, which had few wealthy citizens. The Cajuns of southern Louisiana raised few domestic animals but lived well by hunting plentiful wild game. Nonslaveholders and small slaveholders, no less than planters, considered hunting a sport and recreation as well as a means for getting rid of pests and supplying meat for their families. They ate the squirrels and birds that preyed on crops, but even the crude

[27] Eron Rowland, ed., *Life, Letters and Papers of William Dunbar of Elgin, Mississippi: Pioneer Scientist of the Southern United States* (Jackson, MS, 1930), 243–244, 264, 301; Olmsted, *Back Country*, 225; William Elliott, *Carolina Sports by Land and Water* (New York, 1977 [1846]), 83–96, 150–153; J. G. Guinard to John M. Richardson, Sept. 28, 1852, in Arney R. Childs, ed., *Planters and Businessmen: The Guignard Family of South Carolina, 1795–1930* (Columbia, SC, 1957), 74; Edwin Adams Davis, ed., *Plantation Life in the Florida Parishes of Louisiana, 1836–1846, as Reflected in the Diary of Bennet H. Barrow* (New York, 1943), May 8, 1841 (230); for alligators, see July 4, 1843 (295);. Taylor Diary, 1794; Cecile Hulse Matschat, *Suwannee River: Strange Green Land* (New York, 1938), 31; Bradley G. Bond, *Political Culture in the Nineteenth-Century South: Mississippi, 1830–1900* (Baton Rouge, LA, 1995), 20; James A. Shackford and Stanley J. Folmsbee, eds., *A Narrative of the Life of David Crockett of the State of Tennessee* (Knoxville, TN, 1976 [1834]), 62–63; T. Hunter, "The Turkey Hunter in His Closet," *SLM*, 17 (1851), 659; Captain Flack, "Turkey Hunts in Texas," in Gohdes, ed., *Hunting in the Old South*, 11–36. On partridge hunting, see the diaries of J. A. F. Coleman, Dec. 17–18, 1849, and Henry Craft, Oct. 29, 1848, in Stephen Berry, ed., *Princes of Cotton: Four Diaries of Young Men in the South, 1848–1860* (Athens, GA, 2007), 362, 474. On bear hunting and bear baiting, see *TCWVQ*, 3:915; Phipps, *Genteel Rebel*, 73.

drew the line at the plentiful rats. In 1828, the *Southern Agriculturalist* reported that rats were overrunning the low country and the Sea Islands, especially damaging corn crops. The finest of country houses had to battle infestation of rats as well as mice. Slaves killed hundreds and thousands and used dead rats for fertilizer. On the Savannah River in the early 1840s, specially trained "rice curs" killed thousands every year. Rachel O'Connor of Louisiana depended on her "little rat dog ... the rats are so bad." Rat-killing became a steady pursuit in town and country. Planters paid old slaves a pound of tobacco for every 100 rats they killed. One killed 30 to 40 daily for a total of 2,700 during one winter, but his brother took the palm with 4,000. On many rice-coast plantations, masters and especially mistresses spread poison to kill rats and mice.[28]

"Rice birds" (reed birds in Philadelphia, bobolinks in New England) and other destructive birds arrived in the low country during the spring and remained until autumn. Thomas Rutledge, James Sparkman, and R. F. W. Allston lost the better part of their crops, and some planters were

---

[28] George Gillman Smith, *The Story of Georgia and the Georgia People*, 2 vols. in 1 (Macon, GA, 1900), 476–477; Mary L. Edgeworth, *The Southern Gardener and Receipt Book*, 3rd ed., Philadelphia, 1859), 428–429; Carl A. Brasseaux, *Acadian to Cajun: Transformation of a People, 1803–1877* (Jackson, MS, 1992), 22; *SA*, 1 (1828), 189–190; Mart A. Stewart, "*What Nature Suffers to Groe": Life, Labor, and Landscape on the Georgia Coast, 1680–1920* (Athens, GA, 1996), 161; Lyle Saxon, et al, *Gumbo Ya-Ya: A Collection of Louisiana Folk Tales* (New York, 1945), 183–184; Charles W. Turner, ed., *Old Field School Teacher's Diary (Life and Times of Jeremiah C. Harris)* (Verona, VA, 1975), 35 (Jan. 15, 1853); A. R. Bagshaw to Charles Manigault, Aug. 14, 1844, in James M. Clifton, ed., *Life and Labor on Argyle Island: Letters and Documents of a Savannah River Rice Plantation, 1833–1867* (Savannah, GA, 1978), 15, also 9; Albert Virgil House, ed., *Planter Management and Capitalism in Georgia: The Journal of Hugh Fraser Grant, Ricegrower* (New York, 1954), 35 and the plantation accounts for 1841–1843; George Skipwith to J. H. Cocke, June 17, 1847, Lucy Skipwith to Cocke, Oct. 2, 1859, in Randall M. Miller, ed., *"Dear Master": Letters of a Slave Family* (Ithaca, NY, 1978), 155, 225; "Life, Letters, and Papers of William Dunbar," in Alan Gallay, ed., *Voices of the South: Eyewitness Accounts, 1528–1861* (Athens, GA, 1994), 164; Maggie Davis to Jefferson Davis, Jr., in Hudson Strode, ed., *Jefferson Davis: Private Letters, 1823–1889* (New York, 1966), 141; Rachel O'Connor to David Swayze, Nov. 28, 1829, in A. B. W. Webb, ed., *Mistress of Evergreen Plantation: Rachel O'Connor's Legacy of Letters, 1823–1845* (Albany, NY, 1983), 40. For rat infestation of plantation homes, see Anna Matilda King, *Anna: The Letters of a St. Simons Plantation Mistress*, ed. Melanie Pavich-Lindsay (Athens, GA, 2002), 352. For rat poisoning, see Weymouth T. Jordan, ed., *Herbs, Hoecakes and Husbandry: The Daybook of a Planter of the Old South* (Tallahassee, FL, 1960), 31–32; Tryphena Fox to Anna Rose Holder, September 8, 1850, in Wilma King, ed., *A Northern Woman in the Plantation South: Letters of Tryphena Blanche Holder Fox, 1856–1876* (Columbia, SC, 1993), 39; and Robinson Diary, Mar. 2, 13, 1855, in Joan E. Cashin, ed., *Our Common Affairs: Texts from Women of the Old South* (Baltimore, 1996), 147.

ruined. Rice planters armed slaves, who shot staggering numbers of birds, some edible. In North Carolina, masters distributed guns to trusted slaves to fight off the eagles that preyed on their pigs. Plump rice birds offered some compensation. Coastal Southerners ranked rice birds as a delicacy and cooked them with their heads on. The baking and eating followed strict rules. For one, they were eaten by hand, without utensils, in accordance with a ritual that required the plunging of teeth into the bird's brain, which was especially valued. David Holt wrote from Wilkinson County, Mississippi, that "passenger pigeons in immense flocks" settled "in the trees at their regular roosting places, and in such numbers as to often break large limbs by their weight."[29]

Since squirrels ravished crops, hunting became a necessity. In 1793, Kentucky required each white male to kill a certain number each year. Squirrels and wild turkeys offered farmers and planters popular foods. Davy Crockett recalled frontier days in early nineteenth-century Tennessee, when two parties vied on two-day hunts for the greater kill of squirrels. Squirrels, easily caught, became a regular part of the diet of farmers and small slaveholders. Opossum and raccoon became fair game, hunted primarily by slaves but also by young well-to-do whites. In fact, a recipe for roast possum appeared in Martha McCulloch-Williams's popular *Dishes and Beverages of the Old South*. In East Tennessee, as elsewhere, slaves loved to hunt, and masters allowed them to keep hunting dogs to procure food. Peyton, a slave on M. W. Philips's plantation in Mississippi, killed fifty-two raccoons in one outing. On the Curry plantation in northeast Georgia, slaves separated into two teams to hunt troublesome rabbits. Lowcountry masters provided older black men with guns to kill rice birds, opossum, and raccoons. Black women cooked animals for their own families, frying the fat birds in their grease and sending some of the cooked possum and raccoon to the Big House, where the children relished them. In the 1830s, a northern traveler reported on the enthusiasm and success of plantation slaves in hunting raccoon and opossum. City-bred foreigners had embarrassing moments. Thomas

---

[29] Richard Barry, *Mr. Rutledge of South Carolina* (New York, 1942), 53; Anna Wells Rutledge, ed., [Sarah Rutledge], *The Carolina Housewife* (Columbia, SC, 1979 [1847]), viii–ix; James L. Michie, *Richmond Hill Plantation, 1810–1868* (Spartanburg, SC, 1990), 135; Snyder Papers, *passim*; Mordecai, *Gleanings*, 35; Harriet Ross Colquitt, *The Savannah Cookbook: A Collection of Old Fashioned Receipts from Colonial Kitchens* (Atlanta, GA, 1960), 66–67; Thomas D. Cockrell and Michael B. Ballard, eds., *A Mississippi Rebel in the Army of Northern Virginia: The Civil War Memoirs of Private David Holt* (Baton Rouge, LA, 1995), 3.

Ansell, a prominent English-born lawyer in Missouri, became an object of sustained ridicule when he shot a buzzard, thinking it a wild turkey, and instructed his landlady to prepare it for dinner.[30]

The Massenburg Farm Journal in Franklin County, North Carolina, reveals the extent and variety of hunting:

> March 5, 1835: I kill 11 partridges at one shot & kill 21 in all during the day & 1 dove–Overseer & myself kill & catch 15 rabbits & I was at the killing of 12 of them, he having caught 3 before I got with him.
>
> Sept. 22, 1841: I go with W P Wms. to Warren to a deer hunt.
>
> Sept. 24, 1841: Mr. E A killed a fine Buck–Dr Brodie & T. Alston had a shot & I snapped up a fine buck.
>
> Dec. 10, 1841: I go with T N. F. A[lston], Dr. Brodie at my plantation to have a turkey hunt–and stay all night with him.
>
> Dec. 11, 1841: I hunt Turkeys with T N. F. A & Dr Brodie on Mr. Spruills and & go to Sister M K Wm at night.
>
> Jan. 29, 1842: [Another turkey hunt with Alston and Brother.

Between these adventures the gentlemen went fishing together.[31]

From Washington County, Mississippi, Frank F. Steel explained to his sister in Ohio that he spent an hour or two hunting every morning and always came back "with a brace of ducks, a goose or an equivalent in smaller game. Indeed, I am already growing tired of this sport and meditating a bear hunt in the cane-brake a few miles from here." "Come down"

---

[30] Alvey, *Kentucky Bluegrass*, 201; Shackford and Folmsbee, eds., Life of David Crockett, 139–140; Sarah McCulloh Lemmon, *Parson Pettigrew of the 'Old Church': 1744–1807* (Chapel Hill, NC, 1970), 94; Baker Diary, March 15, Oct. 23, 1849; Morrison Journal, Aug. 8, 1845, Jan. 28, 1846; Martha McCulloch-Williams, *Dishes and Beverages of the Old South* (Knoxville, TN, 1988 [1913], 175–176; J. C. Webster, *Last of the Pioneers; Or, Old Times in East Tenn.: Being the Life and Reminiscences of Pharaoh Jackson Chesney (Aged 120 Years)* (EE: 2003 [1902]), 99; Coleman Diary, Sept. 23, Oct. 15, 1849, in Berry, ed., *Princes of Cotton*, 390, 391; Aug. 14, 1850, in Franklin L. Riley, ed., "Diary of a Mississippi Planter," in *Publications of the Mississippi Historical Society*, 10 (1909), 434; D. Maitland Armstrong, *Day before Yesterday: Reminiscences of a Varied Life* (New York, 1920), 76–77; Jesse Pearl Rice, *J. M. L. Curry: Southerner, Statesman and Educator* (New York, 1948), 6; Edward J. Thomas, *Memoirs of a Southerner, 1840–1920* (Savannah, GA, 1923), 11–13, 22; "G. M.," "South-Carolina," *New-England Magazine*, 1 (1831), 338–339; for the buzzard story see W. V. N. Bay, *Reminiscences of the Bench and Bar of Missouri* (St. Louis, MO, 1878), 180. See also, Forman Diary, Nov. 21, 1814, in W. Emerson Wilson, ed., *Plantation Life at Rose Hill: The Diaries of Martha Ogle Forman, 1814–1845* (Wilmington, DE, 1976), 5; Rosalie Roos, *Travels in America, 1851–1855*, tr. Carl L. Anderson (Carbondale, IL, 1982), 96–97.

[31] Massenburg Farm Journal.

y'all, Simms wrote to James Lawson of New York: "You shall have a frequent deer hunt, and we will give you plenty of Turkey, Woodcock, snipe,
partridge & dove shooting – and fishing to your heart's content." Simms
did not mention that the prey would fill his table.[32]

Clergymen shared the passion for hunting. Episcopal Bishop J. H. Otey
of Tennessee shot opossum and pigeons as well as deer. Hunting trips
brought together clergymen, college professors, and rustics in a spirit
of camaraderie. The Presbyterian Reverend Benjamin Morgan Palmer
joined with Baptists and Methodists in advocating "healthy recreations."
Although northern clergymen preached the virtues of a strenuous outdoor
life, passion and opportunity receded. The Methodist Reverend W. H.
Milburn, a Northerner who rode circuit in all sections, complained that
wealthy Northerners "rarely hunt and are seldom good riders. Rural life
has few charms for our educated women." In Virginia, the Presbyterian
Reverend Robert L. Dabney of Union Theological Seminary used hunting
as a metaphor for preaching. He referred to Christmas hunts on which
boys took untrained hound-whelps, only to see them scatter in every
direction, catching no hares.[33]

The nineteen-year-old Robert Philip Howell, miserably ill, spent the
autumn of 1859 fox hunting with a relative and a friend, "which perfectly
restored my health, as well as afforded me infinite pleasure." Edward
L. Wells, a New Yorker with southern roots and sympathies, remarked

---

[32] Frank Steel to Anna Steel, Dec. 15, 1859; Simms to Lawson, Sept. 20, 1850, and Simms
to E. A. Duyckinck, Nov. 12, 1850, in Oliphant et al., eds., *Letters of Simms*, 3:66,
74. Charles P. Rowland suggested that as late as the 1920s, the South probably had
more hunters and fishermen than any population of comparable size in the world: "The
South of the Agrarians," in William C. Harvard and Walter Sullivan, eds., *A Band of
Prophets: The Vanderbilt Agrarians after Fifty Years* (Baton Rouge, LA, 1982), 25.
José Ortega y Gasset speculates that a sporting hunter has an uneasy conscience when
faced with the death of the enchanting animal he is about to kill. In contrast, a utili-
tarian hunter seeks and values the death of his prey. I find no such distinction among
Southerners: Ortega y Gasset, *Meditations on Hunting*, tr. Howard B. Wescott, 102,
110; cf., John Mayfield, *Counterfeit Gentlemen: Manhood and Humor in the Old South*
(Gainesville, FL, 2009), xv.

[33] Otey Diary, Nov. 29, 1854; Thomas Cary Johnson, *The Life and Letters of Benjamin
Morgan Palmer* (Richmond, VA, 1906), 33; William Hatcher, *Life of J. B. Jeter, D. D.*
(Baltimore, 1887), 25; Peter Walker, *Moral Choices: Memory, Desire, and Imagination in
Nineteenth-Century American Abolition* (Baton Rouge, LA, 1978), 42; John C. Spurlock,
Free Love: Marriage and Middle-Class Radicalism in America, 1825–1860 (New York,
1988), 130; William Henry Milburn, *Ten Years of Preacher Life: Chapters from an
Autobiography* (New York, 1859), 324; Robert L. Dabney, *Sacred Rhetoric: A Course of
Lectures on Preaching* (Richmond, VA, 1870). For interclass camaraderie, see also Wilma
Dykeman, *The French Broad* (New York, 1955), 65–66.

that in southern Georgia the great sport fox hunting followed the English fashion. In *De Bow's Review*, J. T. Wiswall of Alabama exulted that fox hunting revealed the aristocratic warmth of a southern people who spurned Yankee coldness. As an example, Wiswall cited George Noble Jones, a big planter in Florida who lived in Savannah and owned a fine fowling piece, pedigree dogs, and a well-stocked wine cellar. "Fox hunting," DeLeon wrote, "came first in the love of all," and every plantation had its pedigree hounds and horses for the chase. Young men, Hundley suggested, predominated by the 1850s, and despite British precedent, few women participated. Buckingham acknowledged, "Fox hunting is as well understood, as skillfully practised, and as completely enjoyed here, in the mountains of South Carolina, as in England." Missourians considered Virginians born fox hunters, attributing their passion and proficiency to their English origins. Neither Missourians nor Virginians would have appreciated Oscar Wilde's famous description of the English gentlemen's fox hunt: "the unspeakable in pursuit of the uneatable."[34]

Gentlemen invited less-affluent neighbors, yeomen, and even some "respectable poor" to participate and bring their own hounds to fox and deer hunts. The Baptist Reverend Hardin E. Taliaferro reported that the country folks of northwestern North Carolina loved fox hunting, although few had the requisite hounds. The reputation for hospitality among poor farmers in upcountry Georgia rested in part on the ease with which they fed travelers off plentiful deer and bear hunting, a popular sport in the hills. The skins of foxes and other animals were used in clothing. The less affluent organized their own hunts or hunted deer singly whenever they got a yen for venison.[35]

[34] Howell Memoirs (ms.), 3; Edward L. Wells to Mrs. Thomas L. Wells, Mar. 4, 1861, in Daniel E. Huger Smith et al., eds., *Mason-Smith Family Letters, 1860–1868* (Columbia, SC, 1950), 8; Wiswall, "Causes of Aristocracy," *DBR*, 28 (1860), 564–565; Ulrich Bonnell Phillips and James David Glunt, eds., *Florida Plantation Records from the Papers of George Noble Jones* (St. Louis, MO, 1927), 21–22; Dixon Diary, June 20, 1860, in Berry, ed., Princes of Cotton, 127; Buckingham, *Slave States*, 2:177; Agnew "Journal" (with the Diaries), 1856; De Leon, *Belles, Beaux, Brains*, 24; Hundley, *Social Relations*, 31–39. Also, Bills Diary, Sept. 16, 1843, Dec. 24, 1844; Bay, *Reminiscences of the Bench and Bar of Missouri*, 245–246. For casual accounts of fox hunts see Donald Jackson and Dorothy Twohig, eds, *The Diaries of George Washington* (Charlottesville, VA, 1978), Dec, 22, 1785 (4:254–255), Jan. 28, 1786 (4:267–268).

[35] [Taliaferro], Fisher's River (North Carolina) Scenes and Characters, 149; George White, Statistics of the State of Georgia (Savannah, GA, 1849), 264; Armstrong, *Day before Yesterday*, 78–79; F. L. Steel Diaries, July 28, 1838; Olmsted, *Back Country*, 219. Here and there, notably in the Southwest, women did participate in fox hunts: Ingraham, *Sunny South*, 56, 63–65, 97; Charles Lannum in Edward J. Cashin, ed., *A Wilderness Still the Cradle of Nature* (Savannah, GA, 1994), 182–183; Forman Diary, Mar. 13,

Deer hunting required strength and stamina. "S. L. C." of Virginia called it "an amusement for Youth," suggesting hunts in groups of about six, camped in the mountains for a week or so. Southerners sometimes hunted by "driving" the deer. Hunters rode horses when pursuing deer for sport; they built scaffolds or went on foot when pursuing deer for food. Hundley described another method:

Scholars, and men of quiet contemplative natures, frequently prefer to "still hunt," which is likewise much in favor with all "pot hunters"; these latter adopting such a mode of killing their venison from necessity, and their inability to afford the horses and dogs necessary to a successful drive, while the former, being usually of a taciturn bent of mind, find opportunities in still-hunting to gratify their penchant for meditation and solitude.[36]

Driving was the preferred method in the large expanses of the South in which deer still abounded. William Porcher Miles of South Carolina, bored with legal studies, wrote to Mary McCord, "My chief enjoyment is hunting – I've been about a dozen times, and although I have not yet seen a deer, I enjoy it just as much as if I had killed fifty. Oh, what a glorious thing a camp hunt is!" Dr. Henry Peck noted that hunters in Louisiana, expecting deer to appear at night, considered deer hunting necessary to reduce the destruction of crops. Peck estimated the average weight after butchering at between 100 and 170 pounds. The practice in the low-country and on the southwestern prairies of lighting torches to attract curious deer entranced Matilda Charlotte Houstoun of England: "The sportsman generally fires as soon as he can see the creature's eyes." In the upper South, where deer were disappearing, gentlemen traveled to the mountains to find them, going off on "camp hunts" for two to six weeks at a time. Deer became so scarce in Delaware that the legislature forbade killing them in 1841. But a hunting party in Mississippi in 1850 claimed 100 deer in one night. The southern states had an estimated six to ten million deer in 1860; by 1900, they had a million.[37]

1823, Mar. 26, 1839, in Wilson, ed., *Plantation Life at Rose Hill*, 156, 407. For nonslave-holders, see Lynette Boney Wrenn, ed., *A Bachelor's Life in Antebellum Mississippi: The Diary of Dr. Elijah Millington Walker, 1849–1852* (Knoxville, TN, 2004), July 19, 23, Nov. 21, Dec. 9, 1850, and July 20, 28, 1851 (67, 68, 103, 110, 122).

36 S. L. C., "A Hunting Article," *SLM*, 17 (1851), 47; H., "Deer Hunting," in Gohdes, ed., *Hunting in the Old South*, 148, ed. n.; Hundley, *Social Relations*, 37–39.

37 W. P. Miles to Mary E. McCord, Aug. 16, 1842, in Cheves Collection; Henry J. Peck, "Deer and Deer Hunting in Louisiana," *DBR*, 5 (1848), 222; William Elliott, *Carolina Sports by Land and Water* (New York, 1977 [1846]); Mrs. [Matilda Charlotte] Houstoun, *Hesperos: Or, Travels in the West*, 2 vols. (London, 1850), 2:142n.; William

The big planters had extensive hunting preserves, notably deer parks. Even small planters had enough land to serve the purpose. A few in lower Beaufort District, South Carolina, owned a hunting preserve known as "Hunting Island," a coastal strip six miles long and three-quarters of a mile wide that could only be reached by boat through eight miles of dangerous water. Planters freely acknowledged the skill of the slave boatmen, who taught the white children. George Mason in eighteenth-century Virginia and Wade Hampton II in nineteenth-century South Carolina and Mississippi set the standards. Hampton, not content with extensive deer hunting in the two states in which he had big plantations and wanting to get away from the summer heat, took vacations in the mountains of North Carolina. Associations like the St. John's Hunting Club offered the gentry elaborate hunting parties, and even small groups of middling planters took along champagne, fruit, and assorted delicacies to guarantee a festive atmosphere.[38]

The Diary of Bennett H. Barrow in Louisiana provides an idea of the casual hunting of deer and foxes as a regular feature of plantation life:

> June 5, 1836: Went deering and Killed the largest Deer I ever saw – "poor" and weighed 173 pounds cleaved.
> Oct. 1, 1836: Fox chase – caught it.
> Oct. 10, 1836: Deer hunting with brother-in-law.
> Oct. 11, 1836: Caught fox–3 1/4-hr. run.
> April 2, 1837: Deering – killed two does.
> March 17, 1838: Saw the largest flock of Wild Turkeys in my Field – could have killed 5 or 8 with shot gun at one Fire – Killed one with Rifle.

H. Williams, *Slavery and Freedom in Delaware, 1639–1865* (Wilmington, DE, 1996), 31; Bond, *Political Culture*, 19.

[38] I. Jenkins Mikell, *Rumbling of the Chariot Wheels* (Charleston, SC, 1923), 247–273 (Beaufort planters); Richard Beale Davis, *Intellectual Life in the Colonial South, 1515–1763*, 3 vols. (Knoxville, TN, 1978), 3:1215; Edmund S. Morgan, *Virginians at Home: Family Life in the Eighteenth Century* (Williamsburg, VA, 1952), 19; Wade Hampton to Mary Fisher Hampton, April 22 1855, May 22, Nov. 7, Nov. 8, 1857, in Charles E. Cauthen, ed., *Family Letters of the Three Wade Hamptons, 1782–1901* (Columbia, SC, 1953), 39, 48, 52, 53; also on Hampton, see Stephen Meats and Edwin T. Arnold, eds., *The Writings of Benjamin F. Perry*, 3 vols. (Spartanburg, SC, 1980), 2:336; John B. Irving, *A Day on Cooper River*, 2nd ed. enl. and ed. by Louisa Cheves Stoney (Columbia, SC, 1842 (1932), xii. For Wade Hampton I's income from horse-raising, see Ronald Edward Bridwell, "The South's Wealthiest Planter: Wade Hampton I of South Carolina, 1754–1835" (Ph.D. diss.: University of South Carolina, 1980), 426–428. For deer parks, see McLaughlin et al., eds., *Olmsted Papers*, 2:96.

April 22, 1838: Went hunting. Killed one deer.

Sept. 23, 1838: killed a wild Cow ... Fat as could be.

Sept. 25, 1838: Killed two fawns – and one young buck ... very fat.

Sept. 27, 1838: Went hunting in the swamp ... killed 3 deer.

Sept. 28, 1838: [went hunting while hands picked cotton]

May 2, 1840: Killed fine doe.

May 7, 1840: Went hunting in the swamp yesterday ... killed one deer.
Went driving again today – killed 5 deer ... thick as rabbits.[39]

Planters boasted of having excellent hounds, and some, such as Senator William C. Dawson of Georgia, spared no expense to procure them. Clemson had as many as thirty at a time. In *Harper's New Monthly Magazine* in 1853, Thomas Bangs Thorpe had fun with class lines among dogs in the sugar region of Louisiana, separating them by the race of their owners. Youthful planters, he wrote, spent a lot of money on their hunting dogs but did not trouble to keep them tidy. Planters, accustomed to being obeyed, had no more patience with high-spirited dogs than with high-spirited slaves. Commonly, slaves trained the hunting dogs.[40]

Small slaveholders, needing food for their table, took slaves on hunts. Planters organized larger and well-organized hunts, often with slaves along as well. Some planters assigned slaves to do most of the hunting needed to provide meat. In South Carolina, planters customarily assigned an armed slave to duck hunting. Edward J. Thomas of Georgia warned that plantation runaways posed a special danger because many had experience with guns. The ever optimistic among proslavery commentators saw the bright side. In 1847, the *Southern Quarterly Review* published a review of William Elliott's *Carolina Sports by Land and Water*, which pronounced hunters and fishermen men of a naturally "contemplative spirit." Elliott considered hunting and fishing prime illustrations of master–slave relations. The master succored the slave, and the slave considered his master head and protector of the family. "Their interests are the same. They both look to the harvest for their common support."[41]

[39] Barrow Diary in Davis, ed., *Florida Parishes*, 73, 80, 81, 88, 109, 112, 131, 132, 193, 194.

[40] Stephen F. Miller, *The Bench and Bar of Georgia: Memoirs and Sketches*, 2 vols. (Philadelphia, 1858), 1:299; Alester G. Holmes and George R. Sherrill, *Thomas Green Clemson: His Life and Work* (Richmond, VA, 1937), 37; Thorpe, "Sugar Region of Louisiana," in Schwaab and Bull, eds., *Travels in the Old South*, 2:499–500; Lowery, *Life on the Old Plantation*, 53; Theodora Britton Marshall and Gladys Crail Evans, *They Found It in Natchez* (New Orleans, LA, 1939), 77.

[41] Duncan Clinch Heyward, *Seed from Madagascar* (Chapel Hill, 1937), 124, 127; Mallory to Floyd King, July 11, 1858, in T. B. King Papers; *AS:NC*, 2 (Pt. 2), 428; *AS:Tex.*, I4 (Pt. 1), 67; Norman R. Yetman, ed., *Life under the "Peculiar Institution"* (New York, 1970),

On plantation hunts slaves prepared and served meals, tracked animals, and managed the dogs. Body servants participated in the hunting, boasting of and winning plaudits for prowess. Interracial camaraderie at these outdoor stag parties remains difficult to assess. Slaves ate and drank well and had a good time – within prevailing norms of racial etiquette. R. Q. Mallard, as a plantation youth, joined blacks and whites in hunting and in sports "with the due subordination preserved." Occasionally, lines dissolved: Barrow threw a fit when some chaps in his party allowed their mulatto servant to eat with them. Among whites, class lines blurred. Jefferson recalled that Patrick Henry took special delight in camping out on overnight hunting trips with "overseers and such like people." Planters, small slaveholders, and nonslaveholders participated in interclass hunting and fishing parties.⁴²

Hunting in the South, in the words of Stuart Marks, became for hunters a "bastion of masculinity" and a sign of triumph over technology, wild beasts, and their own dogs. When a young man made his first kill, he signaled his rite of passage by daubing his face with the blood of the deer. William Elliott commended the hunt as a wonderful way to bring men together for healthy social intercourse. Men let their hair down and learned much about their neighbors and themselves. Elliott, echoing Xenophon, called hunting "A preparatory school for war." "The expert hunter will, I doubt not, show himself the superior in the field, to another, every other way his equal, not wanting this experience!" In peacetime, Elliott wrote, hunting put a man to a variety of tests of courage in relation to slaves, for no real man would ask a slave to take a risk he would not take himself. Southern men – by no means only slaveholders – thus reinforced their claims to being the world's last, great Chivalry. And they capped it off with a flourish of largesse. Having hunted for their own table, they sent neighbors large portions of their kill.⁴³

Fishing supplemented hunting as lowcountry sport. There and elsewhere, smaller planters and yeomen depended on local seafood to sustain

---

73, 144; Edward J. Thomas, *Memoirs of a Southerner* (EE: 1997 [1923], 14; "Carolina Sports," *SQR*, 12 (1847), 68, 84.

⁴² *TCWVQ*, 3:1052; for the slaves' hunting prowess see Maria Bryan to Julia Ann Bryan Cumming, Dec. 13, 1829, in Carol Bleser, ed., *Tokens of Affection: The Letters of a Planter's Daughter in the Old South* (Athens, GA, 1996), 111; R. Q. Mallard, *Plantation Life before Emancipation* (EE: 1998 [1892]), 28; Barrow Diary, Nov. 6, 1839, in Davis, *Florida Parishes*, 169–170; Sarah N. Randolph, *The Domestic Life of Jefferson, Compiled from Letters and Reminiscences* (New York, 1871), 35; *TCWVQ*, 1:20.

⁴³ Stuart A. Marks, *Southern Hunting in Black and White: Nature, History, and Ritual in a Carolina Community* (Princeton, NJ, 1991), 6; Elliott, *Carolina Sports*, 282.

their tables. During the summer, planters assigned slaves to keep the Big House well supplied with fish and shellfish. Slaves seized opportunities to fish for themselves, and sensible masters gave them time off for fishing parties. Frequently, masters and slaves fished together, in particular on drum fishing expeditions. Individuals often fished alone. "Went fishing at night," J. F. Comer of Alabama recorded, "Caught some fine Trout." His fellow Alabamian, Isaac Barton Ulmer, found much better fishing at Greene Springs, where he attended school, than back in Dallas County: "For some time past, fish has been a common dish among us .... To day there were some hundred and odd caught."[44]

During the spring, planters in central North Carolina organized their slaves and white folks – women, girls, overseers – for family frolics, at which they displayed ingenious methods for catching herring. Planters encouraged their children to invite the neighborhood's poorer children on fishing trips, with slaves to serve them.[45]

Women frequently accompanied men on fishing trips, although never on the dangerous ones off the Atlantic coast. Occasionally accompanied by male slaves, they went without white men. Fishing parties offered pleasant occasions for parents and children to enjoy each other's company. "I wish very much," Mary Jane Chester, wrote to her mother from school, "to be at home so that I could go fishing with you for we always have so much pleasure." Mary DeWitt of Arkansas went fishing with her young son Clinton, caught quite a few, and had a great time: "I am so afraid the fishing time will soon be over then we'll have nothing amusing." In the spring of 1836, prominent novelist Caroline Lee Hentz, then in Alabama, celebrated the achievements of her husband, who "caught two noble fishes – returned in all the flush & glory of conquest." But also her own: "We took a walk to the creek with a bundle of fishing hooks – The fish were very cunning and hid under the sheltering rocks, but some silly ones came out to bite – I caught a minnow & Half – We

---

[44] Lawrence S. Rowland, et al., *The History of Beaufort County, South Carolina*, 2 vols. (Columbia, SC, 1996), 171; Joe Gray Taylor, *Eating, Drinking, and Visiting in the South: An Informal History* (Baton Rouge, LA, 1982), 3, 9; Greenlee Diary, May 14, 1851; Mallory King to Floyd King, July 11, 1858, in T. B. King Papers; Comer Farm Journal, Jan. 30, 1846; I. B. Ulmer to Abigail Ulmer, June 10, 1860 in Ulmer Papers; also, Cornish Diary, Oct. 24, 1840.

[45] Edward Miles Riley, ed., *The Journal of John Harrower: An Indentured Servant in the Colony of Virginia, 1773–1776*, ed. (Williamsburg, VA, 1963), June 11, 1774 (46); Hudson Diary, Aug. 31, 1856; George C. Osborne, "Plantation Life in Central Mississippi, as Reflected in the Clay-Sharkey Papers," *Journal of Mississippi History*, 3 (1941), 285.

kept poor Charly [slave] running all the time for worms & to disentangle our lines." A month later she and Mr. Hentz took their daughters fishing and "caught a great many little fishes." The next day Mr. Hentz and Charly went off for a more serious effort at the mouth of the creek and got thoroughly soaked by the rain "but [returned] bearing a glorious mess." Caroline Hentz responded gleefully to the fish and teasingly to the exhibition of masculine pride: "Oh! the pleasure of successful exertion! Whether man is engaged in wrestling for empires or watching a bait – he still pants for triumph & feels all the flush of victory."[46]

GUNS

Writing in 1851 in the *Southern Literary Messenger*, "S.L.C." boasted that every American boy learned to shoot as soon as he learned to ride or swim. In the North, not likely. In the West and especially the South, notwithstanding a bit of hyperbole, the statement stands. Every farmer and planter kept guns, if only for hunting. In town and countryside Southerners carried guns, claiming the need for protection as well as for hunting. On the frontier, physicians made house calls armed. Congregants and even clergymen attended church armed, ready for attacks by hostile Indians or white ruffians. Rifle shooting was a great Sunday sport in New Orleans, where men preened over their marksmanship. Target practice and shooting matches constituted a part of everyday life, and college students, much like other country dwellers, loved to hunt and fish. Schools and colleges forbade students to carry weapons on campus, but the policy met with mixed success.[47]

Endless yarns about phenomenal marksmanship strain credulity yet command attention. An Indian fighter had to reload long rifles after each

---

[46] Mary Jane Chester to mother, April 1, 1841; Mary E. DeWitt to Marcus B. DeWitt, Oct. 13, 1852 in Mary Jane Chester Papers; Hentz Diary, March 26, 27, April 15, 16, 1836. Also, Carmac Diary, May 1, 1852; Barrow Diary, April 18, 1841, in Davis, ed., *Florida Parishes*, 227–228.

[47] S. L.C., "A Hunting Article," *SLM*, 17 (1851), 44, 47; Robert E. Nisbett and Dov Cohen, *The Culture of Honor: The Psychology of Violence in the South* (Boulder, CO, 1996), 35–36; William Harris Bragg, *De Renne: Three Generations of a Georgia Family* (Athens, GA, 1999), xviii; William Buell Sprague, *Annals of the American Pulpit*, 9 vols. (New York, 1859–1869), 7:143–144; Jack Kenny Williams, *Vogues in Villainy: Crime and Retribution in Ante-Bellum South Carolina* (Columbia, SC, 1959), 10–11; Silverthorne, *Plantation Life in Texas*, 97, 178; Mrs. [E. M.] Houstoun, *Texas and the Gulf of Mexico; or, Yachting in the Gulf of Mexico* (Austin, TX, 1968 [1845]), 16; John O. Beatty, *John Esten Cooke, Virginian* (New York, 1922), 15; Robert F. Pace, *Halls of Honor: College Men in the Old South* (Baton Rouge, LA, 2004), 59–61.

shot. His first shot had to be good or it might be his last. Kentuckians bragged about being the world's greatest shots, and maybe they were. But Texas lore yielded to the claims of the Tennesseans: "A Texas Ranger can ride like a Mexican, trail like an Indian, shoot like a Tennesseean [sic], and fight like a very devil!" In 1861, "G. P. W." of Savannah sent to the *Spirit of the Times* of New York – America's leading sporting journal – a description of Southerners as a hunting people, armed and experienced with guns. Such was the fact, but some blacks questioned such claims. During the widespread insurrection scare of 1856, Francis Terry Leak of Mississippi reported on a conversation between his slaves and those of Colonel S. B. Jones. Clark, Jones's slave, told Leak's that northern abolitionists would arrive soon to kill the whites and free the blacks. Northern youth "are all trained in the use of firearms since the time they can handle a gun, but these trifling southern boys don't now how to shoot." James R. Gilmore (nom de plume, Edmund Kirke), a northern businessman who traveled through the South, described a game that drew heavy betting. Sharpshooters fired at the head of a live turkey tied to a pole. It was not much of a game, since the sharpshooters never missed. Kirke commented in 1863, "In such schools were trained the unerring marksmen who are now 'bringing down' the bravest youth of our country, like fowls at a turkey match."[48]

Fathers prepared sons for school – not only military school – by teaching them to shoot. The Educational Association of Virginia approved *The Child's First Book* by William A. Campbell and William R. J. Dunn, which freely discussed guns in the hands of children. A German immigrant mother in Texas expressed horror when her husband trained their son to shoot, but she and the family adjusted to the need to fight off wild animals, especially panthers, and Indian horse thieves. The passing of the frontier did not change much.

Fathers taught their sons well. Lowcountry boys rode at seven or eight years of age and began to shoot a few years later. A boy began to feel himself a man when he accompanied his father, gun in hand, on his first partridge or quail hunt. Many youngsters in later life could not remember their first shot. Lowcountry boys learned to shoot by taking down easy prey like the numerous ducks and by shooting reptiles and alligators, which they gave to the slaves for food. N. E. W. Long, CSA, wrote to

[48] W. P. W., "Facts from a Georgia Friend," *Spirit of the Times*, 31 (June 31, 1861), 305; Leak Diary, June 16, 1856; Walter Prescott Webb, *The Great Plains* (New York, 1931), 166; James R. Gilmore [Edmund Kirke], *My Southern Friends* (New York, 1863), 56.

his young son from the front in 1862, "You must be a good boy and take care of your Mother, catch fish and kill squirrels for her ... How many rabbits have you and Henry caught since I left?" C. C. Jones, Jr. of Georgia recalled that his "indulgent father generously supplied his sons with guns, horses, row-boats, sail-boats, and fishing tackle" so they could take advantage of an area that abounded in game and fish.[49]

The Methodist Bishop William Capers recalled that, at age eleven, he learned to shoot on the family plantation near Georgetown, South Carolina: "My father taught me the use of the gun with great care: how to handle it, to load it, to shoot with a true aim, and to keep it in good order; so that before I was twelve years old I believe I was as safe in the use of this dangerous implement as I have since been, and nearly or quite as good a marksman." Joseph LeConte, the distinguished scientist, grew up in a pious Christian family on a large plantation in Liberty County, Georgia:

My father never forbade us the use of firearms, but counseled their careful use. The result justified the wisdom of his method. Four of us boys with guns on our shoulders all the time, and yet never an accident...Guns there were a plenty in the house...rifles and shot-guns, single-barreled guns and medium-sized guns, long guns and short guns. There was a complete armory of them up-stairs in one of the closets, besides several in the hands of the most trusty negro men to shoot game and wild animals of prey and crop-destroying birds. There must have been at least twenty of them.

Planters and farmers taught sons to clean guns. Martin Marshall of Alabama recalled washing them in spirits and turpentine. Yet, despite the care that fathers took, occasionally boys died in hunting accidents.[50]

[49] Wharton Jackson Green, *Recollections and Reflections: An Auto of Half a Century and More* (EE: 1998 [1906]), 94–96; William A. Campbell and William R. J. Dunn, *The Child's First Book* (EE: 2000 [1864]), 15–18; Christina Eudora von Scholl to Oma [Grandmother Lembke], June 17, Sept. 25, 1847, in Marj Gurasich, *Letters to Oma: A Young German Girl's Account of Her First Year in Texas, 1847* (Fort Worth: TX, 1989), 52–53, 57–67, 105–107; Reuben Davis, *Recollections of Mississippi and Mississippians* (Oxford, MS, 1972 [1879], 31; D. E. Huger Smith, *A Charlestonian's Recollections, 1846–1913* (Charleston, SC, 1950), 45–46; N. W. E. Long to My Darling Little Boy, June 14, 1862, in Private Possession; C. C. Jones, Jr. quoted in Stanhope Bayne-Jones, "Special Article – Joseph Jones (1833–1896)," *Bulletin of the Tulane Medical Faculty*, 17 (1958) 223.

[50] John Drayton, "A Traveling Governor's View, 1802, in Thomas D. Clark, ed., *South Carolina: The Grand Tour, 1780–1865* (Columbia, SC, 1973), 28; N. W. E. Long to My Darling Little Boy, June 14, 1862, in Private Possession; Capers, "Autobiography," in William M. Wightman, *Life of William Capers, D. D., One of the Bishops of the Methodist Episcopal Church, South, Including an Autobiography* (Nashville, TN, 1902), 36; William Dallam Armes, ed., *The Autobiography of Joseph LeConte* (New York, 1903), 18; on the cleaning of guns, see Weymouth T. Jordan, ed., *Herbs, Hoecakes*

Lowcountry fathers took sons on hunting trips designed for their instruction, and gentlemen invited families, including ladies and children, to visit and enjoy the hunting of partridges, turkeys, and squirrels. Mothers and sisters worried but proudly encouraged their boys to hunt. Rebecca Bryant thrilled when young Henry had "his first regular deer hunt." By age fourteen a plantation lad expected to have his own horse and several guns. Mrs. H. G. Lewis of Natchitoches, Louisiana, assured her cousin that young Robert "has learned to shoot, we do not trust him by himself with a gun but he handles a gun with a great deal of dexterity, has killed several Squirrels and a number of birds." Georgia King of Georgia wrote to her father that Mallery and Lordy, her brothers, had each killed a deer: "It was Lordy's first deer, and I am so glad he killed one. The shooting is becoming better now, Lordy has killed more than 20 teal besides other game." Lordy's mother appreciated his youthful efforts, delighting at the seven doves he bagged for breakfast. Eliza Quitman wrote of her brother: "Henry enjoyed himself in gunning. He brought home a dozen birds one morning, which was I think, pretty good shooting for so young a sportsman."[51]

The wonder is that accidents did not occur more frequently. Since life's many risks included accidents, no one dreamed of restricting access to firearms. From Francis Taylor of Virginia at the end of the eighteenth century to Francis Terry Leak of Mississippi a half century later, Southerners reported laconically on men who accidentally shot themselves. Occasionally, a white man or slave inadvertently killed someone. Here and there a hunter killed a brother or friend. Careless hunters got a rough time from their fellows, who insisted on high standards of safety. In Louisiana, Barrow fumed about a relative who shot his own horse while going through a thicket: "Will carry his gun cocks down, second horse he has shot." Mr. C. Berwyn of North Carolina suffered severe wounds on

and Husbandry: The Daybook of a Planter of the Old South (Tallahassee, FL, 1960), 26. For accidents among wealthy South Carolinians, see Mary D. Robertson, ed., *A Confederate Lady Comes of Age: The Journal of Pauline DeCaradeux Heyward, 1863–1888* (Columbia, SC, 1992), 3.

[51] Deas, *Recollections of the Ball Family*, 75, 79–80; Rebecca Bryant to Willie Bryant, June 1, 1863, in Arch Fredric Blakely, et al., eds., *Rose Cottage Chronicles: Civil War Letters of the Bryant-Stephens Families of North Florida* (Tallahassee, FL, 1998), 234; A. L. Brent to William Cabell, Nov. 5, 1858, in Cabell-Ellet Papers; Mrs. H. G. Lewis to Mrs. J. M. Hunt, March 1, 1837, in Hughes Family Papers; Georgia King to Thomas Butler King, Oct. 3, 1858, Anna Matilda King to Floyd King, Aug. 29, 1858 in T. B. King Papers; Eliza Quitman to John A. Quitman, March 23, 1843, also Dec. 30, 1845 in J. A. Quitman Papers.

a partridge hunt with four other university students. "That kind of hunting," Charles Lockhart Pettigrew wrote to his father in disgust, "where they shoot entirely on the wing is quite dangerous and more especially when there are several in the company; the animation is so great, and so great quickness is necessary, that they never look what they are about or who is in danger, the bird is the only object that attracts attention."[52]

Dangerous or no, some girls and just about every boy learned to shoot and loved to hunt. Frank Hardin of Texas, a planter, hunted for sport but also to fill his table with ducks, quail, pigeons, plovers, snipes, and geese, as well as deer and stray calves. His daughters, as well as sons, rode and hunted with him, having been fitted with rifles at an appropriate age. Hardin, when hunting, took particular pleasure in the company of his daughters. Young ladies clamored for inclusion. "I am sure you would never guess," Georgia King wrote to her father, "SHOOTING Yes, dear Father I have killed TEN robins – I hope when you return you will allow me to go out shooting HAWKS with you. Will you? I shall be very good & pull the trigger at the right time."[53]

Mistresses professed to trust their slaves but nonetheless proceeded cautiously. Emily Burke reported from Georgia in the late 1840s that some women provided for their own defense with firearms: "I have known ladies that would not dare to go to sleep without one or two pistols under their pillows." That farm girls learned to shoot should occasion no surprise, but the young and reputedly beautiful Anne the Huntress – the only name she went by – was something special. She joined a group of local sharpshooters in a contest, replete with an ornamental rifle to go along with her hatchet and hunting knife, and scored a bull's eye at sixty yards. Another Miss Anne, a local favorite, taught school for seventeen years at Guilford. Ann Bailey, a farmwoman in Allegheny County, Virginia, became a local legend for her prowess in hunting deer and bear after she had won her spurs as an Indian-fighter, and Nancy Hart, an illiterate patriot of Elbert County, Georgia, became famous for her defiance of the British and Tories during the Revolution. The respect

---

[52] Taylor Diary, Sept. 29, 1799; Leak Diary, June 5, 1854; John Davis, *Travels of Four and a Half Years in the United States of America*, ed. A. J. Morrison (New York, 1909 [1803]), 89–90; Barrow Diary, May 25, 1845, in Davis, ed., *Florida Parishes*, 357; Charles Lockhart Pettigrew to Ebenezer Pettigrew, Nov. 7, 1835, in Lemmon, ed., *Pettigrew Papers*, 2:270.

[53] Camilla Davis, Trammel, *Seven Pines: Its Occupants and Their Letters, 1825–1872* (Dallas, TX, 1986), 107, 132; Georgia King to Thomas Butler King, Feb. 22, 1850 in T. B. King Papers.

accorded women who shot well proved something of an anomaly, for, as John Hope Franklin observes, "Not a few Southerners associated good marksmanship with the better attributes of manhood." Gentlemen who dubbed themselves "The Chivalry" had mixed feelings about the spectacle of women with guns.[54]

The War led southern men to take a fresh interest in training young women to shoot. With men at the front, women might well have to protect themselves against Yankees, marauders, or rebellious slaves. Thus, for example, when Mississippi seceded, schools opened to teach young ladies to shoot. When Preston Mangum went to War in 1861, he made sure that he first taught his sister Pattie to fire a pistol. On the eve of secession Edmund Ruffin got in step: "At my instigation, all the young ladies, after dinner, tried (most of them for the first time) firing a revolver at a target. I urged them to make up a "Ladies' Shooting Club," & to practice shooting." A year later, with the War on, he taught his twenty-year-old granddaughter to shoot, but ladies in his family and in the neighborhood resisted. He persisted in thinking, "It would remove all of the small existing danger of insurrectionary and other attacks, of negroes – & would render our women an important portion of a 'home guard.'"[55]

Mr. Junkin did his best to teach fifteen-year-old Sarah Lois Wadley of Mississippi to shoot, but the rifle's recoil threw her. A former slave provided a striking contrast in an account of a young lady in Tennessee. Having great confidence in her ability to handle a rifle, she refused the Confederate army's offer of protection. Thank you, no, she replied, as she asked for ammunition. The father of the young Kate Virginia Cox of Virginia taught her and her brothers to shoot and care for weapons. Proudly she announced that she did as well as they. Taking advantage of the absence of the men at war, a gallant chap in Tippah County, Mississippi, threatened to kill Mrs. Dobbin if she did not allow him to pilfer her home. She ordered a slave woman to fetch her gun. He decided not to test her resolve.[56]

---

[54] Dorothy Lloyd Gilbert, *Guilford: A Quaker College* (Greensboro, NC, 1937), 24; Emily P. Burke, *Reminiscences of Georgia* (Oberlin, OH, 1850), 158; Janet E. Kaufman, "'Under the Petticoat Flag': Women Soldiers in the Confederate Army," *Southern Studies*, 23 (1984), 363–375; Henry Howe, *Historical Collections of Virginia* (Charleston, SC, 1845), 173; for Hart see White, *Statistics of Georgia*, 234–238; John Hope Franklin, *The Militant South, 1800–1861* (Cambridge, MA, 1970), 18.

[55] "Reminiscences of Marie Alma Turner," in Shanks, ed., *Mangum Papers*, 5:761; Feb. 14, 1860, May 30, 1861, in *ERD*, 1:401, 2:38.

[56] Wadley Private Journal, undated probably 1859–1860; Ophelia Settle Egypt et al., eds, *Unwritten History of Slavery: Autobiographical Accounts of Ex-Slaves* (Washington,

Prudent young ladies took up pistols under the supervision of an officer. In 1863, Lucy Breckenridge of Virginia, who had been practicing
for a year with her sister Eliza, cried out: "We have met with so many
disasters of late. I wish the women could fight, and I do think they might
be allowed to do so in the mountains and in the fortified cities." Women's
lives "are no more precious than men's, and they were made to suffer –
so a leg shot off or a head either wouldn't hurt them much. I would
gladly shoulder my pistol and shoot some yankees if it were allowable."
Allowable or no, some women shot Union soldiers.[57]

An amused Louise Wigfall Wright, traveling in Pennsylvania, came
across a girl who thought that all southern girls carried revolvers. And in
fact, many Northerners believed that southern females of all ages went
about armed to the teeth. Sherman's troops in South Carolina acted as if
they expected armed ladies when they entered homes. The fear that counseled this prudence was not always exaggerated. For one, the redoubt-
able teenaged Belle Boyd shot and killed a Union soldier who pushed
her mother. Emma Holmes of Charleston reveled in reports of southern
ladies who drew guns on impertinent Yankee troops. She applauded Miss
Stuart of western Virginia and Mrs. Henry M. Hymans of New Orleans
for shooting Yankee soldiers who grabbed and tried to kiss them.[58]

DC, 1968), 3; Lily Logan Morrill, ed., *My Confederate Girlhood: The Memoirs of Kate
Virginia Cox Logan* (Richmond, VA, 1932), 19; Agnew Diary, April 28, 1863.

[57] Mary D. Robertson, ed., *Lucy Breckinridge of Grove Hill: The Journal of a Virginia
Girl, 1826–1864* (Kent, OH, 1979), Aug. 13, 1863, (140–141); also, Butler Diary, Jan. 8,
1861; Reid Mitchell, *The Vacant Chair: The Northern Soldier Leaves Home* (New York,
1993), 99.

[58] Mrs. D. Giraud Wright [Louise Wigfall], *A Southern Girl in '61: The War-Time
Memories of a Confederate Senator's Daughter* (New York, 1905), 46; "Journal of
P. DeC. Heyward," Feb. 18, 1865, in Robertson, ed., *Confederate Lady Comes of Age*,
65–66; Ruth Scarborough, *Belle Boyd: Siren of the South* (Macon, GA, 1997), xiii; John
F. Marszalek, ed., *The Diary of Miss Emma Holmes* (Baton Rouge, LA, 1979), Aug. 11,
1861, Aug. 20, 1862 (79, 191).

4

Vignettes

Sundry Pleasures

The great science of Christianity consists in the innocent enjoyment of every good which surrounds us.

– *Judge Taylor Beatty of Louisiana*[1]

LADIES OF FASHION

Late eighteenth-century Virginians, entranced with European fashions, bought Italian and French finery from British merchants. Thereafter, the fashion spread across the South. In 1824, Ann Pettigrew found in New Bern, North Carolina, "full extravagance and fine dressing, the poorest people make a show." By the 1830s, wealthy lowcountry planters and the young ladies and gentlemen of the ports had yielded to European tastes, and in 1850s, *Godey's Ladies Book* and other popular journals promoted French fashions. Plantation ladies had cosmetics, colognes, perfumes, hair tonics, powder puffs, curling fluids, oils, toothpaste, and mouthwash. Even in interior Mississippi, gentlemen wore cologne, which some made on their plantations. Everard Green Baker, for example, combined alcohol, lavender, bergamot, essence of lemon, and water. The upcountry gentry followed suit, if slowly.[2]

---

[1] Beatty Diary, Apr. 24, 1843.
[2] Virginius Dabney, *Richmond: Story of a City* (Garden City, NY, 1976), 39–40; Virginia Nonimportation Association, June 22, 1770, in Allen Rutland, ed., *The Papers of George Mason, 1725–1792*, 3 vols. (Williamsburg, VA, 1961), 1970), 1:122; for the 1850s, see Arthur C. Cole, *The Irrepressible Conflict, 1850–1865* (New York, 1934), 164–165; Helen Hill Miller, *George Mason: Gentleman Revolutionary* (Chapel Hill, NC, 1975); Ann Blount Pettigrew to Ebenezer Pettigrew, Dec. 30, 1824, in Sarah McCulloh Lemmon,

French styles in dress swept Washington and spread southward, accompanied by bawdy remarks. Scores of politicians and their wives and children, as well as businessmen, planters, and tourists, returned from Washington with reports of a new cosmopolitan culture. Across the South protests rose against European styles, especially against women's revealing clothes, which provoked disapproval and disgust for their display of female flesh. Fastidious and pious ladies recoiled from lewd dress and risqué deportment. In 1803, Rosalie Calvert wrote from the tidewater to her sister in Belgium: "I wear my sleeves half way up the arm; those who follow the exaggerated fashion wear them even shorter and very transparent," and with gloves that let the skin show through. In 1808, the Methodist Reverend John Early, riding circuit in Virginia, rebuked church women for naked breasts and elbows. In 1840, Robert L. Dabney, a student at the University of Virginia, could hardly believe the "naked hide" in Charlottesville. The Reverend William Nelson Pendleton of Lexington, Virginia, appealed to the ancient Greeks and to Thomas Carlyle's *Sartor Resartus* to identify an "esthesiology" – "the science of clothing, the doctrine of fashions, the philosophy of costumes."[3]

Slaveholders taught their daughters from earliest childhood the quality of fabrics and the fine points of dress. Elizabeth Fox-Genovese comments:

A lady distinguished herself by her observation of fashion's conventions; lavish display for its own sake provided no substitute .... Fashion articulated class position; extravagance defied it. A lady had to know the difference, had to manifest in her person a restrained elegance that simultaneously betokened internal self-control and solid male protection.[4]

---

ed., *The Pettigrew Papers*, 2 vols. (Raleigh, NC, 1971, 1988), 2:51; J. B. Grimball Diary, May 25, 1833; William S. Powell, *When the Past Refused to Die: A History of Caswell County, North Carolina, 1777–1977* (Durham, NC, 1977), 167. Cosmetics: Minnie Clare Boyd, *Alabama in the Fifties: A Social Study* (New York, 1931), 112; Fredrika Bremer, *Homes of the New World: Impressions of America*, 2 vols. (New York, 1853), 1:390; Baker Diary, typed, 1:38.

[3] R. S. Calvert to Isabelle van Havre, Dec. 30, 1803, in Margaret Law Callcott, ed., *The Mistress of Riversdale: The Plantation Letters of Rosalie Stier Calvert, 1795–1821* (Baltimore, 1991), 72; W. P. Mangum to Charity A. Mangum, ca 1826, in Henry Thomas Shanks, ed., *The Papers of Willie Person Mangum*, 5 vols. (Raleigh, NC, 1955–1956), 1:227; Albright Diary, Oct. 20, 1864; Harnett T. Kane, *Natchez on the Mississippi* (New York, 1947), 15, 221; George Green Shackelford, *George Wythe Randolph and the Confederate Elite* (Athens, GA, 1988), 22 (Minor); Charles Fraser, *Reminiscences of Charleston* (Charleston, SC, 1959 [1854]), 108; Early Diary, Aug. 6, 1808; David Henry Overy, "Robert Lewis Dabney: Apostle of the Old South" (Unpubl. Ph.D. diss.: University of Wisconsin, 1967), 24; William Nelson Pendleton, "Philosophy of Dress," *SLM*, 22 (1856), 199–200.

[4] Elizabeth Fox-Genovese, *Within the Plantation Household: Black and White Women of the Old South* (Chapel Hill, NC, 1988), 212–213.

With the introduction of cotton-growing in Texas, homespun became the standard dress for men and women alike. For Sundays and at church the women had calico dresses, although the well-to-do brought silk gowns and hats with them when they arrived from the eastern states. Even before Texas joined the Union, the women of the Southwest were beginning to show up at balls in fashionable clothing. For one, Cynthia O'Brien, visiting from Louisiana, loved the balls and her chance to wear a Swiss net dress and white slippers and gloves.[5]

The Southwest bristled with reports of risqué fashions. Yet, even in New Orleans few women dared to wear low-cut dresses until the early 1850s, when small-breasted young ladies compensated by wearing padded clothing. Attending a ball in honor of John C. Calhoun in Vicksburg, Joseph Davis Howell scorched the behavior of Mrs. William A. Gwin, wife of the future Senator of California. Davis could not look at her without blushing:

She was dressed in black velvet cut so low in the neck that it was absolutely indecent, no sleeves to her dress, neck and arms perfectly bare. She seemed to think, though, that the dress was not low enough and did all in her power by drawing her shoulders out of her dress while waltzing with young Calhoun to expose as much of her person as possible to his view – looking at him all the while with such a licentious, languishing look that it made my blood run cold, I felt like kicking them both out of the room for daring to conduct themselves in such a manner before innocent young girls.[6]

Henry W. Connor of North Carolina described to his mother and sister the clothing worn at a celebration for Lafayette in Charleston. Finding the dresses "most brilliant as well as costly," he speculated, "Some of the trappings of our Nabob daughters must have cost $2[000] to $3,000, or perhaps more." The dresses were all white, some with a netting of steel or gold or silver gauze over a white muslin dress, some with blue or pink trimmings. Diamonds were on display "from the common paste up to the diamond of the 1st water." Yet, Alice Hopeton Middleton insisted – curiously, not to say improbably – that, in the 1840s, Charleston, unlike Boston, "was absolutely indifferent to the world of fashion." She did acknowledge that the Middleton and Pringle girls, who went north to

---

[5] William R. Hogan, *The Texas Republic: A Social and Economic History* (Austin, TX, 1969), 46–48; Camilla Davis Trammel, *Seven Pines: Its Occupants and Their Letters, 1825–1872* (Dallas, TX, 1986), 45.

[6] J. H. Ingraham, *Sunny South; Or, The Southerner at Home* (New York, 1968 [1860], 449–450; Joseph Davis Howell to Margaret Howell [his mother], Nov. 21, 1845 in Hudson Strode, ed., *Jefferson Davis: Private Letters, 1823–1889* (New York, 1966), 35.

Newport for summers and returned via New York, brought the latest fashions back with them, making "a marked appearance in the quiet of the old town." Charles Fraser, the celebrated artist, amused by the fluctuations in fashions, recalled turn-of-the century Charleston, when ladies wore low-necked dresses and sleeveless robes. A lady today at mid-century, he wrote tongue-in-cheek, would be aghast by any such thing, but, then, in the old days she would have been aghast at bustles, "attracting all eyes to a point where they could not meet the reproof of her own."[7]

Protests against ladies' fashions grew especially loud in the towns and villages of North Carolina. Senator Willie P. Mangum, writing to his wife from Washington in the mid-1820s, railed about the behavior of women in the parks, whose steel corsets brushed into passersby: "Really you would think that all modesty was gone & lost if you could see the best bred ladies here, squeezing their way through the crowd." In 1845, William D. Valentine of Hertford County went into a tirade over bustles, which – he felt sure – evoked disgust in well-bred women. "Inexperienced and independent spirited girls, well provided for in property and relatives, are most apt to fall into the error from a false notion of their self importance." Valentine, grousing that young girls mindlessly flew to fashionably revealing clothes, attributed moral courage to women who did not succumb. A few years later in Raleigh, the governor's Christmas party jolted State Senator A. C. McIntosh from rural Anderson County. Writing to his wife, he depicted the ladies as attractive, some very much so: "But I confess there was a little more of the breast and arms naked than would look becoming in the country." Eliza Clitherall complained, "Mothers now lead their young ones in folly's path" by encouraging them to follow "vanities" in dress. Robert Graham Barrett, in his senior class address at the University of North Carolina in 1856, objected to the penchant of southern ladies to spring for every fashion that wafted down from New York. Indeed, young ladies found themselves embarrassed by their out-of-fashion silk dresses with long sleeves and high necks.[8]

---

[7] Theodore D. Jervey, *Robert Y. Hayne and His Times* (New York, 1909), 195–196 (Connor); Alicia Hopton Middleton, "A Family Record," in Middleton et al, *Life in Carolina and New England During the Nineteenth Century* (Bristol, RI, 1929), 61; Fraser, *Reminiscences of Charleston*, 108. For tributes to the elegance and taste of the ladies of Charleston and Savannah, see Joseph Lyons, in Jacob Rader Marcus, ed., *Memoirs of American Jews*, 3 vols. (Philadelphia, 1955), 1:245; J. S. Buckingham, *The Slave States of America*, 2 vols. (New York, 1968 [1842]), 1:124.

[8] W. P. Mangum to Charity A. Mangum, ca 1826, in Shanks, ed., *Mangum Papers*, 1:227; Valentine Diary, Apr. 12, Nov. 14, 1845; A. C. McIntosh to Amanda McIntosh, Dec. 26,

In the 1820s, the corset acquired a steel front, and the waistline decreased in girth. Susan Nye Hutchinson complained that her corset ("a very tight Spencer") distracted her from listening to the sermon in church. The ladies shifted from slim skirts to full-length bell-shaped skirts. Short-waist petticoats became fashionable; some, edged with frills, showed below the outer garment. Harry St. John Dixon of the Mississippi Delta, a planter's teenage son, displayed little patience with the ladies' "tight dressing." In 1864, Sergeant James W. Albright of Greensboro wrote from Richmond: "A great many ladies were on the streets & I was sorry to see that tight lacing is again becoming fashionable. Poor girls! There are too many it is true & it may be as good a way to commit suicide as any other." Meanwhile, the ladies of Natchez, Mississippi, were adorning themselves in tight-waist dresses with expansive skirts.[9]

Irritation and enchantment greeted fashionable dress. Virginia Minor, a seventeen-year-old beauty, sometimes visited relations near Charlottesville, Virginia, captivating the most sedate of parties, presumably by her guitar-playing but possibly also by her low-cut white dress. By 1840, traveling hair stylists were arriving in Athens and other Georgia towns to attend to ladies who increasingly used perfume and jewelry. The young ladies of upcountry Georgia – Petersburg, Milledgeville, Athens – were wearing low-cut white tarlatan dresses with as many as a half dozen stiffly starched white skirts: "The larger we stood out," said Cornelia Jones Pond, "the more stylish we were." A popular Sabbath School teacher in Bibb County, Alabama – a bit too popular with the young men – had two small faults: She could not answer any questions correctly, and she wore dresses with low necks and short sleeves. Lucilla McCorkle of Talladega thought the large church congregation remarkably attentive despite the display of new dresses and bonnets: "O Fashion thou leadest captive silly women." Nannie Cross of Arkansas sarcastically ended a school essay in the mid-1850s: "And the city lady can dress in more costly silks after being '*tired to death*' of the flimsy things we are obliged to wear in summer & of course she must have a new bonnet. It will be so delightful." As

1848 in McIntosh Papers; Clitherall Autobiography (Ms.), Book 5; Barrett, "Tendency of the Human Mind to Extremes," UNC, Senior Speeches, 1856.

9 Josephine Bacon Martin, ed., *Life on a Liberty County Plantation: The Journal of Cornelia Jones Pond* (Darien, GA, 1974), 16; Hutchinson, Oct. 29, 1826; James C. Bonner, *Milledgeville: Georgia's Antebellum Capital* (Athens, GA, 1978), 69; Dixon Diary, June 17, 1860, in Stephen Berry, ed., *Princes of Cotton: Four Diaries of Young Men in the South, 1848–1860* (Athens, GA, 2007), 124; Albright Diary, Oct. 20, 1864; Kane, *Natchez on the Mississippi*, 15, 221.

French styles spread to the Mississippi Delta, wealthy plantation ladies ordered in bulk from New Orleans: hoop skirts and fine cotton and silk, which their seamstresses made into stylish dresses.[10]

The popular Methodist Reverend William Winans of Mississippi had his hands full with female parishioners who outdid each other in expensive clothing and clad their children accordingly. In the low country, the high-church Episcopalian Reverend Mr. Cornish had to listen to irate ladies' "strong reasons for leaving a Church." One raged: "I belonged to the Church – but I did not think the minister was a spiritual man & so I left it and went to the baptists." She elaborated, "I don't think that's right to prescribe what dress one shall wear – especially in the public prints. They can preach about it before their own congregations occasionally, if they choose, but if a minister should insist on it I would *leave his Church*." Cornish sighed, "Oh when shall Zion arise & put on her beautiful garments, & shake herself from the dust?"[11]

Mobile, Alabama, had an impressive community of intellectuals and sophisticated wealthy planters and merchants, and its ladies, led by the internationally renowned Madame Octavia Walton LeVert, maintained a high standard of fashion. Madame Le Vert's soirées included, among other luminaries, Augusta Jane Evans, John Forsyth, Caroline Hentz, Mirabeau B. Lamar, A. B. Meek, and Josiah Nott. "When in Mobile," said Barbara Leigh Smith Bodichon of England in the 1850s, "it is *de rigeur* to meet Madame LeVert, '*the lady of the South*.'" Lady Emmaline Stuart referred to Madame LeVert as "one of the most delightful people in the world." Madame Le Vert took the breath away from young ladies such as Eliza Ripley of New Orleans when they saw her conversing with four gentlemen at a time in four different languages. Benjamin F. Porter

[10] Shackelford, George Wythe, 22 (Minor); Weymouth T. Jordan, *Ante-Bellum Alabama: Town and Country* (Tallahassee, FL, 1957), 34; William Garrett, *Reminiscences of Public Men in Alabama for Thirty Years* (Atlanta, GA, 1872), 318 (Porter), 558 (Smith); William Harris Hardy and Toney A. Hardy, *No Compromise with Principle: Autobiography and Biography of William Harris Hardy* (New York, 1946), 7; Mary R. Bullard, *Robert Stafford of Cumberland Island: Growth of a Planter* (Athens, GA, 1995), 79; Josephine Bacon Martin, ed., *Life on a Liberty County Plantation: The Journal of Cornelia Jones Pond* (Darien, GA, 1974), 16; Hutchinson, Oct. 29, 1826; McCorkle Diary, Nov. 15, 1846; Nannie E. Cross, "The Fall of the Year," 1856–1857), in Edward Cross Papers; Bonner, *Milledgeville*, 69; Coulter, *Old Petersburg*, 135; Ernest C. Hynds, *Antebellum Athens and Clarke County, Georgia* (Athens, GA, 1974), 124; Rhoda Coleman Ellison, *Early Alabama Publications: A Study in Literary Interests* (University, AL, 1947), 114.
[11] Ray Holder, *William Winans: Methodist Leader in Antebellum Mississippi* (Jackson, MS, 1977), 96; Cornish Diary, Dec. 5, 1839.

described her as a "small, active, finely formed lady," with "ease of manners combined with grace of expression," who "never permitted pride to conquer politeness." Charles A. Hentz wrote that his mother, the prominent novelist Caroline Hentz, saw a good deal of Madame Le Vert, whom he described as petite, pretty, and fashionably dressed.[12]

Preachers and prim ladies notwithstanding, fashionable southern belles, with some justification, sang their own praises. Joseph Lyons of Charleston judged the ladies of Philadelphia less beautiful than advertised and much inferior to those of Charleston in grace and symmetry. Worse, he judged the gentlemen of Philadelphia "much superior in appearance" to their ladies. J. S. Buckingham of England compared the ladies of Savannah favorably to their northern counterparts: "in general dressed in better taste, less showily and expensively, but with more elegance in form, and more chasteness in colour." Savannah enchanted Charles Joseph Latrobe as "one of the most striking cities in the Union." Savannah initially disappointed Hiram Fuller of Boston as "over-praised," but its pretty women and fine wines compelled him to revise his opinion. New York journalists recognized that the southern ladies set the tone for Washington's high society in the 1850s.[13]

GENTLEMEN PLAIN AND FANCY

In the 1780s, the ladies and gentlemen of Richmond were wearing "decidedly fancy raiment," as Virginius Dabney termed it. Thomas Jefferson, who notoriously sported slippers in the White House, had been fastidious

---

12 Henry Poellnitz Johnston, *The Gentle Johnstons and Their Kin* (Birmingham, AL, 1966), 197; Philip Graham, *The Life and Poems of Mirabeau B. Lamar* (Chapel Hill, NC, 1938), 67–68; Herman Clarence Nixon, *Alexander Beaufort Meek, Poet, Orator, Journalist, Historian, Statesman* (Auburn, AL, 1910), 10; Barbara Leigh Smith Bodichon, *An American Diary, 1857–8*, ed., Joseph W. Reed, Jr. (London, 1972), Feb. 17, 1858 (111); Lady Emmaline Stuart, *Travels in the United States, Etc., during 1849 and 1850* (New York, 1851), xx, 133–137; Eliza Ripley, *Social Life in Old New Orleans: Being Recollections of My Girlhood*, (New York, 1975 [1912]), 86; Benjamin F. Porter, *Reminiscences of Men and Things in Alabama*, ed. Sara Walls (Tuscaloosa, AL, 1983), 56; Steven M. Stowe, ed., *A Southern Practice: The Diary and Autobiography of Charles A. Hentz, M. D.* (Charlottesville, VA, 2000), 441. Madame Le Vert once appeared with jewelry worth between $6,000 and $8,000: Frances Gibson Satterfield, *Madame Le Vert: A Biography of Octavia Walton Le Vert* (Edisto Island, SC, 1987), 53.

13 Joseph Lyons, in Marcus, ed., *Memoirs of American Jews*, 1:245; Buckingham *Slave States*, 1:124; Charles Joseph Latrobe, *The Rambler in North America*, 2nd ed., 2 vols. (London, 1836), 2:16; [Hiram Fuller], *Belle Brittan on Tour, at Newport and Here and There* (New York, 1858), 119, 122–123, quote at 119; Mary A. H. Gay, *Life in Dixie During the War*, 5th ed. (Atlanta, GA, 1979 [1897]), 81–82.

when, as a young man, he began to notice girls. Yet he grew increasingly irate over the spread of foppery and fashion, associating it with a decline in republican virtue, and he favored legal action to restrict dress. "Harsh as it may seem, it would relieve the very patriots who dread it, by stopping the course of their extravagance because it renders their affairs entirely desperate." In particular, he wanted the state to impose plain, austere, republican costumes on women. His views did not prevail. In *Swallow Barn*, John Pendleton Kennedy called Frank Meriwether "a thoroughbred Virginian" but had him dote on his "fine figure and dress." The well-dressed ladies and gentlemen of Richmond much impressed Olmsted when he saw the Virginia legislature in session in 1853. "Everybody in Richmond seemed to be always in *high dress*. You would meet ladies early on a drizzly day, creeping along their muddy streets in light silk dresses and satin hats; and never a gentleman seemed to relieve himself of the close-fitting, shiny, black, full evening suit, and indulge in the luxury of a loose morning coat."[14]

Even at breakfast, Olmstead noted, the gentlemen appeared "all in full funeral dress, not an easy coat amongst them." At home or on the street the ladies and gentlemen wore silk and satin and, even in the morning, looked as if they were on their way to a dinner party. Olmsted recalled similar scenes in New York, "but the gentlemen carry it further than in New York and never seem to indulge in undress." Indeed, from the early 1800s, formal attire was *de rigueur* at parties and balls in Richmond. The presence of a European aristocrat like Prince Achille Murat anywhere almost guaranteed fancy dress at balls. Until the late 1850s, old and young men dressed pretty much alike, except for the colored cravats worn by the young gentlemen. Then, in the late 1850s, to the displeasure of older gentlemen, the young gentlemen of the large towns started to wear short, double-breasted reefing jackets and trousers immense at the hips and tapering to the ankles.[15] In the 1850s, some of the wealthiest of

---

[14] John Chester Miller, *The Wolf by the Ears: Thomas Jefferson and Slavery* (New York, 1977), 34; Dabney, *Richmond*, 39; Dumas Malone, *Jefferson and His Time*, 6 vols. (Charlottesville, VA, 1948–1961), 1:48. For Kennedy, see Howard R. Floan, *The South in Northern Eyes, 1831 to 1861* (New York, 1958), 90; John S. Wise, *The End of an Era* (Boston, MA, 1900), 67. In eighteenth-century South Carolina, broadcloth was not customary above the low country: John Belton O'Neall, *Biographical Sketches of the Bench and Bar of South Carolina*, 2 vols. (Charleston, SC, 1859), 2:326.

[15] Olmsted, "The South," *New-York Daily Times*, Feb. 19, 1853, in Charles Capen McLaughlin, et al., eds., *The Papers of Frederick Law Olmsted*, 2 vols. (Baltimore, 1977, 1981), 2:96; Daniel R. Hundley, *Social Relations in Our Southern States* (Baton Rouge, LA, 1979 [1860]), 176–177; John Esten Cooke, *The Virginia Comedians*, 2 vols. (New York, 1854), 1:92; John O. Beatty, *John Esten Cooke, Virginian* (New York, 1922),

Virginians, male and female, dressed ostentatiously. Elderly gentlemen wore broadcloth, tall silk hats, high standing collars, and white or black socks. In the countryside, gentlemen preferred broad felt or straw hats and white or nankeen waistcoats.

Yet elsewhere men's dress tended toward a stereotyped plain style. "Virginians," Joseph Story observed, "have some pride in appearing in simple habiliments, and are willing to rest their claim to attention upon their force of mind and suavity of manners." Story elsewhere referred to John Marshall's simplicity of dress, which matched his character. Story adulated Marshall, whom Virginius Dabney later called "perhaps the worst-dressed man in America." Story might have been speaking of John Taylor of Caroline – or Nathaniel Macon of North Carolina – whom he loathed but who also preferred a plain, old-fashioned, rustic style of dress. The men and women of Culpeper County, Virginia, enjoyed their reputation for careless dress, but what, exactly, did careless mean? The Presbyterian Reverend Robert L. Dabney praised John Marshall as a man who exemplified Christian simplicity in his dress and demeanor. Dabney was not likely to have been endorsing carelessness. In Louisa County, from which he hailed, the premium for both sexes was simplicity.[16]

By the 1830s, even in upcountry towns like Athens, Georgia, men were beginning to sport jewelry. More broadly, J. S. Buckingham, in Charleston about 1840, commented, "There is a sort of dandyism, in the dress of the young men especially which is peculiarly southern: short frock-coats, small black stocks, rounded shirt-collars, turned down outside the stock to give coolness to the neck, hair or beard under the throat, low-crowned and broad-brimmed white felt hats, and walking sticks, are among the most striking parts of the costume." No few of the lordly lowcountry Carolina planters dressed foppishly. Columbia, South Carolina, normally a rather sleepy town, came alive during legislative sessions, as upcountry farmers and poor sand hillers rubbed elbows in the streets with the

---

5; Lucy Woods Butler to Waddy Butler, Jan. 21, 1861; A. J. Bailey, "Thomas C. Hindman, in Richard N. Current, ed., *Encyclopedia of the Confederacy*, 4 vols. (New York, 1993), 2:776–777.

[16] Joseph Story to Samuel P. P. Frey, May 30, 1807, in William W. Story, ed., *Life and Letters of Joseph Story*, 2 vols. (Boston, MA, 1851),1:151; William W. Story, ed., *The Miscellaneous Writings of Joseph Story* (Boston, MA, 1852), 679; Virginius Dabney, *Richmond: Story of a City* (Garden City, NY, 1976), 43; Arthur Schlesinger, Jr., *The Age of Jackson* (Boston, MA, 1946), 27 (Taylor and Macon); Daniel E. Sutherland, *Seasons of War: The Ordeal of a Confederate Community, 1861–1865* (New York, 1995), 21 (Culpeper); Harriet Martineau, *Retrospect of Western Travel*, 2 vols. (London, 1838), 1:165. "Principles of Christian Economy," *DD*, 1:20; T. C. Johnson, *Thomas Cary Johnson*, ed. *Life and Letters of Robert Lewis Dabney* (Carlisle, PA, 1977), 54.

Charleston Chivalry, some of whom enjoyed putting-on-the-dog. One such dandy caught the eye of Francis Lieber when he showed up in a green cashmere coat, buff vest, loose-fitting fine linen pantaloons, ruffled shirt, bell-crowned beaver hat, white silk stockings, low quartered pumps, and a black silk Barcelona handkerchief around his neck.[17]

"Raleigh people ape city manners," an amused William Hooper Haigh of North Carolina observed. A Whiggish young lawyer, he attended "a brilliant conversational soiree at Genl. Saunder's" in the mid-1840s:

"Prince Haywood" & his retinue were there dressed out in all the trumpery & gee gaws of fashionable finery – He, the democratic aristocratic gloved up Senator – strutted the room in all the dignity & grandeur of a high born noble–and the creatures of fashion carried his chapeau under his arm the whole evening, ... rigged out in all his senatorial finery and ginger bread work.

[Saunders and Haywood] pursue the two extremes in dressing. Haywood, regardless of fashion, preferring comfort in the other extreme – his "strapless'" nankeens being a source of unbounded merriment during the whole political canvass – and like a genuine Locofoco – he has not discarded them now that he has a due respect for their memory – they having done good service and told well with the profanum vulgus.[18]

William H. Crawford of Georgia hated dandyism, which he considered antithetical to intellectuality, and he knew of only two exceptions, one of whom was probably William Pinkney. Governor Troup had, in the words of Dr. James Holmes, "a superlative contempt for fashions, and whatever the cut of the coat might be, he wore his easy frock with standing collar. He despised a hat and generally wore a fur cap, winter and summer." Still, even in the early years of the nineteenth century, upcountry planters like South Carolina's Wade Hampton, who dressed in the plain style of the yeomanry, disdained the ostentation of the lowcountry planters. The upcountry people, rich and middling, wore gray or brown homespun, while the lowcountry planters and their ladies were wearing the latest English fashions. In later years, John C, Calhoun and Chancellor William Harper dressed carelessly and – allegedly – sometimes in bad taste.[19]

---

[17] Ernest C. Hynds, *Antebellum Athens and Clarke County, Georgia* (Athens, GA, 1974), 124; J. S. Buckingham, *The Slave States of America*, 2 vols. (New York, 1968 [1842]), 1:75; N. R. Middleton, "Reminiscences," in Middleton, et al, *Life in the Carolinas and New England*, 195; Frank Freidel, *Francis Lieber: Nineteenth-Century Liberal* (Gloucester, MA, 1968), 128.

[18] A. C. McIntosh to Amanda McIntosh, Dec. 12, 1848 in McIntosh Papers; Haigh Diary, Apr. 19, 1844.

[19] Stephen Meats and Edwin T. Arnold, eds., *The Writings of Benjamin F. Perry*, 3 vols. (Spartanburg, SC, 1980), 2:134 (Crawford); James Holmes, *"Dr. Bullie's"*

In Marion, a typical black-belt town founded in 1819 as Muckle Ridge in Perry County, Alabama, respectable, churchgoing gentlemen did not much fuss over styles of dress in the mid-1820s, wearing homespun brown jeans, pants, and jackets. At a Baptist meeting in 1832 only three men showed up in broadcloth. But the cotton boom had already begun to change everything. Increasingly, notable public figures in Alabama became known for fashionable dress, among them Benjamin F. Porter, distinguished Alabama jurist from the South Carolina elite. William Russell Smith cultivated the appearance of a Spanish cavalier in the cut and style of his coat. Judge William Harris Hardy took pains to dress meticulously. The more fashionable young gentlemen of Natchez had their suits tailor-made in Philadelphia for $100 each, and they bought their shoes from New York or Paris for $10 to $14 a pair. The gentlemen, whether more or less fashion-conscious, wore one item in common: a whip.[20]

Men who sought office had to be careful to dress in a manner congenial to local taste. Powhattan Ellis ruined his career in Mississippi, where he represented the Democratic Party in a markedly aristocratic style. While fording a stream on the campaign trail, he lost his portmanteau. Franklin Plummer, a rival, thereupon published an advertisement: "Lost by Hon. Powhattan Ellis, in crossing the Tallahala, the following articles: 6 lawn handkerchiefs; 6 cambric shirts; 2 night do.; 1 nightcap; 1 pr. stays; 4 pr. silk stockings; hair brush; flesh-brush; clothes brush; razors and dressing-glass, portmanteau, perfume, Etc. etc." Ellis never recovered.[21]

DANCING

Young gentlemen in colonial Virginia were expected to dance well. "Virginians are of genuine blood," said Philip Fithian. "They will dance or die." Since the eighteenth century, the gentry and the middle classes of the towns encouraged their children to study in flourishing music schools or with private tutors. The College of William and Mary pressured students to dance well, and itinerant dance masters throve in Williamsburg.

Notes: *Reminiscences of Early Georgia and of Philadelphia and New Haven in the 1800s,* ed. Delma Eugene Presley (Atlanta, GA, 1976), 91–92; Rachel N. Klein, *Unification of a Slave State: The Rise of the Planter Class in the South Carolina Backcountry, 1760–1808* (Chapel Hill, NC, 1992), 157; John Niven, *John C. Calhoun and the Price of Union: A Biography* (Baton Rouge, LA, 1988), 26; Clyde Wilson, Introduction to *JCCP,* 14:xii; Lillian Kibler, *Benjamin F. Perry, Unionist* (Durham, NC, 1946), 62 (Harper).

[20] Harnett T. Kane. *Natchez on the Mississippi* (New York, 1947), 15, 221.

[21] J. F. H. Claiborne, *Mississippi as a Province, Territory, and State, with Biographical Notices of Eminent Citizens* (Spartanburg, SC, 1978 [1880]), 426

Sir William Gooch, governor of Virginia, boasted that he had "not an ill dancer in my government." Dancing classes spread across Virginia as part of young people's education. Groups met in a private residence – say, the Carters' Nomini Hall – where participants lodged overnight. Parents and friends often accompanied pupils to classes conducted by dance masters. After the Reverend Hugh Jones, professor at the College of William and Mary, recommended the teaching of music, dancing, and fencing, the college provided facilities for instruction until a dancing school appeared in Williamsburg.[22]

And so in South Carolina, Georgia, and westward. In 1802, Governor John Drayton referred to dancing as "a favorite amusement" and to South Carolina's ladies as excellent dancers. Masters and schools became standard features in Charleston, Columbia, and other towns in South Carolina. Lowcountry women acquired a reputation as the most dance-and-music-loving women in America. Every female academy taught dancing, as did many male academies. Colleges taught dancing or arranged to have students take private lessons off-campus, with or without academic credit. Towns as crude as Atlanta and as elegant as Savannah supported dance instructors and schools for both sexes. The young Langdon Cheves, working as a merchant's apprentice, secured a dance instructor and tutor in French on his rise into the gentry. Occasionally, love affairs began at co-ed dancing schools.[23]

[22] Hunter Dickinson Farish, ed., *Journal and Letters of Philip Fithian: A Plantation Tutor of the Old Dominion, 1773–1774* (Charlottesville, VA, 1957), Aug, 25, 1774 (xxx–xxxi); Gooch quoted in Robert Allen Rutland, *George Mason: Reluctant Statesman* (Baton Rouge, LA, 1961), 7; Edmund Pendleton to William Woodford, June 14, 1777, in Robert Allen Rutland, ed., *The Papers of George Mason, 1725–1792*, 3 vols. (Chapel Hill, NC, 1970), 1:213–214. John Drayton, "A Traveling Governor's View, 1802," in Thomas D. Clark, ed., *South Carolina: The Grand Tour, 1780–1865* (Columbia, SC), 27. Richard Beale Davis, *Intellectual Life in the Colonial South, 1515–1763*, 3 vols. (Knoxville, TN, 1978), 3:1267; Ed.'s Introd. Hugh Jones, *The Present State of Virginia: From Whence Is Inferred a Short View of Maryland and North Carolina*, ed. Richard L. Morton (Chapel Hill, NC, 1956), 11, 111; Dumas Malone, *Jefferson and His Time*, 6 vols. (Charlottesville, VA, 1989), 1:47; Taylor Diary, March 14, 1786, Nov. 14, 1795, Oct. 5, 1787, April 20, 1791; Albert Stoutamire, *Music of the South: Colony to Confederacy* (Rutherford, NJ, 1973), 53, 60–61; D. S. Freeman, "Aristocracy of the Northern Neck," *SBN*, 10:70.
[23] Eola Willis, *The Charleston Stage in the XVIII Century* (Columbia, SC, 1924), 9; Archie Vernon Huff, Jr., *Langdon Cheves of South Carolina* (Columbia, SC, 1977), 25; Walter J. Fraser, Jr. *Charleston! Charleston!: The History of a Southern City* (Columbia, SC, 1989), 131; Ravenel Diary, Jan. 10, 1811, Jan. 15, 1812, Jan. 5, 1813, Henry Edmund Ravenel, *Ravenel Records* (Atlanta, GA, 1898); *DHE*, 1:662–663 (North Carolina); Charles C. Jones, Jr. and Salem Dutcher, *Memorial History of Augusta* (Syracuse, NY, 1890), 229. Also, Willie P. Mangum to Charity Mangum, Jan. 10, 1848, and William

Dance teachers fared well, whether formally attached to a college or conveniently in residence nearby. As a West Point cadet, Thomas ("Stonewall") Jackson learned to dance well in a required course. French refugees, especially exiled nobles, excelled as instructors in dance and fencing in the many private dancing schools. Émigrés from revolution-torn St. Domingue included a large number of musicians or, more likely, dispossessed aristocrats (*grand blancs*), well versed in music, who sought ways to support themselves. Germans accounted for a substantial portion of the makers and tuners of musical instruments, although most settled in the North. In Mississippi, J. J. Audubon, the ornithologist and painter, maintained himself as a dance instructor, sponsored by the prestigious Judge Henry Cage. Calhoun approved when his daughter Anna Maria sent her boys to dancing school: "It is a desirable accomplishment and an almost indispensable appendix to the social intercourse of the two sexes in early life." There were occasional embarrassments. Sara Agnes Rice of Virginia described her French music teacher as a "brilliant pianist" and a "genius," but, unhappily, he squandered his large salary and made himself persona non grata by accumulating IOUs.[24]

Balls and dances provided affluent youth with an early taste of *la dolce vita*. John Howard, a student at the University of North Carolina, attended half a dozen parties in his home town of Nashville in 1845. To his sister he described an impressive evening at Miss Mary Bosnall's, "one of the most beautiful, decidedly the most accomplished and among the richest of the 'upper ten thousand.'" He was "presented (Never say introduced!)" to some of the most beautiful creatures that ever whirled through a cotillion." The hotels, music schools, even courthouses in Nashville, Natchez, and other towns held "cotillion parties" at which admission cost two dollars or so. At courthouse dances in Georgia those with shoes and stockings danced the cotillion, those without danced the "scamper down" (Virginia reel). Bernhard, Duke of Saxe-Weimar Eisenach sniffed at the popularity of the cotillion in upper-class southern circles – danced "in the manner of the tedious German quadrilles." In the South Carolina piedmont and in towns like Greensboro, Alabama, ladies and gentlemen long preferred the Virginia reel and cotillion, but slowly

    Preston Mangum to Martha Mangum, Feb. 10, 1848, in Shanks, ed., *Mangum Papers*, 5:90, 97.
[24] Byron Farwell, *Stonewall: A Biography of General Thomas J. Jackson* (New York, 1992), 28; John Seymour Erwin, *Like Some Green Laurel: Letters of Margaret Johnson Erwin, 1821–1863* (Baton Rouge, LA, 1981), xiv, xv; *JCCP*, 22:263; Roger Pryor [Sara Agnes Rice Pryor], *My Day: Reminiscences of a Long Life* (EE: 1997 [1909]), 49.

warmed up to the round dance introduced by French settlers. Belles and beaux thought St. Valentine's Day a wonderful excuse for a round of balls in town, and it long provided an occasion to pack the theaters in Charleston. St. Valentine's Day became a favorite with the young ladies, who made elaborate preparations at school. Across the South, it provided a spirited holiday on the plantations.[25]

Once or twice a year, elite planters hosted a ball in their plantation homes. Toward the end of the evening formal dancing might give way to free-style dancing copied from the blacks. With the onset of oppressive summer heat, dancing shifted to moonlit lawns. Frequently, slaves congregated to watch, and, if white perceptions were correct, they enjoyed the watching as much as the whites enjoyed the dancing. No one bothered to ask the slaves what exactly they enjoyed. The Virginia version of the African jig became a favorite in the eighteenth century. It became customary for gentleman to kiss their ladies after dancing the jig. Frequent dances on the frontier, as far away as Texas, spiced life despite the shortage of women. Dances in Arkansas tended toward the wild side, featuring an abundance of liquor. Teenage Texans rode for miles to dance to a piano or fiddle at all-night parties, the girls dressed in lace-trimmed pantalets with pierced ears, rings, beads, and pig-tails. In 1848, Rutherford B. Hayes of Ohio visited the plantation of his friend, Guy M. Bryan, in Texas and reported a social life of endless balls and parties. Guests rode ten to twenty miles, arriving in the afternoon and staying overnight. Hayes judged as worthy of sophisticated city life the singing of the young ladies, the amusements, and the refinement of the log-cabin world on the Brazos. From South Carolina to the Mississippi Delta young people seized excuses to dance deep into the night, sometimes till dawn.[26]

---

[25] John Howard to E. R. Howard, May 4, 1845; Garvin Davenport, *Cultural Life in Nashville on the Eve of the Civil War* (Chapel Hill, NC, 1941), 29, 167; Bernhard, Duke of Saxe-Weimar Eisenach, *Travels Through North America during the Years 1825 and 1826* 2 vols. (Philadelphia, 1818), 1:209; on the round dance see Grady McWhiney, *Cracker Culture: Celtic Ways in the Old South* (Tuscaloosa, AL, 1988), 113. Also, Douglas Summers, *A City without Cobwebs: A History of Rock Hill, South Carolina* (Columbia, SC, 1953), 68–69; William Edward Wadsworth Yerby, *History of Greensboro, Alabama from Its Earliest Settlement*, ed. Mabel Yerby Lawson (Northport, AL, 1963 [1908]), 18. For St. Valentine's Day see Burge Diary, Feb. 14, 1847, in James I. Robertson, Jr., ed., *The Diary of Dolly Lunt Burge* (Athens, GA, 1962), 4; Eleanor P. Cross and Charles B. Cross, Jr., eds., *Glencoe Diary: The War-Time Journal of Elizabeth Curtis Wallace* (Chesapeake, VA, 1968), Dec. 14, 1863 (94). Music and dance teachers were often addressed as "Professor."

[26] Alexander MacKay, *The Western World; Or, Travels in the United States in 1846–1847*, 3 vols. (New York, 1968 [1849]), 2:82; J. A. Leo Lemay, ed., *Robert Bolling Woos Anne Miller: Love and Courtship in Colonial Virginia, 1760* (Charlottesville, VA, 1990), 2–4;

Only the worst weather kept large crowds from attending parties and balls. Even the gales and raw cold in Georgia proved no deterrent. Clifford Alexander teased his mother, "You must be getting very gay and dissipated in your tastes to ride forty miles to a party – you go quite ahead of the girls there." In the early days of settlement in the Southwest social life evolved around hamlets and villages, not private parties. Even small towns had public (commercial) balls, which drew young people from thirty miles or more. As early as 1837, Houston's gala "San Jacinto Ball" printed invitations on white satin. Men and women traveled with servants up to sixty miles to attend. Dances, some lavish, became the rage in towns and on large plantations, although in the more frontier-like areas the acute shortage of women compelled men to dance with each other. Methodist and Baptist critics condemned dancing, but to little effect.[27]

Every belle coveted the popularity accorded a superior dancer. "Cousin Sally is too pretty," Saida Bird of Georgia wrote to her father, "and, oh, you just ought to see her dance." Cousin Sally, who knew all the current dances, "taught me the polka, schottisch, mazurka, and is going to teach me to waltz." Sixteen-year-old Louisa Quitman of Mississippi enjoyed herself at Robert Dunbar's delightful party. Dancing continued until 2 A.M., she reported to her father, and, "to add to the fun, for the boys called it fun," a thunderstorm compelled the guests to stay overnight. "Four rooms were filled, two for ladies, and girls, one with boys, and another with gentlemen." Three years later Louisa again wrote to her father: "I expect that you will think I am becoming quite dissipated when you hear that I have been to another party." Maybe she referred to the elite ball in Natchez attended by John Wistar Metcalfe, a young planter, who arrived at 8 P. M. and left at 4 A. M.[28]

John Gould Fletcher, *Arkansas* (Fayetteville, AR, 1989), 84; Camilla Davis Trammel, *Seven Pines: Its Occupants and Their Letters, 1825–1872* (Dallas, TX, 1986 68; Abigail Curlee, "The History of a Texas Slave Plantation, 1831–1863" *Southwestern Historical Quarterly*, 26 (1922), 113–114 (Hayes); Diary of Harry St. John Dixon, Jan. 17, 1860 and Diary of John Albert Feaster Coleman, Feb. 10, 1849, in Berry, ed., *Princes of Cotton*, 33, 313.

[27] Carmichael Diary, Feb. 17, 1838; Clifford Alexander to Mother, in Marion A. Boggs, ed., *The Alexander Letters, 1787–1900* (Athens, GA, 2002), 181; Hogan, *Texas Republic*, 50; Ingraham, *South-West*, 2:206; John Hebron Moore, *The Emergence of the Cotton Kingdom in Old Southwest: Mississippi, 1770–1860* (Baton Rouge, LA, 1988), 187–188.

[28] Sallie (Saida) Bird to Edgeworth Bird, June 21, 1863, in John Rozier, ed., *The Granite Farm Letters: The Civil War Correspondence of Edgeworth and Sallie Bird* (Athens, GA, 1988), 112. Also, Mary Granger, ed., *Savannah River Plantations* (Spartanburg, SC, 1983), 428–429; Louisa Quitman to John A. Quitman, Jan. 9, 1840, May 2, 1843 in J. A. Quitman Papers; Metcalfe Diary, Feb, 22, 1843, also March 3, 1843.

The waltz, which Saida Bird considered perfectly respectable, had a checkered history in the South. British travelers discovered that Americans considered the waltz indelicate. In 1805, the French consul in Charleston appalled Mrs. Manigault, Mrs. Middleton, and other high-society ladies by hosting a ball that featured the waltz. The ladies had seen the waltz in Europe and thought this version indecorous. Americans long objected to the manner in which the waltz paired couples off. By the mid-1830s, New Englanders continued to resist the waltz, but Southerners yielded to what many thought risqué. The Tylers caused something of a stir when they introduced the waltz and polka to the White House. Still, until the War, gentlemen in Charleston kept their wives and sisters from participating, while they danced with other women.[29]

Dancing angered the Protestant clergy. Presbyterians, who prided themselves on orthodoxy and church discipline, came down hard. Ministers pleaded with their flock not to send children to dancing schools – those "nurseries of greater evils" – and some large and genteel parties lacked music and dancing in deference to the clergy and strict communicants. Despite local victories, not even the formidable clergy kept the flock in check. In Columbia, the Reverend Benjamin Morgan Palmer refused to baptize children of parents who taught them to dance, and he threatened to resign as pastor when the Church hesitated to crack down. Church courts proceeded apace with charges against communicants but with indifferent results, especially among the young. Prohibition of dancing at weddings met with stiff opposition. Even the prestigious and intransigent Palmer suffered intense frustration. Prominent laymen and some ministers permitted dancing in their homes. As early as the 1830s, the Church – discernibly if uneasily – was making peace with the inevitable.[30]

[29] George C. Rogers, Jr., *Evolution of a Federalist: William Loughton Smith of Charleston, 1758–1812* (Columbia, SC, 1962), 356–357 (consul); Jane Louis Mesick, *The English Traveller in America, 1785–1835* (New York, 1922), 95; Norma Lois Peterson, *The Presidency of William Henry Harrison and John Tyler* (Lawrence, KS, 1989), 237; Caroline R. Ravenel to Isabella Middleton Smith, Dec. 15, 1862, in Smith, et al., eds., *Mason-Smith Family Letters*, 21.

[30] Thomas Cary Johnson, *The Life and Letters of Benjamin Morgan Palmer* (Richmond, VA, 1906), 94–97, 123; Doralyn J. Hickey, "Benjamin Morgan Palmer: Churchman of the Old South" (Ph.D. diss.; Duke University, 1962), 46–47; Margaret Burr DesChamps, "The Presbyterian Church in the South Atlantic States, 1801–1861" (Ph.D. diss; Emory University, 1952), 44–45, 119–124; William Davidson Blanks, "Ideal and Practice: A Study of the Conception of the Christian Life Prevailing in the Presbyterian Churches of the South during the Nineteenth Century" (Th.D., Union Theological Seminary, 1960), 233–242; Ernest Trice Thompson, *Presbyterians in the South*, 3 vols. (Richmond, VA, 1963), 1:320–322. For a defense of dancing by a pious young South Carolina Baptist, see Kathryn Carlisle Schwartz, *Baptist Faith in Action: The Private Writings of Maria*

Mary E. Moragné much admired "old Doctor [Moses] Waddel" but seemed amused and irritated by his blasts at dancing. She may have known, as Mrs. Roger Pryor did, that Waddel's renowned ancestor, the Reverend James Waddel (the famous "blind preacher"), created a scandal among Presbyterians in Virginia by allowing his daughters to dance: "No parent has a right to make his children unfit for polite society." During the 1840s and 1850s, the Presbyterian stronghold of Lexington, Virginia, failed to suppress dancing among younger communicants. At Georgia's White Sulphur Springs, Mary Dean, a strict Presbyterian, attended balls, not to dance but to hear the sweet music performed by Mr. Bacon's school at LaGrange. She saw, however, a good many Presbyterian and Methodist youngsters dancing.[31]

The Reverend Robert Lewis Dabney, writing on "the dancing question" after the War, reviewed the long-standing objections of the Presbyterian Church. The ancients, he said, considered dancing undignified entertainment fit primarily for slaves and the lower classes, and the early Christian Church rejected it as sinful. The stern Southern Presbyterian churches firmly condemned it down to the middle of the nineteenth century, but Dabney sadly acknowledged that it was slowly yielding to popular pressure and failing to discipline members for dancing. That the Church tolerated sinful behavior was bad enough; worse, Dabney feared an attendant evil – the weakening of the Church's power – its "didactic function" – and a proper understanding of the nature of Christian liberty.[32]

The Episcopalians faced criticism from other churches for their alleged toleration and even encouragement of dancing. Abigail Cattin, writing to fellow Presbyterians from Pensacola in 1838, snippily described the Episcopalian Mrs. Rochester as "quite a dressy woman" who considered dancing parties innocent fun. The Methodist Reverend William Winans went into a towering rage when, espying Episcopalian influence, he found a church "arranged for dancing." In the Carolina low country and parts

Baker Taylor, 1813–1895 (Columbia, SC, 2003), 35–36. For Thornwell's opposition to dancing, see James Oscar Farmer, Jr., *The Metaphysical Confederacy: James Henley Thornwell and the Synthesis of Southern Values* (Macon, GA, 1986), 171–172. In the 1880s, the *SPR* was still debating the Church's position on dancing.

31 Mary E. Moragné Journal, Mar. 28, 1837, in Delle Mullen Craven, ed., *The Neglected Thread: A Journal of the Calhoun Community* (Columbia, SC, 1951), 32; Mrs. Pryor, *Mother of Washington*, 64; Ollinger Crenshaw, *General Lee's College: the Rise and Growth of Washington and Lee University* (New York, 1969), 77–78; Mary Dean to James Norman, July 29, 1851, in Susan Lott, Clark, *Southern Letters and Life in the Mid 1800s* (Waycross, GA, 1993), 85.

32 "The Dancing Question," *DD*, 2:560–593.

of Virginia, although Episcopalian ministers vehemently forbade communicants from dancing and attending horse races, many churchgoers bristled at the clerical hostility. Low-church Episcopalians erupted when citizens of Charleston arranged a ball for Henry Clay in 1844, but they directed their fire against its being scheduled for the Sabbath, thereby winning support from men like J. L. Petigru, who might not have objected on other grounds.[33]

Early in the eighteenth century, the Episcopal Reverend James Blair, president of the College of William and Mary, acted as a judge at a horse race and boasted of the College chapel, "This is the most useful place in the College, for here we sometimes preach and pray, and sometimes we fiddle and dance; the one to edify, and the other to divert us." In the 1820s, Bishop Moore preached against balls and the theater, but, taking the measure of the resistance, reigned himself in. President Thomas Roderick Dew of the College of William and Mary, an Episcopalian, seemed puzzled by the ruckus. In *Digest of the Laws, Customs, Manners, and Institutions of the Ancient and Modern Nations* – his history of Western Civilization – he avoided current controversies but observed, "Some commentators suppose every psalm had an appropriate dance." Ann Maury, who heard the bishop deliver an "excellent sermon" against amusements, "felt smote to think I should be going to a gay party in the evening." Ann Pettigrew declined to participate and did not dance at the one ball she attended. New Bern, she remarked six years later, is "so gay, so hospitable. What a place for rich people this New Bern is."[34]

---

[33] Abigail Cattin to Misses Simpson, Jan. 15, 1838, in Simpson Papers; Ray Holder, *William Winans: Methodist Leader in Antebellum Mississippi* (Jackson, MS, 1977), 170; William Watson Manross, *The Episcopal Church in the United States, 1800–1840: A Study in Church Life* (New York, 1938), 50; Emily Wharton Sinkler to Thomas Isaac Wharton (1851), in Anne Sinkler Whaley LeClerq, ed., *Between North and South: The Letters of Emily Wharton Sinkler, 1842–1865* (Columbia, SC, 2001), 143; James Petigru Carson, *Life, Letters and Speeches of James Louis Petigru: Union Man of South Carolina* (Washington, DC, 1920), 238.

[34] Jones, *Present State of Virginia*, ed. Morton, 11; H. S. Lewis, "Formation of the Diocese," in Lawrence Foushee London and Sarah McCulloh Lemmon, eds., *The Episcopal Church in North Carolina, 1701–1959* (Raleigh, NC, 1987), 163 (Moore); Diary, June 23, 1863, in A. J. L. Fremantle, *Three Months in the Southern States: The 1863 Diary of an English Soldier, April–June 1863* (London, 1863), 234; Thomas Roderick Dew, *Digest of the Laws, Customs, Manners, and Institutions of the Ancient and Modern Nations* (New York, 1884 [1852]), 14; Diary, Mar, 7, 1831, in Anne Fontaine Maury, *Intimate Virginiana: A Century of Maury Travels by Land and Sea* (Richmond, VA, 1941). In Lemmon, ed., *Pettigrew Papers*, see Ann Blount Pettigrew to Ebenezer Pettigrew, Feb. 1, 1818 (1:598), Mar. 12, 1818, Apr. 20, 1824 (1:610).

In North Carolina not only sophisticated New Bern but Locust Hill, Morganton, Warrenton, Fayetteville, and Hillsboro had reading societies, debating clubs, masked balls, and elaborate picnics, which drew praise from European travelers. Susan Nye Hutchinson took a jaundiced view. She "certainly should not want to live in Fayette where every day sees a party somewhere." Evangelicals like Hutchinson gave Charles Biddle Shepard, an Episcopalian, a pain. He was doubly glad that relatives and friends were coming to visit, since a great religious revival was sweeping the usually gay town of New Bern and "has thrown a gloom over the town & I really wish to see some one who can enjoy a laugh without thinking he has committed a sin. Old Madam Mae has been converted. Divers others have given up the pomp & vanity of life to become – I was about to say hypocrites, but I will be more charitable." In 1853, Eliza Quitman of Mississippi complained when the Baptist and Methodist revival in Jackson repressed dancing among the large number of converts. She asked her daughter, "What can the Church be about to let all this happen?" Ellen House found a preacher's condemnation of dancing "perfectly ridiculous." She wished he had "waited till next Sunday for his lecture," for then "it would not have interfered with us, or our dance."[35]

"The bolt has fallen," cried the young Eliza Frances Andrews of Georgia. "Mr. Adams, the Methodist minister, launched the thunders of the church against dancing, in his morning discourse." Adams amused her when he "placed dancing in the same category with bribery, gambling, drunkenness, and murder." She only wished that an Episcopal Church were available "to serve as a refuge for the many worthy people who are not gamblers and murderers, but who like to indulge in a little dancing now and then." Dr. and Mrs. William Butler of South Carolina, regular churchgoing Episcopalians, loved music and dancing, and Judge Huger agreed, believing that people ought "to live for both this world and the next." Pious Episcopalians in the Southwest scoffed at arguments against dancing, card-playing, and other pleasures they dubbed innocent. Dr. David Holt of Wilkinson County, Mississippi, an Episcopalian, invited his children to play cards with him at night, after which he read from the Bible that rested on the same table. The Episcopalian Lucy Breckenridge thought well of the

---

[35] Hutchinson Journal, Apr. 12, 181; Charles Biddle Shepard to Ebenezer Pettigrew, Oct. 26, 1829, in Lemmon, ed., *Pettigrew Papers*, 2:41, 2:125; Daniel E. Sutherland, ed., *The Diary of Ellen Renshaw House* (Knoxville, TN, 1996), Mar. 28, 1865 (166).

Presbyterian Reverend Thomas Grasty but ignored his "severe sermon" against dancing.[36]

Against heavy odds, the Methodist preachers carried their war against dancing to great lengths. Yet in the Southwest, while the Presbyterians were waging a strong and partially successful campaign against dancing, the Baptists and Methodists, who were in principle no less opposed, proved lax in enforcement of discipline. The forty-six-year-old Methodist Bishop George Foster Pierce of Georgia, who earned a reputation for integrity and sophistication, claimed to have seen dancing for the first time in his life on a trip to Kentucky in 1857. Since Pierce had presided over a women's college, what are we to think? The experience of Moncure Conway, while a Methodist minister in Virginia, stands for many others. When he preached against dancing, an irritated family moved to another church. Malinda B. Ray, a Presbyterian schoolgirl in Fayetteville, North Carolina, regularly attended a Methodist church and Sabbath school, but neither kept her from dancing. The girls at her female academy seized every recess to practice dancing. Mary Jeffreys Bethell, a devout Methodist, rebuked herself for letting her daughter attend a dancing party: "I done wrong, and have been sorry for it." That her daughter thereafter quit dancing may be doubted. The editors of the Methodist *Weekly Messenger* of Greensborough, North Carolina, presented a typical church view in 1852: "Social parties might be made the means of doing good, the means of moral and intellectual improvement." But, recalling St. Paul's strictures against jesting and foolishness, the editors protested that current parties lacked devotion and prayer. Unfortunately, they did not suggest how to have a good time at devotional, prayerful parties. The editors acknowledged that youthful readers, thinking them puritanical, pressed for reform.[37]

[36] Eliza Frances Andrews, *War-Time Journal of a Georgia Girl, 1864–1865* (New York, 1907), Aug. 27, 1865 (382); Stephen Meats and Edwin T. Arnold, eds., *The Writings of Benjamin F. Perry,* 3 vols. (Spartanburg, SC, 1980), 2:57 (Huger); Thomas D. Cockrell and Michael B. Ballard, eds., *A Mississippi Rebel in the Army of Northern Virginia: The Civil War Memoirs of Private David Holt* (Baton Rouge, LA, 1995), 4; Mary D. Robertson, ed., *Lucy Breckinridge of Grove Hill: The Journal of a Virginia Girl, 1826–1864* (Kent, OH, 1979), Jan. 20, 1864 (168); Beatty Diary, Apr, 26, 1843.

[37] Walter Brownlow Posey, *Frontier Mission: A History of Religion West of the Southern Appalachians to 1861* (Lexington, KY, 1966), 321–322; George G. Smith, *The Life and Times of George Foster Pierce, Bishop of the Methodist Church, South, with a Sketch of Lovick Pierce, D. D., His Father* (Sparta, GA, 1888), 329. On the Methodist campaign against dancing see, e.g., "Autobiography," in William M. Wightman, *Life of William Capers, D. D., One of the Bishops of the Methodist Episcopal Church, South, Including an Autobiography* (Nashville, TN, 1902), 57; R. H. Rivers, *The Life of Robert*

Religious folks designed parties without liquor or dancing and reproached neighbors who lapsed. David Hays of Haywood County, Tennessee, threw a "Great Tea Party" for his churchgoing neighbors. Lucy Fletcher, from a minister's family, sighed with relief when her visiting friend Charlotte Chapman had a good time without dancing: "She ever seemed happy with us – her presence was like a sunbeam." Upon joining a church, some young people gave up dancing but not the determination to enjoy life. Ferdinand Lawrence Steel, a Methodist farmer, took singing but not dancing lessons. Ella Clanton Thomas gave up dancing when she professed Christianity in 1858, but she spent "a delightful winter as a gay girl of fashion."[38]

Governor David Rogerson Williams of South Carolina, in the last year of his life, looked forward to a wedding or a ball: "A chance to laugh and be fat is a primary duty of life." In Louisiana mirth greeted campaigns against dancing and easy living. The influence of Spanish gayety also lingered in Florida and southern Alabama. St. Augustine sported frequent balls, high-stakes gambling, cock and dog fights, and charivari. Although New Orleans was the great social center, good times in the sugar parishes ran high, with frequent plantation parties and a steady stream of guests.

Cajun communities held Saturday night dances in private homes, open to one and all, provided decently dressed. They forbade alcohol and served chicken gumbo with rice at midnight. When the Americans took possession of Louisiana, the French feared that they would prohibit balls. Governor William Claiborne reassured them after warning Secretary of State James Madison not to take the issue lightly. Hostile Protestant ministers did not hold their congregations. At carnival season the good times rolled, and balls went on even during Lent. The passion for dancing among all classes stunned foreigners. Elite and lower-class youth joined in public dances. Notwithstanding puritanical protests, the Catholic Church did not consider dancing sinful, frowning severely only

---

Paine, D. D., Bishop of the Methodist Church, South (Nashville, TN, 1916), 200–201; Peter Walker, *Moral Choices: Memory, Desire, and Imagination in Nineteenth-Century American Abolition* (Baton Rouge, LA, 1978), 235, n. 21 (Conway); Malinda Ray Diary, Jan. 6, 8, 1861 and generally 1860–1861; Bethell Diary, Feb. 14, 1857; *Weekly Messenger*, June 14, 1852. For a lament at dancing by Methodist youth see, Thomas O. Summers, ed., *Autobiography of the Rev. Joseph Travis* (Nashville, TN, 1854), 232.

[38] John Walker Diary, Feb. 2, 1839; Haralson Diary, Sept. 22, 1846; Fletcher "Autobiography" (ms.), 1841; Steel Diaries, July 5, 1839; Thomas Diary, Apr. 8, 1855. Sarah Childress Polk, a Presbyterian, tolerated no dancing in the White House: Anson Nelson and Fannie Nelson, *Memorials of Sarah Childress Polk* (Spartanburg, SC, 1980 [1892]), 92–93.

on violations of Lent. In New Orleans private and public balls, dance schools, and private teachers became the rage, with boleros, gavottes, cotillions, waltzes, mazurkas, reels, minuets, and especially quadrilles. Before long, New Orleans boasted ballrooms unsurpassed in size and splendor. The elegant St. Charles and St. Louis hotels held special balls for children as young as four prior to the adult balls that attracted prostitutes and invited promiscuity.[39]

The campaign against dancing eventually won support from married women who evinced sour grapes. Yet, at the turn of the nineteenth century in Charleston and Richmond, married women participated freely in the balls. By the 1820s, Mary Hamilton Campbell of Abingdon, Virginia, felt "imprisoned" by rules that excluded married women from the gay life. Even so, she asked rhetorically: "After all, what has a woman of my age to do with the world of fashion?" She did not want to be among those who enjoyed dissipation during the week and then tried to atone on Sunday. "You see," she wrote to her husband David, "I have the happy disposition to make the best of my situation." In the 1850s, Charles Fraser remarked a bit ruefully: "Dancing is now exclusively the amusement of the young." In Mississippi, Flavellus Nicholson and his wife had a sumptuous dinner and a grand time at a party given by Mr. Wingate. Nicholson groaned, "I would not be surprised if this was the last party of any magnitude that I shall be invited to, in a long while, for married people get but few invitations to parties."[40]

Fashionable balls in cities like Charleston and Savannah drew acerbic comments from the more reserved, intellectually inclined, and pious women of the elite, who objected, along with much else, to the popular kissing games. Mary H. Eaton of Tennessee complained that young ladies who aspired to be belles generally turned out to be spoiled and selfish wives whose extravagances propelled their husbands into bankruptcy. The clergy-led campaigns did not eliminate dancing but did encourage

---

[39] Harvey Toliver Cook, *The Life and Legacy of David Rogerson Williams* (New York, 1916), 212; Charles B. Reynolds, *Old Saint Augustine: A Story of Three Centuries*, 5th ed. (St. Augustine, FL, 1891), 117; Carl A. Brasseaux, *Acadian to Cajun: Transformation of a People, 1803–1877* (Jackson, MS, 1992), 28–29; J. Carlyle Sitterson, "The McCollams: A Planter Family of the Old and New South," *JSH*, 6 (1940), 355–356. In general, see Henry A. Kmen, *Music in New Orleans: The Formative Years, 1791–1841* (Baton Rouge, LA, 1966), ch. 1. On the St. Charles and St. Louis hotels, see Buckingham, *Slave States*, 1:331; Mrs. [E. M.], Houstoun, *Texas and the Gulf of Mexico; or, Yachting in the Gulf of Mexico* (Austin, TX, 1968 [1845]), 75, 81–82.

[40] Fraser, *Reminiscences of Charleston*, 106–108; Mary Hamilton Campbell to David Campbell, Dec. 1, 1822 in Campbell Family Papers; Nicholson Journal, Dec. 25, 1860.

parents to undertake closer supervision. Kate Carney of Tennessee saw nothing wrong when young ladies danced into the wee hours of the morning, since they were escorted by trustworthy young men. Fannie Page Hume of Virginia reported that smallholders, too, threw their homes open for parties, inviting nearly all the respectable girls of a village. The prudish Alexander Stephens of Georgia considered even such parties beyond the pale. The "flirts & wriggling of some young ladies" threw him into a rage: "abominable, detestable, just such actions as would expect to see the vilest prostitutes in a whorehouse perform!" During the War, Emma Holmes felt "so mortified at the disgraceful character" of Charleston girls "once considered so modest and refined & well behaved." The "ultra fashionables" now seemed "as fast as young women to be found anywhere."[41]

THEATER AND OPERA

In 1665, Pungoteague, Virginia, hosted the first play recorded in English America. During the second decade of the eighteenth century, Williamsburg opened the first theater in British America; Charleston had a permanent theater fifteen years before New York and thirty years before Philadelphia. By the 1790s, a vigorous French theater supplemented the English in Charleston. Each gave three performances a week on alternate evenings. Under pressure from the prestigious Jockey Club, Race Week included performances of Sheridan's *School for Scandal*, Goldsmith's *She Stoops to Conquer*, and other favorites. Planters and merchants supported the theater. So did artisans and mechanics, who usually occupied the balconies and did not always show the gentry respect. In the early nineteenth century, schoolboys in Virginia went to the theater to see Shakespeare as well as Sheridan's *Rivals* and Goldsmith's *She Stoops to Conquer*, and they put on plays in their homes. Still, as late as the 1850s,

---

[41] Christine Jacobson Carter, *Southern Single Blessedness: Unmarried Women in the Urban South, 1800–1865* (Urbana, IL, 2006), 21–22; Mrs. Mary H. Eaton, "Home Secrets–No. V," *Parlor Visitor* (Nashville), 1 (1854), 2–22. Carney Diary, July 20, 1859; Hume Diary, Dec. 28, 1860; Stephens quoted in Thomas E. Schott, *Alexander Stephens of Georgia: A Biography* (Baton Rouge, LA, 1996), 133; Emma Holmes, June 2, 1863, in John F. Marszalek, ed., *The Diary of Miss Emma Holmes* (Baton Rouge, LA, 1979), 264; also, Steven M. Stowe, *Intimacy and Power in the Old South: Ritual in the Lives of the Planters* (Baltimore, 1987, 71. On the rise of subscription dance halls in Charleston in the early nineteenth century, see Nicholas Michael Butler, *Votaries of Apollo: The St. Cecilia Society and the Patronage of Concert Music in Charleston, South Carolina, 1766–1820* (Columbia, SC, 2007), 246–247.

Charles Richard Weld, historian of the British Royal Society, did not enjoy his visit to the theater in Richmond. The coatless audience heartily applauded "atrocious" acting.[42]

The performances varied from excellent to awful, and the clientele varied from cultured to semi-barbarous. In Columbus, Georgia, Buckingham reported a "wretched" theater that was much better attended than the churches. Races, gambling, and balls substituted for the lowest level of literature and art that he had found in American towns. Yet, small towns slowly followed the example of Charleston and Richmond, attracting audiences from miles around. The strength of an easygoing Anglican [later, the Protestant Episcopal] Church and the presence of Huguenots among the well-to-do seaboard planters facilitated the growth of the theater despite attacks from puritanical evangelicals. Most Protestant denominations considered concupiscence a sin in itself. The Catholic and Episcopal churches did not, thereby leaving room for gayety in everyday life. From early days, New Orleans sported a lively theater that often had standing room only. Augusta, Georgia (ca. 1790), attracted famous actors and actresses to its theater. In time, so did the towns of the Southwest, albeit slowly and with difficulty. As early as the 1830s, Houston and other towns in the Republic of Texas had theaters staffed both with professionals and amateurs. *School for Scandal* scored a notable success.[43]

From the earliest times, Christians tended to view the theater as the devil's playground, replete with makeup, costumes, deceit, and illicit pleasures. Presbyterian preachers mounted a pronounced attack on "the world." They drew on Augustine, who, confessing the sins of his youth,

---

[42] Susie M. Ames, *Reading, Writing and Arithmetic in Virginia, 1607–1699* (Williamsburg, VA, 1957), 65; Willis, *Charleston Stage in the XVIII Century*, 7–8, 274, 296, 300; Charles S. Watson, *Antebellum Charleston Dramatists* (University, AL, 1976), 10, 25–26; James H. Dormon, Jr., *Theater in the Ante-Bellum South, 1815–1861* (Chapel Hill, NC, 1967), 32, 136; Susan Dabney Smedes, *Memorials of a Southern Planter*, ed. Fletcher M. Green (New York, 1965 [1887]), 10, 213; Charles Richard Weld, *A Vacation Tour in the United States and Canada* (London, 1855), 324. August Friedrich von Kotzebue brought tears to the eyes of theatergoers, but southern critics thought his writing dreadful: See, e.g., *SLM*, 24 (1857), 252.

[43] Buckingham, *Slave States*, 1:76; Dormon, *Theater in the Ante-Bellum South*, 9; 46; Stoutamire, *Music of the South*, 64; Davis, *Intellectual Life in the Colonial South*, 3:1120, 1280–1281; Paul Tillich, *A History of Christian Thought: From Its Judaic and Hellenistic Origins to Existentialism*, ed. Carl E. Braaten (New York, 1968), 213; Christina Vella, *Intimate Enemies: The Two Worlds of the Baroness de Pontalba* (Baton Rouge, LA, 1997), 34, 86, 378n. 49; S. A. Ferrall, *A Ramble of Six thousand Miles Through the United States of America* (London, 1832), 192; Charles C. Jones, Jr. and Salem Dutcher, *Memorial History of Augusta* (Syracuse, NY, 1890), 291–292; Hogan, *Texas Republic*, 119–128.

assailed the theater "as full of my own miseries." Confronted with the misfortune of others, people are moved not to help but to grieve. George Whitefield assailed the theater as "the devil's masterpiece." Yet, having been an actor in his youth, he scored his greatest successes in no small part by transforming the pulpit into high theater. Southern criticism of the French theater came early and stayed long. At the turn of the century, Francis Kinloch of South Carolina criticized its morals in letters to his daughter in Virginia. By the 1850s, alarmed evangelicals saw the pulpit being transformed into urban entertainment, with the devil as a figure of mirth. "The stage, it cannot be doubted," wrote the Presbyterian Reverend John N. Waddel, a prominent educator, "has ever been the antagonist of the pulpit." The Presbyterian Reverend William S. Plumer of Virginia recalled that even "Rousseau, the infidel," opposed theatergoing and attacked Molière for making immorality attractive. Rousseau in fact had eminent predecessors in hostility to the theater, among them the formidable Blaise Pascal. Plumer declared that by common consent ministers in all Christian communities denounced theatergoing as the first step in a criminal career on the road to hell. He criticized the stage for "adorning bad characters with specious attractions calculated to ensnare the youthful and unwary into the admiration and imitation of gilded vices."[44]

The Presbyterian Reverend Dr. Thomas Smyth of Charleston delivered two discourses in 1838 on "The Theatre, a School of Religion, Manners and Morals!" in which he recommended that Shakespeare's plays be read but not seen. Smyth, supported by representatives of other denominations, scoffed at attempts to view the theater as a school of moral instruction. In Alabama, newspaper editors stressed moral lessons to be drawn from theatrical productions – for example, plays that showed the ill-effects of drinking and gambling. The Methodist Reverend Joseph Cummings and the Baptist Reverend Abiel Sherwood rejected the claim that "the theatre is a school of morals," arguing that, although not intrinsically bad, the

---

[44] Saint Augustine, *Confessions*, tr. Henry Chadwick (New York, 1991), 35–36; Harry S. Stout, *The Divine Dramatist: George Whitefield and the Rise of Modern Evangelism* (Grand Rapids, MI, 1991); [Francis Kinloch], *Letters from Geneva and France*, 2 vols. (Boston, MA, 1819), 1:196–198; *Pensées*, #11, in *Pensées and The Provincial Letters*, tr. W. F. Trotter and Thomas M'Crie (New York, 1941); John N. Waddell, "The Lecture System – Its Influence upon Young Men," *SPR*, 12 (1859), 260; Andrew Delbanco, *The Death of Satan: How Americans Have Lost the Sense of Evil* (New York, 1995), 27, 96; William S. Plumer, *The Law of God, as Contained in the Ten Commandments* (Harrisonburg, VA, 1996 [1864]), 488–504.

theater fell into bad hands, because "[i]t is better calculated to represent vice and grossness, than virtue; and because the virtuous soonest pass the limit where profit and interest in it cease."[45]

The evangelical campaign to suppress the theater as sinful fared poorly in both North and South, although it succeeded in some small towns. In 1793, George Jones, a prominent planter, resigned from the city council of Savannah under pressure after being rebuked by councilmen for his "illiberal, indecorous" opposition to the theater. Episcopalians like the Reverend Jasper Adams of Charleston, who taught moral philosophy, and Bishop J. H. Otey of Tennessee frowned on theatergoing but refrained from joining the Presbyterians and Methodists in all-out assaults. Yet the charge remained sustainable. The theaters attracted prostitutes and gamblers who plied their trades in the third-tier balconies and basement bars, as well as heavy drinkers who continued their night's indulgence. When the Richmond Theater burned in 1811, with seventy burned or trampled to death, many thought it God's punishment for theatergoing. Prostitutes plagued theaters in every American city. Some theaters in New York permitted sexual intercourse in their upper tiers. Even the elegant Park Theater, owned by John Jacob Astor and John Beekman, did little to discourage prostitution at highbrow performances patronized by the local elite.[46]

Shakespeare's plays dominated theater in the South as readily as elsewhere. Thomas Jefferson valued Shakespeare primarily as a great moralist and commentator on human life, but, as the Presbyterian Reverend Dr. Thomas Smyth of Charleston did in later years, he much preferred that Shakespeare's plays be read rather than seen. George Washington,

---

[45] *TSW*, 5:303–348; J. Cummings, "True Dignity of Human Nature and the Evidences of Man's Progress towards It," *Southern Repertory and College Review* 1 (1851), 152; Rhoda Coleman Ellison, *Early Alabama Publications: A Study in Literary Interests* (University, AL, 1947), 80–81; Adiel Sherwood, *"Suffering Disciples Rejoicing in Persecution": The Introductory Discourse, Delivered before the Georgia Baptist Convention at Americus* (Atlanta, GA, 1861), 4. Also, Hutchinson Journal, Feb. 23, 1828.

[46] Watson, *Antebellum Charleston Dramatists*, xv, 1, 11ff, 21–22, 41, 49, chs. 3–4; Richard Barksdale Harwell, *Brief Candle: The Confederate Theatre* (Worcester, MA, 1971), 57, 61 ff, 80. On prostitution in theaters, see Dormon, *Theater in the Ante Bellum South*, 165, 236–237; William Pease and Jane H. Pease, *The Web of Progress: Private Values and Public Styles in Boston and Charleston, 1828–1843* (New York, 1985), 141–142; Hutchinson Diary, Jan. 20, Feb. 3, 17, 22, 1828; Otey Diary, Jan. 6, 1852; Mark K. Bauman, *Warren Akin Candler: The Conservative as Idealist* (Netuchen, NJ, 1981), 51–53; Gaillard Hunt, *As We Were: Life in America, 1814* (Stockbridge, MA, 1993), 86; Timothy Gilfoyle, *City of Eros: New York City, Prostitution, and the Commercialization of Sex, 1790–1820* (New York, 1992), 110.

on the contrary, loved Shakespearean theater. Jefferson's attitude could not appeal to many common people, for on the southern frontier, as in Shakespeare's England, many of the enthusiasts were illiterate or semi-literate. Enthusiasts throughout the South included many more people than cultural *arrivistes* and snobs. In Baltimore, Richmond, Charleston, New Orleans, Vicksburg, and other cities, audiences were drawn from almost all sections of the population. The finest Shakespearean actors appeared often. In any case, between 1800 and 1860, Charleston produced some 600 performances of 23 of Shakespeare's plays, *Hamlet* being the principal favorite, with *Romeo and Juliet* the runner-up. Despite controversy in some quarters, Southerners generally welcomed "Othello," in part by distinguishing swarthy Near East "Moors" from black "Africans." The popularity of the Shakespearean theater had its unpleasant side. A good many of the plays were bowdlerized, and most were cut since they had to share the evening's program with one or more inferior works.[47]

Throughout America, attendance at the theater, concerts, and the opera often reflected a desire to be seen or to sport latest fashions. In Charleston, New Orleans, and Mobile, ladies and gentlemen avoided the theater because of the influx of transient seamen, local workers, prostitutes, and blacks. Audiences behaved raucously, drowning out the voices on stage, drinking, talking, cracking nuts, and chomping apples. Prices were low – a quarter or half dollar – for a seat in the galleries. Rowdies, knowing that there were not enough serious the-atergoers to sustain a theater night after night, used the power of their patronage to lower artistic standards. All over America some actors appeared on stage drunk. The riverboat men took much of the blame for the rowdiness in ports along the Mississippi, but they did seem to take the theater seriously. They attended performances of Shakespeare as well as lighter fare and performed on their steamboats. Shakespeare remained the great favorite everywhere, and *Macbeth*, *Othello*, and

---

[47] Esther Cloudman Dunn, *Shakespeare in America* (New York, 1939), 97–99, 191, 195; Philip C. Kolin, "Shakespeare in the South: An Overview," in Kolin, ed., *Shakespeare in the South: Essays on Performance* (Jackson, MS, 1983), 10–11, and see Joseph Patrick, Roppolo, "Shakespeare in New Orleans, 1817–1865," 114; Christopher J. Thaiss, "Shakespeare in Maryland, 1752–1860," 47; Woodrow L. Holbein, "Shakespeare in Charleston, 1800–1860," 88–89; 98–99; Linwood E. Orange, "Shakespeare in Mississippi, 1814–1980," 157; Charles B. Lower, "Othello as Black on Southern Stages, Then and Now," 199–228; Sara Nalley, "Shakespeare on the Charleston Stage, 1764–1799," 81–82; all in Kolin, ed., Shakespeare in the South.

other plays, even when bowdlerized, attracted large audiences when nothing else might.[48]

The bright side: Southerners increasingly expressed pleasure at the high quality of the dramatic troupes that visited their towns. Companies of strolling players often performed well, drawing large crowds and winning respect despite frequent complaints about boisterous audiences and the moral looseness of the actors and, especially, actresses. Judge Richard Clark of Georgia thought that Savannah attracted the best talent in the country, and eminent literary personages like Joseph Vallance Bevan of Augusta enjoyed performances by Junius Brutus Booth, among others. Until the coming of the railroad, professional stock companies reached ports in Texas – Houston, Galveston, Jefferson – but the inland towns had to make do with local amateurs. Wealthy planters took their families to New Orleans, where, among other celebrities, they could see James Murdoch do Shakespeare for appreciative audiences that included leading politicians.[49]

Local support sustained theatrical productions, although many theaters with poor actors struggled to survive. Even in Charleston, it usually took a Fanny Kemble or Edwin Forrest to pack the house. The celebrated Thomas A. Cooper and his talented daughter Priscilla, the future wife of President John Tyler, played Shakespeare and other favorites in the South. As Cooper grew older, he toured, sometimes resentfully, such towns as Montgomery, Alabama, not always encountering appreciative audiences. In these respects, Charleston fared no worse than Boston. Still, cities and towns hosted concerts, many of which, like theatrical productions, benefited various charities and drew especially large audiences. Aiken, South Carolina, had a Mozart Society, which offered classical music. The

---

[48] F. Garvin Davenport, *Cultural Life in Nashville on the Eve of the Civil War* (Chapel Hill, NC, 1941), 129, 161, 203–212 and ch. 5; Hutchinson Diary, Jan. 6, 1828; Cornish Diary, April 14, Oct. 18, 1861 (Aiken); Watson, *Charleston Dramatists*, 110; Dormon, *Theater in the Ante Bellum South*, 222–223, 236, 246, 250–251, 257–259, 276–277; Michael Allen, *Western Rivermen, 1763–1861: Ohio and Mississippi Boatmen and the Myth of the Alligator Horse* (Baton Rouge, LA, 1990), 192–193; Franklin M. Garrett, *Atlanta and Environs: A Chronicle of Its People and Events*: vol. 1 (Athens, GA, 1954), 1:540; David Outlaw to Emily Outlaw, 1847–1853 in Outlaw Papers. For disorder and violence in the theaters in the North, see Meade Minnigerode, *The Fabulous Forties, 1840–1850: A Presentation of Private Life* (New York, 1924), 142–209.

[49] Lollie Belle Wylie, ed., *Memoirs of Judge Richard H. Clark* (Atlanta, GA, 1898), 128–129; E. Merton Coulter, *Joseph Vallance Bevan: Georgia's First Official Historian* (Athens, GA, 1964), 48; Elizabeth Silverthorne, *Plantation Life in Texas* (College Station, TX, 1986), 181–182. For the bad reputation of actresses, see John Esten Cooke's novel, *The Virginia Comedians*, 2 vols. (New York, 1854), 1:27, 64.

philanthropic gentlemen of the Thalian Society raised about $5,000 to build a theater in Selma, Alabama, donating its profits to charity. Clinton, Louisiana, sustained two theatrical groups, a Shakespearean society, several poetry-reading circles, and an orchestra. And its citizens benefited from performances at nearby Centenary College and the Silliman Female Institute.[50]

Charleston favored musical performances from its earliest days, issuing its first public announcement in 1733, a year before the opening of its first theater. During the second half of the eighteenth century and first half of the nineteenth, Charleston epitomized the integration of town and country, generating social sophistication and political unity, although in the long run impeding economic regional development. The Charleston elite launched the St. Cecilia Society in 1776, and, as in eighteenth-century England, most subscription concerts took place in taverns and coffee houses, which also accommodated balls, lectures, and other cultural events. The performing artists were initially local amateurs, but, increasingly, professionals were attracted to Charleston as its reputation as a cultural center spread. Charlestonians warmly appreciated performances of Handel, Haydn, Bach, and, to some extent, Beethoven, Mendelssohn, and Mozart. By 1800, Charleston was publishing instructions for a variety of instruments, as well as collections of music. In addition, the newspapers carried a good many advertisements for instruments and concerts. Music stores throve on the selling of scores, Haydn's being especially popular. Southerners received a good deal of information about composers and singers from travelers to Europe, who especially admired the French and Italian opera. A writer in the *Southern Literary Messenger* casually ranked Rossini with Mozart as composers of masterpieces. Charlestonians especially admired Rossini's operas. Other favorites ranged from Mozart's *Marriage of Figaro* to a passing interest in such lesser works as Carl Maria von Weber's *Die Freischutz*.[51]

[50] Elizabeth Coleman, *Priscilla Cooper Tyler and the American Scene, 1816–1889* (University, AL, 2006), 78–79; Carl Kohn to Samuel Kohn, Dec. 2, 1832, praising the acting in New Orleans French Theater, in Carl Kohn Letter Book; Pease and Pease, *Web of Progress*, 141; Cornish Diary, April 14, Oct. 18, 1861 (on Aiken); Hutchinson Diary, Jan. 6, 1828; Davenport, *Cultural Life in Nashville*, 161. Ellison, Early Alabama Publications, 79, n. 154, 84–85; Mary Welsh, "Reminiscences of Old St. Stephens, of More than Sixty-Five Years Ago," *Transactions of the Alabama Historical Society, 1898–99*, 3 (Tuscaloosa, AL, 1909), 210, n.4; Samuel C. Hyde, Jr., *Pistols and Politics: The Dilemma of Democracy in Louisiana's Florida Parishes, 1810–1899* (Baton Rouge, LA, 1996), 6.
[51] S. Max Edelson, *Plantation Enterprise in Colonial South Carolina* (Cambridge, MA, 2006), 137; Butler, *Votaries of Apollo*, 18, 45, 113, 151–153, 170, 217–218, 229;

The rage for opera continued unabated through the 1850s but provoked some harsh words. James Johnston Pettigrew referred to crowds
at the opera that "could not distinguish Yankee Doodle from Mozart's
Requiem." Edmund Ruffin was, if anything, more acerbic. Such occasional outbursts notwithstanding, audiences at concerts and opera did
not replicate the gauche behavior of theater audiences. By common consent they were refined and discriminating.[52]
The colonial South valued religious music but rejected New England's
hostility to the secular. From colonial times to secession, local amateurs
sat in with touring professionals. In Virginia indentured servants worked
as musicians, and in Richmond the amateurs often surpassed the touring professionals. With the coming of the steamboat and the railroad,
accomplished professionals visited the South much more often. Elite
townsmen attended concerts and lionized the musicians but kept them
at a distance socially. In consequence, talented middle-class Southerners
concerned with status lacked incentive to pursue professional musical
careers. Louis Moreau Gottschalk of New Orleans, composer and pianist, alone achieved international repute.[53]
Southern travelers to Italy and Paris learned to appreciate Italian
opera. As concerts gained in popularity, the outstanding Adelina Patti and
Teresa Parodi toured Virginia, creating a sensation with arias from *I puritani, Le nozze di Figaro*, and *Il Trovatore*. Southerners discovered Bellini
and became especially enamored of *Norma*. Ellen Douglas Brownlow
reported from Warrenton, North Carolina – as others did from obscure
southern towns – that Madame Anna Bishop, a celebrated soprano, and
Robert Bochsa, "the great Harpist," gave a "very fine" concert. And the
fabulous Jenny Lind, "the Swedish nightingale," swept all before her. In
particular, she took Nashville by storm. Brownlow pronounced herself

Elizabeth P. Simons, *Music in Charleston from 1732 to 1919* (Charleston, SC, 1927), 33;
John Joseph Hindman, "Concert Life in Ante Bellum Charleston," 2 vols. (Ph.D. diss.:
Chapel Hill, NC, 1972), 1:58, 127. For a report on the Parisian opera and a warm tribute
to the "celebrated Maestro Rossini," see J. L. M., "The Italian Opera," *SLM*, 4 (1838),
673; "Conservative Cookery," *SLM*, 16 (1850), 212. Manuel Garcia brought Italian
singers to New York in 1825. The presentation of Rossini's "Barber of Seville" marked
the first time an American audience heard an opera sung in Italian: Arthur Loesser, *Men,
Women, and Pianos: A Social History* (New York, 1954), 470.
52 Jan. 19, 1859, *ERD*, 1:395; John Joseph Hindman, "Concert Life in Ante Bellum
Charleston," 2 vols. (Ph.D. diss.: Chapel Hill, NC, 1972), 1:62, 99, 128, 155.
53 Willis, *Charleston Stage*, 8; Stoutamire, *Music of the South*, 26–27, 43, 80, 103, 123,
154–155, 233, 252, 254; Huger W. Jervey, "South's Contributions to Music," in *SBN*,
7:372–373; Louis Moreau Gottschalk, *Notes of a Pianist*, ed. Jean Behrend (New York,
1964 [1881]).

"highly gratified" when Lind's concert met her highest expectations: "the matchless sweetness & perfection of her voice." She found Lind's voice "supernatural," worthy of angels and a heavenly choir, something to be felt and beyond her own powers of description. North Carolina Bishop Levi Silliman Ives thought an angel had descended from heaven when he heard Lind sing "I know My Redeemer Liveth." Wealthy planters in Natchez, Alexandria, and other towns in Mississippi and Louisiana traveled to New Orleans to hear her. In 1851, she stopped in Natchez on a swing from New Orleans to St. Louis arranged by P. T. Barnum, her agent. She sang in a Methodist church, and planters flocked into town to pay up to $12 each – all in all, the substantial sum of $6,500 for 770 tickets. Lind drew raves for her singing but also for her contributions to charity in New York and Charleston. Not everyone cheered. Jenny Lind disappointed the cultured but generally sour Margaret Johnson Erwin, who found her "shrill." [54]

French opera became popular in the 1820s, followed by Italian and German. New Orleans' fine opera company toured southern towns and drew raves in New York and elsewhere in the North. By the 1850s, the old French opera house in New Orleans featured Bellini's *Norma*, Donizetti's *Lucia di Lammermoor*, Boïeldieu's *La Dame Blanche*, and Meyerbeer's *Le Prophète*, *Robert le Diable*, and *Les Huguenots*. Washington, Louisiana, added Mozart's Don Giovanni and Verdi's *Il Trovatore*. The patronage and exceptional decorum of the French Creoles, joined by people of color, saved the opera in New Orleans. Its regular company won the admiration of most foreign visitors. The fastidious Amelia Murray had a poor opinion of the American opera, but she made an exception for New Orleans. The French opera in New Orleans much pleased Sir Charles Lyell, who considered the orchestra the best in America. In 1857, Captain Henry A. Murray of the British Royal Navy, one of the few critics, found the New Orleans Tuna Saladpera second-rate, but William Kingsford of Canada exulted in its high quality, observing that even the English-speaking people appreciated it despite the coolness between the

[54] J. M. Martin, "The Italian Opera," *SLM*, 4 (1838), 673–678; *SLM*, 7 (1841), 242–243; Ellen Douglas Brownlow to Mary Eliza Battle, Jan. 5, Feb. 24, 1851, Apr. 26, 1853, in Battle Letters; Lynette Boney Wrenn, ed., *A Bachelor's Life in Antebellum Mississippi: The Diary of Dr. Elijah Millington Walker, 1849–1852* (Knoxville, TN, 2004), Dec. 5, 1850 (88), Jan. 23, 1851 (123); Margaret Johnson Erwin to Caroline Wilson, Dec. 12, 1849, in John Seymour Erwin, *Like Some Green Laurel: Letters of Margaret Johnson Erwin, 1821–1863* (Baton Rouge, LA, 1981), 44. William W. Mann, "From Our Paris Correspondent," *SLM*, 15 (1849), 339–344.

two "races," by which he meant American and French. But New Orleans, adhering to European creations, did not create an American or southern operatic style.[55]

THE CIRCUS

Just as towns and villages had "Court Days," they had "Circus Days." The arrival of the circus, with its Herculean movement of large animals over wretched roads, enchanted communities without zoos. The circus enhanced court weeks in towns like Covington, Georgia, and rivaled the theater during race week in Charleston. Circus business contracted significantly during the depression that followed the financial collapse of 1837 and stretched well into the 1840s. With the return of prosperity, the circus entered the South. To launch a circus required $4,000–5,000, the larger ones as much as $8,000. Businesses often proved lucrative, turning the more able and fortunate entrepreneurs into millionaires (by later standards). Most entrepreneurs lived in the Northeast, where they easily found investors and often became men of political and social standing.[56]

In many southern towns and villages the circus stayed only one day per visit. It announced its impending arrival in newspaper advertisements and leaflets, supplemented by posters in taverns and livery stables. Farmers and village folk traveled up to twenty miles to attend. In the North, admission to the circus cost about twenty-five cents, but in the

[55] Arthur C. Cole, *The Irrepressible Conflict, 1850–1865* (New York, 1934), 231–232; Hume Diary, March 19, 23, 1860; Stoutamire, *Music in the Old South*, 185; Henry A. Kmen, *Music in New Orleans: The Formative Years, 1791–1841* (Baton Rouge, LA, 1966), 58–59, 97, 107, 110, 113, 118, 166, 234; Mary A. H. Gay, *Life in Dixie During the War*, 5th ed. (Atlanta, GA), 31–32; Eliza Ripley, *Social Life in Old New Orleans: Being Recollections of My Girlhood* (New York, 1975 [1912]), 1979 [1897]), 7, 31–34, 65; Agnes Lee Journal, Apr. 11, 1856, in Mary Curtis De Butts, ed., *Growing Up in the 1850s: The Journal of Agnes Lee* (Chapel Hill, NC, 1984), 85; Clyde Lottridge Cummer, ed., *Yankee in Gray: The Civil War Memoirs of Henry E. Handerson* (Cleveland, OH, 1962), 23; George Green Shackelford, *George Wythe Randolph and the Confederate Elite* (Athens, GA, 1988), 62; Emma Holmes, Mar. 11, 1861, in Marszalek, ed., *The Diary of Miss Emma Holmes*, 15; Amelia E. Murray, *Letters from the United States, Cuba, and Canada*, 2 vols. in 1 (New York, 1968 [1856]), 269–270; Henry A. Murray, *Lands of the Slave and the Free: Or, Cuba, the United States, and Canada*, 2nd ed. (London, 1857), 146; [William Kingsford], *Impressions of the West and South* (Toronto, 1858), 55–56, 78; Sir Charles Lyell, *A Second Visit to the United States of North America*, 2 vols. (London, 1855), 2:93; also, Sir Charles Augustus Murray, *Travels in North America during the Years, 1834, 1835 and 1836* (London, 1839), 2:179.

[56] Stuart Thayer, *Annals of the American Circus: Vol. III, 1848–1860* (Seattle, WA, 1992), 9; 11–12, 19, 21, 119.

South, with its sparse population and poor roads, at least twice as much. Those seemingly paltry fees added up to big money. In 1858, a traveling circus at Lockapoko, Alabama, proved nothing special when it grossed about $1,000 a day.[57]

Once a circus made a successful stop, it reappeared annually, drawing large crowds across lines of class, race, and sex. Responses were mixed but, on balance, decidedly favorable. In Mississippi in 1850, Baker found the circus "decidedly the best I ever witnessed, the feats of the cask – the balls, & the suppleness of the limbs transcended anything of the kind I ever witnessed." In contrast, Isaac Ulmer, a student at Mr. Tutweiler's school, thought the circus at Greene Springs, Alabama, in 1860 "very poor." Too bad – since Mr. Tutweiler had graciously allowed his pupils to attend and even waited outside "to keep us 'straight.'" W. W. Holden, editor of the *North Carolina Standard*, choked when the elite of Raleigh turned out to see a juggler, and a poor one at that. In 1856, J. H. Bills reported from Bolivar County, Tennessee: "Delightful day. Great Show of Animals & Circus. Negroes and Children all Crazy to go." Apparently, no few white adults shared the passion, and politicians attended for pleasure and in order to work the crowds to advance personal and political interests. Even John C. Calhoun did not resist. In 1833, he delivered his first public speech on nullification at a reception held at a circus.[58]

CHRISTMAS HOLIDAYS

In colonial times the Christmas holidays presented country gentlemen with a golden opportunity to display affluence and hospitality. The coastal elite's Christmas Eve suppers featured punch made from Irish whiskey, sugar, hot water, and lemons, served from silver pitchers and accompanied by cigars for the gentlemen. And then, there were the special Christmas pies and cakes: the pies filled with beefsteak, turkey, duck, partridge, goose, as well as jelly and hardboiled eggs; the cakes swimming in rum, whiskey, and cordials. British travelers commented disapprovingly on open shops and on the scarce notice paid to Christmas Day, especially in the North. As the evangelicals advanced, Christmas became quieter, and it sometimes appeared that only Episcopalians and Catholics went

---

[57] Stuart Thayer, *Traveling Showmen: The American Circus before the Civil War* (Detroit, MI, 1997), ix., 16, 30–31, 70–71, 74–75; Thayer, *Annals of the American Circus*, 103.

[58] Janet M. Davis, *The Circus Age: Culture and Society under the American Big Top* (Chapel Hill, NC, 2002), 86; Cornish Diary, March 18, 1856; McBryde Diary, April 11–14, 1856.

to church. On Christmas and New Year's Day the evangelical Christians thanked God for having survived another year, and, repenting their sins, prayed for strength to do better in the year ahead. Evangelical ministers campaigned hard to downgrade Christmas as a religious holiday, but their sternest admonitions failed to make many pious Southerners turn Christmas into just another day.[59]

In Mississippi, Baker recounted a sermon by the Cumberland Presbyterian Reverend John Middleton, who ridiculed those who celebrated Christmas: "For said he, we do not know the year much less the day Christ was born – observing Christmas as a feast, or fast day, is all superstition said he." Baker took the sermon lightly. Yet, Christmas dinner among rural folk of all denominations tended to be a quiet affair for family and friends and perhaps a few neighbors. Even the fun-loving French Catholic Creole planters of Louisiana rarely put up Christmas trees. They spent Christmas Day *en famille*, although more likely to attend church than their Protestant neighbors. Yet, during a quiet Christmas, relatives and friends came from some distance and settled in for a visit that might last weeks.

In families that considered Christmas dinner something special, a turkey probably graced one end of the table and a pig, ham, or haunch of venison the other, with a variety of vegetables in between and plentiful desserts afterwards. For the affluent, several wines accompanied the courses. Friends sent food to each other, routinely or on impulse. In North Carolina, Thomas Ruffin regularly sent Kenneth Rayner mutton at Christmas, which Jinny Bond, Rayner's old cook, salted and wrapped in meal to last till New Year's Day. But then, such neighborliness extended beyond holidays. Across the South, farmers lent wagons, oxen, and other essentials to their neighbors. In the low country, Mrs. Langdon Cheves told her aunt that she had just received a basket of turnips and a dish of sausages from friends. Her aunt commented, "This is the custom here." Especially if a family fell ill, another sent one or more servants to assist and do the chores.[60]

---

[59] In general see Penne L. Restad, *Christmas in America: A History* (New York, 1995); Rhys Isaac, *The Transformation of Virginia, 1740–1790* (Chapel Hill, NC, 1982), 80–81; Richard Barry, *Mr. Rutledge of South Carolina* (New York, 1942), 22; Mitchell King Diary, Dec. 24, 25, 1852. For Christmas pies, see [Rutledge], *The Carolina Housewife*, 85; for cake, see Martha McCulloch-Williams, *Dishes and Beverages of the Old South* (Knoxville, TN, 1988 [1913], 145.

[60] Baker Diary, Dec. 30, 1859, Dec. 31, 1854; Mesick, *English Traveller in America*, 85; D. W. Mitchell, *Ten Years in the United States* (London, 1862), 196; Harnett T. Kane, *Plantation Parade: The Grand Manner in Louisiana* (New York, 1955), 37; Kenneth Rayner to Thomas Ruffin, Dec. 25, 1860, Dec. 24, 1861, in *TRP*, 3:204, 206; Franklin

Thanksgiving celebrations also met religious objections, and not only from evangelicals. Thanksgiving fell on various days selected by the governor or a town council, usually in November, sometimes in October or January. Southerners generally marked the day quietly, going to church and having a family dinner that featured the traditional turkey. Among those who disapproved, William Henry Holcombe of Natchez, a Swedenborgian, resented the closing of shops and public offices and grumbled that this New England custom smacked of Judaism and Roman paganism. The state had no business in appointing a special day to honor God. Holcombe nonetheless enjoyed the big turkey dinner that a boarding-house landlady prepared for her twenty-seven guests. Thanksgiving passed more boisterously for the slaves. Many masters, although fewer in the low country, gave their slaves the day off for a big bash. After church, the more affluent whites returned to a dinner at which champagne, other wines, and brandy flowed, while their slaves enjoyed a wide assortment of food and liquor not usually given to them. Whites and blacks would be pretty tight by bedtime. Masters brought their slaves to each other's plantations, making the day a community get-together.[61]

Churches fully attended on Sundays before and after Christmas were often poorly attended on Christmas Day. Evangelicals dampened the social spirit of the day, complaining about the "superstition" of parishioners. The day, not the season. At the end of November or beginning of December the plantations got a taste of the celebrations to come with a joyous festival of hog-killing, which Martha McCulloch-Williams declared almost as sacred as Christmas. High spirits burst forth after Christmas, reached a crescendo on New Year's Eve and New Year's Day, and maintained a high pitch for days or weeks thereafter. Linton Stephens wrote to his brother Alexander from Charlottesville, Virginia, where he was studying law, about "that glorious festive week ... emphatically called 'Christmas holidays,' and which in other places, and even in old

---

M. Garrett, *Atlanta and Environs*, vol 1 (Athens, GA, 1954), 1:543; [Anon.], *The Old Pine Farm: or, The Southern Side* (Nashville, TN, 1860), 52; Mrs. Cheves, quoted in Huff, *Langdon Cheves*, 184; W. Emerson Wilson, ed., *Plantation Life at Rose Hill: The Diaries of Martha Ogle Forman, 1814–1845* (Wilmington, DE, 1976), Sept. 9, 1820 (109).

[61] Holcombe Diary, Jan. 18, 1855; Henry Clay Warmoth Magnolia Plantation Journals, Oct. 4, 1858; J. Carlyle Sitterson, *Sugar Country: The Cane Sugar Industry in the South* (Lexington, KY, 1953), 100; Wendell Holmes Stephenson, ed., *Isaac Franklin: Slave Trader and Planter of the Old South. With Plantation Records* (Baton Rouge, LA, 1938), 112; *AS:Texas*, 4 (Pt. 1), 190, *AS:Tenn.*, 6 (Pt. 2), 53. For the low country, see Louis M. DeSaussure Diary, Nov. 1, 1859; Elizabeth Hyde Botume, *First Days amongst the Contrabands* (Boston, MA, 1893), 247.

Georgia, is devoted to joy over our passage through the toils of another year, and feasting upon the good things it has yielded to the labors of man and beast."[62]

"This is Christmas eve," Elizabeth Graham wrote Edward Graham in 1829, "as you are in a land of Episcopalians, I suppose there are great preparations making for the celebration of tomorrow ... I suppose there will be very little notice of it taken here." Strict Presbyterians did not recognize Christmas as a feast day but did exchange presents, treat their slaves, and let their boys set off "poppers" (firecrackers). In Lynchburg, Virginia, and other towns, festive occasions featured hard drinking. What, after all, did the evangelical preachers expect? Even regular churchgoers needed holidays to relax, the more so in frontier towns like Little Rock, Arkansas, which during the 1830s swayed with balls and parties. G. W. Featherstonehaugh recounted a tavern scene: three women and one hundred gun-toting, heavy-drinking, violence-prone men who danced with each other. Panola, Mississippi, had settled down by 1861 and featured a "tableau" with musical entertainment, acting, supper, and dancing for "a pretty large crowd."[63]

Whites loved to attend the slaves' parties at Christmas and during the year. Often, the slaves welcomed them – or pretended to – but just as often they did not. They tolerated masters and mistresses who showed up as chaperones and enjoyed the scene, but took umbrage at

---

[62] McCulloch-Williams, *Dishes and Beverages*, 39; Davis Diary, Dec. 25, 1838; Clitherall "Autobiography" (ms.), Nov. 25, 1859; Wadley Private Journal Dec. 31, 1860; Taylor Diary, Dec. 25 for the 1780s and 1790s; Morrison Journal, Dec. 24, 25, 1845; Otey Diary, Dec. 25, 1846, 1847; Greenlee Diary, Dec. 25, 26, 1847; Sturdivant Diary, Dec. 24, 25, 31, 1854; Linton Stephens to Alexander H. Stephens, in James D. Waddell, *Biographical Sketch of Linton Stephens, Containing a Selection of His Letters, Speeches, State Papers, Etc.* (Atlanta, GA, 1877), 73.

[63] Elizabeth L. Graham to Edward Graham, Dec. 24, 1829, quoted in Margaret Burr DesChamps, "The Presbyterian Church in the South Atlantic States, 1801–1861" (Ph.D. diss; Emory University, 1952), 128; "C. C." "Christmas Holidays at Teddington, *SLM*, 7 (1841), 219; Sophia E. Pearson to John W. Ellis, Jan. 20, 1848, in Noble J. Tolbert, ed., *The Papers of John Willis Ellis*, 2 vols. (Raleigh, NC, 1964), 1:70; James O. Breeden, *Joseph Jones, M. D.: Scientist of the Old South* (Lexington, KY, 1975), 12; William Davidson Blanks, "Ideal and Practice: A Study of the Conception of the Christian Life Prevailing in the Presbyterian Churches of the South during the Nineteenth Century" (Th.D., Union Theological Seminary, 1960), 153–154.; Maria Bryan Harford to Julia Ann Bryan Cumming, Dec. 21, 1826, Dec. 24, 1840, in Carol Bleser, ed., *Tokens of Affection: The Letters of a Planter's Daughter in the Old South* (Athens, GA, 1996), 320; Joseph Leonard King, Jr., *Dr. George William Bagby: A Study in Virginian Literature, 1850–1880* (New York, 1927), 22; G. W. Featherstonhaugh, *Excursion through the Slave States* (New York, 1968 [1844]), 129; Baker Diary, Dec. 24, 18, 1861; Lyle Saxon et al. *Gumbo Ya-Ya: A Collection of Louisiana Folk Tales* (New York, 1945), 164.

the party-crashing of young sports who came to dance with the black girls. Respectable whites took their enjoyment vicariously. Esther Boyd recalled the fiddles and "some body to *pat*," and a floor full of dancers. At square dances with solo parts, they competed to stand out as the best. Visitors and transplanted Northerners like Julia Tyler interpreted the occasions as testimony to the slaves' contentment under kind masters. Rarely did these observers grasp the satirical treatment of whites in songs and dances.[64]

Masters took pride in their largesse when they held a big barbecue for their slaves, who spiffed up for a good time. Bills threw a big lay-by barbecue and exulted, "All to the number of 45 on that farm appear truly a happy set of people all handsomely dressed with amusements in their own way & all behaving well." T. M. Garrett, a student at the University of North Carolina, took a stroll through Chapel Hill one evening and came upon blacks who were "enjoying the innocent amusement" of singing and playing a banjo, and whose skill impressed him. The scene also inspired "a natural reflection." How happy they were, how carefree: "Their minds never being extracted to dwell upon any distant object." Edward L. Wells of New York wrote that "Great gaiety" prevailed among the slaves at Christmas time even at secession, when disconcerted whites "did not take much notice of it." A year later, Caroline R. Ravenel remarked, "Christmas in Charleston is the saddest day of the year; & is merry only to children and negroes."[65]

An acid observation from Francis de Castelnau, a Frenchman on a trip in Florida:

Nothing proves better the moral degradation of the negro than the joy and contentment he shows in the state of slavery. Draw near a plantation and the noisy outbursts of laughter that you hear there will make you forget the overseer who goes about with a huge whip. Then comes the rest days and all the miseries of the week are forgotten in the wildest dances and the most ridiculous capers.

---

[64] Boyd, "Notes and Recollections" (ms.), 8; Theodore Delaney, "Julia Gardiner Tyler" (Ph.D. diss: College of William and Mary, 1995); C. E. L. Town Diary, Feb. 26, 1853. For the reaction of slaves to white attendance, see *AS:S.C.*, 2 (pt. 1,) 16; *AS:Tex.*, 4 (pt. 2), 243; *AS:Ga.*, 13 (pt. 4), 224; *AS:Ky.*, 16, 23; Orville W. Taylor, *Negro Slavery in Arkansas* (Durham, NC, 1958), 207–208. For the satire, see Leroi Jones, *Blues People: Negro Music in White America* (New York, 1999), 86.

[65] Bills Diary, July 24, 1858; also, Sturdivant Plantation Records, July 12, 1845; Edward L. Wells to Mrs. Thomas L. Wells, Jan. 1, 1861, and Caroline R. Ravenel to Isabella Middleton Smith, Dec. 25, 1862, in Daniel E. Huger Smith, et al., eds., *Mason-Smith Family Letters, 1860–1868* (Columbia, SC, 1950), 7, 23.

Those slaves committed the crime of enjoying each other's company and finding pleasurable moments in a grim world. They thereby condemned themselves in the eyes both of self-righteous proponents of freedom and of self-serving exploiters. At the same time, as Elizabeth Fox-Genovese and I have discussed elsewhere in detail, masters congratulated themselves on their own kindness and generosity and on the presumed gratitude of their slaves.[66]

During the holidays, balls, dances, and regionally preferred pastimes filled the cities and towns much more than the countryside. Richmond boasted oyster suppers. Tallahassee held races, welcomed an occasional traveling circus, and held balls and modest parties. The citizens of Jackson, Mississippi sent printed invitations to Christmas Eve parties open to the public at the city hall or in private accommodations. From the low country to the Southwest, celebrations featured fireworks displays, sometimes interspersed with the firing of cannons. In Texas, fireworks for home entertainment consisted of dried hog bladders, usually held on sticks by the children, who popped them in the fireplace. A darker side: William Gilmore Simms complained that before the Revolution – and even afterwards in some parts of South Carolina – Christmas and New Year's celebrations included "this cruel sport" of cock fighting.[67]

South Carolina's frolicking went on for two weeks. In 1829, John S. Palmer, a student at South Carolina College, referred to Columbia's social season as a "campaign of dissipation." A party at the home of Judge Abraham Nott, crowded to suffocation, boasted "a vast collection of beauty and a splendid display of fashions." B. H. Johnson wrote, "A great number of young ladies spent the Session at this place," with "all the belles of Columbia" attending his mother's ball. Private parties celebrated the newly married. Upcountry yeomen greeted young people with good food and drink as they went from house to house, dancing and fiddling.[68]

---

[66] Castelnau, 1837, quoted in Julia Hering, "Plantation Economy in Leon County," in Elinor Miller and Eugene D. Genovese, eds., *Plantation, Town, and County: Essays on the Local History of American Slave Society* (Urbana, IL, 1974), 33; Garrett Diary, July 2, 1849. cf. Fox-Genovese, *Within the Plantation Household* and Eugene D. Genovese, *Roll, Jordan, Roll: The World the Slaves Made* (New York, 1974).

[67] Catherine Cooper Hopley, *Life in the South from the Commencement of the War*, 2 vols. (New York, 1971 [1863]), 1:164–165; Bertram H. Groene, *Ante-Bellum Tallahassee* (Tallahassee, FL, 1971), 150; Hutchinson Diary, Dec. 25, 1827; see, e.g., the printed invitation for 1850 in J. A. Quitman Papers; Antonia Quitman to John A. Quitman, Jan. 5, 1857 in J. A. Quitman Papers; Silverthorne, *Plantation Life in Texas*, 140; William Gilmore Simms, *The Life of Francis Marion*, 8th ed. (New York, 1844), 68.

[68] John S. Palmer to Esther Simons Palmer, December 8, 1829, in Towles, ed., *World Turned Upside Down*, 33; B. H. Johnson to Edward C. Johnson, Dec. 20, 1828, in Francis

Anna Cheves wrote in 1839 that her brother Langdon had married on Christmas day and that local beaux crowded into the Cheveses' home. "We also had a Christmas tree erected in the middle of the room which we decorated with fruit, sugar plums, candy & cakes, & which was brilliantly lighted with candles ... We had all determined beforehand to exert ourselves as much as possible to prevent it from becoming stiff and tiresome." Anna Cheves's casual mention of a Christmas tree disguised a tangled history. Masters in Mississippi provided Christmas trees for the black children, only occasionally for themselves. Christmas trees at home became popular in Western Europe and America during the nineteenth century. The medieval Church tried, with indifferent results, to curb pagan merriment in irreverent celebrations. Popular enthusiasm proved hard to contain, but Christmas only slowly became a grand holiday. In the southern colonies, the Anglican establishment looked the other way when Christmas provided a wonderful excuse for a good time.[69]

The legacy of Puritanism was another matter. Puritans banned Christmas and saints' days from their calendar – along with gambling, cock fighting, fox hunting, and horse racing. The effects lingered well into the nineteenth century. Mass participation in an increasingly secular and coarsely commercial Christmas did not sweep the country until after the War. Indeed, during the War, the Natchez *Daily Courier* espied a Yankee plot:

Christmas has been celebrated from time immemorial by the believers in Christ, and many times the Roundheads of ancient puritanical stock attempted its suppression. Some of these same Roundhead descendants, at the North, are now the prime movers of the destruction of the South; and should they succeed, it would not astonish us at all to hear of their making, as in ancient days, one grand attempt to destroy the time-honored institution of Christmas.[70]

The Christmas holidays brought loved ones home, but also lured them away. Some children celebrated in the homes of friends, some of whose family members were visiting their own parents or other relatives. In the

---

Johnson Scott, ed., "Letters and Papers of Governor David Johnson and Family, 1810–1855," Appendix to *Proceedings of the South Carolina Historical Association* (1941); Lillian Kibler, *Benjamin F. Perry, Unionist* (Durham, NC, 1946), 25.

[69] Anna Cheves to Anna Dulles, Dec. 29, 1839 in Langdon Cheves Collection; *Natchez Daily Courier*, Dec. 25, 1862, in John K. Bettersworth, ed. *Mississippi in the Confederacy: As They Saw It* (Baton Rouge, LA, 1961), 312; Smedes, *Memorials of a Southern Planter*, 149.

[70] Restad, *Christmas in America*, especially ch. 1; Smedes, *Memorials of a Southern Planter*, 149.

Mississippi Valley, affluent ladies had their turn. Mothers and daughters went off to the great social whirl in New Orleans, shopping and attending the opera and balls. State legislatures sometimes remained in session during the Christmas holidays, keeping members away from home despite unwritten laws that arranged to have legislators join their families during the holidays. With husbands away, wives visited friends or entertained themselves. Being away at school proved trying for the young. James Iredell, Jr. of North Carolina wrote to his parents from Princeton in 1805 that he missed the seasonal gaiety, since his fellow students treated Christmas "with perfect indifference." The indifference visibly disgusted the numerous southern students. In contrast, the University of Virginia made a great fuss at Christmas, at least before 1840, when a railroad made it easy for students to go home. Despite the efforts to accommodate students, turbulence often accompanied the imposition of rules to rein in their efforts to have a good time. Students chafed all the more since slaves were enjoying themselves under fewer restraints.[71]

At Oglethorpe College near Atlanta, Isaac Barton Ulmer candidly wrote to his father in Columbus, Georgia, exulting over the great success of the Christmas Eve party for the students: "Most of the young people of Midway, and some of Milledgeville attended." Some students experienced celebrations at school as a treat, since, despite efforts to restrain them, they reveled in ways not permitted at home. In 1850, the Board of Trustees of the College of South Carolina asked President William C. Preston to explain his having excused students during Christmas holidays. He replied:

I knew it was a prevalent custom in the State to have a family reunion on that day ... and I acceded to the desire of the parents to have them in the family circle .... Besides, the Christmas holidays in a village like Columbia are always attended by

---

[71] T. B. Thorpe, "The Sugar Region of Louisiana" (1835), in Schwaab and Bull, eds., *Travels in the Old South*, 2:518; James Iredell, Jr. to Ebenezer Pettigrew, Jan. 11, 1805, in Lemmon, ed., *Pettigrew Papers*, 1:357; Thomas Jefferson Wertenbaker, *Princeton, 1746–1896* (Princeton, NJ, 1946), 210; Phillip Alexander Bruce, *History of the University of Virginia, 1819–1919: The Lengthening Shadow of One Man*, 5 vols. (New York, 1920–1922), 2:266; also, Sarah Clifton Southall Diary, Dec. 22–25, 1855, in Southall and Bowen Papers. Louisiana declared Christmas a legal holiday in 1837, and by 1860 thirteen states had followed suit. On state legislators, see William Henry Trescot, *Memorial on the Life of J. Johnston Pettigrew, Brig.-Gen. Of the Confederate States Army* (Charleston, SC, 1870), 30; R. F. W. Alston to Adele Petigru Alston, Dec. 20, 1840, in J. H. Easterby, ed., *The South Carolina Rice Plantation, as Revealed in the Papers of Robert F. W. Allston* (Chicago, 1945), 87–88; Antonia Quitman to John A. Quitman, Jan. 5, 1857 in J. A. Quitman Papers.

a series of low and vulgar dissipation – drinking, gaming, cock fighting &c Lewd & exhibitions – from which I thought it was well the boys should be abstracted & placed under Parental guardianship.[72]

Giles Patterson, a twenty-year-old student at the College from an upcountry planter family, remained misty-eyed at "the great holiday of my youth which I always looked forward to ... with the pleasurable emotions of a child." Mary Jane Chester, at Columbia (Tennessee) Female Institute, wrote to her sister, "I wonder how I shall spend my Christmas, the first one that I ever spent away from home. You will all be so happy *at home* – the very name of home makes me feel happy." Jacob Rhett Motte, a student at Harvard in 1831, fancied himself back in Charleston: "Nothing is heard, thought, or dreamt of, but pleasure and enjoyment; from the proudest aristocrat to the humblest negro, everyone devotes his time and money to the sole engrossing subject – pleasure."[73]

On plantations preparations began weeks in advance. With November came prettification of Big House and slave quarters. Slaves saw to such tasks as butchering hogs, smoking hams, stacking firewood, laying carpets, hanging curtains, and putting up evergreen branches, holly wreathes, candles, and Christmas trees. During the two weeks or so before Christmas, mistresses and slaves seeded raisins, cut citron, washed and dried currants, mixed apple toddy, baked pies, and made puddings. Slaves cleaned up the plantations, making everything shipshape. As William Gilmore Simms's fiction revealed, the cost of the holidays drained wealthy but cash-poor planters.[74]

Belles and beaux tramped from plantation to plantation. "Storm parties" became the rage in Mississippi, as crowds of young people, determined to dance all night, descended on the home of a planter or

---

[72] Isaac Barton Ulmer to Col. I. B. Ulmer, Dec. 25, 1860, in Ulmer Papers; W. C. Preston to Gentlemen, March 2, 1850, in Preston Papers.

[73] Giles Patterson, *Journal of a Southern Student, 1846-1818, with Letters of a Later Period*, ed., Richmond Croom Beatty (Nashville, TN, 1944), 42; Mary Jane Chester to Martha Butler Chester, Dec. 19, 1840, in Chester Papers; J. R. Motte, July 4, 1831, in A. H. Cole, ed., *Charleston Goes to Harvard: The Diary of a Harvard Student of 1831* (Cambridge, MA, 1940), 52.

[74] "Sketches of South-Carolina," published in *Knickerbocker Magazine* in 1843 and reprinted in Schwaab and Bull, eds., *Travels in the Old South*, 2:317–318; Silverthorne, *Plantation Life in Texas*, 135; Alan Grubb, "House and Home in the Victorian South," in Carol Bleser, ed., *In Joy and in Sorrow: Women, Family, and Marriage in the Victorian South, 1830–1900* (New York, 1991), ch. 10; and Lemmon, ed., *Pettigrew Papers*, vols. 1–2.

well-to-do professional, expecting him to offer hospitality even if not forewarned. In rural Georgia, men, masked as women or grotesque creatures, went door-to-door to entertain neighbors, spreading "great merriment." Christmas in the countryside featured hunting parties as a principal entertainment for men, some of whom engaged in solitary hunting: "Another Christmas come and I am still alive," wrote Henry William Harrington of North Carolina, "rather dull time tho – Rode out with the Hounds this morning and walked out with my gun in the evening." More gregarious North Carolinians organized elaborate fox hunts. Throughout the South fastidious ministers disapproved of holiday hunts, which in various sizes and degrees of formality remained common.[75]

The pious John Walker usually kept a quiet Christmas, in accordance with the preaching at his Methodist church, but then his nineteen-year-old niece Frances Walker married Hill Lipscomb, a thirty-year-old widower with two children. John Walker commented: "It was the gayest company I have been in for many years. If we have done wrong Lord Jesus Master forgives us." Masters who gave their slaves wedding parties, as many did, had the double satisfaction of congratulating themselves on their largesse and of having a good time. On the larger plantations several couples wed simultaneously, providing an excuse for a big party that included neighbors, white and black.[76]

For masters who heeded their preachers' admonitions against "idolatry" and attendant dissipation only reluctantly, the determination of the slaves to have their barbecues, parties, and dances came as a godsend. Masters showed their hardworking "people" a good time and seized the excuse to have one themselves. Sally Baxter, who married into a planter family in Mississippi, wrote to her relatives in New York, "You know

---

[75] *Plantation Life: The Narratives of Mrs. Henry Schoolcraft* (New York, 1969 [1860]), 22; E. Grey Dimond and Herman Hattaway, eds., *Letters from Forest Place: A Plantation Family's Correspondence* (Jackson, MS, 1993), 96; [Henry Benjamin Whipple], *Bishop Whipple's Southern Diary, 1843–44* (New York, 1968), 53, 55, 57 ("great merriment."); Harrington diary quoted in Stuart A. Marks, *Southern Hunting in Black and White: Nature, History, and Ritual in a Carolina Community* (Princeton, NJ, 1991), 26–27; Zebulon Vance to Harriett Newell Espy, Dec. 24, 1852, in Elizabeth Roberts Cannon, ed., *My Beloved Zebulon: The Correspondence of Zebulon Vance and Harriett Newell Espy* (Chapel Hill, NC, 1971), 166; Cornish Diary, Dec. 25, 1840; Baker Diary, Dec. 25, 1852.

[76] John Walker Diary, Dec. 25, 1832, and Christmas entries for 1824–1846. For slave weddings, see Genovese, *Roll, Jordan, Roll*, 475–481; S. R. Jackson Journal, May 26, 1836, in Jackson-Prince Papers; Mary Petigru to Adele Petigru Allston, Dec. 27, 1860, in Easterby, ed., *South Carolina Rice Plantation*, 171.

that Xmas is the Negroes particular festival." The scandalized Reverend Mr. Hanscombe failed to prevent Simms from providing a high time for family, friends, and servants as a matter of *noblesse oblige*. The family of John Brown, a planter in Arkansas, usually spent a quiet day at home, but his slaves made it a celebration. In 1853, Brown mused:

> This day which has for centuries been dedicated as a holyday is in our retired situation but little noticed .... It is a human as well as a wise regulation to allow them a few days as a Jubilee, and they enjoy it. All are brushing up, putting on their best rigging, and with boisterous joy hailing the approach of the Holy days, which we are in some degree relieved of the particular oversight of them. So we are all happy.

William A. Graham of North Carolina, Jeremiah Harris of Virginia, and the Associated Presbyterian Reverend Mr. Agnew of Mississippi said much the same: For many white adults, the season proved dull; for blacks, it proved an occasion for a good time.[77]

The slaves' holidays ran three or more days, which Johann David Schoepf, traveling in Virginia in the 1780s, thought excessive: "for at no time do they (white and black) work so hard as to need a long rest." Despite accusations, the slaves were not a hard-drinking people, but at Christmas the liquor flowed. For blacks and whites, Christmas required a liberal disbursement of eggnog. Texans punned about the "Holy Daze." Judge Richard Clark of Savannah grumbled about the heavy consumption of eggnog and stronger spirits during the holidays, and, indeed, the shops in town did a smashing business in whiskey and brandy, as well as in fruit, oysters, fowl, premium beef, and fireworks. Eggnog consisted of brandy or whiskey and egg whites and yolks beaten separately with milk. The ladies often substituted syllabub or spiced wine for hard liquor. Varina Davis willingly paid a high price for a bottle of brandy to make eggnog for her servants at the Confederate White House but was aghast when she thought she would not have enough eggs. To her relief, she got

---

[77] Sally Baxter to George Baxter, Dec. 22–23, 1860, in Ann Fripp Hampton, ed., *A Divided Heart: Letters of Sally Baxter Hampton, 1853–1862* (Spartanburg, SC, 1980), 8; D. F. Jamison to G. F. Holmes, Jan. 28, 1847, in Oliphant, et al., eds., *Letters of Simms*, 2:252; Thompson, *Presbyterians in the South*, 1:464; Brown, quoted in Joe Gray Taylor, *Negro Slavery in Louisiana* (Baton Rouge, LA, 1963), 206–207; W. A. Graham to J. W. Bryan, Dec. 28, 1843, in Henry Thomas Shanks, ed., *The Papers of Willie P. Mangum*, 5 vols. (Raleigh, NC, 1955–1956), 2:465; Jeremiah Harris Diary, Dec. 29, 1860, in Charles W. Turner, ed., *An Old Field School Teacher's Diary (Life and Times of Jeremiah C. Harris)* (Verona, VA, 1975), 77; Agnew Diary, Dec. 25, 1860, Dec. 25, 1861, Dec. 25, 1862. Also, Ervin Diary, Christmas entries for 1839–1860.

them, for she knew that without eggnog the servants would have considered Christmas a failure.[78]

Christmas day belonged to the children, black and white, who clamored for and received gifts and pampering. For adult slaves the day included gifts and the distribution of clothing and "luxuries." Masters settled business accounts, paying slaves the small amounts of money they had earned for extra work and for chickens or vegetables from the slaves' gardens and distributing bonuses for superior work. Bills sighed, "My Negroes from both farms are in. We are much crowded & Christmas is anything but fun for me – I divide $150 among my slaves." For slaves with "'broad wives,'" women who lived on other plantations, the holidays meant passes to spend half a week or more with their families. House servants and coachmen counted on tips. The days after Christmas tried whites, since they had to eat cold dinners. Many masters routinely gave house servants leave to enjoy the holidays and shifted for themselves with previously prepared meals.[79]

The slaves rose early on Christmas day, marching to the Big House to call for gifts. Masters and mistresses knew that refusals or expressions of annoyance would have been singularly inappropriate. If anything, mistresses rose earlier to tend to the sick and supplicants. If plans went awry or slaves had a special request, responsible masters went to town for last-minute purchases. It was always one thing or another. A planter in Mississippi wrote: "Killed a sheep and a hog for my negroes ... Spent the day waiting on the negroes and making them as comfortable as possible." In the low country a "killing of the beef" for the slaves became a Christmas ritual. The overseer of a large plantation wrote that he killed a number of cattle for the slaves: "I can do more with them in this way

---

[78] Johann David Schoepf, *Travels in the Confederation, 1783–1784*, tr. Alfred J. Morrison (New York, 1968 [1788]), 2:118; Camilla Davis Trammell, *Seven Pines: Its Occupants and Their Letters, 1825–1872* (Houston, TX, 1986), 56; Wylie, ed., *Memoirs of Judge Richard H. Clark*, 76; Davenport, *Cultural Life in Nashville*, 204–205; Silverthorne, *Plantation Life in Texas*, 140; Katharine M. Jones, ed., *Ladies of Richmond: Confederate Capital* (Indianapolis, IN, 1962), 247. Also, Hilliard Diary, Dec. 25. 1849; John Q. Anderson, ed. *Brokenburn: The Journal of Kate Stone, 1861–1868* (Baton Rouge, LA, 1955), Dec. 22, 1861 (77); Hopley, *Life in the South*, 1:165–168.

[79] John Witherspoon DuBose, "Recollections of the Plantations," *Alabama Historical Quarterly*, 1 (1930), 63–75; 115; "Plantation Accounts," Dec. 25, 1833, in Jackson-Prince Papers; Bills Diary, Dec. 26, 1856; Greenlee Diary, Dec. 25, 1850, Dec. 25, 1854; Expenses for 1854 in Stirling Papers; W. C. Harrison to William H. Taylor, Jan. 26, 1857, in Dromgoole-Robinson Papers; Taylor, *Negro Slavery in Louisiana*, 200; Mrs. Roger Pryor [Sara Agnes Rice Pryor], *My Day: Reminiscences of a Long Life* (EE: Chapel Hill, NC, 1997 [1909]), 7.

than if all the heads of cattle were made into lashes." Custom required invitations to slaves from nearby plantations. Christmas dinners were often staggered – scheduled for a day other than the 25th – so that slaves might attend each other's festivities.[80]

In Louisiana, where the exigencies of the sugar harvest compelled a delay in the celebration of Christmas until January, Eliza Ann Marsh wrote, "This morning I commenced preparation for the Negroes dinner that I came on to superintend. In the morning I made about a bushel of ginger cakes, & made old Jane commence making the bread, after dinner I made a flag for the Negroes, & two large pitchers of hot whisky punch, with which I treated them when they came up to see me." Phanor Proudhomme did not specify his activities precisely, but he spent the three-day holiday almost entirely with his slaves.[81]

Baker began the three-day holiday:

I have endeavored too to make my Negroes joyous and happy,–& am glad to see them enjoying themselves with such a contented good will .... I have recommenced work today – I called all hands up last night, told them the work we had before us compelled our hollidays to close, & made a few remarks to them as to their duties the following year. They seemed thankful for the favor I had extended to them & eager to commence work. I gave them from Thursday night last – Thus I commenced another year under favorable auspices as far as my domestic affairs are concerned – I did all I could to make their hollidays pleasant to them & they seem to appreciate my endeavors.[82]

Masters doubtless gave their slaves an elaborate holiday with a view toward reconciling them to their lot and improving their productivity and discipline but also to reassure themselves of their own kindness and sense of Christian responsibility. Louis Manigault remarked on a "pleasant Christmas" on his plantation: "All the people are quite well which is the principal thing." Many of the rural whites seem to have enjoyed the slaves' holiday events much more than their own modest efforts. Ostensibly, they attended because the slaves expected them to, because they considered it a duty, because they had to provide supervision against the threat of excessive drinking and carrying-on. Still, a reading of their

---

[80] Newstead Plantation Diary, Dec. 25, 1858; Smith, *Charlestonian's Recollections*, 48; overseer quoted in Ulrich B. Phillips, "Plantations with Slave Labor and Free," *AHR*, 30 (1925), 742; Foby, "Management of Servants," *Southern Cultivator*, 11 (Aug. 1853), 227–228; Magruder Diary, Dec. 19, 23, 1846; Hutchinson Diary, Dec. 25, 1837; McCall Plantation Journal and Diary, Dec. 25, 1852. Also, Joan Caldwell, "Christmas in Old Natchez," *Journal of Mississippi History*, 21 (1959), 264.

[81] Marsh Diary, Jan. 8, 1850; Prudhomme Papers, Dec. 24–26, 1860.

[82] Baker Diary, Dec. 25, Dec. 28, 1852.

private comments encourages the thought that, mostly, they hoped to have a good time as observers if not participants.[83]

During the War, Edward McGehee Burrus, serving with Longstreet's corps, wrote to his sisters back home in Woodville, Mississippi, that he had had a deluxe dinner in camp, provided for him by Claib, his devoted body-servant, who was pining for his wife and children. He then inquired about the scene at home:

Who 'caught' you & who did you 'catch'? What presents were revealed to inquisitive young eyes when the napkins were removed at breakfast? Who did Papa bestow his *inevitable knife* upon – his left-hand man (or as *some* might prefer to have it, boy) being absent? Was little William as fidgety as the occasion required or did the gravity & importance of his position as Major-domo & chief maker of ceremonies weigh down any inclinations he might have had toward levity or hilarity? Did the negro women assemble as usual around the black gallery to receive their brilliant colored drew patterns & was the distributor of *coffee, flour, sugar*, etc. as liberal as usual? ... In short, what kind of a Christmas was it–merry or dull?[84]

For the slaveholders, celebrations principally came with the New Year holiday. New Year's Eve was a big event in the cities, replete with parades and balls. On New Years Day the young gentlemen called on the ladies. The rounds started at about 11 A.M., since days were short and courting took time. Gentlemen joined their ladies in New Year's Day festivities but also had work to do in settling the year's business accounts. And that made it a grim day for slaves who faced sale to cover heavy debts and for slaves hired out, who had to leave families and friends for a year's work elsewhere. The wonderfully festive spirit shown by the slaves during the Christmas holidays had a dark side – apprehension of a bad ending to the great week.[85]

---

[83] Louis Manigault to Charles Manigault, Dec. 28, 1852, in James M. Clifton, ed., *Life and Labor on Argyle Island: Letters and Documents of a Savannah River Rice Plantation, 1833–1867* (Savannah, GA, 1978), 133. For planters' enjoyment of their slaves' holiday, see also, Nevitt Diary, Dec. 27, 1858; Catherine Carson to W. S. Waller, Jan. 26, 1836, in Carson Family Papers; Journal of Araby Plantation, Sept. 25, Dec. 27, 1843, in Nutt Papers; J. F. Corsbee to Newton D. Woody, Dec. 31, 1857, in Woody Papers; Judith Page Rives to Alfred L. Rives, Jan. 12, 1858, in Alfred L. Rives Papers; Bond Diary, Jan. 6, 1862; Solomon Northup, *Twelve Years a Slave* (New York, 1970 [1854]), 213–215, 220–221; Barrow, Dec. 24, 1839, in Davis, ed., *Plantation Life in the Florida Parishes*, 175. Many planters spent the holidays on plantations rather than in town. See e.g., J. B. Grimball Diaries, Dec. 25, 1837; and the items for 1848–1849 in the Henry Papers.

[84] Edward McGehee to his sisters, Dec. 29, 1862, in Lester Collection.

[85] Harriet Elizabeth Amos, "Social Life in an Antebellum Cotton Port: Mobile, Alabama, 1820–1860," (Ph.D. diss.: University of Alabama, 1976), 182; Eliza Ripley, *Social Life in Old New Orleans: Being Recollections of My Girlhood*, (New York, 1975 [1912]),

"My servants have a 'Candy pulling' tonight," J. H. Bills wrote on New Year's Eve. "They are as happy as Lords at 11 P.M." Simms delighted in providing entertainment for his slaves – and himself. One year he staged a *tableau vivant*, replete with costumed queens, princes, sultans, and what not: "The whole plantation gathered to the Spectacle. You should have seen our negroes," he wrote to a northern friend, "our piazza was crowded with them, leaping over each other's heads & much more delighted than you & I have ever been." The slaves seized every opportunity to have a good time, and we have no reason to doubt the veracity of their masters' accounts. Baker and others thought they saw grateful slaves delighted to return to work. Gustave Breaux of Louisiana commented on New Year's Day: "The hands as usual came in to greet the New Year with their good wishes – the scene is well calculated to excite sympathies: notwithstanding bondage, affections find roots in the heart of the slave for the master." But Breaux knew that thousands of slaves were hired out by the year; that the date of their departure was January 1; and that slaves referred to it – a day of heavy transactions in slave sales – as "heartbreak day."[86]

Former slaves may well have been right to suggest that they had a better time than their masters on holidays, at least in areas in which stern preachers had their way with white Protestants. White and black sources both hint, when they do not shout, that much of the whites' enjoyment came from observing blacks parties, which especially delighted the white children. Protestant masters may have taken Easter lightly, but they generally gave their slaves a holiday, which, in Virginia at least, stretched from midday Saturday through Tuesday morning.[87]

Holidays did not provide the only occasions for masters and mistresses to enjoy their slaves' entertainment. Slaves formed two rival groups at corn-shucking and, after the awarding of prizes, ended with dancing and feasting. Then, as at other times, adventurous masters chose the best performers and challenged other masters to test the talents of their own slaves, wagering on the outcome. Slave children, like children everywhere, loved to show off their talents, begging for a chance to sing,

51; John W. Blassingame, ed., *Slave Testimony: Two Centuries of Letters, Speeches, Interviews, and Autobiographies* (Baton Rouge, LA, 1977), 161; Herschel Gower and Jack Allan, *Pen and Sword: The Life and Journals of Randal W. McGavock* (Nashville, TN, 1959), 450; Botume, *First Days amongst the Contrabands*, 90.

[86] Bills Diary, Dec. 30, 1843; Simms to James Lawson, April 30, 1848, in Oliphant, et al., eds., *Letters of Simms*, 2:410; Breaux Diaries, Jan. 1, 1859.

[87] Hopley, *Life in the South*, 1:233; "Sketches of South-Carolina" (1847), in Schwaab and Bull, eds., *Travels in the South*, 2:317.

dance, and strum the banjo in the Big House as well as the quarters. Masters and mistresses were pleased to accommodate them. Some, like the Cheves family of South Carolina, expected adult slaves to show up on Sunday morning to "sing and shout for us." Slave children, in turn, expected sugar and biscuits for services rendered. Masters called on their slaves for entertainment from dancing contests to wrestling matches. Here and there, masters encouraged malevolent rivalries among male slaves in approximations of Roman gladiator contests.[88]

---

[88] Annie Laurie Broidrick, "A Recollection of Thirty Years Ago" (typescript), 7; Huff, *Langdon Cheves*, 11; Leslie Owens, *This Species of Property: Slave Life and Culture in the Old South* (New York, 1976), 117–118; Silverthorne, *Plantation Life in Texas*, 183. On corn shucking see Roger D. Abrahams, *Singing the Master: The Emergence of African American Culture in the Plantation South* (New York, 1992), 3–4, 67.

5

Vignettes

Charms of High Life

The Platonists, indeed, are not so foolish as, with the Manicheans, to detest
our present bodies as an evil nature.

– Saint Augustine[1]

SCANDALS

The most eminent southern families had their full share of scandals. William
D. Valentine, a prudish thirty-year-old son of a planter, taught school in
Windsor, North Carolina, where he found himself surrounded by vice. He
lamented that gentlemen with wives and daughters tolerated it. Valentine
believed the ladies in town to be virtuous but puzzled over their apparent
lack of concern: "Fornication and adultery and leching are boldly practiced
by the youth without fear of shame, regard of respect for themselves or
decency of society; and if their obscene indulgence happens to be social –
they take pride and the greatest pleasure in telling it to every body, interlacing
their narrations if possible with implications of persons innocent." Valentine
could have cited Mary Henderson, his fellow North Carolinian: "Poor Mrs
Barkin is making herself the town talk by going to the NU[?] alley and other
places of dissipation after her drunken gambling husband."[2]

---

[1] Saint Augustine, *The City of God*, tr. Marcus Dods (New York, 1950), 447, also 470–472,
also, Saint Augustine, "On the Holy Trinity," *Nicene and Post-Nicene Fathers*, ed. Philip
Schaff (Peabody, MA, 1995), 141.

[2] Valentine Diaries, April 8, 1838; Henderson Journal, Aug. 20, 1855, in Henderson Papers;
also, Hutchinson Journal, Feb. 15, 16, 1838; Serena R. Lea to Martha Jackson, July 5,
1840, in Jackson-Prince Papers.

Few doubted that young men were likely to have a rakish streak, and parents devoted much effort to keeping their sons' indiscretions within tolerable bounds. Young ladies from "respectable" families lived under formidable restraints, but audacious young gentlemen claimed to have little trouble finding bed partners. Letters of young gentlemen to each other discussed adventures with poor whites, blacks, prostitutes, and young ladies of the ostensibly well-chaperoned elite. Many of the letters contained coarse language.[3]

With or without issue, illicit liaisons gave the churches a headache, for they adjudicated many more cases than the courts did. Bishop Meade of Virginia moaned about "certain offences against good morals," singling out "a lady of respectable family" who "broke the seventh commandment." The churches aired such matters and pondered cases in which spiteful women filed dubious charges against men they resented. The Associated Presbyterian Reverend Samuel Agnew did not like what he found in Madison County, Mississippi: "dissipated young men and wild, careless frolicsome girls." He was sure that he had not yet seen the worst: "Some of the young people of both sexes are hard cases, but the Spirit of God can work a change." In Lee County before and during the War, Agnew bemoaned the decline in female morals: "Some of the women of that county, despairing of husbands have given indulgence to loose habits. Jim Pratt's widow is one of the frail ones. Some of the old men fear that a general defection of this kind will prevail in consequence of the scarcity of men."[4]

When Augustus Baldwin Longstreet became president of Emory College at Oxford in 1840, Middle Georgia had changed considerably since his youth in the 1820s. It now harbored a good deal of quasi-oriental mores. Leading gentlemen flaunted concubines, and the clergy had its hands full in a fairly successful work of reformation that significantly curbed at least outward behavior in the 1850s.[5]

J. S. Buckingham, among other foreigners, thought that Americans generally had few seductions and incidents of adultery. Since he doubtless had comparison with England and France in mind, he may have been right. Still, southern proslavery ideologues made much of their

---

[3] Steven M. Stowe, *Intimacy and Power in the Old South: Ritual in the Lives of the Planters* (Baltimore, 1987), 81–82.

[4] William Meade, *Old Churches, Ministries, and Families of Virginia*, 2 vols. (Berryville, VA, 1978 [1857]), 1:365; Agnew Journal, Dec. 26, 1856, June 13, 1863.

[5] John Donald Wade, *Augustus Baldwin Longstreet: A Study of the Development of Culture in the South* (New York, 1924), 242–243.

"traditional values" and could hardly complain when their enemies recited the litany. To cite some of the more flamboyant cases: Nancy Randolph, John Randolph's cousin, never stood trial for the murder of her bastard child by Richard Randolph, his brother. Richard Randolph was acquitted of the murder and probably had not been an accomplice, if in fact one took place. John Randolph also accused Nancy of sleeping with a black servant. The truth of any of the accusations against her remains moot, but the local folks believed the worst. Jefferson, in a moving letter to his daughter, Martha Jefferson Randolph, appealed to her to reflect on human frailty and not judge Nancy too harshly.[6]

After the Revolutionary War, Nathanael Greene and "Mad Anthony" Wayne, two of the most famous northern Revolutionary War generals to lead commands in the South and fast friends, would have shot it out, had not Greene died before he could challenge Wayne to a duel for having dallied with his beautiful and charming wife, Catherine. In 1833, Senator John Tyler of Virginia opposed a consulship in Algiers for ("Black Horse Harry") Henry Lee, son of Light-Horse Harry Lee, for having seduced his sister-in-law. Indignantly, Lee asked how Tyler could be so fussy, since Mr. Jefferson himself had done something of the sort. Richard Henry Wilde of Georgia, accomplished poet, scholar, and congressman, created a stir with his all-too-open affair with the notoriously flirtatious wife of Representative Joseph White of Florida. In 1838, Thomas Holly Chivers, Georgia's celebrated poet, was living in New York, where he could play more freely. He asked Alexander Stephens to defend him against his wife's suit for bigamy, admitting, "I have been intimate with more ladies than one, since I left the state of Georgia, and expect to be with many more before I die. It is all the fashion here."[7]

---

[6] J. S. Buckingham, *The Slave States of America*, 2 vols. (New York, 1968 [1842]), 1:127; William Cabell Bruce, *John Randolph of Roanoke, 1773–1833: A Biography Based Largely on New Material*, 2 vols. (New York, 1970 [1922]), 1:108 ff, 119–120, 2:275 ff. The facts remain obscure. Nancy Randolph moved to New York and married old Gouveneur Morris.

[7] Mary Granger, ed., *Savannah River Plantations* (Spartanburg, SC, 1983), 73–74, 121–122; Oliver Perry Chitwood, *John Tyler: Champion of the Old South* (New York, 1939), 102; on Wilde, see Maria Bryan Harford to Julia Ann Bryan Cumming, Mar 17, 1834, in Carol Bleser, ed., *Tokens of Affection: The Letters of a Planter's Daughter in the Old South* (Athens, GA, 1996), 169; Chivers to Stephens, Sept. 19, 1838, in Thomas Holley, et al., eds., *The Complete Works of Thomas Holley Chivers: The Correspondence of Thomas Holley Chivers, 1838–1858* (Providence, RI, 1957), 2. The sexual adventures of Edgar Allan Poe, a long-time friend of Chivers, titillated the gossip mill in Charleston as well as Richmond. See, e.g., Simms to E. A. Duyckinck, March 27, 1846, in Mary C. Oliphant et al., eds., *The Letters of William Gilmore Simms*, 6 vols. (Columbia, SC, 1952–1982), 2:157–159.

In Charleston, where upper-class mores and much else veered toward the standards of Bordeaux and other Atlantic ports, Charles Pinckney flaunted his love affair after the death of his wife in 1794. In later years, a daughter of the eminent James L. Petigru faced accusations of having had an illegitimate child by a well-known Charlestonian. Among lesser lights, Colonel John Cunningham, scion of a noted loyalist family, would have been at the center of society in upcountry Abbeville and in Charleston, if his frequent adulterous escapades had not raised eyebrows. In later decades proslavery Southerners enjoyed the exploits of Cassius Clay, Kentucky's famed abolitionist, whose philandering in Moscow while serving as American minister led to his divorce. The ravishingly beautiful Mary Boozer took Columbia, South Carolina, by storm, notwithstanding the scandals that swirled around her and her mother. "Big Dave" Boozer, a wealthy widower in the village of Newberry, married Mrs. Peter Burton, known as a gold-digging widow. She thereupon conducted an affair openly. The magnanimous and forgiving Big Dave adopted Mary, his wife's daughter. But then he either committed suicide or was murdered, and the gossip mill throve. Mother and daughter moved to Columbia, where they remained until they accompanied Sherman's army northward. Achieving celebrity status on three continents, they appeared as the subject of novels and stories.[8]

Already privately condemned for his omnivorous sexual appetites, Governor James H. Hammond of South Carolina made himself publicly odorous by being caught engaging in sexual play with his teen-age nieces. He then made himself wholly ludicrous by proclaiming, wide-eyed, that, after all, he had stopped short of intercourse. His antics would have been wonderfully funny if they had not crippled the political career of one of the South's ablest and most intelligent leaders, and if they had not ruined the girls' chances of ever marrying, notwithstanding their being Hamptons – that is, daughters of one of the wealthiest, most powerful, and most respected planters in the South. The legislature again heard about the scandal in 1857, when Hammond and Francis Pickens vied

---

[8] Clement Eaton, *The Mind of the Old South* (Baton Rouge, LA, 1967), 30 (Petigru); Mark A. Kaplanoff, "Charles Pinckney and the American Republican Tradition," in Michael O'Brien and David Moltke-Hansen, eds., *Intellectual Life in Antebellum Charleston* (Knoxville, TN, 1986), 113; Ernest McPherson Lander, Jr., *The Calhoun Family and Thomas Green Clemson: The Decline of a Southern Patriarchy* (Columbia, SC, 1983), 189 (Cunningham); Paul E. Fuller., *Laura Clay and the Woman's Rights Movement* (Frankfort, KY, 1992), 2; Thomas H. Pope, *The History of Newberry County, South Carolina*, 2 vols. (Columbia, SC, 1973), 1:102. Nell S. Graydon suggests the Boozers were the victims of slander for their northern origins and pro-Union sympathies: *Tales of Columbia* (Columbia, SC, 1964), 125–127.

for election to the U.S. Senate. Pickens took high ground: "The line was drawn distinctly between virtue and honor on one side, and open vulgar blagardism [sic] on the other." No one accused Pickens, who became South Carolina's wartime governor, of blackguardism or sexual impropriety, but he had his own personal miseries. He had a daughter whose marriage brought pain and mortification to her father. Pickens thereupon exacerbated his pain by marrying a coquettish spoiled brat whose deportment left him open to derision.[9]

Incest ranked among matters rarely discussed outside the courts. It occurred infrequently but frequently enough to catch the attention of state legislatures. As traditionalists, legislators as well as judges had to uphold male authority in the family; as civilized men, they could hardly countenance violation of daughters. They were pitiless toward rogues who forced daughters, handling them roughly. But evidence was hard to come by, and men easily assumed that young women who did not resist had made themselves accomplices. The legislatures responded by making incest a crime and restricting marriage between kin, but they had to do so carefully, since judges were loathe to interfere with the autonomy of families. And here they invoked the common law, which did not recognize incest as a crime. Peter Bardaglio, who has investigated these matters, suggests that, in effect, the social commitment to hierarchy and patriarchy undermined action against offenders and offered little protection to victims. He doubtless has a point, but little can be said with assurance. The hush-hush that has always accompanied incest may well have disguised much. Despite stories of men like Hammond, who had as a mistress an enslaved daughter by an enslaved black mistress, and despite the modern understanding that incest does not respect class, there is little to suggest that it occurred often in planter families – the description of the low country as one vast cousinage notwithstanding. Yet comments about family trees in remote populations not having enough branches hint at perduring popular perceptions that other southerners saw a good deal of incest that never resulted in trials.[10]

Southerners gossiped while they made valiant efforts to pretend not to know what they knew. Protection of family name and honor remained the principal point for both men and women, and even in the sophisticated

---

[9] Carol Bleser, ed., *The Hammonds of Redcliffe* (New York, 1981), 28–33; Drew Gilpin Faust, *James Henry Hammond and the Old South* (Baton Rouge, LA, 1982), 32.

[10] Peter W. Bardaglio, "'An Outrage upon Nature,'" in Carol Bleser, ed., *In Joy and in Sorrow: Women, Family, and Marriage in the Victorian South, 1830–1900* (New York, 1991), 32–51.

circles of the low country and the cities, aristocratic ladies did not escape rebuke for easy morals. William Gilmore Simms, no prude, exploded in 1858 that Charleston was "wonderfully healthy this season" but also "ineffably stupid." He mentioned "thirty-six fast women, who would like to do any amount of whoring if they could escape the consequences; and who abuse the men terribly because they don't operate in spite of their difficulties, though with their free will & consent; and at the risk of a bullet for adultery, & gallows for rape." Simms surely knew that Sullivan's Island, off the coast, served as a refuge for young ladies and gentlemen anxious to get free of the conventions that bound them in Charleston and on their plantations.[11]

A letter from William H. Trescot to William Porcher Miles of Charleston – with James D. B. DeBow, classmates at the College of Charleston – illuminated the underside of elite life in the port cities. Miles had returned from Norfolk, Virginia, where he had performed heroically as a volunteer nurse during the epidemic of 1855. But subsequently he began an affair with a woman who, while young and innocent, had married a man with nothing to offer except "gold." The wags in Charleston, to say nothing of his unionist political enemies, had a field day. Trescot wrote his "dear friend," then mayor and congressional candidate, that, emphatically, he had no wish to be judgmental but had to counsel an end to the affair:

Now my friend as a man of the world you know this cannot continue – If this be an ordinary liaison the publicity of the thing is in very bad taste and is moreover demanding from you entirely too great a sacrifice – You are not bound to ruin a whole life for the possession of any person however charming and the public proclamation of such damned folly is unworthy of you and unpardonable in the freshest fool that ever fancied he could be *[illegible]* himself.

Fooling around could have damaging effects on a political career, if word circulated too freely. Trescot claimed to be sure that Miles was innocent of such folly:

[But] if then you have one spark of real attachment to the unfortunate lady – save her from herself – think for her – act for her. It *is* in *your* power if not to stop

---

[11] W. G. Simms to M. C. M. Hammond, Sept. 18, 1859, in Oliphant et al., eds., *Letters of Simms*, 4:176. According to Bishop Elder, Catholics and Protestants alike in the Delta readily violated the sanctity of marriage: William Henry Elder, *Civil War Diary, 1862–1865* (Natchez, MS, n.d.), 74 (Jan. 31, 1864). On Sullivan's Island, see Steven M. Stowe, "City, Country, and the Feminine Voice," in O'Brien and Moltke-Hansen, eds., *Intellectual Life in Antebellum Charleston*, 300.

this torrent of evil-speaking, at least to put in safely by putting out of the way the poor victim whose life is endangered. Refuse to her the pleasure of your society if that can only be purchased by her at the expense of character.[12]

SEXUAL BOUNDARIES

Much idle conjecture has arisen from the undeniable sexual exploitation of black women by men who prated endlessly about the purity of their white women. In one preposterous version, ice-cold ladies assigned sexual pleasure to racially inferior black "wenches" and degraded lower-class white women. Those who believe that the ladies were frigid produce no evidence, whereas the ladies' diaries and correspondence contain frequent expressions of loving marriages. No doubt, Eliza Wright was not alone in approaching her wedding bed in fear: "I am sure I would have died if my husband had not been *particularly* kind." Direct reference to sexual pleasure appeared rarely in letters between wives and husbands, but frequent teasing and discreet allusions hardly suggested prudery. Occasionally, as John Rozier says about Edgeworth and Sally Bird: "Their correspondence was astonishingly frank and their love not only romantic but openly and candidly physical."[13]

Flippant generalizations nonetheless floated about and still float about. In the 1790s, the Marquis de Chastellux found that the women of Virginia shared little in the amusements of the men and were "often coquettish and prudish before marriage, and dull and tiresome afterwards." Having slaves to care for them and their children, some judged, made women indolent. In the 1830s, Charles N. Mosely complained of the want of an interesting unmarried lady in New Market, South Carolina. They were "all straight creatures" who preferred "Hymens slavery." Yet the literature of southern humor was rich in accounts of female sexual appetites.[14]

---

[12] Trescot to Miles, April 13, 1856, in W. P. Miles Papers.

[13] Eliza L. W. Wright Journal, Jan. 15, 1836, in Joan E. Cashin, ed., *Our Common Affairs: Texts from Women in the Old South* (Baltimore, 1996), 54; John Rozier, ed., *The Granite Farm Letters: The Civil War Correspondence of Edgeworth and Sallie Bird* (Athens, GA, 1988), xxviii; Elizabeth Fox-Genovese, *Within the Plantation Household: Black and White Women of the Old South* (Chapel Hill, NC, 1988), 235–236, 240–241; Stowe, *Intimacy and Power*, 126.

[14] Marquis de Chastellux, *Travels in North America in the Years 1780, 1781, and 1782*, 2 vols., rev., tr. H. C. Rice, Jr. (Chapel Hill, NC, 1963), 2:441–442; Hennig Cohen and William A. Dillingham, eds., *Humor of the Old Southwest*, 2nd ed. (Athens, GA, 1964), xix.

Gentlemen indulged in the lewd jokes common at stag gatherings, but, more revealingly, they joked about their own ladies. The Reverend James S. Lamar of Georgia, speaking of log-rolling, recounted, "Woe to him who is tardy! He joked about his wife's powerful attractions holding him back." In upcountry Carolina during the eighteenth and early nineteenth centuries, female *arrivistes* ruffled lowcountry sensibilities with frank, even crude discussions of sex. Miss Pitt married, and Martin Gordon recounted to Benjamin Tureaud – both wealthy sugar planters – a story about a wife's waking her husband: "Oh my dear, don't you hear a rat!" To which her husband replied, "No, my darling – I do not – but I smell a rat." The rat, according to Gordon, "was run back to his 'hole' – and the loving couple went to sleep."[15]

Nothing indicates that men or women, high or low, separated love from physical passion. In 1844, the *New Orleans Medical and Surgical Journal* endorsed monogamy as morally and physically the best state but rejected abstinence as unnatural and unhealthful for both sexes. Ministers spoke more delicately but, drawing on Augustine's attack on Manichaeism, encouraged women to seek sexual pleasure. Thus the Presbyterian Reverend Dr. James Henley Thornwell of South Carolina: "There is nothing virtuous or vicious in any of the naked appetites, but virtue or vice may attach to the methods of their gratification." Episcopal Bishop J. H. Otey of Tennessee reserved his ire for illicit methods of gratification, as when he exploded at Mrs. Mix in Natchez. Although married, she brazenly lived in sin with Judge Debuisson: "Shameless profligacy & licentiousness! Such alas! is human nature!"[16]

Despite his many affairs in the quarters, Hammond, in his reply to the antislavery Thomas Clarkson, dismissed the charge of Abolitionists that masters slept with their slaves. Appealing to a wide audience of southern ladies as well as gentlemen, he ridiculed Harriet Martineau for her "grand charge": "The constant recurrence of the female Abolitionists to this topic, and their bitterness in regard to it, cannot fail to suggest to even the most charitable mind that 'Such rage without betrays the fires within.'" In Baltimore, Ernest Duvergier de Hauranne, a young Frenchman, discreetly referred to the sexual abuses that slavery permitted. The ladies

---

[15] Lamar, in Edward J. Cashin, ed., *A Wilderness Still the Cradle of Nature* (Savannah, GA, 1994), 35; William Dusinberre, *Them Dark Days: Slavery in the American Rice Swamps* (New York, 1996), 31; Martin Gordon to Benjamin Tureaud, Sept. 19, 1850, in Tureaud Papers.

[16] *New Orleans Medical and Surgical Journal*, 1 (1844), 110–111; "Discourses on Truth" in *JHTW*, 2:479; Otey Diary, Jan. 15, 1852.

laughed: "Oh! it isn't always the best men we love the best." Southern women of various attitudes took for granted that young men sowed wild oats. They tried to keep their men on the straight and narrow but took a less harsh view of men's transgressions than men took of women's. Anna Matilda King of Georgia happily told her son that Tootie "looks prettier & is MORE HAPPY now than since her marriage." It seems that her husband "has CONFESSED HIS sins & implored her pardon for all the CAUSES he has given her for unhappiness." Everard Green Baker of Mississippi did some confessing of his own on "a memorable day in my existence." He prayed:

> Oh my God enable me to keep good my holy resolves ... that I may never become cold or indifferent upon that most of important of subjects – the salvation of my soul – Oh my God enable me to live as a Christian should live to be a faithful husband, a kind father & master & an exemplary Christian .... Dear Laura [and I] rode out this eve, we had much serious talk, – & I am more & more convinced of the pure & unsullied piety of my dear wife – while I have ever been too much taken up with the world she has never failed to offer up her prayers, to our common Savior that I might turn from my evil ways to those paths of pleasantness & peace, & now I trust the prayers of that dear one are answered, & that I may never cause her heart to bleed again for my waywardness.[17]

VICISSITUDES OF COURTING

Custom in the colonial South required children to have parental consent to marry. In the early eighteenth century, wedding announcements in newspapers often mentioned the size of the estate a woman brought to her marriage. Some fathers wrote wills that left property to a son provided he renounce interest in a particular young lady. For those with substantial property, the disposition of that property held central importance; marriage concerned the family at least as much as the individual. Without having to worry about the disposition of substantial property, lower-class children had more room to do as they pleased.

Southerners juggled a strong sense of family responsibility with a no less strong sense of respect for the feelings of young people who wanted to marry for love. In the late eighteenth century, John Rutledge's widowed mother faced declining fortunes in the South Carolina low country.

---

[17] [William Gilmore Simms, ed.] *Selections from the Letters and Speeches of James H. Hammond* (Spartanburg, SC, 1978 [1866]), 134–135; Ernest Duvergier de Hauranne, *A Frenchman in Lincoln's America*, 2 vols. (Chicago, 1974), 2:482; Anna Matilda King to Lord King, Sept. 28, 1848, in T. B. King Papers; Baker Diary, Sept. 4, 1859.

She worried about one son who needed capital to start a business and about the lack of marriage proposals for a daughter perceived to be stuck in a financially precarious family. She had a solution. She asked John to marry a wealthy young lady, mentioning one of the Horry girls. He acknowledged his responsibilities but thought to find another way. The demand of the southern well-to-do for parental consent remained powerful, but parents, bending to creeping romanticism, eased pressure on children. In Louisiana, the Cajuns, who considered marriage a family concern, did not bend. A suitor needed permission from the women's family, including cousins. Anglo planters solved the problem, if imperfectly, in the manner of the planters of the Southeast: They did everything possible to have their children associate with members of their social circles. At church, academies, colleges, resorts, and balls – even at quilting parties, corn-shuckings, and log-rollings – they met members of their own class or at least of "respectable" families. Children had stratagems for breaking free of parental restraint, and parents had stratagems for reining them in. John Houston Bills of Tennessee, visiting Charlottesville, Virginia, met Miss Juliet A. Gilmer, "with whom I fell in love, also Miss Margaret Walker for whom I entertain the same kind of affection & so advise one or both to await the Coming of my sons whom I shall certainly advise to court them." Daughters sometimes accepted marriage proposals without consulting parents, confident of their approval. Polly Jefferson did not consult Thomas Jefferson, her father, but she knew of his high opinion of John Eppes.[18] In short, the elite tried to live in accordance with a Spanish adage: *Dime con quién andas y te diré quien eres* [Tell me with whom you associate, and I shall tell you who you are].

Circumstances encouraged love at first sight. Teenaged Reuben Davis of Mississippi and a young friend visited his friend's uncle. The family and friends were returning from church: "I asked Glover who the girl was who wore the white frock and big Leghorn hat with roses on it, and he told me it was his eldest cousin. Miss Halbert was about sixteen then, and I thought her the most beautiful and fascinating girl I had ever

[18] Richard Barry, *Mr. Rutledge of South Carolina* (New York, 1942), 30–31; Carl A. Brasseaux, *Acadian to Cajun: Transformation of a People, 1803–1877* (Jackson, MS, 1992), 39; Bills Diary, May 16, 1851; Dumas Malone, *Jefferson and His Time*, 6 vols. (Charlottesville, VA, 1948–1961), 3:239. For eastern low country friends and cousins, see Dusinberre, *Them Dark Days*, 37. For shifting attitudes in historical context, see Elizabeth Fox-Genovese, *Marriage: The Dream that Refuses to Die* (Wilmington, DE, 2008).

seen." Davis resolved, then and there, to marry her, and the feeling was mutual. A risk but within limits. Each came from an established, respectable family and trusted Glover's assurances of good character. The means of "presentation," as introductions were called, varied; one of the more acceptable was an invitation to Sunday dinner that included an invitation to attend church together.[19]

When children, especially daughters, married without parental consent, family relations could be poisoned for life, even severed. An irritated Bennett H. Barrow of Louisiana cried out: "Marry a Daughter against the mother's will – hatred or dislike remains with her forever." John Walker, a planter in Virginia, recounted the marriage of Ethelin Walker to James Croxton, who faced "the great opposition of her parents [who] were distressed more than my pen or words can express." Some irate fathers turned out of their homes young women, girls really, who refused to marry decrepit old men, but the women had a chance of being taken in by sympathetic families in their communities.[20]

Young people did fall in love with and marry outsiders. Sometimes, they defied their parents' wishes because of conflicting estimates regarding the character of the young lady or gentleman. The first Pierce Butler, stationed in South Carolina during the Revolutionary War, eloped with fifteen-year-old Betsey Izard only to have her father's friends frustrate the affair. A wag quipped that Major Butler "will never make a good general, unless he can conduct his Coups de Main with more secresy [sic]." Butler did better on the next round, marrying Mary Middleton from a leading lowcountry family. Eighteen-year-old Letitia Watkins of Mississippi turned down numerous marriage proposals before she eloped, perhaps not voluntarily. Her mother had always insisted that she marry up to the family's station. In this respect, Letitia proved a dutiful daughter when she ran off with William Martin Walton, a planter, but her father never forgave her. John Stanly may have forgiven his daughter for eloping with Colonel Armstead, but how it must have rankled. Still, what else could the poor woman have done? Armstead's character and family connections were in order, but he and Stanly were

---

[19] Reuben Davis, *Recollections of Mississippi and Mississippians* (Oxford, MS, 1972 [1879], 46; Mitchell D. King to John W. Ellis, Oct. 5, 1849, in ed., *The Papers of John Willis Ellis*, 2 vols. (Raleigh, NC, 1964), 1:81.

[20] Barrow Diary, Nov. 6, 1839, in Edwin Adams Davis, ed., *Plantation Life in the Florida Parishes of Louisiana, 1836–1846, as Reflected in the Diary of Bennet H. Barrow* (New York, 1943), 170; John Walker Diary, March 15, 1837; Clitherall "Autobiography." 1810 (ms.). Book 5.

political enemies. Most parents did not persist in opposition, especially after grandchildren arrived.[21]

To prevent a young lady's rush into marriage, parents were likely to send her to boarding school to give her time to cool off. A determined daughter who merely hinted at elopement likely got her way. Even the imperious Charles Carroll of Carrolton yielded to his daughter's threat to elope with Robert Goodloe Harper, despite his firm objections to her seeing him at all. If a young man had tact and skill, no threat of elopement need arise. Thus, William J. Hanna won over his father-in-law, John Craig, a prominent lawyer in the Chesterfield District of South Carolina, who had strongly opposed the marriage. Hanna turned out well and rose to become brigadier general of militia, a state senator, and a district solicitor. The two men became warm friends.[22]

Young lovers maneuvered tactically around testy parents, sometimes enlisting slaves in their efforts. Lucy Breckenridge and her fiancé devised a secret code in which to write each other. The less imaginative chose trusted maids and valets to carry love letters back and forth. Plantation maids knew each other and checked out the reputations of their mistresses' swains. More drastically, mammies drove off undesirable suitors for their young mistresses. Ever since Roman times, as delineated by Ovid, slave confidantes exercised formidable power by protecting secret liaisons and carrying rumors of bad character and assurances of good. Thomas Bayne of Georgia learned to cherish his stepmother despite earnest efforts by the old family servants to sabotage his father's marriage to the nineteen-year-old Mary Green. The practice of confiding in servants in the pursuit of love affairs infuriated Eliza Barnwell, who charged that it led to gossip, quarrels, and family estrangements. Yet, only occasionally did someone object strongly to the intervention of servants. Belles easily

---

[21] Fox-Genovese, *Within the Plantation Household*, 207–210; Stowe, *Power and Intimacy*, 84; William Harris Hardy and Toney A. Hardy, *No Compromise with Principle: Autobiography and Biography of William Harris Hardy in Dialogue* (New York, 1946), 16; Lewright B. Sikes, *The Public Life of Pierce Butler, South Carolina Statesman* (Washington, DC, 1979), 2–3; see the extended correspondence in E. Grey Dimond and Herman Hattaway, eds., *Letters from Forest Place: A Plantation Family's Correspondence* (Jackson, MS, 1993); William Shepard to Ebenezer Pettigrew, Dec. 22, 1814, in Lemmon, ed., *Pettigrew Papers*, 1:476–477. Kate Stone's sister, who married at sixteen, turned down ten proposals: John Q. Anderson, ed. *Brokenburn: The Journal of Kate Stone, 1861–1868* (Baton Rouge, LA, 1955), 345.

[22] David Hackett Fisher, *The Revolution of American Conservatism* (New York, 1965), 38; John Belton O'Neall, *Biographical Sketches of the Bench and Bar of South Carolina*, 2 vols. (Spartanburg, SC, 1975 [1859]), 2:105 (Hanna).

turned to favorite slaves to assist in courtship. After all, black women taught elite young ladies proper deportment. Sara Agnes Rice's servant refused to let her do work like spinning. Why? "Ain't I done tole you? Ladies don't nuvver do them things." Well, bu, then, why could Miss Sara help with the laces and muslins? "Cause – ladies *does* do dem things?"[23]

Parents, especially among the well-to-do, did not easily dictate their children's love lives. Most knew that their sons and daughters combined family pride and respectful deference with strong wills. They knew that, more often than not, their children would marry whom they wished. Hence an accommodation of sorts: The young ladies selected their husbands, but their parents did everything possible to make sure that their choices moved in respectable circles. Marrying within a close social circle carried a special advantage. The interlocking of families smoothed the rationalization and sharing of plantation finances and production.[24]

Swains took the measure of the romantic streak in young ladies – all the more so since many had a streak of their own. Routinely, they sent the young ladies whom they courted poems of their own creation. The young ladies manifestly appreciated the thought and effort, however they judged the poetry. More soberly, the editors of *Oakland College Magazine* in Mississippi instructed young ladies in 1858: "In marriage there should be congeniality of affection, religion, and education ... No lady should ever pledge her hand to one who has not her heart. From this principle she should not be seduced by wealth or fame or talents, nor misled by officious friends, or awed by the authority of mistaken parents." Ministers had a problem when parental objections arose from differences of religion or denomination. The ladies had a cushion: A lady might withdraw her acceptance of a marriage proposal, but law as well as mores forbade a gentleman from doing so.[25]

---

[23] Robertson, ed., *Lucy Breckinridge Journal*, Nov. 23, 24, 1863 (157); Bayne Autobiographical Sketch (ms.), 4; A. L. Broiderick, "A Recollection" (ms.), 5; Thomas Diary, Sept. 16, 1866; Stephen B. Barnwell, *The Story of an American Family* (Marquette, MI, 1969), 120; Mrs. Roger Pryor, *My Day: Reminiscences of a Long Life*, 16.

[24] Philip Hamilton, "Gentry Women and the Transformation of Daily Life in Jeffersonian and Antebellum Virginia," in Angela Boswell and Judith N. McArthur, eds., *Women Shaping the South: Creating and Confronting Change* (Colombia, MO, 2006), 9.

[25] See Louisa Quitman's correspondence, 1848–1851, in J. A. Quitman Papers; Robertson, ed., *Lucy Breckinridge Journal*, Nov. 1863 (157); Baker Diary, June, 1849. Robert Tyler may not have qualified as a good poet, but his ardent prose in his letters to Priscilla Cooper, the actress, was itself poetic: Elizabeth Coleman, *Priscilla Cooper Tyler and the American Scene, 1816–1889* (University, AL, 2006), 67. "On Marriage," *Oakland College Magazine*, 3 (1858), 23; W. W. Sweet, *Religion on the American Frontier: The*

Mollie Mitchell of Alabama surprised "Mag," her sister, with news of her marriage. Choosing Mr. Mitchell, she refused to submit to reigning attitudes or fuss about inessentials: "I am nearly an inch taller than he is – he is a fine figure and upon the whole Mag, he is a fine looking Gentleman. He is a farmer – he is *not* rich, neither is he poor – and had he not one Dollar in the world, I should consider him a fortune within himself for he knows how to make it and have it made and then to take care of it after it is made." She allowed that he was not as well educated as she would wish, "though I would not be ashamed of him in any crowd."[26]

Mary Moragné, having determined to marry a man of modest means, feared disappointing and displeasing her mother and friends. She had no intention of displaying "cold & miserable pride" and playing the fool: "Last night when I happened to give Mother a hint of Mr ___ intentions towards me, she appeared surprised; & her countenance grew heavy with apprehension: – she could not smile – they have been looking for *wealth* & *rank* & *fame* for me; but pride cannot now influence my resolves; the first duty I owe in this respect, is to my own heart." Two weeks later she regretted having provoked her mother to "bitter & unusual reflection" about marrying Mr. Davis. She registered her mother's anxiety about her having to face the risks and hardships of life. "Here is the radical error: – I have been *raised for a rich man's wife!* from what height am I fallen then – to resolve to be *always poor* – ha! ha!" For her, the tower that supposedly loomed over her as a prison appeared as a castle in the air: "a phantasmagoria ... I have borne with my friends long enough: they must now bear with me."[27]

A strong current ran counter to class prejudice. Southern society prided itself on having room at the top for "respectable" and "industrious" young men likely to climb the ladder with a little help. Tally Simpson, from a planter family in upcountry South Carolina, ridiculed the "silly fools" who refused to let daughters marry men of poor origins. He cited C. G. Memminger and J. L. Orr – prominent politicians – to insist that society needed talent, not class pretensions. Tellingly, according to postwar reminiscences of men from all classes in Tennessee, sons of small slaveholders and nonslaveholders, especially in regions with few big planters, wooed and wed the rich men's daughters with whom they

Methodists (New York, 1946), 131; Eleanor M. Boatwright, *Status of Women in Georgia, 1783–1860* (Brooklyn, NY, 1994), 38.

[26] Mary Jane Allen Mitchell to Margaret Stevens Browne, Oct. 12, 1853, in Browne Papers.
[27] Mary Moragné, in Delle Mullen Craven, ed., *The Neglected Thread: A Journal of the Calhoun Community* (Columbia, SC, 1951), 43 (Feb. 26, 1842), 46 (March 12, 1842).

attended school or church. James T. McColgan, from a planter family, recalled that a poor girl, if pretty, had a better chance of marrying into wealth than a (presumably plain) wealthy girl did, but planters doubtless knew those poor girls mostly as products of "respectable" families.[28]

Courting was tricky for swains. Intentions could easily be misunderstood or manipulated. James Garnett warned the young ladies of Virginia to avoid "Platonic friendships" with men: Only coxcombs approached young ladies in that way, for they sought something other than marriage. The seventeen-year-old John wanted to be Sarah Lois Wadley's beau. He proceeded carefully with all the correct moves, which probably marked him as a good friend rather than a lover. ("Lover" did not designate, as it does now, sexual intimacy.) Sarah thought him "nice" in his dress and smooth and glossy hair. He corrected the children when they did not speak grammatically and entertained her with his gift for punning. "He is very kind to drive us wherever we wish to go, and makes no objection to any of our arrangements." Octavia Bryant explained that she was not engaged, for while every girl has a "sweetheart," that does not mean he is "an accepted *Lover*." Even at the Virginia Springs, where visitors let their hair down a bit, a gentleman did not hold a lady's hand in public unless betrothed. Belles nonetheless were great flirts. Lucy Walton recalled that Cary Bryan, "one of our loveliest girls," said that she intended to have many declared lovers to sustain her reputation as a belle. Walton, sensitive to the potential damage, avoided playing the tease: "I never allowed any gentleman to commit himself by the SERIOUS expression of sentiment when it was possible to avoid it." Mary Easton of Tennessee added in 1854 that spoiled and vain belles generally turned out to be irresponsible wives and mistresses.[29]

Young gentlemen prided themselves on their prowess at winning hearts, but they cautioned each other against leading a young lady to think their intentions more serious than they were, lest they become, in the words of John Cunningham of Abbeville Court House, "an object

[28] Tally Simpson to Caroline Simpson, May 29, 1863, in Guy R. Everson and Edward W. Simpson, eds., *"Far, Far from Home": The Wartime Letters of Dick and Tally Simpson, Third South Carolina Volunteers* (New York, 1994), 238; TCWVQ, 1:127, 399; 2:695, 752; 3:1034, 1098, 1219; 4:1373, 1426 (McColgan); 5:1794.

[29] James M. Garnett, *Lectures on Female Education*, 3rd ed. (Richmond, VA, 1825), 196; Wadley Private Journal, Jan. 4, 1861; Octavia Bryant to Winston Stephens, Feb. 15, 1858, in Arch Fredric Blakely et al., eds., *Rose Cottage Chronicles: Civil War Letters of the Bryant-Stephens Families of North Florida* (Tallahassee, FL, 1998), 34; Fletcher Autobiography, Winter, 1843 (ms.); Mrs. Mary H. Eaton, "Home Secrets–No. V," *Parlor Visitor* (Nashville), 1 (1854), 2-2.

of execration from being the memento of disappointment." Only a fool would send a young lady a love letter unless sure of her confidence. She would probably reply curtly, if only to end matters before her brother intervened. Perceived impertinence to a lady invited a challenge to the field of honor or to a shootout or caning in the street. Anna Matilda King of St. Simon's, Georgia, fretfully cautioned her sons about flirting without serious intentions, deploring the cruelty to the young ladies. The Presbyterian Reverend Robert L. Dabney of Virginia broadened the condemnation of seduction as the worst of sins, both in its general and specifically sexual forms:

The honorable mind justly condemns it as the most loathsome combination of treachery, cruelty, and selfishness which can be exhibited toward a fellow creature. The victim is one whose feebler sex should have appealed to every manly instinct for honorable protection instead of wrong; and whose love, stronger than the instinct of life, creates of itself a sacred obligation to refrain from injury.[30]

Everything had to be done to protect a woman's reputation. A chap in Tennessee made the mistake of impugning the "fair name" of some thirty young ladies in Bristol. He got off with a $1 fine and court costs, but the local gentlemen tarred and feathered him. Women's reputations had to be preserved even with reference to seeming trifles. "A good white lady told me one time," Sena Moore, an ex-slave, reported, "dat a bad white woman is a sight worser and low down than a bad nigger woman can ever git to be in dis world." Mary Eliza Eve Carmichael of Georgia was "much mortified at my Cattys coming home with a certain gentleman when she had two brothers that went with her – spoke to my boys about it, seems very sorry it happened so." A woman did not easily live down a reputation for looseness.[31]

Even gentlemen who scrupulously observed local mores risked unforeseen consequences. Thomas Anderson Holcombe, a notable lawyer and preacher in lower Virginia and the uncle of W. H. Holcombe of Natchez, was summoned to the bedside of a Miss Royall, "a homely old maid,

---

[30] J. Cunningham to B. C. Yancey, Oct. 1, 1839, in Yancey Papers; Mrs. Roger Pryor, *My Day: Reminiscences of a Long Life*, 95; Anna Matilda King to Lordy King, August 10, 1854, in Anna Matilda King, *Anna: The Letters of a St. Simons Plantation Mistress*, ed. Melanie Pavich-Lindsay (Athens, GA, 2002), 241, and see 243, n. 1; *DD*, 1:631; cf., Elise Pinckney, ed., *The Letterbook of Eliza Lucas Pinckney, 1739–1762* (Columbia, SC, 1997), 159.

[31] Herschel Gower and Jack Allan, *Pen and Sword: The Life and Journals of Randal W. McGavock* (Nashville, TN, 1959), Nov. 16, 1858 (497); *AS: S. C.*, 3 (pt. 3), 211; Carmichael Diary, Feb. 24, 1838; Walker-Reid Memoranda, n.d.

10 years older than himself with whom he had a slight acquaintance." To his amazement, the dying Miss Royall bequeathed him most of her estate, confessing "vast and unappeasable love" for him. She could not die in peace unless he accepted her offer. A miracle ensued. Miss Royall recovered. Gratitude and common decency required that he marry her.[32]

From colonial times to deep into the nineteenth century, foreigners thought southern young ladies had too much freedom to meet their young gentlemen for walks or church or lectures without chaperones and to indulge in smooching and kissing games. Eliza Frances Andrews of Georgia, a teenager during the War, commented: "Under no other social *régime*, probably, have young girls been allowed such liberty of intercourse with the other sex as were those of the Old South – a liberty which the notable absence of scandals and divorces goes far to justify."[33]

Parson Weems, in his popular *Life of Washington* (1809), extolled marriage for love. Among Weems's predecessors, the Presbyterian Reverend William Graham told his students in 1796 that natural rights include the right to marry whom one chose. Increasingly, preachers denounced men who married for money. Prominent ministers like the Methodist Reverend R. H. Rivers insisted that men marry for love, but within "the same class" and, so far as possible, have equal property and fortunes. "There must be mutual love. Without this as an all-pervading principle, they can in no circumstances be either moral or happy." From a British perspective, Buckingham thought that the penchant for marrying for money accounted for many unhappy marriages.[34]

John C. Calhoun wanted his sons to marry good women whom they loved, but, aware of their impecuniousness, guided them toward rich

---

[32] W. H. Holcombe Autobiography (ms.), 1:24.

[33] J. A. L. Lemay, ed., *Robert Bolling Woos Anne Miller: Love and Courtship in Colonial Virginia, 1760* (Charlottesville, VA, 1990), 5–6; Mary Ann Cobb to Howell Cobb, Jan. 21, 1863, in Kenneth Coleman, ed., *Athens, 1861–1865: As Seen Through Letters in the University of Georgia Libraries* (Athens, GA, 1969), 58; Sheila R. Phipps, *Genteel Rebel: The Life of Mary Greenhow Lee* (Baton Rouge, LA, 1994), 62; Eliza Frances Andrews, *War-Time Journal of a Georgia Girl* (New York, 1907), 39. Rosalie Roos, deeply committed to women's rights, reported elopements in Charleston as by no means rare: *Travels in America, 1851–1855*, tr. Carl L. Anderson (Carbondale, IL, 1982), 66.

[34] Mason Locke Weems, *The Life of Washington. A New Edition with Primary Documents* (Amonk, NY, 1996 [1809]), 6; "Lectures on Human Nature Aula Libertatis, Delivered by Wm. Graham: Notes taken by Joseph Glass, 1796," 139; R. H. Rivers, *Elements of Moral Philosophy* (Nashville, TN, 1859), 293–295; Harold W. Mann, *Atticus Haygood: Methodist Bishop, Editor, and Educator* (Athens, GA, 1965), 36–37; Ray Holder, *William Winans: Methodist Leader in Antebellum Mississippi* (Jackson, MS, 1977), 31; Buckingham, *Slave States*, 2:196.

young ladies. After all, a good, lovable young lady might just as well be rich as poor. From Texas, Alfred Howell wrote home to Virginia to ask his father, a Baptist minister, if the belle he had his eye on "is actually worth $40,000." Marrying for money cut both ways. Mary Barrey married old Mr. William Jessee of Middlesex County, Virginia. "She has married a rich man," John Walker commented, "I wish it may not cast her soul in hell."[35]

J. H. Ingraham, surveying Natchez in the 1830s, noticed that men waited to marry until well-off – until they had made enough money to provide properly for a lady with sensible tastes. He fretted about the many who remained bachelors and fell into dissolute male society. A lawyer, looking for a rich wife, finally caught one. A wag remarked, "He would have married her in her winding sheet if she had been as ugly as original sin, and only had enough breath in her to say yes to the preacher." A gentleman from an inland town told Olmsted that he had only one slave but would have to buy three more to accommodate a wife, and "that alone would withdraw from my capital at least three thousand dollars." Simms wrote to Mary Lawson of New York that marriage was too expensive. He teased that if northern women's rights advocates wanted to accomplish something, they should convince women to desire less and make marriage cheaper. Planters, in their wills urged executors to protect their daughters against fortune-hunting suitors.[36]

Busybodies thought they knew mercenary marriages when they saw them, and doubtless they were often right. Caroline Lee Hentz did not find Doctor Dickey's bride "handsome – not even pretty – nor witty, but her father has 4 or 500 negroes and that makes her lovely in this southern land." The wealthy Pauline Heyward clucked, "Capt. Milledge, they say, has married for money,' his bride possessing $100,000 in *gold*. I hear she is very ugly. I always thought he'd marry a fortune or – a beauty." Basil Gildersleeve wrote a friend in 1855, "If I do marry, I must marry a

35 Lander, *Calhoun Family and Clemson*, 41; Howell quoted in Maxwell Bloomfield, "Texas Bar in the Nineteenth Century," *Readings in the History of the American Legal Profession*, ed. Dennis R. Noland (Indianapolis, IN, 1980), 273 (Eventually, he married the daughter of a well-to-do planter and merchant in Fort Worth); John Walker Diary, Dec. 18, 1832.

36 [Joseph Holt Ingraham], *The South-West. By a Yankee*, 2 vols. (n.p., 1966 [1835]), 2:46–47; Harnett T. Kane, *Natchez on the Mississippi* (New York, 1947), 9; Frederick Law Olmsted, *A Journey in the Seaboard Slave States* (New York, 1968 [1856]), 66 n; Simms to Mary Lawson, July 26, 1859, in Oliphant et al., eds., *Letters of Simms*, 4:163; William Warren Rogers, Jr., *Black Belt Scalawag: Charles Hays and the Southern Republicans in the Era of Reconstruction* (Athens, GA, 1993), 4.

fortune – as my patrimony is almost nothing." Willie Mangum's nephew responded angrily when his uncle called him "foolish" and "a simpleton" for planning to marry "a fine, fashionable & poor lady." Did he not know "he had decreed for himself a life of misery & suffering." Fashionable and poor meant morally loose and prone to spend money one did not have. The strictures fell on both sexes. Keziah Brevard huffed, "Mrs. Willson is an old fool for marrying a man who has nothing but himself to give her." Brudder Coteny, a venerable black preacher on the Sea Islands, roasted the white folks who, instead of behaving like Christians, mocked marriage by caring about money rather than love.[37]

Southern mothers encouraged daughters to marry an affluent man or one with good prospects. Some pushed their daughters to think big. A fine young man worth some $15,000 doted on Mary Stevens of Alabama. Her mother discouraged her: "For you must go far above that it is said you are the prettiest girl ever was in Shelby." Respect for parents notwithstanding, children sometimes proved defiant. Campbell Robert Bryce of South Carolina expected his father to object to his marrying Sarah Henry of Mississippi, who was neither rich nor beautiful. Marry her he did. Sarah Knox Taylor, daughter of General and Mrs. Zachary Taylor, married Jefferson Davis over their objections. Since they had objected to her marrying a soldier, Davis resigned his commission. Before losing her to malaria three months later, a grateful Davis wrote to her, "Often I long to lay my head upon that breast which beats in unison with my own, to turn from the sickening sights of worldly duplicity and look in those eyes, so eloquent of purity and love." Maria Bryan of Georgia married a respectable physician against the wishes of her parents, who long remained estranged from her. Much annoyed, John Cunningham complained to a friend, "Mother seems determined that I shall marry no one of my own choosing, who is not particularly of her own. D___n it, I feel distressed to oppose her."[38]

37 Hentz Diary, May 26, 1836; "Journal of P. DeC. Heyward," July 13, 1865, in Mary D. Robertson, ed., *A Confederate Lady Comes of Age: The Journal of Pauline DeCaradeuc Heyward, 1863–1888* (Columbia, SC, 1992), 83; Basil Gildersleeve to Emil Hübner, Oct. 10, 1855, in Ward W. Briggs, Jr., ed., *The Letters of Basil Lanneau Gildersleeve* (Baltimore, 1987), 20; W. P. Mangum to Charity Mangum, Jan. 25, 1853, in Shanks, ed., *Mangum Papers*, 5 vols. (Raleigh, NC, 1955–1956), 5:264–265; Keziah Brevard Diary, Jan. 21, 1861; John G. Williams, *"De Ole Plantation"* (Charleston, SC, 1897), 21–22 (Brother Coteny).

38 Mother to Mary Stevens, January 24, 1841, in Browne Papers; Ethel Trenholm Seabrook Nepveux, *Sarah Henry Bryce, 1825–1901: A Glimpse at a Remarkable Woman in the Turbulent Civil War Era* (Charleston, SC, 1994), 3; Clement Eaton, *Jefferson Davis* (New York, 1977), 22; Bleser, ed., *Tokens of Affection: The Letters of a Planter's*

Marriage for money came with risks. The brother of Benjamin Palmer suffered a diminution in prestige and respect when he married a rich but unintelligent, spoiled, party-loving young lady. The Lees of Virginia put it this way: "Never marry unless you can do so into a family which will enable your children to feel proud of both sides of the house." And yet, wealthy parents proved a handicap to some daughters. A young lawyer in Raleigh, North Carolina, shook his head over the fate of the daughters and heiresses of the wealthy, much respected, and widely influential Judge Duncan Cameron: "No one has brass enough to acknowledge himself a suitor for favor." The judge, it seems, was "a high Churchman – & yet so cold & forbidding."[39]

Pity the young gentlemen: They did not find it easy to live up to the beau ideal of the young ladies they put on a pedestal. The ladies expected their men to be strong, commanding exemplars of chivalric virtues. They often referred, semi-facetiously, to husbands as "lords and masters." Sarah Morgan explained her reluctance to marry: "I have yet to meet the man I would be willing to acknowledge as my lord and master." One young teenage girl wrote to another: "Miss Lucy Copeland was married lately to Mr. Gardiner of Nashville and immediately went up to the mansion of her lord." Elizabeth Ruffin of Virginia in 1827 and Kate Carney of Tennessee in 1859 sang the same tune. Elizabeth preferred celibacy to "that CHARMING SERVITUDE under a lord and master ... I dread to yield freedom, render obedience, and pay homage to any ONE." Kate Carney turned seventeen and resolved not to marry soon, although she was older than her sister and the same age as her mother when she "took upon herself 'to love, honor, and obey.'"[40]

Thomas Cumming of Augusta, Georgia, sent his wife detailed instructions for everything – what, how, with whom. His attitude, perhaps common in the eighteenth-century South, faded in the nineteenth. Yet, Mary Hamilton Campbell of Abingdon, Virginia, asked her husband's advice on buying horses but did not stop there:

Daughter in the Old South (Athens, GA, 1996), xxvii; John Cunningham to B. C. Yancey, Feb. 24, 1839, in Yancey Papers.

[39] B. M. Palmer to R. H. Reid, May 1, 1850, in Thomas Cary Johnson, *The Life and Letters of Benjamin Morgan Palmer* (Richmond, VA, 1906), 145; Thomas L. Connelly, *The Marble Man: Robert E. Lee and His Image in American Society* (New York, 1977), 171; Haigh Diary, Jan. 17, 1844.

[40] Sarah Morgan quoted by Anne Firor Scott, *The Southern Lady: From Pedestal to Politics, 1830–1930* (Charlottesville, VA, [1970] 1995), 23, and Scott's perceptive remarks; M. M. Drane to Susan Henry, Feb. 17, 1849, in Henry Papers; Elizabeth Ruffin Diary, Feb. 8, 26, 1827; Carney Diary, July 25, 1859, also Jan. 5, 1859.

I shall be guided by your advice in every thing. I know your judgment and experience are far superior to my own, and that our happiness is equally your care. Don't let your tenderness and anxiety for me prevent you from pursuing the course you wish ... My heart is tender and affectionate, but it does not want a proper elevation of spirit. I have as great a regard for your honor as your life, and it will never be marred by me ... I will hold myself in readiness for your orders.

A month later she added, "I have determined to lay no plans of my own but to be governed strictly by your advice."[41]

David Outlaw of North Carolina replied with annoyance when his wife asked permission to give a party for their daughter: "Really I shall quarrel with you if you do not quit asking my advice and permission about matters of this kind .... Ours is a partnership of equals at least such I have always considered it and such I wish you to consider it – and to act accordingly. I have the utmost confidence in your prudence and discretion." Henry A. Wise of Virginia, having his own ideas of proper marital relations, thought he detected an assault when Mary, his second wife, seemed most deferential. He rebuked her after two years of marriage:

I would give anything if you will only cease to think and say anything to me about such matters as changing your habits and character so as better to conform to my wishes. Why mar your letters, or your conversation or your looks even with what reminds me of my weakness? Why appeal to God to attest your innocence of an intention to offend me, when you know that annoys me itself? I implore you to drive away such thoughts and feelings and never to express them to me.

James Henley Thornwell took a different view. He had "one of the best wives in the world, for she manages every thing and just leaves me to my books and study ... She manages pretty much my worldly affairs for me."[42]

Husbands did expect deference in everything they deemed essential. But since not all ladies proved self-denying, nor all gentlemen authoritative, tensions emerged. William Schley, who generally referred to his wife, Elizabeth, affectionately and without complaint, burst forth to her uncle that she had defied his wishes and gone to spend the summer in Athens, Georgia, without him: "She is not what I would have her to be

---

[41] Thomas Cumming to wife, Nov. 24, 1788, in W. Kirk Wood, ed., *A Northern Daughter and Southern Wife: The Civil War Reminiscences and Letters of Katherine H. Cummings, 1860–1865* (Richmond, VA, 1976), 103, n. 9; Mary Hamilton Campbell Letter Book, Aug. 22, Sept. 4, 1812, in Campbell Family Papers.

[42] David Outlaw to Emily Outlaw, Dec. 13, 15, 1849; Craig M. Simpson, *A Good Southerner: The Life of Henry A. Wise of Virginia* (Chapel Hill, NC, 1985), 97; J. H. Thornwell to James Gillespie, March 4, 1837, in Thornwell Papers.

and fondly hoped she was. Sir, my anticipations have not been realized ... When she chooses to get angry, and as I would say without cause, she forgets that virtue, called prudence, and talks before negroes, children &c &c – enough – I feel conscious of my own rectitude, and will endeavor to be resigned to my fate, be it what it may." Archibald D. Murphey of North Carolina wrote to his wife, Jane, that he would never ask her to do anything she would find disagreeable, but he was sure that her affection for him would usually make compliance with his wishes a pleasure for her. Benjamin F. Perry hoped his wife would acknowledge him as a splendid husband: "I am a good husband in all things, except that I will not sometimes yield my opinion to yours; but in this you afterwards admit me to be right, and like a good wife ... acknowledge yourself to be wrong." Lucilla Agnes McCorkle deplored "the warmth" with which she argued with her husband, praying to God that she not continue a "lunacy" that threatened her marriage to a "husband for whom I bless the Lord." How could she have picked flaws in his manner and disposition, especially after he had warned her against her penchant for carping? God heard her prayers: "I thank thee O Father that thou hast rescued me from such a snare – I feel less prone to carp after the manner of worldly fools." She knew she had "a nervous husband and that all my patience will be required or our fireside will become a bedlam I have been trying to convince him of his errors – and that spirit of debate was itself alone a kin to the error I opposed."[43]

Deference came in various forms. Martha Jefferson probably never called her famous husband anything but "Mr. Jefferson." Such formalities became less common but never disappeared during the antebellum years. Lucy Wood Butler never called her husband by his first name. He asked her to, but she did not think it proper. Neither did the wives of such clerical luminaries as the Reverend Richard Furman and Bishop George Foster Pierce. Elizabeth Curtis Wallace may have called her husband by his first name in bed – who knows? – but he was "Mr. Wallace" in her diary. The letters of Amanda McIntosh to her husband and his to her could hardly have been more loving, but she always addressed him as "Mr." and signed "Amanda C. McIntosh." More

---

[43] William Schley to Henry Jackson, Feb. 18, 1824, in Jackson-Prince Papers; Archibald D. Murphey to Jane Murphey, Aug. 18, 1807, in William Henry Hoyt, ed., *The Papers of Archibald D. Murphey, 1777–1832,* 2 vols. (Raleigh, NC, 1914), 1:14 Perry to wife, 1846, quote in Lillian Adele Kibler, *Benjamin F. Perry: South Carolina Unionist* (Durham, NC, 1946), 189–190; McCorkle Diary, entries "Sabbath," Nov., 1857, Nov., 1848, Dec., 1850.

frequently, young ladies expected their fiancés to address them by first name, but they addressed their fiancés formally until requested not to. "You may call me Will if you wish," William Walton of Mississippi wrote to his fiancé. "I am tired of cold Mr. Walton. Don't it look so formal?"[44]

Gentlemen often married mid-teen young ladies many years their junior. In 1822, the legislature of Mississippi gravely debated whether to void elopements of girls under fourteen. Mrs. H. G. Lewis of Natchitoches, Louisiana, described the "genteel" wedding of Miss Sarah Ann Tortson, age fourteen, to Mr. Patrick C. Williams in 1837 without a hint of disapproval. Much less did John Berkeley Grimball of the South Carolina low country disapprove when William Elliott's seventeen-year-old daughter, Harriet, married the thirty-five-year-old General Gonzalez, "a Cuban gentleman ... well known throughout the country from his connection with the disastrous Lopez."[45]

Men in their thirties or much older who married teenagers or even women of twenty or so could expect deference normally accorded fathers. Perry, who sternly lectured his wife on obedience, had married Elizabeth Frances McCall when he was thirty-one. He reflected on his young bride in a manner that suggests she might have been his daughter: "She is too particular – more attention being paid to her hair than is necessary. This fault will be cured with age, as I believe all of her faults will be – Her mind is good & may be characterized for good sense and a quickness of perception – She has a retentive memory & recollects well all that she reads or that I read to her." In Mississippi, Hiram Cassedy, upon marrying the fifteen-year-old Mary Proby, enrolled her in the Elizabeth [female] Academy. Charles Manigault welcomed his son, Louis, and new daughter-in-law to the old family home, writing to Louis, "What a fine chance you have now (when all alone in the evenings) of giving your wife

---

[44] Butler Diary, July 19, 1861, and editor's note; Carolyn L. Harrell, *Kith and Kin* (Macon, GA, 1984), 18 (Furman); George G. Smith, *Life and Times of George F. Pierce* (Sparta, GA, 1888), 75–76; Eleanor P. Cross and Charles B. Cross, Jr., eds., *Glencoe Diary: The War-Time Journal of Elizabeth Curtis Wallace* (Chesapeake, VA, 1968), 123 (Aug. 8, 1864); correspondence of A. C. McIntosh and Amanda C. McIntosh, 1848; William Walton to Letitia Watkins, Feb. 21, 1853, in Dimond and Hattaway, eds., *Forest Place*, 63. Dumas Malone, Jefferson's great biographer, told his graduate seminar that he felt certain Jefferson always remained "Mr. Jefferson" to his wife.

[45] Dunbar Rowland, *Courts, Judges, and Lawyers of Mississippi, 1798–1935* (Jackson, MS, 1935), 34; Mrs. H. G. Lewis to Mrs. J. M. Hunt, June 29, 1837, in Hughes Family Papers; J. B. Grimball Diary, April 18, 1856. Grimball referred to the filibustering Lopez expedition to seize Cuba from the Spanish.

some lessons in French. It will be awkward if she don't understand our family Colloquial language."[46]

Ellen Douglas Brownlow of North Carolina learned of the impending marriage of her friend, Mary Eliza Battle. She teased about the exchange of freedom and lightness of heart for the stern and forbidding life of a matron – reminiscent "of a regiment of round heads in Cromwell's time." Elizabeth Mayo Fulton mocked her newly married sister with an indirect message for her brother-in-law: "Tell Brother T. to send me word if you are an obedient wife. I have some curiosity to hear, for you know I always said you would make your Old Man walk chalk."[47]

Yet, gentlemen, clerical and lay, preferred wives to be strong and to influence them positively. How, with all the clamors for deference, did the ladies turn that trick? John Stark Ravenscroft of North Carolina and Nathaniel Russell Middleton of South Carolina had complementary explanations. When Ravenscroft married Anne Spotswood, of the Virginia elite, he put aside his rakish ways and began the career that led him to become Episcopal bishop of North Carolina. Of her influence, he wrote:

She was a woman of high principle and of a very independent character; what she did not approve of she would not smile upon, yet she never gave me a cross word or an ill-natured look in her life, and in the twenty-three years it pleased God to spare her to me, such was her discretion that, though I often acted otherwise than she could have asked me to do, and though she was faithful to reprove me, there never was a quarrel or temporary estrangement between us.[48]

Middleton recalled his childhood, when his father wanted him to ride along on the usual Sunday expeditions but his mother did not:

I learned a lesson which has influenced my life. My mother made no factious opposition. She never forgot or tried to evade the promise to obedience to which she had committed herself without any mental reservations; she simply expressed

---

[46] Perry quoted in Kibler, B. F. Perry, 183; Holder, *William Winans*, 139; Charles Manigault to Louis Manigault, Dec. 30, 1857, in James M. Clifton, ed., *Life and Labor on Argyle Island: Letters and Documents of a Savannah River Rice Plantation, 1833–1867* (Savannah, GA, 1978), 257.

[47] Ellen Douglas Brownlow to Mary Eliza Battle, Jan. 28, 1853, in Mary Eliza Battle Letters, and for a teasing reference to fiancés and husbands as lords and masters, see Brownlow to Mary Eliza Battle, Jan. 7, 1857; Elizabeth Mayo Fulton to Lucy Taylor, Nov. 22, 1834, in Catherine Thom Bartlett, ed., *"My Dear Brother": A Confederate Chronicle* (Richmond, VA, 1952), 16.

[48] Ravenscroft quoted in Marshall DeLancey Haywood, *Lives of the Bishops of North Carolina from the Establishment of the Episcopate in that State Down to the Division of the Diocese* (Raleigh, NC, 1910), 46.

her dissent and was silent, but the look in her eye, the sadness in her countenance, the grief which she did not pretend to repress, did her work far more effectually than if she had made the most powerful and demonstrative opposition; I turned to my father and declined to accompany him.[49]

Thus did gentlemen pay tribute to wives and mothers who guaranteed family stability and good order by remaining acquiescent while leading their men down the right path by force of moral example. Tributes no less touching spoke well for gentlemen as well as ladies. But an unsympathetic critic might wonder at the ease with which men acknowledged their own frailties and counted on their women to call them to the straight and narrow. It seems that mature men never lost the need, even when playing father to adolescent wives, to have mother at hand. The women did their best to obey their husbands but did not always succeed. No few, having grown up with fathers they adored, came to think less of their husbands. "The union formed by marriage," wrote Elizabeth Eve Carmichael, "can neither slacken nor dissolve those ties which bind us to our parents." How fortunate that Langdon Cheves and David McCord never fell out, for Louisa Susanna McCord loved her husband but worshiped her father. Young women expected to marry a man worthy of their fathers and even the brothers they doted on. From the earliest years, manliness – understood primarily as strength – meant everything. Girls expected their brothers to protect them, and boys expected to do so. Catherine Couper Lovell recalled that, as a child, she took for granted that her five-year-old brother shielded her against any threat.[50]

Malachi Foy exemplified brotherly guidance of younger sisters. Foy, with Lee's army in Virginia, wrote to his sister and younger brothers, "You must take the Bible and read a chapter for us every night and, my sweet little Sister, you must be a good girl and say your little prayers for us every night before you lie down." B. F. Doswell, a student at Washington College, gently chided his younger sister for the lack of "neatness" in her letters and asked that she work to improve. Her reaction is not on record, but his chicken-scrawl may have made her cavil. When Thomas J. (later "Stonewall") Jackson converted, relations with his sister reversed. She had encouraged his conversion but increasingly slid into doubt. For years, he worked to strengthen her faith. Pauline DeCaradeuc Heyward

[49] N. R. Middleton, "Reminiscences," in Alicia Hopton Middleton et al., eds., *Life in Carolina and New England During the Nineteenth Century* (Bristol, RI, 1929), 190.
[50] Carmichael Book, 1803; Catherine Couper Lovell, *The Light of Other Days* (Macon, GA, 1995), 6.

of Aiken, South Carolina, tutored her young brothers in history and literature – subjects she continued to read avidly. With Sarah Morgan, the reverse: Her brother and father pushed her hard to read widely. She did.[51]

To some extent a good academic education blended with ladylike graces. William J. Grayson approvingly reported that J. L. Petigru demanded that his daughters read not only French but Italian and Spanish. Petigru described Italian as the language of Dante and Spanish as the language of Cervantes, whose *Don Quixote* he read with them. Kitty Mangum wrote to cousin Martha in 1850, "I am still taking Music lessons and progress tolerably well, but find some difficulty in it for Father will not let me go on without understanding the principals [sic]." Calhoun took the same view. While pursuing your studies, he wrote to Anna Maria, "You must not neglect musick and the other accomplishments." Anna Maria did not resist her father. The Calhouns sent her to a fine school in Edgefield, where she lived with Francis W. Pickens's family, and then moved on to a more advanced academy in Columbia – to the great irritation of her father, whom Floride had neglected to consult. Anna Maria pursued the ladylike accomplishments but made clear that she cared much more about politics.[52]

A PLAYFUL PROVOCATION

Early in the War, two impish belles, probably the Ramsey sisters of Charlotte, North Carolina, "refugeeing" in Knoxville, Tennessee, had sport with the mores of the elite:

To the Editor of the Democrat:

Two young ladies of admitted beauty and accomplishments, connected with one of the most ancient and respectable families in North Carolina, identified thus

[51] Malachi Foy to his brothers and sisters, June 18, 1862, in Mills Lane, ed., *"Dear Mother, Don't Grieve About Me. If I Get Killed, I'll Only Be Dead"* (Savannah, GA, 1990), 134; B. F. Doswell to Emma Doswell, Sept. 16, 1848; James I. Robertson, Jr., *Stonewall Jackson: The Man, the Soldier, the Legend* (New York, 1997), 139, 153; "Journal of P. DeC. Heyward," in Robertson, ed., *Confederate Lady Comes of Age*; Charles East, ed., *The Civil War Diary of Sarah Morgan* (Athens, GA, 1991), xvi, xix.

[52] William J. Grayson, *James Louis Petigru: A Biographical Sketch* (New York, 1866), 106–107; Kitty Mangum to Martha P. Mangum, June 14, 1850, in Shanks, ed., *Mangum Papers*, 5:176; J. C. Calhoun to Anna Maria Calhoun, Feb. 13, 1832, in J. Franklin Jameson, ed., *Calhoun Correspondence* (Washington, DC, 1900: "Annual Report of the American Historical Association for the Year 1899," vol. 2), 312; Charles M. Wiltse, *John C. Calhoun: Nullifier* (Indianapolis, IN, 1949), 165–168.

with the independence and glory of the country, are not unwilling to enter into the matrimonial relation with some gentleman of congenial taste and sentiment of a good family, good looking if not handsome – tall, slender, graceful, industrious frugal intelligent moral a stranger to gambling and other fashionable vices and especially intemperance not affluent but still rich enough to support a wife like a Lady, in comfort, ease and elegance and willing in case of his death to settle on us for Life ten thousand dollars and to leave no poor Kin dependent on us or their estate for a living. Such gentlemen as want to get married as much as we do will please address us on this subject. No yankee need apply nor any one who was not in the Confederate army. This is indispensable to a successful application.

Respectfully,

YLA,

Charlotte, NC
    PS. YLA prefers a red-headed gentleman.[53]

[53] Editor's note: I have not been able to locate the source of this letter.

6

Home Away from Home

The gentry of the Old South outside their own homes, were seen at their best when Carolina planters resorted to Charleston in the sickly season; when Lexington, Ky., was the refuge of dwellers in the Lower Mississippi Valley from disease and torrid heat; when the small theatre of a city was crowded ... and when at the White Sulfur Springs, Va., Madison Springs, Ga., the Warren Springs, N. C., Harrodsburg, Ky., Biloxi, and Pass Christian on the Gulf, and other resorts .... They were exponents, sometimes to an exaggerated degree, of the virtues and faults of the gradations of the ruling class.

– Edward Ingle[1]

Virginia planters took their families on two- or three-month vacations, often spending a portion at the springs, which family and community networks gave a special character. Julia Marsh Patterson of Crawford County, Georgia, traveled with husband and servant to visit kin near Montgomery, Alabama. On the trip she reestablished contact with the "many delightful acquaintances from there at the Watering Places in Georgia." Old friends like Jefferson's biographer Henry Stephen Randall of New York and Hugh Blair Grigsby of Virginia found the Virginia Springs an ideal place to get together as did old college chums who sought to renew acquaintances. Episcopal Bishop J. H. Otey of Tennessee and

---

[1] Edward Ingle, *Southern Sidelights* (New York, 1896), 20. Ingle added that at southern springs ladies and gentlemen "presented charms of manner and gifts of mind" that entranced northern acquaintances. The low country's "sickly season" lasted about half the year; planters scurried to the up country or the coastal islands: Lawrence Fay Brewster, *Summer Migrations and Resorts of South Carolina Lowcountry Planters* (Durham, NC, 1947), 9, 22–23; Peter McCandless, *Slavery, Disease, and Suffering in the Southern Lowcountry* (Cambridge, 2011) 249–270.

Julia Gilmer of North Carolina, among many, stopped at a spa only to find it full of strangers, but new friendships followed quickly. Southern travelers to the Virginia Springs often curtailed expenses by stopping at the estates of wealthy planters along the route. For those from the far-away lower tier of the Southwest, trips to the springs punctuated visits to relatives in Virginia or northward. The prominent Bones Family of Augusta, Georgia and Winnsboro, South Carolina, traveled to Virginia Springs, which they thought a good place for branches of the family to get together. Dr. Josiah Nott of Mobile and others from the eastern states who lived in the Southwest also relished their visits to the Virginia Springs, where they met kin, friends, and members of the social and political elite, northern and southern.[2]

The world-famous springs of Virginia became a summer world unto themselves. White Sulphur Springs ("the White") stood out, but hundreds of lesser springs dotted the southern landscape. About fifty miles west of Washington, Fauquier White Springs, held the most prestigious of the chivalric tournaments, at which the legendary Turner Ashby, among others, held forth. Wealthy lowcountry planters flooded into the springs of North Carolina and Georgia as well as Virginia. For months at a time, the gayety from the low country brightened many a dull community. "Our village is very gay indeed at this time," Zebulon Vance of North Carolina wrote his fiancée, Harriett Newell Espy, in August, 1852. "The S[outh] Carolinians are crowding both our Hotels to over flowing ... We have had dancing at the Hotel incessantly for the last two weeks."[3]

---

[2] Catherine Cooper Hopley, *Life in the South from the Commencement of the War*, 2 vols. (New York, 1971 [1863]), 1:102; Julia Marsh Patterson Journal, 1850 (ms. p. 41), in Benjamin C. Yancey Papers; H. S. Randall to H. B. Grisby, Feb. 15, 1856, in Frank J. Klingberg and Frank W. Klingberg, eds., *The Correspondence between Henry Stephens Randall and Hugh Blair Grigsby, 1856–1861* (Berkeley, CA, 1952), 34; Otey Diary, Aug. 12, 1852; Julia A. Gilmer Diary, 1860; Abram Pollock, "Biography of Thomas Gordon Pollock (ms.), 211, in Pollock Papers; Daniel Kilbride, "Cultivation, Conservationism, and the Early National Gentry: The Manigault Family and Their Circle," *Journal of the Early Republic*, 19 (1999), 228; Leak Diary, Sept., 1854; E. G. Baker, June 7–July 31, 1857; for the Bones, see the correspondence in the Hughes Family Papers for 1825–1829; Reginald Horsman, *Josiah Nott: Southerner, Physician, and Racial Theorist* (Baton Rouge, LA, 1987), 75, 229; for Jewish families with cross-country connections, see, e.g., Rebecca Gratz to Solomon Gratz, July 17, 1859, in David Philipson, ed., *Letters of Rebecca Gratz* (Philadelphia, 1929), 411–412. For Alabamans who stopped at Virginia Springs on the way north for vacation or business, see Harriet Elizabeth Amos, "Social Life in an Antebellum Cotton Port: Mobile, Alabama, 1820–1860," (Ph.D. diss.: University of Alabama, 1976), 209.

[3] Vance to Espy, Aug. 16, 1852, in Elizabeth Roberts Cannon, ed., *My Beloved Zebulon: The Correspondence of Zebulon Baird Vance and Harriett Newell Espy* (Chapel Hill, NC, 1971), 115; on Fauquier, see Elizabeth Fox-Genovese and Eugene D. Genovese, *The Mind*

Alabama's many springs, including the fashionable Ashford, Bladon, and Chandler Springs, arose to accommodate nearby planters, and Bailey Springs and Valhermoso Springs won reputations for their curative waters. Bladon Springs lured the fastidious Madame Octavia LeVert of Mobile, who described it as "a perfect balm in Gilead." When the Bladon Springs Hotel opened in 1846 to accommodate two hundred guests from Alabama, Mississippi, and Louisiana, a village grew up around it as planters built homes nearby. Butler Springs had its own attractions, but the vulgar speech and blasphemy Mary Lides heard there shocked her. Josiah Nott and Eliza Clitherall were among the thirty or so elite families that lived at Spring Hill, enjoying excellent springs that attracted the well-to-do who fled the yellow fever epidemic of 1853. In Mississippi, the yellow fever of 1855 ruined the popular resort of Coopers Well – a favorite spot for Natchez nabobs and such distinguished personages as Henry Foote and Henry Watkins Allen. In its glory days some five hundred ladies and gentlemen crowded its ballrooms.[4]

In the early nineteenth century, Virginians and South Carolinians constituted most of the visitors to Virginia Springs. Whatever the medicinal advantages of the springs, the atmosphere long remained dull. William J. Clarke insisted that Blue Sulphur Springs had better water than the White, and others considered the waters at Warm Springs and Mineral Springs in western North Carolina especially healthful. In 1832, cholera and yellow fever epidemics greatly increased the popularity of the Virginia Springs, and southern planters poured in. Within a few years New Orleans' proverbially beautiful belles began to arrive in force, and wealthy upcountry and lowcountry South Carolinians found a summer home away from home. In the social whirl at Virginia Springs, Octavia Le Vert of Mobile, playing her guitar and singing Spanish love songs, enhanced her reputation

of the Master Class: History and Faith in the Southern Slaveholders' Worldview (New York, 2005), ch. 10. See also Clitherall "Autobiography," Book Six (ms.). For springs in Georgia, see George White, *Statistics of the State of Georgia* (Savannah, GA, 1849), 179, 190, 584–585; Claude Henry Neuffer, ed., *The Christopher Happoldt Journal: His European Tour with the Reverend John Bachman (June–December, 1838)* (Charleston, SC, 1960), 85.

4 James F. Sulzby, Jr., *Historic Alabama Hotels and Resorts* (Tuscaloosa, AL, 1960), 27–37, 53, 85; W. Stuart Harris, *Dead Towns of Alabama* Tuscaloosa, AL, 2001), 60, 62–63, 70; Thomas McAdory Owens, *History of Alabama and Dictionary of Alabama Biography*, 4 vols. (Spartanburg, SC, 1978 [1921]), 2:992–999; Horsman, *Josiah Nott*, 162–163; H. G. Evans Diary, Sept. 5, 1855; Vincent H. Cassidy and Amos E. Simpson, *Henry Watkins Allen of Louisiana* (Baton Rouge, LA, 1964), 23.

as an enchanting presence, "the South's most famous belle," and "the most charming woman in the world."[5]

With better roads and means of transportation, people came from as far away as Texas, but "better" was not good enough for some. The condition of the dusty roads in Virginia much annoyed the ladies of John C. Calhoun's family. Martha Calhoun Burt declared that nothing would induce her to return to the Virginia Mountains. The Calhouns seemed in a bad mood. They thought the expense excessive, and, although they wound up with decent accommodations, they considered their quarters close to intolerable. Probably, the family shared the endless complaints of flies and bedbugs. Then too, the growing numbers of people from outside Virginia and Carolina became an irritant to the old-timers, drawing them together against interlopers. Leticia Burwell reported that Virginians and Carolinians coalesced in resenting the influx. Meanwhile, the Virginians and Carolinians drew return fire. Mary Telfair, from an elite Savannah family, speaking for many Georgians, Alabamans, and Mississippians, disapproved of South Carolinians as full of "pomp and parade" and too conscious of their wealth.[6]

HUNTING AND ENTERTAINING

Hunting was a favorite sport for the gentlemen, as well as for black servants, some of whom acquired a mastery of the terrain that they put to good use in guiding Confederate deserters and Yankee stragglers to safety during the War. The White and other springs made a fine pack

[5] Percival Reniers, *The Springs of Virginia: Life, Love, and Death at the Waters, 1775–1900* (Chapel Hill, NC, 1941),ch. 5; William J. Clarke to Mary Bayard Clarke, Nov. 14, 1861, in Terrell Armistead Crow and Mary Moulton Barden, eds., *Live Your Own Life: The Family Papers of Mary Bayard Clarke, 1854–1886* (Columbia, SC, 2003), 96; John Hill Wheeler, *Historical Sketches of North Carolina from 1584 to 1851*, 2 vols. in 1 (Baltimore, 1964 [1851]), 2:92.

[6] Caldwell Delaney, Madame Octavia Walton Le Vert: The South's Most Famous Belle (Mobile, AL, 1861), 4; Frances Gibson Satterfield, *Madame Le Vert: A Biography of Octavia Walton Le Vert* (Edisto Island, SC, 1987), 72; Lt. Patrick Calhoun to J. C. Calhoun, July 14, 1846, in *JCCP*, 23:313–314; Letitia A. Burwell, *A Girl's Life in Virginia before the War*, 2nd ed. (New York, 1895), 117–118; Charles J. Johnson, Jr., *Mary Telfair: The Life and Legacy of a Nineteenth-Century Woman* (Savannah, GA, 2002), 64–65. Also, Ethel Trenholm Seabrook Nepveux, *Sarah Henry Bryce, 1825–1901: A Glimpse at a Remarkable Woman in the Turbulent Civil War Era* (Charleston, SC, 1994), 29 (bedbugs). On the response to the cholera and related matters, see also Cecil D. Eby, Jr., "*Porte Crayon*": *The Life of David Hunter Strother* (Chapel Hill, NC, 1960), 7; Jacob Bond I'on [sic] to J. S. Palmer, July 14, 1821, in Louis P. Towles, ed., *A World Turned Upside Down: The Palmers of South Santee, 1818–1881* (Columbia, SC, 1996), 67.

of hounds available for guests attracted by the numerous deer. Philip Holbrook Nicklin [Pelegrine Prolix] reported, "Everyone who likes can join in this spirit-stirring sport, provided he can beg, borrow, or steal a horse." President Martin Van Buren made a big hit with his sumptuous stag parties at the White, at which gentlemen feasted on venison, pheasants, chickens, turkey, trout, and even squirrels, but he made an even bigger hit with his hunting party.[7]

A romantic aura hung over the springs, which provided marvelous places to meet eligible bachelors and prospective brides, and young ladies and gentlemen made the most of the opportunity. That a certain amount of hanky-panky went on need not be doubted, but it rarely came to much. The young, seizing the chance to let their hair down, added kissing games to their masquerade balls. In a macabre twist on slave auctions, young ladies and gentlemen were "sold" to the highest bidder, who would acquire "ownership" of these "slaves" – up to a point never crossed, at least in public view. Young people who visited Shocco, North Carolina, and other springs, did not always succeed in their quests. Ellen Douglas Brownlow reported, "very few persons were there; the girls were literally belles without beaux." Flirting was the rage, but there were few opportunities for sexual liaisons. Ladies either went to the springs with fathers, brothers, or husbands or in the care of reliable family friends. Unmarried men lodged on the White's "Alabama Row," where, presumably, the nervous parents of the belles kept an eye on them. The socially prominent women who graced the springs in the 1850s included such belles as Ella Eaton, from one of the richest families in North Carolina, and such matrons as Susan Dabney Smedes of Mississippi. Women did go off to the springs without their husbands, though, often, with children in tow. Young ladies especially looked forward to the gay social life, however much conducted under the sharp eyes of their mothers.[8]

---

[7] Pelegrine Prolix [Philip Holbrook Nicklin], *Letters Descriptive of Virginia Springs. The Roads Leading Thereon and the Doings Thereat, 1834 and 1836*, 2nd ed. (Austin, TX, 1978), 20; John Stewart Oxley to Thomas Henry, Sept. 9, 1853, in G. A. Henry Papers; Marianne Finch, *An Englishwoman's Experience in America* (New York, 1969 [1853]), 327; John C. Inscoe, *Mountain Masters: Slavery, and the Sectional Crisis in Western North Carolina* (Knoxville, TN, 1989), 89; Reniers, *Springs of Virginia*, 123–124.

[8] Volumnia Barrow to R. R. Barrow, July 18, 1859 and correspondence for 1859–1860, in R. R. Barrow Residence Journal; Ellen Douglas Brownlow to Mary Eliza Battle, Sept. 4, 1851, Sept. 22, 1854, in Mary Eliza Battle Letters; Elizabeth Silverthorne, *Plantation Life in Texas* (College Station, TX, 1986), 184; Edward M. Steel, Jr., *T. Butler King of Georgia* (Athens, GA, 1964), 124; Featherstonhaugh, *Excursion through the Slave States*, 16; Reniers, *Springs of Virginia*, 184–185 (Eaton); and see Joe Gray Taylor, *Eating, Drinking, and Visiting in the South: An Informal History* (Baton Rouge, LA, 1982), 75. On the

In 1816, James Kirk Paulding, a friendly northern literary man, observed on a tour of southern springs, "A man who goes to a watering-place to get a wife deserves to be – married; a folly which, as Sir Peter Teagal says, 'always brings with it its own punishment.' " Courting nevertheless often led to marriage and the forging of a family alliance. Among the outstanding matchmakers at the Virginia Springs, William Pope of Huntsville, Alabama, held pride of place in the 1830s. Ten matches had been consummated in 1835, with some fifty others in the offing, and Colonel Pope thought he could safely predict the consummation of twenty, since his vast experience had shown the survival rate of courtships to be about 40 percent. Courtships also figured in the lives of Southerners who went to northern springs. Newport, Rhode Island, and Saratoga and Ballston Spa in New York (the favorite watering place for the Telfairs of Savannah) hosted an East Coast elite that transcended sectional differences and provided meeting places for romances and future marriages.[9]

A spectacular event at the White: The forty-two-year-old Francis Pickens won the heart of nineteen-year-old Lucy Petway, a much coveted Texas beauty. She had wanderlust – apparently in more ways than one – and agreed to the marriage on condition that Pickens accept one of the diplomatic posts he had routinely turned down. Off they went to the court of the Tsar of All the Russias. George Wythe Randolph met Mary Adams Pope at the springs and subsequently married her. A rich young widow, she set out for a lengthy visit to the springs, if not to find a husband, at least to brighten a lonely life. And the Virginia Springs were wonderful places for honeymoons. Isaac Franklin, one of the South's leading slave traders, and James H. Hammond were among the more prominent men who took their brides on honeymoons there.[10]

---

supervision of mothers, see Charlotte Ann Allston to R. F. W. Allston, Sept. 27, 1818, in J. H. Easterby, ed., *The South Carolina Rice Plantation, as Revealed in the Papers of Robert F. W. Allston* (Chicago, 1945), 50–51. A common case: Floride Calhoun and the children went off to the White for an extended stay; John joined them only briefly: Lander, *Calhoun Family and Clemson*, 101.

[9] [James Kirk Paulding], *Letters from the South*, 2 vols. (New York, 1819), 1:173; Reniers, *Springs of Virginia*, 80; Johnson, *Mary Telfair*, 56–57, 68–69.

[10] Nell S. Graydon, *Tales of Columbia* (Columbia, SC, 1964), 60 (Pickens); George Green Shackelford, *George Wythe Randolph and the Confederate Elite* (Athens, GA, 1988), 29; Caldwell Delaney, *A Mobile Sextet* (Mobile, AL, 1981), 9; Drew Gilpin Faust, *James Henry Hammond and the Old South* (Baton Rouge, LA, 1982), 62–63; Wendell Holmes Stephenson, ed., *Isaac Franklin: Slave Trader and Planter of the Old South. With Plantation Records* (Baton Rouge, LA, 1938), 19.

The White became a center of fashion in the 1830s, although much of the fashion struck the more austere as outlandish. Arthur Middleton, an internationally famous Charleston dandy, showed up to catch the eye of Miss Anna May, a great beauty. Other visitors included Cora Livingston, hailed as the belle of belles from Natchez, along with Virginia's Miss Carleton, Miss Barbour, and Miss Randolph, as well as Reverdy and Mrs. Johnson, the Claibornes of Louisiana, and Robert Stannard of Richmond. Middleton was something else: He wore what Mary Middleton described as a "screaming check suit and a velvet shirt that stunned New York and a full set of whiskers and mustachios." Presumably less garish were gentlemen like Colonel Richard Singleton, the master of seven plantations between Charleston and Camden, who was esteemed for his sobriety, devotion to family, and managerial efficiency. None of which kept him from spending two hours on careful preparation to face the day faultlessly dressed while his wife read the Bible and newspapers.[11]

A bemused Buckingham remarked about 1840, "Female dandies we saw were not so ridiculous as the males; their peculiarities consisting chiefly in the extravagant excess to which they pushed every style of dress beyond its usual limits; extremely compressed waists, very low bodies [sic], greatly exposed back, and perfectly naked shoulders, highly protruding bustles, added to the most beseeching coquetry of attitude and manner." He thought southern, like northern, women generally reserved but inclined to go to extremes when given a chance. Still, as late as the 1850s, northern ladies at the springs appeared at breakfast in silk, whalebone, and jewelry, whereas their southern sisters still wore uncomfortably long muslins. Conditions varied considerably from one spa to another. In Alabama, the ladies who gathered at Bailey Springs dressed fashionably in the "Darro" (white taffeta adorned with needlework), as well as such styles as the "Marion" and the "Nightingale." But confusion reigned at Butler Springs. Mary Lide came upon some ladies dressed well and others inappropriately.[12]

The White – like springs across the South – featured a ball almost every night, much to the delight of William Battle and James Johnston Pettigrew, students at the University of North Carolina. Battle thought

[11] Reniers, *Springs of Virginia*, 85, 52; Eliza Cope Harrison, ed., *Best Companions: Letters of Eliza Middleton Fisher and Her Mother, Mary Hering Middleton, from Charleston, Philadelphia, and Newport, 1839–1846* (Columbia, SC, 2001), 55, n.4; Graydon, *Tales of Columbia*, 51.

[12] Buckingham, *Slave States*, 2:338; Reniers, *Virginia Springs*, 193–194; Sulzby, *Alabama Hotels*, 30, 85.

the five-man band less than first-rate and much of the dancing unorganized and ludicrous. No matter: "The dance was graced by some of New Orleans's loveliest daughters." Since beauty is in the eyes of the beholder, not everyone agreed. Mrs. Lovell Murran found few invalids but many fashion-plates – "quite a display of fashion, though I am sorry to say not of beauty. I do not think I ever saw so many really homely persons as are congregated here."[13]

Percival Reniers, the premier historian of Virginia Springs, has described the social scene in a manner that sheds light not only on the different dancing styles of the Virginians and South Carolinians but on their mutual antagonism, which had a political parallel: "The Balls were mostly Virginia reels and square dances, with an occasional cotillion thrown in when there were enough sophisticates to carry it off. The South Carolina girls could rise to stardom then, being more experienced in the fashionable world than most of their Virginia sisters." The discomfiture of the Virginia belles amused Mrs. Allston of the Georgetown crowd, making her feel superior, as Rice-coast Carolinians usually did. "I have heard a great Deal often of the Virginia Girls' Dancing," she wrote her son Robert, the future governor, "but they sit down here and look Panic Struck, when our Girls get the floor – they dance nothing here but Reels and Jigs, our dancing you know is Cotillions and Country Dances, they cant go it, one young Lady got up tryed a Cotillion Blundered got Vexed and walked out of the Room." The mutually irritating airs of Rice-coast Carolinians and Tidewater Virginians encouraged social knifing. The Virginians dominated the Sweet and felt a proprietary interest. The South Carolinians claimed the Salt Sulphur for their own and – with some reason – felt that they had the better of the bargain.[14]

South Carolinians and Virginians displayed different sensibilities in more ways than one. Grimball, vacationing at the White in 1835 with Meta and the children, noted in his diary that the entertainment included a mulatto who sang the Marseillaise, which proved unobjectionable, but also "love ditties." To make matters immeasurably worse, "He sings them uncommonly well." Mr. [Whitemarsh?] Seabrook and Mr. [Isaac?] Holmes had taken their families, and "they were so shocked by this exhibition – a Black man in a slave country singing love songs in the presence of their wives & daughters, that they, and with them, all the other

[13] Battle quoted in Reniers, *Springs of Virginia*, 78; Mrs. Lovell Murran to Eliz[abeth] Quitman, July 19, 1838, in J. A. Quitman Papers.
[14] Reniers, *Springs of Virginia*, 44–45.

Carolinians, marched out of the room." They protested loudly but to no avail: "Slavery in this part of the country is a very different thing from Slavery in So.Ca." The Virginians, he feared, were reconciling themselves to emancipation.[15]

The nearby environment had its seedy side. In the 1830s, the White's "Wolf Row" became notorious for noise, frolics, and wildness. Buckingham's British reserve did not take well to the drunkenness and debauchery among many of young people in the area, who attended the public balls at the Cave despite the high cost of $2.50 per person. The young men were chiefly sons of planters from the surrounding country, with some Southerners from Virginia Springs, all brought up in the tainted atmosphere of slavery; and the female visitors were mostly farmers' daughters, from the neighborhood, who looked to this annual illumination of the Cave as young country-girls in England do to the recurrence of an annual fair; at many of which, it is to be feared, similar scenes to those described, very frequently occur. Buckingham took an even dimmer view of the atmosphere at the springs into which parents plunged scores of seven- to twelve-year-old children for three months a year:

[It is] absolutely pernicious, introducing them thus early into the very hot-bed of dissipation; the chief occupation of such children being that of eating and drinking uncontrolled at every meal, playing chequers or backgammon, and reading fashionable novels during the day, and dancing with partners of the opposite sex at night; by all which health is impaired, bad tastes are formed, and a premature development is given to those very passions, which it ought to be the duty of all parents to curb and restrain.

Parents did not need Buckingham to tell them of the dangers, and some made an effort to have their children attend local schools during these summer months. Numbers and the extent of success cannot be ascertained.[16]

Gambling, sometimes ruinous, provoked much grumbling. Robert Bailey, a well-known gambler-turned-innkeeper, arrived at the Virginia Springs from Philadelphia with Ann Turnbull, his mistress and coworker, whom local folks called a "notorious whore." His fine brandies, wines, whiskeys, cheeses, coffee, chocolates, and cigars overwhelmed the local population. Bailey ruined himself by gambling and had to depart, but

[15] J. B. Grimball Diaries, July 28, 1835.
[16] Featherstonhaugh, *Excursion through the Slave States*, 17 ("Wolf's Row"); Buckingham, *Slave States*, 2:392, 2:348. For parents' efforts, see, e.g., the accounts of trips to the springs in Norton-Chilton-Demeron Papers for 1844 and 1859. For schools at the springs and in upcountry villages, see Brewster, *Summer Migrations*, 75.

not before he helped make high-stakes gambling part of the ambience. Thereafter, professional gamblers crowded into the springs, looking for and finding easy marks among wealthy planters, who had little experience with fixed games. In the 1820s, when men outnumbered women five to one, drunks, gamblers, and hell-raisers predominated, but conditions improved steadily thereafter. By the 1850s, proprietors segregated gamblers in a few cottages, but teetotaling never became the fashion. The first round of organized drinking took place between six and seven in the morning, the second under the dome in the afternoon ("evening"), and the third between six and seven at night. Prudence generally prevailed, but excesses there were. Conditions outside western Virginia may have been rougher, if only because less in the spotlight. The Reverend Henry Ruffner of Virginia observed that Lewisburg, Kentucky, owed its prosperity largely to its proximity to the springs, but to his disgust, some nearby springs welcomed gamblers and swindlers who preyed on unwary guests. Still, the editor of *Transylvania Journal of Medicine and the Associated Sciences* recommended Harrodsburg Springs as the best in Kentucky from a medicinal point of view but also highly rated White Sulphur Springs as comparable to the famous springs of that name in Virginia.[17]

Horse racing invited heavy betting at more fashionable springs like Virginia's White. Other activities proved more edifying. The Virginia Springs lay close enough to Charlottesville to encourage visitors to look in at the University of Virginia and to encourage the professors to drop in. Friendships and professional relations grew. Georgia's distinguished Joseph LeConte visited the springs in the 1850s and met William Holmes McGuffey, J. H. Holcombe, Albert Taylor Bledsoe, George Frederick Holmes, and Basil Lanneau Gildersleeve. The professors added to the life of the springs by giving evening lectures on various subjects.[18]

Despite charms, the hustle and bustle proved a bit much. Some visitors to the Virginia Springs in the 1850s found the journey from one to another trying as well as expensive. Ellen Douglas Brownlow, who regularly visited the springs at Shocco, would have liked to accompany a

[17] Herbert Asbury, *Sucker's Progress: An Informal History of Gambling in America from the Colonies to Canfield* (New York, 1939), 256; Patricia C. Click, *The Spirit of the Times: Amusements in Nineteenth-Century Baltimore, Norfolk, and Richmond* (Charlottesville, VA, 1989), 59; Reniers, *Springs of Virginia*, 17, 21–22, 38–41, 55–56; Henry Ruffner, "Notes of a Tour," *SLM*, 5 (1839), 44–45; The Editor, "An Account of Some of the Principal Mineral Springs of Kentucky," *Transylvania Journal of Medicine and the Associated Sciences*, 5 (1832), 375–401.

[18] William Dallam Armes, ed., *The Autobiography of Joseph Le Conte* (New York, 1903), 168–169; J. H. Otey Diary, Aug. 13, 1852

friend to Virginia, but could not: "It is too expensive a trip for my purse in these hard times." At the White, J. W. Alexander thought the treatment of visitors "all but inhuman." The Presbyterian Reverend Thomas Smyth of Charleston reported to his daughter that conditions were much better at the smaller springs. But then, much depended on taste. In 1825, Bernhard, Duke of Saxe-Weimar, considered Warm Sulphur Springs much underestimated and destined to rival New York's Saratoga Springs. The White and some other springs attracted those who wanted a gay time, whereas the Red Sweet Springs attracted those who, like James C. Furman and Edmund Ruffin, preferred a quieter environment. During the 1850s, the Virginia Springs became more crowded than ever. J. H. Ingraham of Natchez discovered no few seekers after health and pleasure who were glad to go home. Thomas ("Stonewall") Jackson reported differently. At Alum Springs in 1852, he found some four hundred people crowded into facilities designed to accommodate three hundred maximum. He had to share a bed and spend ten dollars a week for board. Yet, he thought the accommodations fine and heard no complaints from others. "This water I consider the water of waters," he wrote, regretting he could stay only a week. Virginia Springs complicated the lives of many who rarely if ever stayed at them. At Monticello, Jefferson had his hands full with an endless string of travelers on their way to the springs, and everywhere travelers from one part of the South on their way to another destination stopped briefly at the springs. The springs provided opportunities for local people to supplement their incomes. They provided markets for farmers, who raised meat and vegetables; people for miles around provided lodgings for those crowded out of the springs' cottages; and others made money by providing various small services.[19]

[19] Ellen Douglas Brownlow to Mary Eliza Battle, Aug. 24, 1854, in Mary Eliza Battle Letters; W. Alexander to Thomas Smyth, Aug. 15, 1855 and Thomas Smyth to Sarah Ann Smyth, Sept. 14, 1857; and accounts for 1857 and 1859, in Thomas Smyth, *Autobiographical Notes, Letters, and Reflections* (Charleston, SC, 1914), 187, 461; Bernhard, Duke of Saxe-Weimar Eisenach, *Travels Through North America during the Years 1825 and 1826*, 2 vols. (Philadelphia, 1818), 1:188; on Red Sweet Springs, see Harvey Tolliver Cook, *The Life Work of James Clement Furman* (Greenville, SC, 1926), 48; Sept. 9, 1858, in *ERD*, 1:229; George P. R. James, "Virginia Country Life," in Eugene L. Schwaab and Jacqueline Bull, eds., *Travels in the Old South, 1783–1860: Selected from Periodicals of the Times*, 2 vols. (Lexington, KY, 1973), 2:525–526; J. H. Ingraham, *Sunny South; Or, The Southerner at Home* (New York, 1968 [1860], 206, 217; L. M. W. Fletcher "Autobiography" (m. s), Aug.-Sept., 1844; T. J. Jackson to Laura Jackson, July 12, Sept. 7, 1852, in Thomas Jackson Arnold, *Early Life and Letters of General Thomas J. ("Stonewall") Jackson* (Richmond, VA, 1957 [1916]), 190. For the neighboring area, see Susan P. Hopewell to My Dear Cousins, n.d., in Leah and Rebecca

Buckingham contrasted the springs of Virginia favorably with those of Saratoga: a better climate and less bother. Since the cost of travel to the Virginia springs ran high in the 1840s, the clientele came primarily from the more affluent classes, whereas the clientele of Saratoga came from the middle classes, especially those of upstate New York. Yet Buckingham complained that Saratoga had more "dandies" than anywhere else. Alexander Mackay, an acute British traveler, agreed: "Many families, from all parts of the Union, prefer the quiet and retirement of the springs of Virginia, to the hurry-scurry life and fashionable vortex of Saratoga." Once a place for the elite, Saratoga now attracted people from all walks of life, although it remained "to a considerable extent, a place of fashionable resort." Once a place for invalids, it now catered primarily to partygoers. The hotels were big, dining halls crowded, prices high. The weather? Cloudy nine months a year.[20]

A good many Southerners continued to find Saratoga Springs pleasant, among them Caroline Bird Yancey Beman, mother of the secessionist W. L. Yancey and wife of the abolitionist N. S. S. Beman. She seems to have enjoyed talking about her marital woes and confessing her own (unspecified) faults. As a boy, Frederick A. P. Barnard, a great educator in Alabama and Mississippi and later in his native New York, visited his grandfather at Saratoga Springs, admiring the "beautiful manners" and "elegant way of life" of the Southerners there. In 1836, Charles Lockhart Pettigrew of North Carolina drew back from the two thousand or so people "of all sorts and descriptions; every one seemed disposed to exhibit him or her self to the best advantage; only a few invalids were there. I suppose it was too gay." Pettigrew reported three balls a week, in addition to three "hops." A hop, he explained, was an "inferior ball." In 1850, Julia Marsh Patterson visited Saratoga Springs with her husband and did not have a good time. Although people gathered from every state, she did not know any of them, and unlike her experience at the springs in her native Georgia, she did not find it easy to make friends there. The highborn predominated, she observed, but, in addition to diseased, maimed, and deformed who were there for the waters, there were "mendicants

Simpson Papers; Carney Diary, Aug. 22, 1859; Kenneth W. Noe, *Southwest Virginia's Railroad: Modernization and the Sectional Crisis* (Urbana, IL, 1994), 65; on Jefferson see Alexander Ormond Boulton, "The Architecture of Slavery: Art, Language, and Society in Early Virginia" (Ph. D. diss.: College of William and Mary, 1991), 277.

[20] Buckingham, *Slave States*, 2:316–318, 336; Alexander MacKay, *The Western World; Or, Travels in the United States in 1846–1847*, 3 vols. (New York, 1968 [1849]), 2:88, 3:197–198.

soliciting charity." The way the women dressed appalled her, especially the matrons who tried to look girlish in – would you believe? – sleeveless gowns. "On the whole, there was little gallantry displayed, the young ladies, generally speaking, taking care of themselves. Yet the natural beauty of Saratoga overwhelmed her: "Never have I witnessed a more charming retreat." Some comparisons seem wide of the mark, for the southern springs also shifted from a focus on invalids to the fashionable, and no less than Saratoga featured women in sleeveless gowns, although perhaps not in Julia Patterson's Georgia.[21]

COSTS: FINANCIAL AND POLITICAL

By 1830 and steadily thereafter, southern editors and politicians cried out against summer treks to the North. Journal articles, communications, and editorials boosted the southern springs and recommended books. *De Bow's Review* applauded the emergence of springs on the Gulf Coast, singling out Alabama's "seats of fashion and pleasure" and noting Mary J. Windle's "pleasant" *Life at White Sulphur Springs*. The *Southern Literary Messenger* warmly recommended J. J. Moorman's *The Virginia Springs.*[22]

The journals appealed to southern pride and material interest, arguing that expenditures in the North hurt the southern economy badly. Estimates of southern expenditures on trips to the North for social, business, and educational purposes varied considerably and remain untrustworthy. But they ran high enough to provoke political alarm and contention. In 1832, the *Georgia Telegraph*, in an estimate credited by *Niles' Register*, asserted that Southerners spent $500,000 a year on social trips to the North. In 1838, *Niles' Register* estimated that fifty thousand

---

[21] Maria Bryan Harford to Julia Ann Bryan Cumming, Aug. 5, 1839, in Carol Bleser, ed., *Tokens of Affection: The Letters of a Planter's Daughter in the Old South* (Athens, GA, 1996), 254 (Beman); William J. Chute, *Damn Yankee! The First Career of Frederick A. P. Barnard. Educator, Scientist, Idealist* (Port Washington, NY, 1978), 77; C. L. Pettigrew to William Shepard Pettigrew, Aug. 20, 1836, in Sarah McCulloh Lemmon, ed., *The Pettigrew Papers*, 2 vols. (Raleigh, NC, 1971,1988), 2:309; Julia Marsh Patterson Journal (1850), in Benjamin C. Yancey Papers, 108. Also, Meade Minnigerode, *The Fabulous Forties, 1840–1850: A Presentation of Private Life* (New York, 1924), 90–91. John and Eliza Quitman also spent almost $1,500 on a trip to the North in 1825 that included Saratoga Springs: Robert E. May, *John A. Quitman: Old South Crusader* (Baton Rouge, LA, 1985), 27.

[22] Southern Agriculturalist and Register of Rural Affairs, 8 (1835), #3, 9 (1836), #2 and #4; *DBR*, 21 (1856), 323–329, *DBR*, 9 (1850), 349–350; 23 (1857), 444; *SLM*, 20 (1854), 447; also, *SQR*, 2 (1842), 540.

people from the cotton states went north each year and spent about $500 each. In the 1840s William Gregg, the industrialist, complaining about the lack of investment capital in the South, thought Southerners spent $12 million per year in the North. The cost of northern trips varied widely, but a wealthy planter like Grimball spent $3,238 in 1856 for a trip that included Montreal and Boston as well as Saratoga, New York City, and Niagara. Costs to planters who spent three or more months in the North ran high.[23]

Behavior at northern springs upset southern gentlemen, especially when their families traveled without them. R. D. Arnold of Savannah warned his daughter, who was vacationing in New Jersey in 1852, to be careful at the beach. He had heard reports of libertines and gamblers who preyed on unsuspecting young ladies. He understood that southern young ladies showed greater reserve than northern but still cautioned her. Ella Arnold thereupon shocked him with reports of public displays of affection between men and women.[24]

Increasing numbers of Southerners received hostile receptions at northern springs. Stonewall Jackson, who had had pleasant experiences in the North as a West Point cadet and army officer, took his wife to Vermont and Massachusetts for her health. There they met resentment, insults, and South-baiting. Francis Terry Leak, a Mississippi planter, expressed a growing attitude in 1855: "It would be better to see Southern men & Ladies, visiting the Lakes & Prairies of the West, to hunt & fish, and overlook plantations, than idling months at the North among the abolitionists." South Carolinians continued to go to Saratoga even in the late 1850s, but relations with Northerners there grew tense. Increasingly, Northerners and Southerners kept to themselves and interacted with cold formality. Indeed, something of the sort was also taking place at the Virginia Springs. Another southern complaint: Speaking in Richmond in the mid-1850, Virginia, R. G. Morris – seconded by George Fitzhugh – claimed that Southerners were abandoning Saratoga Springs in no small part because of the "treatment they have received in the last few years from the free negroes." Northern newspapers commented on the absence of Southerners at Newport and Saratoga, but the extent of the diminution

[23] See e. g., *SQR*, 18 (1850), 24; J. A. Turner, "What Are We to Do?" *DBR* 29 (1860), 72–77; and, generally, Avery O. Craven, *The Coming of the Civil War* (Chicago, 1942), 296–297; J. B. Grimball Account, Oct. 10, 1856. Grimball spent $2,500 in New York state; Louis De Saussure Plantation Book (1837), 7.

[24] R. D. Arnold to Ella Arnold, July 30, Aug. 22, 1852, in Richard H. Shryock, ed., *Letters of Richard D. Arnold, M. D., 1808–1876* (Durham, NC, 1929), 61–62.

remains unclear. The growing conflict in the courts over interstate comity especially discouraged Southerners, for they could no longer safely take their slaves on trips.[25]

Yet, northern springs remained attractive, perhaps as much for the radical change of pace and manner as for the weather. What could Virgil Maxcy of South Carolina do when his doctors urged that he take his wife to Saratoga for her health? Jefferson Davis continued to summer at the "southern community" in Newport, and Southerners went to Newport and Bristol to visit relatives. During South Carolina's long "sickly season," a good many wealthy and socially prominent lowcountry planters went to Newport – a pattern started well before the Revolution and resumed immediately after it. Despite the diminution of travel to the North, possibly half of the Southerners who traveled to summer vacation spots in the 1850s still went north.[26]

SUMMER ADJUSTMENTS

Many black-belt planters chose nearby pine barrens rather than go up country or out-of-state. They rode out to their plantations once or twice

[25] John Bowers, *Stonewall Jackson: Portrait of a Soldier* (New York, 1989), 93; Leak Diary, Nov. 29, 1855; Avery O. Craven, *The Growth of Southern Nationalism, 1848–1861* (Baton Rouge, LA, 1953), 256–257, 271; R. G. Morris, "Southern Educational and Industrial Development," *DBR*, 20 (1856), 625; George Fitzhugh, "Southern Thought," *DBR*, 23 (1857), 340; Brewster, *Summer Migrations*, 102, 116; Harold M. Hyman and William M. Wiecek, *Equal Justice under Law: Constitutional Development, 1835–1875* (New York, 1982), 99; Sarah Chilton to Mary P. Norton, Aug. 16, 1844, in Norton-Chilton-Demeron Papers. Resistance to northern travel made the plantations more attractive in summer. Planters with access to spring water and financial means installed hydraulic rams to bring running water into their homes, and they devised ingenious methods for reducing the insect nuisance: James C. Bonner, *A History of Georgia Agriculture, 1732–1860* (Athens, GA, 1964), 183–184.

[26] Virgil Maxcy to John C. Calhoun, Aug. 6, 1843, in *JCCP*, 17:336; also George Warren Cross to Calhoun, Aug. 11, 1818, in *JCCP*, 3:23. For the continued popularity of Saratoga among Southerners, see, e.g., William Hooper Haigh Diary, Aug. 28, 1843; Herschel Gower and Jack Allan, eds., *Pen and Sword: The Life and Journals of Randal W. McGavock* (Nashville, TN, 1959), 145. On Newport, see Arthur C. Cole, *The Irrepressible Conflict, 1850–1865* (New York, 1934), 203. On southern family ties at Newport see Brewster, *Summer Migrations*, 30–34. George C. Rogers, *Evolution of a Federalist: William Loughton Smith of Charleston, 1758–1812* (Columbia, SC, 1962), 54; Alicia Hopton Middleton, "A Family Record," in Alicia Hopton Middleton et al., *Life in Carolina and New England During the Nineteenth Century* (Bristol, RI, 1929), 79; James David Glunt, eds., *Florida Plantation Records from the Papers of George Noble Jones* (St. Louis, MO, 1927), 21–22; Elliott Ashkenazi, *The Business of Jews in Louisiana, 1840–1875* (Tuscaloosa, AL, 1988), 41.

a week to keep an eye on their overseers and slaves. In Carolina and Georgia, a number of the lowcountry planters, perhaps most, created summer communities not far from the coast. A case in point: Walterboro, South Carolina, provided a place of refuge in the early nineteenth century and after. John Hamilton Cornish, newly arrived from New England, described Walterboro as "like all their summer retreats built among the pine trees, the Native forest is scarcely molested. The houses are set among the trees with very little if any signs of cultivation about them." Eliza Clitherall found life at Walterboro "plain & social – no city airs or excitement." The community's one store satisfactorily met local demand and had an upper room to accommodate social events and church services. Summer homes were modest one-story cottages with large porches and just enough room to squeeze in the inevitable guests. In low country and up country, places like Walterboro, McPhersonville, and Springville blossomed as centers of genteel social life. Even on the Sea Islands, from which most planters fled during the summer, some built health resorts on the island's seaward bluffs. Ministers, too, took summer vacations, and many summer communities engaged one for weekly services. Residents of some small communities settled for services led by a layman.[27]

Summer communities rose together with the springs and had a similar effect on politics and social life. Planters who spent several months a year in summer homes participated in local affairs, building churches and schools and earning a reputation for generous treatment of the nearby and transient poor. Healthful places of refuge made life possible for lowcountry planters in more ways than one, including the feeding of illusions. Well-policed summer communities, Samuel DuBose remarked, had "an obedient, well-ordered, and happy body of slaves." Whigs and

---

[27] Robert Q. Mallard, *Plantation Life before Emancipation* (Electronic ed.; Chapel Hill, NC, 1998 [1892]); Guion Griffin Johnson, *A Social History of the Sea Islands, with Special Reference to St. Helena Island, South Carolina* (Westport, CT, 1969), 75; Easterby, ed., *South Carolina Rice Plantation*, 9; Ralph Betts Flanders, *Plantation Slavery in Georgia* (Chapel Hill, NC, 1933), 225; Josephine Bacon Martin, *Midway Georgia in History and Legend, 1852–1869*, 2nd, ed. (Darien, GA, 1961), 8; Cornish Diary, December 24, 1839; [Anon.], "Tour in the Interior of South Carolina" [1825], in Schwaab and Bull, eds., *Travels in the old South*, 1:183; Clitherall "Autobiography" (ms.), Book 5; Simpson, *Cokers of Carolina*, 4–5. For preaching, see Mary E. McGrath, "Sketch of Major Jas. Lovell" (ms.), in West Manuscripts, n. d.; R. F. W. Alston (1838), in Easterby, ed., *South Carolina Rice Plantation*, 9; Albert Sidney Thomas, *A Historical Account of the Protestant Episcopal Church in South Carolina, 1820–1857: being a Continuation of Dalcho's Account, 1670–1820* (Columbia, SC, 1957), 197; Thomas Cary Johnson, *The Life and Letters of Benjamin Morgan Palmer* (Richmond, VA, 1906), 31; Middleton et al., *Life in Carolina and New England*, 153.

Democrats, unionists and radicals, clustered together. Camden County, Georgia, for example, attracted Whig families like the Clinches, who had a better chance than at other times of the year to exchange views and plan activities. When, in August 1840, the Clarksville Tippecanoe Club invited Willie P. Mangum of North Carolina to speak at Buffalo Springs, Virginia, S. H. Harris explained, "You may expect at any rate a large collection as the Springs is at this time a place of considerable resort and the people of the neighborhood can be very readily collected.²⁸

Visitors to the springs, even the White, met planters from far away who built summer homes nearby. Lowcountry Carolinians built summer homes in Flat Rock, North Carolina, and Indian Springs and Rowland Springs, Georgia. Carolinians and Georgians built "The Hill," a community near the popular spa at Summerville. Others repaired to summer homes at Waynesville, southwest of Brunswick. By the 1840s, Rowland's Springs in Cass County (later, Bartow) and Warm Springs in South Central Georgia became fashionable for well-to-do Southeasterners. John Bachman of Charleston favored Madison Springs, as did William C. Richards, who pronounced it Georgia's Saratoga. George White, in his *Statistics of Georgia* (1849), added Sulphur Springs in Hall County as "among the most delightful spots in Georgia."²⁹

---

²⁸ S. H. Harris to W. P. Mangum, August 10, 1840, in Shanks, ed., *Mangum Papers*, 3:43; also, Stephen H. Long, "Hot Springs of Arkansas," in Schwaab and Bull, eds., *Travels in the Old South*, 1:135; Samuel DuBose, "Reminiscences of St. Stephen's Parish," in T. Gaillard Thomas, ed., *A Contribution to the History of the Huguenots of South Carolina* (New York, 1887), 82; Rembert W. Patrick, *Aristocrat in Uniform: General Duncan L. Clinch* (Gainesville, FL, 1963), 209; Albert Virgil House, ed., *Planter Management and Capitalism in Georgia: The Journal of Hugh Fraser Grant, Ricegrower* (New York, 1954), 22.

²⁹ Mitchell King Diary, 1853–1856. King had a lot of distinguished company at Flat Rock, including Huger, Memminger, Preston, Middleton, Rhett, Pringle, Allston, Pinckney, and Clingman. See also J. B. Grimball Diaries, July 16, 1836; Carmichael Diary, July 17, 1840; James Graham to W. A. Graham, Oct. 29, 1830, in J. G. deRoulhac Hamilton, ed., *The Papers of William Alexander Graham*, 5 vols. (Raleigh, NC, 1957–1973), 1:193; Lester D. Stephens, *Joseph LeConte: Gentle Prophet of Evolution* (Baton Rouge, LA, 1982), 169, 26; John N. Waddel, *Memorials of Academic Life* (Richmond, VA, 1891), 44; David Wyatt Aiken Autobiography (ms.), 12–13; Middleton et al., *Life in the Carolinas and New England*, 150–155; Frederick Law Olmsted, *A Journey in the Back Country* (New York, 1970 [1860]), 251; Inscoe, *Mountain Masters*, 209; William Harris Bragg, *De Renne: Three Generations of a Georgia Family* (Athens, GA, 1999), 102–103; [William C. Richards], "Notes of a Summer Tour, *Orion*, 2 (1843), 181; White, *Statistics of the State of Georgia*, 151, 308, 424. On Summerville, see W. Kirk Wood, ed., *A Northern Daughter and Southern Wife: The Civil War Reminiscences and Letters of Katherine H. Cumming, 1860–1865* (Augusta, GA, 1976), 105, n. 5; Steel, *T. Butler King*, 6.

Beersheba Springs, about thirty miles north of Sewanee in Tennessee, hosted four hundred or so Gulf Coast planters at a time. Mayor Randal W. McGavock of Nashville and Colonel Armfield, the big slave-trader and planter, mixed with prominent men from Mississippi and Alabama. Armfield spent a small fortune on his visits to Beersheba, while Isaac Franklin, his partner in the slave trade, preferred Tennessee's popular Borean, Bovair, and Tyree Springs. Montvale Springs in east Tennessee accommodated three to four hundred people primarily from Georgia, Alabama, and Louisiana. What the pinebarrens gained, the towns lost. Alexandria, Louisiana, did not initially much impress Bishop Leonidas Polk; it impressed him less during the summer when half its population of eight hundred left for the pine barrens.[30]

In Mississippi, the Anglo planters of Madison County repaired to summer homes on the Gulf Coast, near Biloxi and Mississippi City; the French to Shieldsborough, along with Biloxi. Duncan McAlpin advised Mangum that Mississippi Springs ranked as "the most fashionable and celebrated Watering place in this part of the world." In the 1850s, Lafcadio Hearn, noting the large number of Texans and the beautiful white sand at Last Island, southwest of New Orleans, pronounced it the most fashionable watering place in the South. In the Delta's Washington County, where blacks outnumbered whites ten to one, wealthy planters could afford to head north to the expensive springs of Virginia or Saratoga. They packed up their families in mid-May and did not return until mid-October. Not only southern planters but affluent Northerners established seasonal homes in Florida. Bel Air, in the piney woods outside Tallahassee, arose in the wake of the cholera epidemic of 1841 to permit the wealthy to spend three or four months a year in a healthful climate and recuperative waters. Planters built summer homes nearby, and Tallahasseans, who had habitually gone north until the late 1830s, began to favor the area. The waters proved efficacious for many and not at all for many others, doubtless according to the nature of the malady. Welak, too, became a place of retreat for Northerners, especially merchants who combined business with pleasure. In addition to advertising the miraculous cures effected by

---

[30] McGavock, Aug. 19, Sept. 5, 1858, in Gower and Allan, eds. *Pen and Sword*, 483, 486; George R. Fairbanks, *History of the University of the South at Sewanee, Tennessee* (Jacksonville, FL, 1905), 29, n.; Stephenson, *Isaac Franklin*, 16–17; Thomas Perkins Abernethy, *From Frontier to Plantation in Tennessee: A Study in Frontier Democracy* (Chapel Hill, NC, 1932), 281; William Dillon, *Life of John Mitchel*, 2 vols. (London, 1888), 2:96 (Montvale); William M. Polk, *Leonidas Polk, Bishop and General*, 2 vols. (New York, 1915), 83.

climate and water, citizens advertised Welaka as a hunting and fishing paradise. Some Northerners who went to southern springs doubtless felt like those of whom Lord Bryce spoke in the 1880s. They go, he wrote, "to know the South, and themselves diffuse new ideas among the backward populations of those districts."[31]

The "summer people" brought seasonal commercial booms to sleepy areas and did much to beautify bedraggled settings by building attractive cottages. They enhanced social and cultural life with dances, parties, lectures, and intellectual circles. All in all, vacationing planters enlivened the life of the pine barrens and up country.[32]

SUMMERTIME POLITICS

The springs and summer communities figured large in southern politics, although historians have taken little notice. The first rule at the White and at other springs was known as "the truce of the waters: no politics." The second rule, harder to enforce: no nasty gossip or personal altercations. Violations usually occurred in private conversations while public decorum was upheld. Ladies and gentlemen did not bring their political animosities to the springs, did not proselytize, did not quarrel, and did not spread scandal, although George Wythe Randolph thought the springs a place for picking up juicy tidbits of scandal about social lions and lionesses of southern high society. Whigs and Democrats, Southrons and Yankees, unionists and secessionists obeyed the truce of the waters, but not quite everyone. The irrepressible Edmund Ruffin recounted his visit to the White in 1857, "where of course I met with numerous persons and ... used every suitable occasion to express my opinion, & the grounds thereof, that the slave-holding states should

---

[31] Belle Kearney, "Patrician Days of Madison County" (ms.); Charles S. Sydnor, *A Gentleman of the Old Natchez Region: Benjamin L. C. Wailes* (Durham, NC, 1938), 1190; McAlpin to Mangum, Sept. 5, 1849, in Shanks, ed., *Mangum Papers*, 5:163. On Hearn, see Camilla Davis Trammell, *Seven Pines: Its Occupants and Their Letters, 1825–1872* (Houston, TX, 1986), 87. See Hearn's novel *Chita* in Hearn, *American Writings*, edited by Christopher Benfey, (New York, 2009); Bern Keating, *A History of Washington County, Mississippi* (Greenville, MS, 1976), 32; Bertram H. Groene, *Ante-Bellum Tallahassee* (Tallahassee, FL, 1971), 54–55, 165 (Bel Aire); George Lee Simpson, Jr., *The Cokers of Carolina: A Social Biography of a Family* (Chapel Hill, NC, 1956), 29–30; Arch Fredric Blakely et al., eds., *Rose Cottage Chronicles: Civil War Letters of the Bryant-Stephens Families of North Florida* (Tallahassee, FL, 1998), 14; James Bryce, *The American Commonwealth*, 3rd ed., 2 vols. (New York, 1895), 2:487.

[32] For an account with special reference to the up country of western North Carolina, see Inscoe, *Mountain Masters*, 8–9, 30–34.

speedily separate from the others & form a separate confederacy." In 1861, Ruffin and Judge Perkins reminisced about their meeting at the White in 1840, when they had been "concerting plans to preach dis-union, & when we had not half a dozen there to sustain us." For years Ruffin had been cajoling everyone in sight with his secessionist doc-trines. He succeeded only in getting himself in bad odor even with those who agreed with him. Political proselytizing fell into the category of things just not done.[33]

Yet politics was everywhere. Who knows how many politicians cau-cused behind closed doors, negotiated alliances, and hatched schemes? Do it they did, year after year. The significance of the springs for south-ern politics can hardly be exaggerated, however much it proceeded *sotto voce*. The most famous stories of wheeling and dealing probably never happened. The tradition that Madison secured Baptist support for ratification of the Constitution when he met the Reverend Mr. Leland at Gum Springs was a good story long circulated but unverified. John Breckenridge got the draft of the famous Kentucky Resolutions, which he introduced into the Kentucky Legislature, at the Virginia Springs. Or was it at Monticello?[34]

In the late 1850s, George Fitzhugh attributed the throngs at south-ern spas to mounting resistance to trips to the North, where they were "insulted by the helps in hotels" and threatened by the prevailing hostil-ity to southern institutions and values. Fitzhugh exulted, "These Southern watering places annually bring together persons from various States of the South, who form friendships, unite various sections in stronger bonds of amity, and confirm each other in the support of Southern institutions, by comparison and concurrence of opinion." John Randolph of Roanoke, Abel P. Upshur, and other Virginians did go to the springs in part to meet political allies. Men who first met each other at the springs – Daniel Moreau Barringer and James Johnston Pettigrew, for example – some-times became fast friends, creating or strengthening political alliances. At Greenbrier White Sulphur Springs, Thomas Caute Reynolds, a prominent Richmond intellectual and diplomat, met George W. Goode, originally of Virginia, who persuaded him to move to St. Louis, where Reynolds

---

[33] Shackelford, *G. W. Randolph*, 42; Aug. 21, 1859, *ERD*, 1:332; retrospective of 1857 in 1:16; Dec. 33, 1861 (2:181).
[34] Francis Taylor Diary, 1797; James C. Klotter, *The Breckenridges of Kentucky, 1760–1981* (Frankfort, KY, 1986), 20. In the 1920s, Ulrich Bonnell Phillips called attention to the political importance of the springs, but his lead has gone uninvestigated: Ulrich Bonnell Phillips, *Life and Labor in the Old South* (Boston, MA, 1948 [1929]), 127.

became United States District Attorney and then lieutenant governor of Missouri.[35]

Politicians did not violate the truce when they spoke against the advent of militant abolitionism in the 1830s, since they did not consider the defense of slavery partisan politics. In fact, the springs provided material for proslavery propaganda. A Charlestonian wrote from Red Sulphur Springs about the wonderful appearance of the black servants. Abolitionist fanaticism "must abandon her extravagant theories" when it "compares the happy, smiling countenances of the African race – their superior intelligence and civilization – with the care-worn features, lumbering bodies, squalid wretchedness, and disgusting rusticity of the European peasantry." Thomas Roderick Dew, on the "undoubted authority of Mr. Barbour," reported that "a negro gentleman from Liberia, who lately visited the Virginia Springs, for the purpose of re-establishing his health," had regaled the planters with stories of the miserable failure of the Liberian experiment.[36]

The truce applied to public, not private, behavior, and politicians knew how to profit from the springs without violating the rule. In the late 1830s, northern conservatives like James Tallmadge of New York and southern conservatives like Hugh Legaré of South Carolina and W. C. Rives of Virginia met at the White. Martin Van Buren went there in 1838, largely in an unsuccessful effort to convince Rives to help rebuild his unraveling coalition. On the radical side, in 1845 Robert Barnwell Rhett, lobbying for the Bluffton movement, returned from Washington to South Carolina via the Virginia Springs, where he had some tough discussions with Polk's representatives over the tariff and the threat of secession.[37]

In 1840, Robert Ransom reported to Mangum from Virginia, "Our watering places are filled to overflowing & a large majority for Clay."

[35] Fitzhugh, "Southern Thought," *DBR*, (1857), 340; Claude H. Hall, *Abel Parker Upshur: Conservative Virginian, 1790–1844* (Madison, WI, 1963), 148; Wilson, *Carolina Cavalier*, 55; T. C. Reynolds to G. W. Goode, Feb. 4, 1849, in "Glimpses of the Past: Letters of Thomas Caute Reynolds, 1847–1885," in *Missouri Historical Society*, 19 (1943), 14–15. Henry L. Benning, in a prosecession speech at Milledgeville in 1860, cited Kettel to charge that 50,000 Southerners were going north every year and spending $1,000 per person: Benning in William W. Freehling and Craig M. Simpson, eds., *Secession Debated: Georgia's Showdown in 1860* (New York, 1992), 139–140.

[36] A Visitor, "Virginia Springs," 3 *SLM*, (1837), 281–284, quote at 281; Thomas Roderick Dew, "Essay on Slavery," in *The Pro-Slavery Argument, as Maintained by the Most Distinguished Writers of the Southern States* (Philadelphia, 1853), 433, n.

[37] Michael O'Brien, *A Character of Hugh Legaré* (Knoxville, TN, 1985), 236; Charles Henry Ambler, *Thomas Ritchie: A Study in Virginia Politics* (Richmond, VA, 1913), 204–205.

Three years later, when the aging Henry Clay's presidential ambitions were again running high, he made a point of displaying himself on tour, with spots at the watering places, to demonstrate his physical vitality. The gossip mill served him well, as reports crossed the country of his good health. Calhoun reported that John Tyler's vetoes of Whig party measures had provoked supporters and opponents to caucus at the springs to plan their next moves. In 1844, Whitmarsh Seabrook asked Calhoun to return from Washington via Warm Springs, North Carolina, for he was anxious to discuss important matters with him; and in 1849, Richard K. Crallé urged Calhoun to visit the Virginia Springs for his health, adding that he would find much in the way of political doings.[38]

At the White in 1846, the Presbyterian Reverend Robert L. Dabney found too much politics for his taste, but he was probably referring merely to the presence of politicians. Dabney was too shy to approach Calhoun, whom he noted had a reputation for being especially accessible to all. Die-hard Calhoun supporters, hoping to rekindle his presidential prospects, had huddled at the White the previous year. When James Hamilton, Jr. learned that John C. Calhoun was going to the Virginia Springs, he wrote that the trip would improve Calhoun's health and "enable the public men of Virginia, who congregate there to make what many of them so much desire, your acquaintance." On his way to and from the springs, Calhoun was deluged with invitations to meet with assorted politicians, not all of them his supporters. The intensification of sectional antagonisms, provoked by the Mexican War and the Wilmot Proviso, sent leading Southerners to the springs to consult on necessary measures. Calhoun received reports both from Eustis Prescott of Kentucky on discussions at nearby Blue Licks Springs, and from Franklin Elmore on the plans of Robert Turnbull to go to the Virginia Springs to confer with planters and politicians of Mississippi and Louisiana.[39]

---

[38] Robert Ransom to W. P. Mangum, September 12, 1844, in Shanks, ed. *Mangum Papers*, 4:193; for Clay's 1848 visit to White Sulphur Srings, see Michael Holt, *The Rise and Fall of the American Whig Party: Jacksonian Politics and the Onset of the Civil War* (New York, 2003), 276; Calhoun to Richard Crallé, Oct. 8, 1841, in *JCCP*, 15:785; Whitemarsh Seabrook to J. C. Calhoun, July 17, 1844, in *JCCP*, 19:382; R. K. Crallé to J. C. Calhoun, Sept. 23, 1845, in *JCCP*, 22:163; James Hamilton, Jr., to J. C. Calhoun, Aug. 2, 1846, in *JCCP*, 23:384; Richard K. Crallé to Calhoun, Feb. 27, 1849, in *JCCP*, 26: 323–324; also, Charles M. Wiltse, *John C. Calhoun: Sectionalist* (Indianapolis, IN, 1944), 229.

[39] Thomas Cary Johnson, ed. *Life and Letters of Robert Lewis Dabney* (Carlisle, PA, 1977), 102.

In 1851, John Slidell of Louisiana and Albert Gallatin Brown of Mississippi, two of the tougher Democratic politicians in the Southwest, spent a good deal of time together at the White. No one thought they were discussing the latest fashions in ballroom dancing. Slidell moved around. In 1851 he also went to Saratoga Springs to meet with Robert J. Walker of Mississippi and William Marcy, supporters of James Buchanan's political ambitions. Two years later former president Tyler met with President Franklin Pierce at the White by prearrangement, although neither publicly engaged in politicking. The normally suspicious Ruffin may have been right that Banks, editor of the *Cincinnati Enquirer*, went to the White in 1859 primarily to line up support for Stephen Douglas. In 1860, with the threat of secession in the air, John Letcher, Virginia's new governor, spent a week at the White with Company F of the Richmond Volunteers: a message not hard to read.[40]

Political meetings took place at springs across the South. In South Carolina, lowcountry planters flocked to Greenville in the piedmont during the summer, where they got to know the people of the upcountry. It became a summering place for such distinguished personages as Governors Henry Middleton and Joseph Allston in early days and then Joel Poinsett, John Belton O'Neall, and others. Michael Tuomey, South Carolina's state geologist, in a letter to his wife, expressed admiration of the Poinsetts for maintaining a summer home near Greenville and socializing with the local folk instead of isolating themselves with other wealthy people at some spa. Radicals like Robert Y. Hayne went there, but Greenville especially attracted unionists, providing an opportunity for Petigru, Poinsett, and Daniel Huger of the low country and Benjamin F. Perry and John Belton O'Neall of the up country to exchange ideas and coordinate plans. Unfortunately, some lowcountry planters developed a bad reputation for overbearing and boorish behavior at Greenville and other upcountry summering places. The common folk took umbrage, as did Perry and others of the upcountry elite.[41]

[40] James Byrne Ranck, *Albert Gallatin Brown: Radical Southern Nationalist* (New York, 1937), 133; Allan Nevins, *Ordeal of the Union*, 2 vols. (New York, 1947), 2:12; Lyon Gardiner Tyler, *The Letters and Times of the Tylers*, 3 vols. (Williamsburg, VA, 1884–1896), 2:505. Buchanan favored Bath Springs in Virginia as a vacation spot: Lavender Ray to His Brother, Jan. 12, 1862, in Mills Lane, ed., *"Dear Mother, Don't Grieve About Me. If I Get Killed, I'll Only Be Dead"* (Savannah, GA, 1990), 92; *ERD*, Aug. 20, 1859 (1:31); F. N. Boney, *John Letcher of Virginia: The Story of Virginia's Civil War Governor* (University, AL, 1966), 97.
[41] Archie Vernon Huff, Jr., *Greenville: The History of the City and County in the South Carolina Piedmont* (Columbia, SC, 1995), 89–95; Michael Tuomey to Sarah E. Tuomey,

Social class strains at Greenville suggest as yet unstudied problems elsewhere. Elite families from the South Carolina low country built summer homes in western North Carolina – with slave labor. They employed local people for menial services, holding them at a distance. Bad feelings grew. During the War, some old accounts were settled. At Beersheba Springs in the eastern highlands of Tennessee rebellious poor whites plundered planters who had been spending summers there since the 1850s.[42]

Glenn Springs, between Spartanburg and Unionville in South Carolina, attracted the Calhouns, among those who sought to recover from illness, but it served other functions as well for the two hundred or so who gathered there at any one time. "In a few days," William Gilmore Simms wrote Hammond in 1847, "I shall go over to Glenn Springs where I shall probably see many persons with whom I may speak of the future of our State." In 1850, Simms published an article in the *Southern Quarterly Review* that recommended Glenn Springs to those who wished to meet the flower of the gentry of the middle and up country, "with a slight sprinkling of others from the seaboard." You will find them, he beamed, "courteous, intelligent, and frank; easy in their manners, and prompt and graceful in their hospitalities."[43]

Shocco Springs throve in the 1840s and 1850s. "The refined and cultivated society that frequented Jones and Shocco springs," exulted Mary Norcott Bryan, "cannot be excelled." In 1842, Calhoun broke his long-standing rule against accepting a dinner in his honor outside South Carolina. He did so at Shocco Springs during the summer, when people from long distances had gathered. By his account, some five to six hundred people attended, "embracing the entire population for a considerable distance round, and many who had come from a considerable distance." Ellen Douglas Brownlow reported "an immense crowd at Shocco – about 700 persons at one time and I now presume there are 550

Aug. [no date], 1845, in Lewis S. Dean, ed., *The Papers of Michael Tuomey* (Spartanburg, SC, 2001), 68–69; Lillian Kibler, *Benjamin F. Perry, Unionist* (Durham, NC, 1946), 83–84; Brewster, *Summer Migrations*, 61, 64, 89, 114, but generally, for Greenville as summer resort, see especially 58–61; J. J. O'Connell, *Catholicity in the Carolinas and Georgia: Leaves of Its History* (Westminster, MD, 1964 [1879]), 443.

42 Steven V. Ash, *When the Yankees Came: Conflict and Chaos in the Occupied South, 1861–1865* (Chapel Hill, NC, 1995), 192–193; Lucy Virginia French Diary, July 26, 1863.

43 *JCCP*, 16: 439, 443; Simms to Hammond, Aug. 21, 1847, in Mary C. Oliphant et al., eds., *The Letters of William Gilmore Simms*, 6 vols. (Columbia, SC, 1952–1982), 2:344; article from *SQR* quoted, 2:344–345, n 229; Brewster, *Summer Migrations*, 80–83.

or 600 more." She regretted that so many strangers crowded in, making old friends hard to find.[44]

The sons of Zachary Taylor and Martin Van Buren, worn out by the campaign of 1848, chose Virginia for rest and recuperation. Politicians did, however, have to watch themselves, for everyone knew everyone else's business, and the gossip mill throve. R. M. Johnson of Kentucky became a target for those who objected to his having a colored mistress, whom he apparently barely kept under wraps on his visits to the Virginia Springs. Rising sectional tensions sometimes caused bigger trouble. An amused William E. Seward told Perry about his political adventure at Virginia Springs. When a gentleman from South Carolina freely abused Van Buren, Seward gave tit-for-tat by abusing Calhoun. The gentleman from South Carolina did not take it well, and a fight was only narrowly averted.[45]

H. L. Hunley of New Orleans, who hated the Virginia Springs but had to accompany his sister and her children, wrote to R. R. Barrow, his brother-in-law: "I hear much of politics here. The Bell & Everett men seem in the ascendant here – The Virginians contend however that Breckinridge will carry the state." Meanwhile, Edmund Ruffin was meeting with R. F. W. Allston and other secessionists at the White on the eve of secession. After the War, Robert E. Lee, Alexander Stephens, P. G. T. Beauregard, and other Confederate leaders met at White Sulphur Springs to hear an appeal from William Rosecrans, a Union general turned Democratic politician, to enter the lists in Seymour's presidential campaign.[46]

Religious leaders, congregating at the springs, discussed church affairs and secular politics. If nothing else, religious leaders met politicians and cemented personal and political ties. The Methodist Bishop George Foster Pierce described the White as "the great resort of all the Southern people." Presbyterian divines like James Henley Thornwell

---

[44] Mary Norcott Bryan, *A Grandmother's Recollection of Dixie* (Electronic ed.; Chapel Hill, NC, 1998 [1912]), 13; see *JCCP*, 16: xxi–xxii, 440–441 (account of speech), 481 (Calhoun to R. M. T. Hunter, Sept. 30, 1842); Ellen Douglas Brownlow to Mary Eliza Battle, June 1, Aug. 24, 1854, in Mary Eliza Battle Letters.

[45] T. Michael Parrish, *Richard Taylor: Soldier Prince of Dixie* (Chapel Hill, NC, 1992), 22; Stephen Meats and Edwin T. Arnold, eds., *The Writings of Benjamin F. Perry*, 3 vols. (Spartanburg, SC, 1980), 3:265–266; Robert Gary Gunderson, *The Log-Cabin Campaign* (Frankfort, KY, 1957), 80 (Johnson).

[46] H. L. Hunley to R. R. Barrow, Aug. 9, 1860, in R. R. Barrow Residence Journal; William M. Mathew, ed., *Agriculture, Geology, and Society in Antebellum South Carolina: The Private Diary of Edmund Ruffin* (Athens, GA, 1992), 298; T. H. Williams, *Beauregard: Napoleon in Gray* (Baton Rouge, LA, 1955), 267.

and Dr. William S. Plumer and Methodists like the Presbyterian-hating Parson Brownlow could not avoid running into each other in 1859 or other years, although Brownlow may well have decided to skip Thornwell's sermon. Sundays featured well-attended religious services, generally Episcopalian and Presbyterian. Philip Holbrook Nicklin observed of the White: "On Sunday, the barroom is converted into a chapel for the nonce, and the gay into the devout." Preaching at the springs generally drew high praise. Bishop Otey and the Reverends Benjamin Morgan Palmer, James Henley Thornwell, William S. Plumer, and William G. Brownlow often preached at the Virginia Springs. However much vacationers congratulated themselves on their displays of piety, the more devout Southerners remained unconvinced. The Baptist Hannah Lide Coker wrote to the Reverend James C. Furman from Red Sulphur Springs in 1835: "The visitors here are for the most part gay and thoughtless, though we have met with a few who appear to be truly pious."

Like most southern states, Georgia had its own "White Sulphur Springs," located near Gainesville in Meriwether County. It became a celebrated fashionable community, replete with a post office, Masonic Hall, railroad depot, large general store, blacksmith services, and a Presbyterian church. Despite muddy roads that made access difficult, it drew people from as far west as Louisiana. Georgia's White Sulphur Springs arose in the 1850s to accommodate the more pious folks, especially the Presbyterians, who considered – in the words of the Associate Reverend Samuel Agnew – the majority of visitors to the various springs "pleasure hunters, instead of health hunters."[47]

---

[47] Eustis Prescott to Calhoun, Aug. 20, 1847, Franklin H. Elmore to Calhoun (on Turnbull), Aug. 25, 1857, in *JCCP*, 24:498, 510; George G. Smith, *The Life and Times of George Foster Pierce, Bishop of the Methodist Church, South, with a Sketch of Lovick Pierce, D. D., His Father* (Sparta, GA, 1888), 326; *ERD*, Aug. 20, 1859 (on Plumer), Sept.5, 1859 (on Brownlow), 1:337–335; notes on Thornwell's preaching at the White in Thornwell Papers, April 16, 1859; W. G. Brownlow, *Sketches of the Rise, Progress, and Decline of Secession* (Philadelphia, 1862), 58; Reniers, *Springs of Virginia*, 145; Nicklin ["Prolix"], *Virginia Springs*, 20. See the Otey Papers for the 1840s and 1850s – e. g., Sept.–Oct. 1840 and Aug, 15, 1852; Buckingham, *Slave States*, 1:307; on Palmer and Mrs. Hannah Lide Coker to J. C. Furman, Sept. 5, 1835, see Cook, *Life Work of Furman*, 47; James Stacy, *A History of the Presbyterian Church in Georgia* (Atlanta, GA, 1912), 315–316; Agnew Diary, Dec. 3, 1856; also, Greenlee Diary, Aug. 13–17, 22, 1853. For Georgia's White Sulphur Springs, see also Susan Lott Clark, *Southern Letters and Life in the Mid 1800s* (Waycross, GA, 1993), 49; Olin Jackson, ed., *A North Georgia Journal of History*, 2 vols. (Alpharetta, GA, 1992), 1:129–135 and on Limestone Springs in Hall County 2:93.

From the 1820s, the Virginia Springs brought together past and future presidents of the United States (Tyler, Van Buren, Pierce), governors (Barbour, Gilmer, Allston, Manning, McDuffie, Quitman), political leaders (Clay, Calhoun, Alexander Stephens, Jacob Thompson, Charles Conrad), social and economic leaders (Petigru of South Carolina, Mercer of Mississippi, Perkins of Louisiana), literary leaders (De Bow, Gayarré), joined by such northern luminaries as Daniel Webster, Rufus Choate, and Abbott Lawrence. In the 1850s, Lord Acton, visiting New York City, noted that the well-to-do scattered in June, many on their way to Saratoga, but others to the Virginia Springs. Where else was the father of the youthful James Johnston Pettigrew likely to meet Chief Justice Roger Taney and thereby help set his son's career in motion? And where else were ordinary folks like Fannie Page Hume of Virginia likely to meet the Hugheses of Texas? After the War, Northerners flocked to the Virginia Springs in larger numbers than ever before, establishing friendships with Southerners that eased, if slightly, the way to sectional reconciliation.[48]

---

[48] Reniers, *Springs of Virginia*, 7, 49, 65, 170, 188; *ERD*, Aug. 18–21, 1859 (1:332); "Lord Acton's American Diaries," *Fortnightly Review* 110 (1921), 730; Wilson, *Carolina Cavalier*, 25; Fannie Page Hume Diary, June 28, 30, 1860; E. Merton Coulter, *The South During Reconstruction, 1865–1877* (Baton Rouge, LA, 1947), 307–308.

7

Matters Not So Sweet

To be ignorant of what occurred before you were born is to remain always
a child. For what is the worth of human life, unless it is woven into the life
of our ancestors by the records of history.

– Cicero, Orator[1]

THE MANGUM SAGA

Representative David Outlaw of North Carolina seethed. His fellow
Whig, Senator Willie P. Mangum, remained in Washington Christmas
after Christmas instead of returning home to his family. Outlaw wrote
to Emily, his wife, in December, 1848, "Well you think Judge Mangum
is ashamed of his wife – I think his conduct totally inexcusable, and the
more so from his age [mid-fifties] and his high official station." Alluding
to General William T. Haskell of Tennessee, Franklin Welch Bowdon of
Alabama, and James D. Westcott, Jr. of Florida, who had not returned
home since arriving in Washington, Outlaw fumed: "I regret to say there
are several other cases of a similar character, and perhaps more than
I know of. The people ought not to tolerate such conduct in their representatives." A month later Outlaw wrote to Emily that during every congressional session, politicians committed adultery with married women.[2]

[1] Cicero, Orator, tr. H. M. Hubbell (LCL), §113.
[2] David to Emily Outlaw, Dec. 17, 1848, Jan. 27, 1849. See Elizabeth Fox-Genovese,
Within the Plantation Household: Black and White Women of the Old South (Chapel
Hill, N. C., 1988), 237–240.

By October 1849, Outlaw softened: "I have felt sorry for Judge Mangum since my arrival here. He looks dejected, as though he was conscious he had done wrong, and was mortified about it. I have made no allusion to it myself. Haskell of Tennessee is still here. He has abandoned his family altogether." Two months later Outlaw wrote:

Judge Mangum is keenly sensitive upon the subject of his remaining here all the year. I am satisfied great injustice has been done him. His pecuniary embarrassments are the cause. From what I can learn his habits, if not exemplary, have been better than heretofore. I do not wish to be understood as excusing him. It is unmanly for a husband to shrink from any difficulties, and have his wife to encounter them, but his remaining for such is much less censurable than those which have been attributed to him. He spoke to me yesterday with great feeling on the subject, and I could not but feel deep sympathy for him. He said that I had avoided him since my return (perhaps I had to some extent for I could not feel the same respect for him as formerly, especially if his absence from home was the result of dissipation and debauchery) and seemed to be much mortified at it.[3]

Mangum's continued absence from home became a political embarrassment for the Whigs, who also questioned his firmness in defense of slaveholders' rights. Vice President Millard Fillmore left Washington, and the Senate considered Mangum for its president pro tem. The Whig Party had more than one scandal in North Carolina. The wife of George Badger, one of North Carolina's most powerful politicians, died, and he married her sister. When she gave birth to twins prematurely, Outlaw and Kenneth Rayner, Badger's party rivals, jumped on it.[4]

Mangum received word that his wife had fallen ill and needed him, but he stayed put. Outlaw thought he was now too ashamed to go home: "I really pity him, for all his faults he has many good qualities, though I must say, his long absence, amounting to a virtual abandonment of his family, is inexcusable." A few days later Mangum finally

---

[3] David to Emily Outlaw, Oct. 3, Dec. 9, 1849. Before the War, between a third and a half of residents of northern cities – families as well as individuals – lived in boardinghouses, some for many years: see, Wendy Gamer, *The Boardinghouse in Nineteenth-Century America* (Baltimore, 2007), 3, 9, ch 2.

[4] Gregg Cantrell, *Kenneth and John B. Rayner and the Limits of Southern Dissent* (Urbana, IL, 1993), 66. For Whig concern about Mangum's politics, see W. A. Graham to James Graham, March 24, 1850, and Arthur F. Hopkins to William A. Graham, April 6, 1852, in J. G. DeRoulhac Hamilton, ed., *The Papers of William Alexander Graham* 5 vols. (Raleigh, NC, 1957–1973), 2:319.

left for home, and Outlaw chided Emily for her harsh view of him and politicians in general. He himself would never do such a thing – as she knew – but if he ever did succumb to temptation, he knew she would forgive him. A few months later he reported on a chap who, suspecting his wife of having an affair, shot her suspected lover to death on a street in Washington: "If all men who have cause to be jealous, were to shoot a man in this city, there would be a very considerable mortality here." Outlaw reassured Emily about her own husband. Well he might have, since his own political responsibilities kept him away from home for as long as ten months a year. She wanted him to fix a date for his return home:

It is impossible *now* for me to do so. I will come whenever and as soon as I can ... I know your sex needs all the attention which kindness and love can bestow – I would that I could be with you, to share your cares and make you as happy as I could – But this is to me painful subject – as I cannot do what I so earnestly desire – Give my love to the children and be assured of the unabated love of your husband.[5]

Meanwhile, Mangum continued to write pathetic if affectionate letters to Charity, his wife. Ever since the 1820s he had been moaning about the absences required by his career. April, 1849:

I feel that you have many reasons to complain of me – & yet, *you have not* – I am unhappy. I am embarrassed. I have suffered *everything*. I know you have *always* been *mine*, & true to me; & I would suffer more than martyrdom not to be true to you – I *love you*, my Love. My *dear Love* – my *dear Wife* – I would suffer death, rather than not be your husband while you live – & after your death, I would die rather than have another – if I survive you.

During the spring of 1851, Mangum hoped to go home, but he suffered a bad fall that led to paralysis and contributed to his death some years later. Despondent over his brother's death, he suffered physically and emotionally. As his health improved, he hoped to return home but could not. For the next two years he wrote painful letters, lamenting his neglect of Charity and his inability to get his affairs in order.[6]

5 David Outlaw to Emily Outlaw May 5, June 11, June 17, Sept. 26, 1850, May 6, 1852; Stephen W. Berry II, *All that Makes a Man: Love and Ambition in the Civil War South* (New York, 2003), 114–116, 123, 135–136. Years later, Clingman praised Mangum's character: *Selections from the Speeches and Writings of Hon. Thomas L. Clingman of North Carolina* (Raleigh, NC, 1877), 259.
6 See esp., W. P. Mangum to Charity Mangum, April 15, May 19, Sept. 29, 1851, Jan. 25, 1853, in Henry Thomas Shanks, ed., *The Papers of Willie P. Mangum*, 5 vols. (Raleigh, NC, 1955–1956), 5: 153–154, 5:141–142, 207, 215–216.

CASH-POOR RICH MEN

As Mangum's travail suggests, supposedly wealthy Southerners often lived on a financial margin. Much of the local trade in cash-starved towns like Chapel Hill, North Carolina, and Williamsburg, Virginia, had to be conducted by barter or by borrowing trifling amounts. Corn functioned as a means of exchange in much of the up country. Piney Woods land-holders practiced "safety-first" production of family foodstuffs, but mar-ket relations increased during the prosperous 1850s, as roads improved and railroads expanded. The extent and significance of market relations continue to provide fuel for speculation.[7]

Planters and farmers regularly borrowed from and lent neighbors a few dollars at a time. They might need $25 to $100 to move their cotton, or buy bacon, or for any other purpose. In 1850, Philip Henry Pitts, a cotton planter with nineteen slaves near Selma, Alabama, sent his father, who raised as much cotton as he did, $7 to attend a railroad convention. "Papa" repaid the loan and lent Pitts a dollar. In 1860, Pitts borrowed $11 for journal subscriptions and incidentals. John Walker of Virginia cosigned a note for $500 but borrowed and lent $10 or $20 at a time. Planters had other ways of surviving without ready cash. In the towns, slaveholders lent house slaves to friends or neighbors who occasionally needed help, but probably not on Saturdays, which was a day busy with sweeping yards, washing clothes, and cleaning.[8]

In cash-starved eighteenth-century Charleston, the well-to-do lived off credit, and the poor to middling folks lived in part by barter. The socially and politically prominent John Rutledge, with two hundred slaves but little liquidity, ran up tabs for months for rent, transporta-tion, labor, food, laundry, and barbering, paying in cash at Shepherd's Tavern. The shortage of cash among planters persisted during the nine-teenth century. Thomas E. Cox owned twenty-four slaves but had to

---

[7] Kemp P. Battle, *History of the University of North Carolina*, 2 vols. (Spartanburg, SC, 1974 [1907]), 1:313; Parke Rouse, Jr., *Cows on the Campus: Williamsburg in By-Gone Days* (Richmond, VA, 1973), 46; Charles Yancey in *U. S. Commissioner of Patents, Report on Agriculture, 1849* (Washington, DC, 1850), 137; Gary J. Battershell, "Upcountry Slaveholding: Pope and Johnson Counties, Arkansas, 1840–1860" (Ph. D. diss.: University of Arkansas, 1996), 66; [Anon.], *The Old Pine Farm: or, The Southern Side* (Nashville, TN, 1860), 22–23; Damon R. Eubank, *In the Shadow of the Patriarch: The John J. Crittenden Family in War and Peace.* (Macon, GA, 2009), 27.

[8] Franklin Account Books, 1842–1843, 1847–1855, Greenlee Diary for the 1850s, esp. Nov. 7, 1851, Nov. 6, 1858, July 1, 1859; Pitts Diary and Account Book, Sept. 29, Oct. 1, 11, 1850, May 26, 1860; J Walker accounts for 1835–1837, esp. Feb. 18, 1837; also, *TCWVQ*, 4:1603.

send one of them to town regularly to sell small quantities of produce for a few dollars. John S. Palmer, a wealthy lowcountry planter, apologized to his wife and son in 1848 for being strapped and "at a loss to know what sort of Christmas presents to get for the children." Wealthy plantation mistresses like Henrietta Tilghman scrounged for a few dollars to pay hired help, sometimes borrowing $5 or $10 to do so. More than once, John G. Guignard, managing a plantation for his wealthy father, asked him for $25 pocket money. Edwin F. King of Alabama, owner of six plantations, borrowed $3 to $10 at a time to pay bills. In 1832, the prosperous John Berkeley Grimball, out of funds, struggled to meet his family's summer expenses. He grumbled over bills: $9.25 for taxes, $4.30 for board. He lost $4 or $5 at the lottery but consoled himself with the $5 he earned for jury duty. Grimball wanted to help Jehu Jones and his family to emigrate to Liberia, "but I can scarcely support my own family by the practice of the most rigid economy." Charlotte Ann Alston could not provide her son at West Point the money to keep his horse and servant properly and hoped R. F. W. Allston could help out. Thomas Clemson wrote to John C. Calhoun, his father-in-law, that the overseer needed a $50 debt covered. Clemson did not have $50 and wondered if Calhoun could help. Meanwhile, Clemson cried about having to subsidize Andrew Pickens Calhoun, John's perpetually indebted son. Floride Calhoun's brother, John Ewing Colhoun, Jr., squandered his estate in high living. John C. Calhoun, with eighty slaves, borrowed the $600 he needed to send his wife and children to Europe. John A. Quitman, in Washington, sent his wife, Eliza, "a check for $100 for market money."[9]

---

[9] Richard Barry, *Mr. Rutledge of South Carolina* (New York, 1942), 40; Cox Account Books, 1853–1854; John S. Palmer to Esther Simons Palmer and John S. Palmer, Jr., Dec. 15, 1848, in Louis P. Towles, ed., *A World Turned Upside Down: The Palmers of South Santee, 1818–1881* (Columbia, SC, 1996), 144; Henrietta Kerr Tilghman to Tench Tilghman, [undated in 1840s] in Joan E. Cashin, ed., *Our Common Affairs: Texts from Women of the Old South* (Baltimore, 1996), 138–139; John G. Guignard to James S. Guignard, Feb. 18, 1818, April 22, 1829, in Arney R. Childs, ed., *Planters and Businessmen: The Guignard Family of South Carolina, 1795–1930* (Columbia, SC, 1957), 43, 57–58; Weymouth T. Jordan, *Ante-Bellum Alabama: Town and Country* (Tallahassee, FL, 1957), 51 (King); J. B. Grimball, Diary, June 1, May 10, June 1, 16, Oct. 5, 1832; Charlotte Ann Allston to R. F. W. Allston, June 8, 1823, in J. H. Easterby, ed., *The South Carolina Rice Plantation, as Revealed in the Papers of Robert F. W. Allston* (Chicago, 1945), June 8, 1823; Clemson to Calhoun, Dec. 22, 1840, in *JCCP*, 15:395–396; Ernest McPherson Lander, Jr., *The Calhoun Family and Thomas Green Clemson: The Decline of Southern Patriarchy* (Columbia, SC, 1983), 9, 37, 154; J. A. Quitman to Eliza Quitman, 1857, in J. A. Quitman Papers. *DBR* estimated credit charges at 15–20%: 4 (1847), 221.

Country storekeepers, tavern owners, and physicians extended credit to rich and poor, expecting to collect when crops were sold. In close-knit towns and villages, storekeepers depended on their reputations for honesty and fair dealing. They summarily dismissed clerks who took advantage of customers. Numerous planters, including big ones, operated stores in nearby towns to supplement even substantial incomes. Why, then, should not a big planter like Francis Taylor of Virginia dine at the home of the owner of the general store?[10]

The frustrations of the southern market drove Mathew Carey of Philadelphia and other northern publishers to distraction. Planters and "middling folk" did buy books; Bibles and atlases sold especially well. The southern market proved lucrative in the early decades of the nineteenth century, as the career of Mason Locke ("Parson") Weems demonstrated. But chronic indebtedness and swings in cotton prices resulted in considerable difficulty in bill collection. The Presbyterian Reverend A. A. Porter of South Carolina, noting the influence of population density and urbanization, acknowledged that the North easily outran the South in number of authors and publications. But the South "reads and studies books, if she does not make them." Southerners read much more widely than Northerners knew. But publishers like Lippincott groaned over losses incurred by inability to collect debts. Southern journals faced similar difficulties, since many subscribers failed to pay on time or, too often, at all. The immense circulation of printed sermons and religious tracts by the churches arose primarily from pressure among the laity, which displayed a considerable thirst for them. The sale of sermons and tracts remains unmeasured, but reports on colporteurs suggest a large circulation. Ministers and ladies' church groups provided religious tracts for yeomen without the cash to buy books.[11]

---

[10] James D. Watkinson, "'Fit Objects of Charity': Race, Faith, and Welfare in Antebellum Lancaster County, Virginia, 1817–1860," *Journal of the Early Republic*, 21 (2001), 54; Gerald M. Capers, Jr., *The Biography of a River Town. Memphis: Its Heroic Age* (Chapel Hill, NC, 1939), 57–58. Edwin J. Scott, *Random Recollections of a Long Life, 1806 to 1876* (Columbia, SC, 1884), 95–96; Henry Boley, *Lexington in Old Virginia* (Richmond, VA, 1936), 158; Taylor Diary, Nov. 23, 1796, March 11, 1798, Sept. 2, 1798. For a sampling of storekeepers, see G. W. Sargent to Winthrop Sargent, March 2, 1853; Greenlee Diary, Feb. 21, 1859; Baker Diary, June 29, 1864; George Lee Simpson, Jr., *The Cokers of Carolina: A Social Biography of a Family* (Chapel Hill, NC, 1956), 8, 25, 35.

[11] William Charvat, *The Profession of Authorship in America 1800–1870* (Durham, NC, 1970), ch. 3. On debts to northern publishers, see [A. A. Porter], "North and South," *SPR*, 3 (1850), 363. On southern journals, see Francis Elliott Hall McLean, *Periodicals Published in the South Before 1800* (Charlottesville, VA, 1928), 2–10; Bertram Holland Flanders, *Early Georgia Magazines* (Athens, GA, 1944), 207; Rhoda Coleman Ellison,

When Chief Justice Frederick Nash of North Carolina died heavily in debt, his wife and daughters opened a school to survive. The old families of Virginia, Thomas Jefferson among them, became notoriously impecunious. John Randolph of Roanoke, with 300–400 slaves and 8,000 acres of productive land in the 1820s, ceaselessly complained: "A Virginia estate has plenty of serfs, plenty of horses, but not a shilling." For spending money he relied on his hardly munificent congressional salary. John Tyler provided a case study of Virginia's genteel poverty-in-affluence. He owned between thirty and fifty slaves from the 1820s to the 1850s but was always strapped for cash, hurt badly by entertainment and other expenses as governor in the 1820s. His son and daughter-in-law, who served as political advisers, lived off him. In 1827, he sold a slave to meet the expenses of a seat in the U.S. Senate. In 1851, he suffered the indignity of asking the editor of the *Southern Literary Messenger* to wait for a few dollars for a subscription. He and his adored young wife spent lavishly to furnish their home and live in a style appropriate to a venerable Virginia family – venerable but financially shaky.[12]

In the late 1850s, William Gilmore Simms wailed to Mary Lawson that he owed $5,000 and was "poor in pocket" despite having $70,000 in capital. James Henry Hammond owed considerable debts in "'petty sums' which I have been compelled to meet or evade." John Esten Cooke, a leading Virginia poet and novelist, had to sell off books to pay his bills – Milton for a bushel of corn, Shakespeare for a bushel of onions, Chaucer for a string of fish, Bacon for a bushel of beans. Simms's wailing had countless precedents. In 1813, William Garrett, owner of forty slaves, complained that he hated his life of imprisonment to endless debts. The Episcopalian Reverend John Hamilton Cornish reported during the long depression of the late 1830s and 1840s that fortunes disappeared, reducing even wealthy lowcountry planters to

Early Alabama Publications: A Study in Literary Interests (University, AL, 1947), 91–97; Elizabeth Fox-Genovese and Eugene D. Genovese, *The Mind of the Master Class: History and Faith in the Southern Slaveholders' Worldview* (New York, 2005), 438–440.

[12] Anne Strudwick Nash, *Ladies in the Making (also a Few Gentlemen) at the Select Boarding and Day School of the Misses Nash and Miss Kolloch, 1859–1860 Hillsborough, North Carolina* (Hillsborough, NC, 1964), 9; William Cabell Bruce, *John Randolph of Roanoke, 1773–1833: A Biography Based Largely on New Material*, 2 vols. (New York, 1970 [1922]), 1:343, 2:118 (quoted), 358; Oliver Perry Chitwood, *John Tyler: Champion of the Old South* (New York, 1939), 72, 85–86; Frank Luther Mott, *A History of American Magazines, 1741–1850, vol. 1* (Cambridge, MA, 1938), 647; Julia Gardiner Tyler to Alex Gardiner, Apr., 1845, in Tyler Family Papers.

poverty. Even in flush times the wealthy nabobs of Natchez carried stag-gering debts and had little cash.[13]

Crop failures and natural disasters plunged planters into debts that took years to pay off. In 1820, a big loan from Joel Poinsett rescued Calhoun after his cotton crop and a gin house burned. Terrible storms hit the Sea Islands in 1804, 1813, and 1824, costing big planters like Thomas Spaulding of Sapelo a fortune. David Rogerson Williams lost a 350-acre cotton crop in 1829. Floods on South Carolina's Peedee River in 1819 and 1852 left planters in dire straits. A hailstorm wrecked homes, sugarhouses, and crops in Louisiana in 1850, with an estimated loss to Episcopalian Bishop Leonidas Polk of $100,000. Storms and epidemics badly hurt wealthy residents of Savannah, Charleston, and other cities. George W. Featherstonhaugh, the geol-ogist, blamed lavish personal expenditures for much of the planters' economic troubles, adding that southern politicians blamed northern exploiters.[14]

One man's difficulty created another's opportunity. Rather than invest in surplus land or slaves, some planters lent money at interest. Francis Terry Leak of Mississippi, a successful planter, supplemented his income from the interest on loans of several hundred dollars at a time: "Wrote to W. R. Cole that I had $4,000 to $5,000 to spare, which any of his punctual friends could have if they would apply for it soon." In 1858, he had $14,500 out in loans. Columbus Morrison, a small slaveholder in Alabama, lent hundreds of dollars at a time, commenting, "It is a pleasant thing to have another resource – the interest of good

---

[13] In Mary C. Oliphant et al., eds., *The Letters of William Gilmore Simms*, 6 vols. (Columbia, SC, 1952–1982), see: Simms to Mary Lawton, June 25, 1858 (4:7), Simms to Hammond, July 10, 1858 (78), Simms to Cooke, April 14, 1860 (215–216). William Garrett to Thomas Ruffin, Dec. 2, 1813, in *TRP*, 1:137; Cornish Diary, Jan. 9, 1843; also, Mary Maxcy Leveret to Edward Leverett, Aug. 26, 1858, in Frances Wallace Taylor et al., eds., *The Leverett Letters: Correspondence of a South Carolina Family, 1851–1868* (Columbia, SC, 2000), 73. For a delightful sketch of the Natchez nabobs, see Theodora Britton Marshall and Gladys Crail Evans, *They Found It in Natchez* (New Orleans, LA, 1939), ch. 8.

[14] Charles M. Wiltse, *John C. Calhoun: Nationalist* (Indianapolis, IN, 1944), 315, 433, n. 1; Mart A. Stewart, *"What Nature Suffers to Groe": Life, Labor, and Landscape on the Georgia Coast, 1680–1920* (Athens, GA, 1996), 20; Harvey Toliver Cook, *The Life and Legacy of David Rogerson Williams* (New York, 1916), 170, 173; William M. Polk, *Leonidas Polk: Bishop and General*, 2 vols. (New York, 1915), 1:206–207; Mary Granger, ed., *Savannah River Plantations* (Spartanburg, SC, 1983), 12–13; George W. Featherstonhaugh, *Excursion through the Slave States* (New York, 1968 [1844]), 156.

notes amounts to about $600." John Blackford in Maryland lent up to $1,000.[15]

Gentlemen lost estates because they unwisely endorsed friends' notes. Thomas Jefferson set a bad example in cosigning notes. Wilson Cary Nicholas bailed him out financially and then asked to have the favor returned. Jefferson obliged by cosigning a big note. Nicholas failed, and Jefferson took a bath. The wealthiest and most socially prominent families watched one or more members lose a patrimony by endorsing a note. Chief Justice William L. Sharkey resigned from Mississippi's Supreme Court in 1850 to recoup financial losses from signing notes for friends. A. L. Bingaman, a wealthy planter-politician known for his drinking, gambling, and wild largesse, died insolvent after having to sell his estate, including a fine library. He might have survived this if he had not endorsed friends' notes with abandon. The $400,000 in debts carried by the fabulously wealthy Wade Hampton of Mississippi and South Carolina arose in part from his cosigning notes. Benjamin Allston lost his estate early in the nineteenth century, and Joseph Waties Allston saved himself in 1834 only by selling half of his slaves. Gentlemen met these obligations even when they were victims of fraud. A friend defaulted on a note that Hezekiah Anderson had endorsed. Anderson sold his estate and personal property, leaving his wife and ten children impoverished. Others did not lose everything but suffered painful setbacks. James Louis Petigru lost a plantation in the 1830s largely because of defaulted notes he had endorsed. Abel P. Upshur lost $5,000 through the "misfortune" of one friend and the "baseness" of another. Tongues wagged at Virginia Springs when the wealthy Richard Singleton of South Carolina almost ruined himself by signing notes and lending money never repaid. Considered a model of good sense and practicality, Charles Pettigrew of North Carolina endured severe embarrassment by the default of friends in the 1850s. David Vance lost most of his property and left little to his children. He had generously bought the auctioned property of straitened neighbors and then returned it to them.[16]

---

[15] Leak Diary, April 17, 1857, also, June 26, July 3, 7, 1841; Morrison Journal, Dec. 23, 1845; Fletcher M. Green, ed., *Ferry Hill Plantation Journal* (Chapel Hill, NC, 1961), 43, n. 13.

[16] Dumas Malone, *Jefferson and His Time*, 6 vols. (Boston, MA, 1962–1981), 6: esp. chs. 21 and 30 and the Appendix on "Jefferson's Financial Affairs." Jeffrey Doyle Richardson, "Nothing More Fruitful: Debt and Cash Flow on the Antebellum Rice Plantation" (masters thesis, University of North Carolina, 1995); James D. Lynch, *The Bench and Bar of Mississippi* (New York, 1881), 194; Harnett T. Kane. *Natchez on the Mississippi* (New York, 1947) 150–158; Charles E. Cauthen, ed., *Family Letters of the Three Wade Hamptons, 1782–1901* (Columbia, SC, 1953), xiv, xvii; Easterby, ed., *South Carolina Rice Plantation*, 12, 36; Lincoln Lorenz, *The Life of Sidney Lanier* (New York, 1935), 8

Debts brought families anguish. Howell Cobb, a wealthy planter, married a young lady who brought $100,000 worth of property with her. He managed the country's finances as James Buchanan's Secretary of the Treasury but could not balance his own books. A spendthrift, who forever hoped for a great crop to pull him out of debt, Cobb owed a fortune to his relatives, the Lamars. In Virginia the third William Byrd of Westover committed suicide after he incurred enormous debts and squandered the family fortune on gambling. Harry Manigault lost at cards the fortune his mother had marked for him. His irresponsibility led to an unseemly lawsuit by his brother. In Mississippi, Samuel Davis, father of Jefferson and Joseph, found himself desperate in 1822 after he unwisely underwrote the debt of a son-in-law. He had to sell his plantation, which, fortunately, Joseph Davis was able to buy.[17]

A number of men went on to distinguished careers after their fathers had lost their estates. Light-Horse Harry Lee, a Revolutionary War hero and Robert E. Lee's father, spent himself into a debtor's prison and then abandoned his family for the West Indies. William H. Crawford's father moved from Virginia to Georgia in the wake of financial failure. Benjamin Mell, father of the Baptist Reverend P. J. Mell of Georgia, was, according to his grandson, "a very liberal man, sympathetic by nature, and generous to a fault." A defaulting friend left him with a ruinous bill. Thomas ("Stonewall) Jackson grew up poor because his father squandered his estate by cosigning, gambling, and dissipation. Petigru exploded at his father for frittering away a fortune on horse racing. Occasionally, a scoundrel, with a reputation as an upright man, obtained a loan, convinced a local farmer to cosign, and absconded.[18]

(Anderson); William J. Grayson, *James Louis Petigru: A Biographical Sketch* (New York, 1866), 136–140; Claude H. Hall, *Abel Parker Upshur: Conservative Virginian, 1790–1844* (Madison, WI, 1963), 109; Percival Reniers, *The Springs of Virginia: Life, Love, and Death at the Waters, 1775–1900* (Chapel Hill, NC, 1941), 56–57.

[17] James C. Bonner, *Milledgeville: Georgia's Antebellum Capital* (Athens, GA, 1978), 141–142 (Cobb); John Spencer Bassett and Sidney Bradshaw Fay, eds., "The Westover Journal of John A. Selden, Esqr., 1858–1862," in *Smith College Studies in History*, 6 (Northampton, MA, 1921), 259; William Dusinberre, *Them Dark Days: Slavery in the American Rice Swamps* (New York, 1996), 36; William C. Davis, *Jefferson Davis: The Man and His Hour* (New York, 1991), 23. For a poignant account of the tension between brothers, see the letters of Julia Ann Bryan Cumming in Carol Bleser, ed., *Tokens of Affection: The Letters of a Planter's Daughter in the Old South* (Athens, GA, 1996), ch. 11.

[18] Charles Royster, *Light-Horse Harry Lee and the Legacy of the American Revolution* (New York, 1981), ch. 5; Chase C. Mooney, *William H. Crawford, 1772–1834* (Lexington, KY, 1974), 15; P. H. Mell, Jr., *Life of Patrick Hues Mell* (Louisville, KY, 1895), 9–10; R. L. Dabney, *Life and Campaigns of Lt. Gen T. J. (Stonewall) Jackson*, (Harrisonburg,

Politicians needed a reputation for generosity and willingness to help those in distress. They had to spend freely on entertaining supporters and could not easily refuse to endorse their notes. Benjamin H. Hill of Georgia made a fortune as a lawyer but died poor. He had spent lavishly on hospitality and the beautification of his mansion, but he had also signed notes for friends. Thomas Butler King of Georgia lost $12,000 when a friend defaulted on a promissory note. The mercurial S. S. Prentiss of Mississippi gambled and drank away his fortune but also took big losses from endorsements. Judah P. Benjamin of Louisiana could afford the $60,000 loss from a note he had cosigned, but it hurt. David Outlaw felt compelled to "lend" $50 to a constituent who showed up in Washington and, more seriously, "Mangum's debt I consider as lost." Francis W. Pickens of South Carolina wrote to Calhoun that he had – in terror – signed a $5,000 note, which he feared he would have to pay. Bishop Leonidas Polk found himself strapped when a friend illegally manipulated his accounts. Notably, Polk, refusing to prosecute, paid the debt.[19]

The financial irresponsibility of masters threatened their slaves. "Stood Lawson Williford Security for 400 Dollars," E. E. Ervin wrote, "Borrowed Money he says I shall not be disturbed about given a lien on a negro for the same." Addison Lea asked his father to bail him out of a financial mess, for he did not want to have to sell his slaves: two of whom were old, another young, and all faithful. Slaves often went as collateral for debts, and not every slaveholder had Lea's scruples. And besides, many had no choice. Even Lea needed his father's help.[20]

Planters did not easily refuse to endorse the notes of friends. Grimball, with about 150 slaves, contributed only $100 to Calhoun's campaign in 1843. He wished he could have contributed the requested $500, but did not have that much to spare. Meanwhile, although

VA, 1983 [1865]), 9; Lacy Ford, "James Louis Petigru," in Michael O'Brien and David Moltke-Hansen, eds., *Intellectual Life in Antebellum Charleston* (Knoxville, TN, 1986), 158; [Anon.], *The Old Pine Farm: or, The Southern Side* (Nashville, TN, 1860), 68–69.

19 *Senator Benjamin H. Hill of Georgia: His Life, Speeches and Writings* (Atlanta, GA, 1891), 85–86; Edward M. Steel, *T. Butler King of Georgia* (Athens, GA, 1964), 34; Dallas C. Dickey, *Seargent S. Prentiss: Whig Orator of the Old South* (Baton Rouge, LA, 1945), 285; Robert Douthat Meade, *Judah P. Benjamin: Confederate Statesman* (New York, 1943), 90; David Outlaw to Emily Outlaw, June 10, 1848; Pickens to Calhoun, May 16, 1844, in *JCCP*, 18:525; Polk, *Leonidas Polk*, 1:208.

20 Ervin Diary and Account Books, April 17, 1851; Addison Lea to William Lea, July 5, 1856, in Lea Family Papers. For slaves in payment for debts, see Comer Farm Journal, July 28, 1856.

$14,000 in debt, he endorsed notes of between $2,000 and $5,000. Grimball was particularly annoyed to have to endorse a note for a Mr. Wilkes, who wanted to take his wife on an excursion: "Though reluctant to do so, I could not decline." Bennet Barrow of Louisiana, worth at least a quarter of a million dollars and with almost 350 slaves, never got out of debt. He constantly plowed funds into expansion of his plantation but suffered from his passion for horse races and unwillingness to refuse to endorse notes. In one case he might have recouped by taking a slave held as mortgage, but he could not in good conscience deprive the poor widow of her services. In 1842, he lamented, as many others did: "My situation is very critical & all from assisting what I thought my friends – d___ such___ owe no money myself yet have to work 4 years to pay others debts – or sacrifice my land." Then too, Barrow had thought J. Desmont, an English physician, a perfect gentleman, but Desmont slipped out of St. Francisville for parts unknown, leaving between $10,000 and $16,000 in debts. Barrow paid $200 when Desmont forged his name to a note. From colonial times onward, frustrated factors complained about planters who scurried west when financially embarrassed; factors risked millions of dollars, since their agreements with planters often took place under gentlemen's agreements. Stealing off to the west grew worse after the crash of 1837. In later years the Barings and other firms chose to buy cotton outright rather than on advances.[21]

In the 1850s, Northerners turned heavy southern indebtedness to political advantage, attributing to slavery the South's weak economic development, lack of cash, and inadequate credit. Then, too, frequent litigation over debts added substantially to business costs. Northerners complained to Joseph Sturge of England that planters manipulated them politically by threatening to default on heavy debts. Ernest Duvergier de Hauranne sympathized with the Southerners whom Yankee creditors fleeced on interest charges, but he believed that much of the difficulty arose from the planters' penchant for living beyond their means. Sounding like an abolitionist, he maintained that when planters crashed, their slaves suffered catastrophe: "It is on such occasions that one may

---

[21] J. B. Grimball Diary, Aug. 21, 1843, Feb. July 28, 16, 1844 (quoted); Edwin Adams Davis, ed., *Plantation Life in the Florida Parishes of Louisiana, 1836–1846, as Reflected in the Diary of Bennet H. Barrow* (New York, 1943), Jan. 19, 1842 (251); Ralph W. Haskins, "Planter and Cotton Factor in the Old South: Some Areas of Friction," *Agricultural History*, 29 (1955), 180; Ralph W. Hidy, *The House of Baring in American Trade and Finance* (New York, 1970), 403–405, 436–438.

see in all its horror the true character of the holy, patriarchal institution of slavery."[22]

The ladies swayed between sympathy for their husband's plight and bitter rebuke at their constant indebtedness. They took umbrage at cosignings that risked their families to help friends, especially when they did not much like or trust the friends. Few ladies joined Mary Watters in attributing the hated indebtedness to slavery. Watters wrote to a kinsman from Wilmington, North Carolina, in 1835, "We cannot reasonably expect that permanency of happiness we so much desire – Your property situated as it is, is a powerful obstacle ... Oh! How much suffering have I seen! Oh! How many evils originate from this source! From the possession of such property in such a place!" The separation of black families made her ill: "I do think a curse attends it." The planters kept their way of life "with a pertinacity worthy of a better cause." What could be done when custom, habit, prejudice, and even education promote "principles imbibed early and never contrasted, and daily association with persons whose views are the same?" She pleaded, "To break loose from *all the fetters* – would evidence a strength of intellect which would do honor to any man."[23]

LURE OF THE TURF

Various forms of gambling throve, none more than betting at the numerous racetracks. From the early eighteenth century Virginians and North Carolinians traveled considerable distances to attend races. The governor of Maryland staged a horse race in 1754 that drew some 2,000, and the South Carolina Jockey Club held its first race in February 1793. Wags censured rakes for risking their fortune on a single race, but local races drew whole families, including tutors and indentured servants. No censure applied to the two prominent Virginia gentlemen who pitted their horses in a race for $1,500 in 1797.[24]

---

[22] G. W. Daniels "Entrepreneurship in the Old South," in W. B. Moore, Jr. and J. F. Tripp, eds., *Looking South: Chapters in the Story of an American Region* (Westport, CT, 1989), 165; Joseph Sturge, *A Visit to the United States in 1841* (New York, 1969 [1842]), 157; Ernest Duvergier de Hauranne, *A Frenchman in Lincoln's America*, 2 vols. (Chicago, 1974), 2:463.

[23] Mary Watters to Richard Quince, Feb. 16, 1835, in Quince-Watters Papers.

[24] John Brickell, *The Natural History of North Carolina* (Murfreesboro, NC, 1968 [1737]), 39; *The Journal of John Harrower: An Indentured Servant in the Colony of Virginia, 1773–1776*, ed. Edward Miles Riley (Williamsburg, VA, 1963), Oct. 4–8, 1774 (65); Eleanor Parke Curtis to Elizabeth Bordley Gibson, Apr. 24, 1797, in Patricia Brady, ed.,

During the nineteenth century, a racetrack of sorts in frontier Georgia arose wherever a crossroads grocery appeared. Just about every eminent personage from the Blue Ridge to the Chesapeake attended when Virginia's Jeter's Racecourse opened in 1822. The Presbyterian Reverend William S. White considered the track's influence on morals deplorable but attested to a wholesome change after the religious revivals of the mid-1830s. Paltry races in, say, Pineville, South Carolina, entertained lesser folks but did not attract the gentry and lacked the customary dinners and balls. In the Texas Republic plantations and smaller towns had racecourses, some individually owned, some sponsored by jockey clubs. John Eaton, territorial governor of Florida, doubled as president of a local racing club. Exclusive clubs in lowcountry South Carolina included St. John's Hunting Club (which had little to do with hunting), St. Stephen's Club, and St. Thomas Club. St. Stephen's planned two-day races. The Agricultural Society of South Carolina featured horse racing from the Society's inception in the 1780s.[25]

Churches disciplined members for participating, abetting, or wagering, but even the most fervent clergymen had difficulty in curtailing enthusiasm. Preachers and teachers raged at the "unmitigated evil." Schoolboys went off anyway, and some placed bets. Lowcountry boys staged their own competitive races. Warnings of violence at the tracks – knifings, eye gouging, ear biting, and worse – threw young hotspurs into the briar patch. In the Southwest white boys from "respectable families" envied hard-drinking young gamblers. Robert Patrick recalled village life in Louisiana: "They were looked up to by the balance of us." Young men carried and sometimes used pistols, especially if they wandered into the gambling houses described by Giles Patterson, a student at South Carolina College in 1847: "The first house we arrived at was what is

George Washington's Beautiful Nelly: The Letters of Eleanor Parke Custis Lewis to Elizbeth Bordley Gibson, 1794–1851 (Columbia, SC, 1991), 33–34.

[25] *"Stonewall" Jackson's Pastor: Rev. William S. White, D. D. and His Times: An Autobiography* (Harrisonburg, VA, 2005 [1891]), 55–56; Elizabeth Palmer Porcher to Harriet R. Palmer, Jan. 25, 1856, in Towles, ed., *World Turned Upside Down*, 195; William R. Hogan, *The Texas Republic: A Social and Economic History* (Austin, TX, 1969), 132–135; John Marszalek, *Petticoat Affair: Manners, Mutiny and Sex in Andrew Jackson's White House* (Baton Rouge, LA, 2000), 213; Tamara Miner Haygood, *Henry William Ravenel, 1814–1887: South Carolina Scientist in the Civil War Era* (Tuscaloosa, AL, 1987), 22; Burnette Vanstory, *Georgia's Land of the Golden Isles* (Athens, GA, 1956), 15–16; Chalmers S. Murray, *This Our Land: The Story of the Agricultural Society of South Carolina* (Charleston, SC, 1949), 31. By 1840, races had become a standard part of agricultural fairs in the Northwest.

called the Gambling House, where was the bar room, and the numerous modes of losing money arranged around the room to suit every man's taste, or so that no man could go home with any money in his pocket with an excuse."[26]

John Davis of England remarked at the beginning of the nineteenth century, "Cotton in *Carolina* and horse raising in *Virginia* are the prevailing topics of conversation." In Richmond during and after the Revolutionary era, nothing dimmed the popularity of the races – not the heavy drinking, the gambling, the brawling, or the prostitution. Robert Baylor wrote to R. M. T. Hunter that the races in Fredericksburg attracted gamblers, slave traders, blacklegs, and the lower classes but also judges, chancellors, and respectable planters. Benjamin F. Perry of South Carolina refused to attend the races: "I consider them demoralizing & ruinous ... They bring together a set of black guards." Yet not even the politically entrenched Perry swayed his upcountry neighbors. Reformers fumed, but the lure of the racecourse proved irresistible. Citizens feared the Lord but remained unconvinced that their peccadilloes ranked high in the book of sins.[27]

In 1828, Miss Margaret, playing the belle, wrote to her brother:

The Jockey Club are now holding their annual races, & the town is very full of strangers, all the planters too are in with their families, and quite gay – I never knew more public amusements at one time in the place: besides the different balls, theatre & Circus, which we have not attended this winter, there is David's splendid Painting of the Coronation of Bonaparte .... There is for lovers of music, a treat in the Panharmonican, which we visited last evening, it is a combination of 206 wind Instruments of 13 different kinds forming a complete Band.

26 Edward L. Ayers, *Vengeance and Justice: Crime and Punishment in the Nineteenth-Century South* (New York, 1984), 119; Anson West, *A History of Methodism in Alabama* (Spartanburg, SC, 1983 [1893]), 152–154; R. H. Rivers, *The Life of Robert Paine, D. D., Bishop of the Methodist Church, South* (Nashville, TN, 1916), 196–199; Phillip Alexander Bruce, *History of the University of Virginia, 1819–1919: The Lengthening Shadow of One Man*, 5 vols. (New York, 1920–1922), 2:336; Daniel Walker Hollis, *University of South Carolina*, 2 vols. (Columbia, SC, 1951), 1:154–155; F. Jay Taylor, ed., *Reluctant Rebel: The Secret Diary of Robert Patrick, 1861–1865* (Baton Rouge, LA, 1959), 9; Giles Patterson, *Journal of a Southern Student, 1846–1848, with Letters of a Later Period*, ed., Richmond Croom Beatty (Nashville, TN), 48 (Jan. 19, 1847). For boys' races, see D. E. Huger Smith, *A Charlestonian's Recollections, 1846–1913* (Charleston, SC, 1950), 38–39, 62–63.

27 John Davis, *Travels of Four and a Half Years in the United States of America*, ed. A. J. Morrison (New York, 1909 [1803]), 104–1205; Harry M. Ward and Harold E. Greer, Jr., *Richmond during the Revolution, 1775–83* (Charlottesville, VA, 1977), 52; Robert Baylor to R. M. T. Hunter, May 20, 1826, in Charles Henry Ambler, ed., *The Correspondence of Robert M. T. Hunter, 1826–1876* (Washington, DC, 1918), 28; Lillian Kibler, *Benjamin F. Perry, Unionist* (Durham, NC, 1946), 190.

Four years later she wrote to her husband, the Presbyterian Reverend John Adger: "The Races are over, large sums of money have changed owners – & more has left the state now, than went to the valley of the Mississippi – the town was crowded with strangers, the hotels overflowing. Theatre – Balls – Concerts & all kinds of dissipation in abundance."[28]

Horse racing became a national mania, but nowhere on so grand a scale as in the South. New England frowned on it. Boston's race in 1862 was the first in a half century and had little effect elsewhere in the region. A startled Hugh Legaré arrived in Washington in the 1830s to find that Congress had difficulty in getting a quorum when the National Course was open. The national racing calendar for 1851 showed thirty-six events, twenty-one of them in the South. It was ever thus in Virginia even more than in South Carolina – which is saying a lot. Rhys Isaac, describing the "quarter race" as colonial Virginia's sport par excellence, writes, "A distinctive form of horse racing had evolved in the Chesapeake region during the seventeenth century that clearly indicated the prevailing taste for strong self-assertion and aggressive contest. The race was a violent duel that tested not only the speed of the horses but the daring and skill of the riders."[29]

In the seventeenth and early eighteenth century, the poorer folks were fined for presuming to enter a horse in races considered affairs of gentlemen. In Virginia, writes Randy J. Sparks, a horse "was an emblem of wealth and status and a proud extension of his owner." Hence, the indignation of the York County Court in 1674 at the news that James Bullicke, a tailor, had arranged a high-stakes race: "It being contrary to Law for a Labourer to make a race, being a sport only for Gentlemen." The poor had to go to their own races, which often ended in drunken brawls. At mid-century, racecourses were segregated by class.[30]

By the turn of the century, more polite, stylized races became the norm, but something of the old spirit remained. Replacement of quarter racing by course racing compelled concentration on improved breeds, and large importations from England and Spain ensued. Jefferson, an enthusiast,

---

[28] Margaret Adger to brother Feb. 27, 1828, and to John Adger, Feb. 23, 1832, in Thomas Smyth, *Autobiographical Notes, Letters, and Reflections* (Charleston, SC, 1914), 77.

[29] Arthur C. Cole, *The Irrepressible Conflict, 1850–1865* (New York, 1934), 192–193; Linda Rhea, *Hugh Swinton Legaré:* (Chapel Hill, NC, 1934), 160–161; W. T. Porter, ed., *Racing Calendar, 1851* (n.p., 1851); Rhys Isaac, *The Transformation of Virginia, 1740–1790* (Chapel Hill, NC, 1982), 98–101; Pierre Marambaud, *William Byrd of Westover* (Charlottesville, VA, 1971), 200.

[30] Randy J. Sparks, "Gentleman's Sport: Horse Raising in Antebellum Charleston," *South Carolina Historical Magazine* (93 (1992), 15–16.

opened his *Farm Book* with a list of horses with pedigrees, including twenty-eight breeding mares. John Randolph of Roanoke, who loved the races and traveled to Charleston for Race Week, complained to St. George Tucker in 1790, "If report does not lie greatly, the Blacklegs have had a fine harvest during the Races." The blacklegs, it seems, "have been employing their talents to great advantage in plucking a young pigeon who ranks very high among the would-be nobility of our country, and shines forth, a very luminous constellation in the horizon of the fashionable world."[31]

In 1860, Samuel Mordecai limned the Jockey Clubs and their spring and autumn races at Richmond, Petersburg, and elsewhere. Gentlemen arrived in coaches and four, phaetons, chariots, and gigs, with wives and daughters in the latest fashions:

[The racecourse] presented a brilliant display of equipages, filled with the reigning belles and their predecessors. Many were the pairs of gloves lost and won between them and their beaux .... The race week was a perfect carnival. The streets were thronged with equipages and the shops with customers. Not only taverns and boardinghouses were filled, but private families opened their hospitable doors to their country friends. Among the week's amusements was the *Race Ball* .... [But] The sports of the turf have so degenerated of late years, that few ladies of the present generation ever saw a race. The field is now chiefly in possession of a class, termed in softened phrase, 'sporting characters,' in the same way that negro-traders are called 'speculators.' ... The field presents a scene of the lowest gambling and dissipation; but there is now a prospect of the sport being more respectably patronized and conducted.[32]

Charleston boasted America's greatest Race Week. Lowcountry gentry and the common folk went race-crazy. Charles Fraser, the artist, recalled Charleston of the 1790s: "Clergymen thought it no impropriety to see a well-contested race and the Race Ball, given by the Jockey Club was always the most splendid of the season." People poured into town from all quarters, and the theater as well as the circus throve. Those with interests other than the races sensibly adjusted. "The best idea we can give of the *moral influence* of race-week (as exerted formerly)," John B. Irving wrote in 1857, "is to state that the courts of justice used daily to adjourn and all the schools were regularly *let out*, as the hour for starting the

<hr />

[31] Edwin Morris Betts, ed., *Thomas Jefferson's Farm Book: With Commentary and Relevant Extracts from His Writings* (Charlottesville, VA, 1987), 87–88; Bruce, *Randolph of Roanoke*, 1:130, also, 131, 136–137.

[32] Samuel Mordecai, *Richmond in By-Gone Days* (Richmond, VA, 1946 [1860]), 252–255; Virginius Dabney, *Richmond: Story of a City* (Garden City, NY, 1976), 86.

horses drew near." Businesses closed. The Episcopal Church and the Carolina Medical Association scheduled their meetings to coincide with Race Week. In 1853, Governor John L. Manning led a memorable parade of the militia to the Washington Race Course. Even Edmund Ruffin, who cared little for the races, did not pass up the opportunity to meet friends and associates. A grim feature: Between racecourses the track held slave auctions. As professional gamblers and rowdies appeared in ever larger numbers, the enthusiasm of the gentry for the races, or at least for open Race Weeks, receded. The jockey clubs intervened, with some success, to control events. The scene became more genteel but still sometimes rowdy. For all the complaints, Race Week continued to flourish.[33]

For a long time Charleston's Washington Course hosted the only substantial races in South Carolina. W. Rand wrote from Washington in 1802: "I wish to visit the Southern races again, the people are rich & easy to milk having plenty of that much Admired (evil) Cash." In the early nineteenth century, the Georgetown elite revived its dormant Jockey Club and put on its own Race Week. Columbia, Camden, and Newberry District followed suit. Private companies advertised booths that served dinners, suppers, fresh fruit, sweets, and abundant liquor. Mainly an affair of the elite, all classes came in numbers that made Race Week a community project. In every part of the South the wealthy bet staggering amounts, losing plantations and fortunes more often than seems imaginable. Racing bets often ran higher than a poor man's crop, but poor as well as rich bet anyway. Betting in the South, especially on the Sabbath, appalled Henry Benjamin Whipple, future Episcopal bishop of Minnesota. With tempers short, duels and challenges to the field of honor

[33] Rosser H. Taylor, *Ante-Bellum South Carolina: A Society and Cultural History* (New York, 1970), 51ff; Eola Willis, *The Charleston Stage in the XVIII Century: With Social Settings of the Time* (Columbia, SC, 1924), 160, Fraser quoted at 196; J. L. Petigru to Hugh Legaré, Feb. 17, 1836, in James Petigru Carson, *Life, Letters and Speeches of James Louis Petigru: Union Man of South Carolina* (Washington, DC, 1920), 181; D. Maitland Armstrong, *Day before Yesterday: Reminiscences of a Varied Life* (New York, 1920), 82–83. [John B. Irving], *The South Carolina Jockey Club* (Charleston, SC, 1857), 11; George C. Rogers, Jr., *Charleston in the Age of the Pinckneys* (Columbia, SC, 1980), 71; Jean Martin Flynn, *The Militia in Antebellum South Carolina Society* (Spartanburg, SC, 1991 [1917]), 1; A. J. McElveen to Z. B. Oakes, Feb. 7, 1854, in Edmund L. Drago, ed., *Broke by the War: Letters of a Slave Trader* (Columbia, SC, 1991), 71; Linda Rhea, *Hugh Swinton Legaré: A Charleston Intellectual* (Chapel Hill, NC, 1934), 67; William M. Mathew, ed., *Agriculture, Geology, and Society in Antebellum South Carolina: The Private Diary of Edmund Ruffin* (Athens, GA, 1992), Feb. 22–25, 1843 (103); Patricia C. Click, *The Spirit of the Times: Amusements in Nineteenth-Century Baltimore, Norfolk, and Richmond* (Charlottesville, VA, 1989), ch. 4.

occurred frequently. The Savannah Jockey Club had its hands full with duel-provoking charges of cheating and unfair practices.[34]

Tallahassee, Florida's capital, emulated Charleston in the 1830s, but by 1842, the devastation of the Seminole War and the nuisance of a reform government effectively ended the gaiety. Race Week had offered a carnival atmosphere replete with elaborate balls. Hotels and private homes overflowed with guests from long distances. In North Carolina, a number of taverns had racetracks that featured fine horses and provided an excuse for galas. Taverns packed up oysters and suppers to send to the track. They made big money during the racing season by raising rents and prices to four or five times the normal rates. In Georgia, the Petersburg Jockey Club held three-day races as early as the 1790s, the Augusta Gentlemen's Driving Park Association from about 1810, the Fairfield Jockey Club near Athens from 1831. Lowcountry races welcomed people from other states, inviting them to lavish private dinner parties.[35]

Racing swept westward. The racing season in Huntsville, Alabama, attracted Andrew Jackson, who arrived in 1816 to race his horses and resume contact with the local folks. But Mobile became Alabama's great racing center, and, as elsewhere, the Jockey Club included much of the planter and merchant elites. Natchez, Mississippi, riding the crest of the "Flush Times," emerged as a racing center in the 1830s. Gentlemen took their places at the track, while their ladies, equipped with umbrellas, watched from carriages placed to afford a good view and permit their occupants' shouts to carry. The northern-born J. H. Ingraham thought the main racecourse at Natchez the finest in the South. The Mississippi Chivalry gathered at St. Catherine racecourse. England's J. S. Buckingham visited the Natchez Jockey Club at the end of the decade and estimated at

---

[34] George C. Rogers, Jr., *The History of Georgetown County, South Carolina* (Columbia, SC, 1970), 95–96, 222; Nell S. Graydon, *Tales of Columbia* (Columbia, SC, 1964), 48; W. Rand to John Steele, June 8, 1802, in H. M. Wagstaff, ed., *The Papers of John Steele*, 2 vols. (Raleigh, NC, 1924), 1:282; Isaac, *Transformation of Virginia*, 100; [Henry Benjamin Whipple], *Bishop Whipple's Southern Diary, 1843–44* (New York, 1968), 116; Thomas Gamble, *Savannah Duels and Duellists* (Savannah, GA, 1974 [1923]), 156.

[35] Bertram H. Groene, *Ante-Bellum Tallahassee* (Tallahassee, FL, 1971), 154–155; William S. Powell, *When the Past Refused to Die: A History of Caswell County, North Carolina, 1777–1977* (Durham, NC, 1977), 159–160; E. Merton Coulter, *Old Petersburg and the Broad River Valley of Georgia: Their Rise and Decline* (Athens, GA, 1965), 151; Charles C. Jones, Jr. and Salem Dutcher, *Memorial History of Augusta* (Syracuse, NY, 1890), 293–294; Ernest C. Hynds, *Antebellum Athens and Clarke County, Georgia* (Athens, GA, 1974), 128; Charles Manigault to Louis Manigault, Feb. 7, 1859, in James M. Clifton, ed., *Life and Labor on Argyle Island: Letters and Documents of a Savannah River Rice Plantation, 1833–1867* (Savannah, GA, 1978), 277.

least $10,000 laid on bets in a race for which the prize was $400. Here, he snorted, "sportsman" is a euphemism for gambler. What would he have thought if he had visited Huntsville, where the prizes ran to $20,000? The racetrack at Natchez Under-the-Hill appealed to both unsavory locals and the most respectable gentlemen from the sedate bluff. Local proprietors draped their notorious saloons in bunting. Gamblers, sailors, and brawlers met in the streets with reserved planters to discuss odds and make side bets – meetings that often ended in shootouts. Less prestigious racecourses appeared elsewhere in Mississippi, including Evergreen Race Course, just south of Vicksburg, which ran weekly contests at $400 a purse.[36]

Racecourses in New Orleans and nearby Metairie attracted big-time gamblers. Money and liquor flowed as planters, merchants, and well-to-do professionals joined poor and middling folks there during festive Mardi Gras. Every April in the 1840s, the racing season of one or two weeks drew thousands. Reduced to but one race a day by 1861, it lost some of its luster. The Metairie Jockey Club boasted some of the biggest planters of the lower Mississippi Valley – Duncan Kenner, William J. Minor, Thomas Walls. Kenner had a private track as well as impressive stables for his Kentucky and English thoroughbreds. Routinely, he bet several thousand dollars on his own horses. And why not? Kentucky's fine horses sold well as far away as Russia. Wealthy planters built private racecourses for families and friends. Adam L. Bingaman of Mississippi, a powerful Whig, became famous as the magnate of the celebrated St. Catherine racecourse. The Cajuns of Louisiana, reputedly great riders, held frequent private races among themselves. In the Southeast, Henry McAlpin and John Ewing Calhoun had popular tracks.[37]

---

[36] William H. Brantley, Jr., *Three Capitals: A Book About the First Three Capitals of Alabama: St. Stephens, Huntsville and Cahawba, 1818–1826* (University, AL, 1947), 54; Kane, *Natchez*, 154–155; Harriet Elizabeth Amos, "Social Life in an Antebellum Cotton Port: Mobile, Alabama, 1820–1860," (Ph.D. diss.: University of Alabama, 1976), 193–194; [Joseph Holt Ingraham], *The South-West. By a Yankee*, 2 vols. (n.p., 1966 [1835]), 2:219; J. S. Buckingham, *The Slave States of America*, 2 vols. (New York, 1968 [1842]), 1:456, 2:213; James F. Sulzby, Jr., *Historic Alabama Hotels and Resorts* (Tuscaloosa, AL, 1960), 146; Edith Wyatt Moore, *Natchez Under-the-Hill* (Natchez, MS, 1958), 9; James T. Currie, *Enclave: Vicksburg and Her Plantations, 1863–1870* (Jackson, MS, 1980), 22. According to Cynthia A. Kierner, jockey clubs in eighteenth-century Virginia and South Carolina arranged for women bettors: "Hospitality, Sociability, and Gender in the Southern Colonies," *JSH* (1996), 462.

[37] Whipple, *Southern Diary*, 116; Harnett T. Kane, *Plantation Parade: The Grand Manner in Louisiana* (New York, 1955), 192–193; on Kenner and the Metairie Jockey Club, see T. Michael Parrish, *Richard Taylor: Soldier Prince of Dixie* (Chapel Hill, NC, 1992), 64–66; for Russian and Kentucky horses, see Robert L. Kincaid, *The Wilderness*

Subject to regional exceptions, the ladies attended with gusto. Eliza Ripley of Louisiana recalled that the ladies of the lower Southwest considered the races no place for them, but that "every Kentucky woman loves a horse." The Kentucky ladies arrived in droves for big races near New Orleans, while the Creole ladies generally stayed away. In North Carolina and Virginia, the ladies participated in family visits, and the more fashionable turned out to see the star attraction: the penning of wild horses. Solomon Rothschild of France, disappointed by race week in New Orleans in 1861, found a large throng of ladies, who got more attention than the horses. In Texas, flirtatious and gaily dressed ladies turned out in force, becoming magnets of attention.[38]

There is no record of a lady's losing a plantation or an eye-catching amount of money, but they did enjoy prudent betting. In Irving's account,

First is seen, in the ladies' stand, a galaxy of beauty – Matrons and Demoiselles – mothers in the full bloom and maturity of their loveliness; and daughters, exceedingly beautiful, and *very much like their mothers*; the animation of the scene greatly augmented by those 'who come to be *seen* as well as *to see*'; vying with each other in the little coquetries every accomplished belle knows well how to avail herself of, to secure the devotion of some popular beau – among other things, *betting* upon some pending event.

Plain-folk women matched the enthusiasm of the high-toned ladies. During the eighteenth century, races on the Georgia frontier figured as high sport, and large numbers of white women and blacks and Indians of both genders came from miles around. The dinking and hell-raising disgusted Parson Weems. Nothing much changed in Georgia or anywhere else in the first half of the nineteenth century.[39]

Road (Indianapolis, IN, 1947), 206; Bonner, *Milledgeville*, 94; Dunbar Rowland, ed. *Mississippi: Comprising Sketches of Counties, Towns, Events, Institutions, and Persons, Arranged in Cyclopedic Form*, 4 vols. (Spartanburg, SC, 1976 [1907]), 1:243–244; Carl A. Brasseaux, *Acadian to Cajun: Transformation of a People, 1803–1877* (Jackson, MS, 1992), 30; Granger, ed., *Savannah River Plantations*, 318; Charles M. Wiltse, *John C. Calhoun: Nullifier, 1782–1829* (Indianapolis, IN, 1949), 162.

[38] Eliza Ripley, *Social Life in Old New Orleans: Being Recollections of My Girlhood*, (New York, 1975 [1912]), 245 and ch. 30; DHUNC, 2:212; T. Holmes, "The Wild Horses of the Sea islands of Virginia and Maryland," in Schwaab and Bull, eds., *Travels in the Old South*, 1:227; Barbara Hull, *St. Simons: Enchanted Island: A History of the Most Historic of Georgia's Fabled Golden Isles* (Atlanta, GA, 1980), 44; Solomon de Rothschild in Jacob Rader Marcus, ed., *Memoirs of American Jews*, 3 vols. (Philadelphia, 1955), 3:103; Elizabeth Silverthorne, *Ashbel Smith of Texas: Pioneer, Patriot, Statesman, 1805–1886* (College Station, TX, 1982), 53.

[39] [Irving], *South Carolina Jockey Club*, 13; Weems, in Edward J. Cashin, ed., *A Wilderness Still the Cradle of Nature* (Savannah, GA, 1994), 55–57.

In colonial Virginia, ownership of a racehorse signaled a gentleman of substance – a signal that Virginians carried to the Southwest thereafter. The Kentucky Bluegrass slowly replaced Virginia in horse racing and in supplying southern planters with horses for the race track as well as for personal use. The Bluegrass has a saying: "Every man needs a wife, a gun – and a good horse." Henry Clay and other horse raisers and track enthusiasts formed the Kentucky Association in 1826. The sporting buffs of eastern North Carolina drooled over the horses raised by Stephen Wright Carney, a legislator, general of the militia, and scion of a wealthy family, who brought good breed stock home from European trips. Leading families like the Minors displayed trophies and hung paintings of the region's great horses in their homes. The fortune of William Ransom Johnson ("the Napoleon of the Turf"), one of Virginia's wealthiest planters, rested on horse breeding. His son-in-law, James West Pegram, had a sign at the main entrance of his own plantation: "There is nothing so good for the inside of a man as the outside of a horse." Bennet Barrow spent $3,000 for a horse in 1837, $6,000 for another in 1838. His brother William paid $7,000 for "Mad Anthony." Thomas Kirkman of Nashville, planter and businessman, imported thoroughbreds and raised some of the finest horses of the day. According to legend, he won $100,000 at a race on Long Island in 1844.[40]

Benjamin Disraeli characterized horse racing as "the noble pastime of an aristocracy." John B. Irving, who quoted Disraeli in 1857, stated an ideal more than a reality: "No Carolina Turfman prepares his horses and brings them to the Starting Post, as a *business*, but only as a *recreation*." Southern planters, like horse breeders everywhere, doted on their truly great horses as they doted on little else. Prominent planters, merchants, and politicians in every part of the South raised and ran fine horses. Daniel Ravenel, who pioneered in horse breeding in the low country, refused to run his racers for money. Josiah Nott reported from Mobile, "The mania for racing & stock here is tremendous, & as soon as they get

---

[40] Malone, *Jefferson*, 1:8; R. Gerald Alvey, *Kentucky Bluegrass Country* (Jackson, MS, 1992), 127–128, 133–135; *DNCB*, 1:328 (Carney); William Garrett, *Reminiscences of Public Men in Alabama for Thirty Years* (Atlanta, GA, 1872), 342; Kane, Natchez, 155; Marshall and Evans, *They Found It in Natchez*, 199–200; Davis, ed., Florida Parishes, 57–61, 80, 112; Peter S. Carmichael, *Lee's Young Artillerist: William R. J. Pegram* (Charlottesville, VA, 1995), 8, 12; Hennig Cohen and William A. Dillingham, eds., *Humor of the Old Southwest*, 2nd ed. (Athens, GA, 1964), 60 (Kirkman).

out of debt every body will go into it – but they know good things & will have none other."[41]

Towns of all sizes turned main streets into racing turf, sometimes with unpleasant consequences. About 1820, three years before it incorporated, Greensboro, Alabama, outlawed horse racing through Main Street. It had become the favorite pastime of hoodlums, who scorned the ordinance and outgunned the authorities. The gentlemen of Greensboro, staunch supporters of law and order, intruded, announcing that they would shoot to kill at the next offense. Gentlemen again upheld law and order in 1833, when some $60,000 went on the throw of the dice on a riverboat. A player had cheated. Outraged citizens tossed him overboard. He drowned.[42]

Joseph Mabry of Alabama had, among other racing horses, "Hugh Lawson White" ($6,410) and "Cholera" ($520). Pierce Butler and Hammond paid $8,000 for a horse that won purses of $1,000 and more. In 1853, Joseph Jones visited eight livery stables in Philadelphia at the request of his father in Georgia and reported pairs at $800–1,500, according to trotting ability. At Milledgeville, Georgia – not a principal center for horse racing during the 1830s – the entrance fee ran as high as $1,000. Costs included the training and maintenance of specialized slaves to care for the horses. From the earliest days, slaves trained and attended to racehorses. "Fidelity unto death" was the charge masters and mistresses gave to grooms trusted with the care of their favorite horses. Expensive racing horses required the painstaking attention of several well-trained slave grooms and jockeys.[43]

HIGH ROLLERS AND LOW

During the seventeenth and eighteenth centuries, gambling flourished among the gentlemen of Virginia to an extent well beyond anything in

---

[41] [Irving], *South Carolina Jockey Club*, 205, 209; Henry Edmund Ravenel, *Ravenel Records* (Atlanta, GA, 1898), 47; Nott quoted in Reginald Horsman, *Josiah Nott: Southerner, Physician, and Racial Theorist* (Baton Rouge, LA, 1987), 67.

[42] William Edward Wadsworth Yerby, *History of Greensboro, Alabama from Its Earliest Settlement*, ed. Mabel Yerby Lawson (Northport, AL, 1963 [1908]), 15, 33.

[43] Rebecca Hunt Moulder, *May the Sod Rest Lightly: Thomas O'Connor* (Tucson, AZ, 1977), 27; Drew Gilpin Faust, *James Henry Hammond and the Old South* (Baton Rouge, LA, 1982), 158–159; Joseph Jones to C. C. Jones, Dec. 13, 1853, in Joseph Jones Collection; Bonner, *Milledgeville*, 94; [Irving], *South Carolina Jockey Club*, 45; Donald G. Morgan, *Justice William Johnson, The First Dissenter: The Career and Constitutional Philosophy of a Jeffersonian Judge* (Columbia, SC, 1954), 8. For expert slave jockeys, grooms, and doctors, see Wilma A. Dunaway, *Slavery in the American Mountain South* (New York, 2003), 86–87. J. B. Grimball reported that "Poor Pompey" was deeply fond of the carriage horse and terribly distressed at its death: Diaries, Nov. 18, 1843.

the North. George Washington forbade gambling in the Revolutionary army primarily because it ruined some of his best officers. Alas, subsequently, gambling flourished among the politicians and businessmen in the national capital named for him. Thomas H. Palmer, a northern editor, commented on the Virginians in 1814, "Their vices are such as arise from the same temperament of mind which produces their virtues. The most striking to a stranger is a spirit of gambling." Gambling swelled in the Confederate army, and whenever possible, troops flocked to a local racecourse. Francis W. Dawson, a startled Englishman, reported losses up to $2,000 in poker games. Gambling went hand in hand with heavy drinking, creating a problem for the army. In Confederate hospitals gambling seriously threatened recoveries and good order. The gambling mania even carried into the Union's prisoner-of-war camps. Confederate generals replicated Cromwell's generals, who, motivated by security considerations rather than religious zealotry, suppressed horse racing and bear-baiting in the 1650s.[44]

Widespread, high-stakes gambling plagued the South, even as measured against standards on the northern frontier. E. S. Abdy, a Fellow at Jesus College, Cambridge, wrote in the early 1830s: "The spirit of gambling seems to possess a vast number of the 'higher orders' in Richmond." He might have included the lower orders, black and white. St. George Tucker, a hanging judge in gambling cases, told a grand jury in 1802 that habitual gambling and drunkenness threatened community morals more than violent crime did. He probably assumed – with most critics – that the one often caused the other. In 1834, Lucian Minor claimed that Massachusetts, Connecticut, and Rhode Island had no racecourses and probably less than a fourth of the crime and vice of his native Virginia.[45]

Americans imported games of chance but made no important contribution of their own. They gambled democratically. French aristocrats and

44 T. H. Breen, "The Cultural Significance of Gambling among the Gentry of Virginia," *William and Mary Quarterly*, 34 (1977), 239–257; Henry Chafetz, *Play the Devil: A History of Gambling in the United States from 1492 to 1955* (New York, 1960), 29, 179–183; T. H. Palmer, "Observations of Virginia," in Schwaab and Bull, eds., *Travels in the South*, 1:94; Bell Irvin Wiley, *The Life of Johnny Reb: The Common Soldier of the Confederacy* (Baton Rouge, LA, 1978), 37–41; Francis W. Dawson, *Reminiscences of Confederate Service, 1861–1865*, ed. Bell I. Wiley (Baton Rouge, LA, 1980 1882]), 87; H. H. Cunningham, *Doctors in Gray: The Confederate Medical Service*, 2nd ed. (Baton Rouge, LA, 1986), 91. For POW camps, see John G. Barrett, ed., *Yankee Rebel: The Civil War Journal of Edmund DeWitt Patterson* (Chapel Hill, NC, 1966), 98.

45 E. S. Abdy, *Journal of Residence and Tour in the United States of North America*, 3 vols. (New York, 1969 [1835]), 2:270; Lucian Minor, "New England," *SLM*, 1 (1834), 84–88; also, James M. Denham, *"A Rogue's Paradise": Crime and Punishment in Antebellum Florida, 1821–1861* (Tuscaloosa, AL, 1997), ch. 2.

grand bourgeois shot craps, which steadily became a pastime for poor whites and blacks. Faro, a French creation and a favorite among crooks, became the most popular card game in America. The house had the customary advantage of a modest return from an honest game, but it also had an incentive to cheat, since the host dealt the cards. Gaming houses in Monte Carlo banned it; those in the United States did not. Gambling, a minor vice in most places, grew into a big business as well as a means of recreation in New York and other big cities. Southern politicians led the field in Washington, but southern gamblers relied on the productive capacity, entrepreneurship, and professional skills of the North. Only New Orleans approached New York's expertise in producing marked cards for professionals. Almost all of the famous gamblers of the Flush Times learned their trade in New York.[46]

State legislatures tried to ban gambling, at least on the Sabbath. Louisiana repeatedly did so without effect in New Orleans. Unwilling or unable to enforce regulations, authorities levied registration fees and taxes. In consequence, respectable men invested in the business, congratulating themselves on their philanthropy, since fees and taxes supported the Charity Hospital, provided at least 20 percent of the money for the College of New Orleans, and supplied substantial aid to other charities. Laws designed to suppress gambling in the Republic of Texas fed its increase, with more Texans indicted for gambling than any other crime. Reformers had a hard time. In the American Southwest, discipline, like charity, began at home, and legislators were not famous for self-discipline. They relaxed by playing cards, especially high-stakes faro. Whenever state legislatures met, professional gamblers, prostitutes, and petty swindlers swarmed into town, infesting the sea and river ports and working boats on the Mississippi and off the coast. During the Flush Times, New Orleans, Natchez, and Vicksburg teemed with professional gamblers, desperadoes, and murderers.[47]

Early in the nineteenth century, professional gamblers infected Richmond and other cities. Mrs. Thomas Elston Randolph went to Norfolk in a boat filled with gamblers and suspicious-looking women. Offended by the

---

[46] The discussion draws freely on Herbert Asbury, *Sucker's Progress: An Informal History of Gambling in America* (New York, 1939).

[47] [Ingraham], *South-West*, 1:128–135; Abdy, *Journal of Residence and Tour*, 2:271; John Duffy, ed., *Parson Clapp of the Strangers' Church of New Orleans* (Baton Rouge, LA, 1957), 32; Dennis C. Rousey, *Policing the Southern City: New Orleans, 1805–1889* (Baton Rouge, LA, 1996), 46–48; Grady McWhiney, *Cracker Culture: Celtic Ways in the Old South* (Tuscaloosa, AL, 1988), 134–135; Lyle Saxon, et al., *Gumbo Ya-Ya: A Collection*

horrid language, she tossed all night. Alexander MacKay noted that even reserved, respectable people succumbed to the temptation to gamble with evil-looking professionals on riverboats. These desperadoes, he wrote, "form so large an ingredient in the population of the South." Yet desperadoes probably did not do as much damage as the new class of gentlemen gamblers – men like Wylly Barron of Georgia, who dressed and behaved respectably, ran clean games, and excluded minors from the table.[48]

Lotteries – genteel gambling – became common in North and South and helped finance colleges, academies, and charities. Virginia treated private lotteries as criminal but sanctioned public lotteries. The authorities in Columbia, South Carolina, cracked down on gambling houses from time to time, but those in Charleston looked the other way. The presence of South Carolina College probably accounts for the difference, since professional gamblers preyed on students. Even the strict Presbyterians of Lexington, Virginia, raised no objection to municipal lotteries in the 1830s. The Agricultural Society of South Carolina financed its activities by raising large sums through a lottery. North Carolina legislatures designated particular academies to conduct lotteries, some of which fell flat, although lottery tickets sold for as little as 76 cents. Until the 1830s, even religious educators, North and South, approved lotteries to finance schools, and New York and Pennsylvania ran them on a large scale. A reaction ended the practice in Virginia and Louisiana, but most slave states continued it until the 1850s. Then came the abolition of official lotteries throughout the North and most of the South; Georgia, Kentucky, Missouri, and Delaware retained them. Only after the War did the Protestant churches emphatically denounce lotteries as un-Christian, although some prominent clergymen, such as Jasper Adams, president of the College of Charleston, had done so long before.[49]

of Louisiana Folk Tales (New York, 1945),126–127; Hogan, *Texas Republic*, 128–130, 261; Bonner, *Milledgeville*, 71–72; R. D. Arnold to his wife, Dec. 6, 1837, in Richard H. Shryock, ed., *Letters of Richard D. Arnold, M. D., 1808–1876* (Durham, NC, 1929), 17.

[48] Ward and Green, *Richmond during the Revolution*, 52; Robert McColley, *Slavery and Jeffersonian Virginia* (Urbana, IL, 1964), 41; Mrs. Nicholas Trist to Mrs. T. J. Randolph, Oct. 17, 1829, in Randolph Whitfield and John Chapman, *The Florida Randolphs, 1829–1978*, 2nd ed. (Atlanta, GA, 1987), 51; "Autobiography of George Tucker," *Bermuda Historical Quarterly*, 18 (1961), 134; Alexander Mackay, *The Western World; Or, Travels in the United States in 1846–1847*, 3 vols. (New York, 1968 [1849]), 2:267, 320; Click, *Spirit of the Times*, 58–59; on Barron, see Lollie Belle Wylie, ed., *Memoirs of Judge Richard H. Clark* (Atlanta, GA, 1898).

[49] Click, *Spirit of the Times*, 63; Jack Kenny Williams, *Vogues in Villany: Crime and Retribution in Ante-Bellum South Carolina* (Columbia, SC, 1959), 47–50; Frederick

Cock fighting rivaled horse races as high sport well into the nineteenth century. In Virginia it began as the sport of small slaveholders, yeomen, and lesser folks but soon attracted gentlemen. Horse races and cock fights brought men together to talk politics, do business, and strengthen social ties. Gentlemen traveled thirty or forty miles to bet liberally. Some brought their own cocks and even their own food, since inns were likely to be jammed, with many crowded into one room, sleeping on the floor. Young gentlemen in Virginia displayed a penchant for escaping to the high-stake cock pits. In the South Carolina low country in the 1730s, cock fights scored high among pleasures and remained in vogue for more than a century in the up country. The son of J. Marion Sims explained: "Only the rich and cultivated bred cocks for fighting, and, like fox-hunting, it was an expensive sport." Cock fights in New Orleans attracted gentlemen, especially among the French.[50]

Those who found cock fights insufficiently exhilarating turned to gander pulls, which startled travelers. Tied to the top of a post, the greased gander's head and neck were stripped of feathers. Young gentlemen, riding at full speed, grasped at the greased gander. A half dollar spectator's entrance fee went into the purse of the chap who pulled off the head.

Southerners of all classes bet on anything and everything. Gabriel (Valcour) Aime of Louisiana boastfully wagered a "perfect dinner" for

Rudolph, *The American College and University: A History* (Athens, GA, 1990), ch. 9; Henry Boley, *Lexington in Old Virginia* (Richmond, VA, 1936), 32. Murray, *This Our Land*, 66–67. Also, Charles L. Coon, ed., *North Carolina Schools and Academies: A Documentary History, 1790–1840* (Raleigh, NC, 1915), 15, 139–142; Asbury, *Sucker's Progress*, ch. 5; William Davidson Blanks, "Ideal and Practice: A Study of the Conception of the Christian Life Prevailing in the Presbyterian Churches of the South during the Nineteenth Century" (Th.D., Union Theological Seminary, 1960), 243–245; Charles Reagan Wilson, *Baptized in Blood: The Religion of the Lost Cause, 1865–1920* (Athens, GA, 1980), 88–89; Jasper Adams, *Elements of Moral Philosophy* (Philadelphia, 1837), Part 6, ch. 4.

[50] Taylor Diary, Apr. 9, 1798; Isaac, *Transformation of Virginia*, 101-102,404; Albert T. Beveridge, *The Life of John Marshall*, 4 vols. (Boston, MA, 1916), 1:283–284; Marquis de Chastellux, *Travels in North America in the Years 1780, 1781, and 1782*, 2 vols., rev. tr. H. C. Rice, Jr. (Chapel Hill, NC, 1963), 2:386–387; D. S. Freeman, "Aristocracy of the Northern Neck," *SBN*, 10:70–71; Rogers, Jr., *Charleston in the Age of the Pinckneys*, 113; Edwin L. Green, *A History of Richland County: Vol. 1, 1732–1805* (Columbia, SC, 1932), 142–143; H. M. Sims, Introduction to J. Marion Sims, *The Story of My Life* (New York, 1884), 36; Jean Boze to Henri de Ste Gemé, March 10, 1832, in St. Geme Papers. Cock fighting originated in ancient Persia and spread to Greece: Judith M. Barringer, *The Hunt in Ancient Greece* (Baltimore, 2001), 90–93.

fellow planters entirely from the products of his own plantation, including shrimp, crabs, quail, snipe, wild duck, bananas, pineapples, and tobacco. They covered his $10,000 bet. He won.[51]

Lowcountry planters loved the boats they relied on for local transportation, and they took great pride in the skill of their black boatmen. Hence, they raced against each other's boats and slaves, with masters in the coxswain seats. Then came a feast, to which the losers contributed the wine. Well-to-do citizens of Glynn County, Georgia, gave their beautiful boats names like Lady Love, Star, Lightning, and Lizard. "A boat race," George White commented in 1849, "is an exciting occurrence to all classes, but especially to the slaves, who really think that the reputation of the plantations to which they belong depends upon the swiftness of their masters' boats." In 1857, the Aquatic Club of Georgia challenged all comers to race a boat with the stakes at $10,000. Thomas Butler King doubtless enjoyed the prestige accorded him as president of the club, but his wife did not enjoy his large gambling losses. The three-day regatta in January excited the ladies in whose honor the concluding ball was given. Everyone, said Florence King, enjoyed the regatta. At Pass Christian, yacht races attracted a wealthy elite and a curious community.[52]

Gaming houses included prostitution, drunkenness, and frequent violence. In Vicksburg, the patience of "the respectable portion of society" ran out. A blood purge of miscreants followed. Elsewhere, reform governments cleaned up towns and cities or at least reduced the evils and kept them out of sight. Where the authorities failed, the good citizens lent a hand. The mayor of Richmond stood for law and order, which sometimes required extralegal force. So he joined the vigilantes who burned down seven or eight gambling houses in the early 1830s. In subsequent years, citizens of Richmond, Norfolk, and New Orleans determined to end prostitution and violent crimes associated with gambling. The fate of gamblers and assorted criminals depended on the vicissitudes of public opinion and the peculiar circumstances of each incident. In Memphis in the 1850s, a gambler killed someone and got off. A few years later, his son

[51] Saxon, *Gumbo Ya-Ya*, 214–215; Burnette Vanstory, *Georgia's Land of the Golden Isles* (Athens, GA, 1956), 81.

[52] George White, *Statistics of the State of Georgia* (Savannah, GA, 1849), 284; Florence King to Fuddy King, Dec. 18, 1857, in T. B. King Papers; Steel, *T. Butler King of Georgia*, 2; Susan Dabney Smedes, *Memorials of a Southern Planter*, ed. Fletcher M. Green (New York, 1965 [1887]), 83.

did the same and barely escaped a lynching. Outraged citizens ordered all gamblers to leave town.[53]

Astonishing losses had dire consequences. The former slave and abolitionist Austin Steward considered Captain William Helm a kind, pleasant, indulgent master. Fond of the turf and a devoted fox hunter, Helm also played cards for high stakes, and on one occasion lost $2,700. As a young lawyer, Nathan Green, who became the jewel of Tennessee's Supreme Court, probably lost as much by high-stakes gambling as he made by practicing law. Philip Porcher reported a "sad event" in Columbia: A young man blew his brains out after losing all his money at the races. Although New Orleans abounded with wild exaggerations, plausible reports circulated of gambling losses of $100,000 at a time, and the recklessness of some big planters lent credibility to stories of their losing plantations at poker in a single night.[54]

When slaves gambled among themselves and with the poor whites, they risked little. When their masters gambled, they put their slaves at risk. Heavy losses invited sales of slaves to cover debts, as well as sale of plantations and probable separation of slave families. At such moments masters, kind or brutal, looked alike to their slaves. Wealthy planters made easy marks for seasoned criminals. The number of wealthy and socially and politically prominent Southerners who lost fortunes and plantations at the races and gambling tables will never be known, but they sprinkled the records and community lore. Rhys Isaac's remark on eighteenth-century Virginia applies well beyond: "To lose in a world where personal prowess was of great consequence would mean a momentary taste of annihilation." People crowded the events "as much for the excitement of seeing some laid low by defeat, as they did for the celebrating with the winners."[55]

---

[53] Brian Steel Wills, *A Battle from the Start: The Life of Nathan Bedford Forrest* (New York, 1992), 38–39; Asbury, *Sucker's Progress*, 125–126, 228–229; Abdy, *Journal of Residence and Tour*, 2:270.

[54] Austin Steward, *Twenty-Two Years a Slave and Forty Years a Freeman* (Reading, MA, 1969 [1857]), 16–17, 27–28; John W. Green, *Lives of the Judges of the Supreme Court of Tennessee, 1795–1947* (n.p., 1947), 92–93; Philip E. Porcher to Elizabeth Palmer Porcher, Sept. 22, 1856, in Towles, ed., *World Turned Upside Down*, 204; "Autobiography of George Tucker," 108; Stephen F. Miller, *The Bench and Bar of Georgia: Memoirs and Sketches*, 2 vols. (Philadelphia, 1858), 1:23; Bonner, *Milledgeville*, 72; Malone, *Jefferson*, 1:75–78; Emory M. Thomas, *Bold Dragoon: The Life of J. E. B. Stuart* (New York, 1968), 5–7; Henry S. Foote, *The Bench and Bar of the Southwest* (St. Louis, MO, 1876), 94–98; Saxon, *Gumbo Ya-Ya*, 222; Asbury, *Sucker's Progress*, ch. 8.

[55] Isaac, *Transformation of Virginia*, 119. For slave testimony on slave sales provoked by gambling debts see John W. Blassingame, ed., *Slave Testimony: Two Centuries of Letters, Speeches, Interviews, and Autobiographies* (Baton Rouge, LA, 1977), 212, 505; Benjamin

GOOD WINE AND MEAN WHISKEY

Between 1790 and 1830, Americans consumed more alcohol per capita than before or since, although less than Swedes and Scots. To astonished foreigners, Americans floated on a sea of alcohol, imbibing more than four and a half gallons per capita in 1825. Drunkenness rose to unprecedented heights during the first two decades of the century, before the rise of great cities and urban slums. From 1792 to 1810, when the population doubled, use of distilled spirits tripled.[56]

During the late eighteenth century, southern backcountry farmers made brandy and whiskey in quantity, often to pay preachers and teachers. By 1800, improvements in distillation brought whiskey drinking into vogue. For the next half-century, more-or-less decent whiskey sold for about 50 cents a gallon and the meanest whiskey as low as 15 cents, which even the poor could afford. Nonslaveholders and small slaveholders made hard liquor from any available fruit. Teetotalers kept liquor available for guests, slaves, and medicinal purposes. Public drunkenness shocked Yankee travelers to the South, but planters ignored drunken poor whites unless they drew slaves into gambling or illicit trade.[57]

Did Southerners drink more than Northerners? Henry Howe, Virginia's historian, and Michael Tuomey, South Carolina's state geologist, espied much heavier drinking in the North, but most observers disagreed. In 1842, James Louis Petigru told his sister of two lawyers killed in one week: "Oliver Smith, so notorious for a certain sort of practice, was it seems equally out of money and carousing." The drunken Smith crashed his gig and died. The other lawyer, a twenty-five-year-old son

Drew, *A North-Side View of Slavery: The Refugee, or, the Narrative of Fugitive Slaves in Canada* (New York, 1968 [1857]), 264; Francis Fedric, *Slave Life in Virginia and Kentucky; Or, Fifty Years of Slavery in the Southern States of America* (EE: Chapel Hill, NC, 1999 [1863]), ch. 3. For racing debts see Alonzo Thomas Dill, *Carter Braxton: Last Virginia Signer* (Richmond, VA, 1976), 8; W. P. Cresson, *James Monroe* (Chapel Hill, NC, 1946), 371; "Autobiography," 21, in Holcombe Papers.

56 W. J. Rorabaugh, *The Alcoholic Republic: An American Tradition* (New York, 1979), ch. 1; and generally, Paul Johnson, *The Birth of the Modern: World Society, 1815–1830* (New York, 1991), 78–761. The United States produced 90 million gallons of whiskey in 1860: Emerson David Fite, *Social and Industrial Conditions in the North During the Civil War* (Williamstown, MA, 1976), 81. Distilleries increased from 2,500 in 1792 to 14,000 in 1840.

57 Powell, *When the Past Refused to Die*, 66–67; Frank L. Owsley, *Plain Folk of the Old South* (Baton Rouge, LA, 1949), 116; Ephraim Lawrence and Nellie Lloyd, in *AS: S. C.*, 3 (pt. 3), 128–129; on medicinal purposes see Jordan, *Alabama: Town and Country*, 76; D. D. Hall, "A Yankee Tutor in the Old South," *New England Quarterly*, 33 (1960), 87; *SBN*, 10:567–581; Jane Louise Mesick, *The English Traveller in America, 1785–1835*

of the prominent Josiah Taylor, apparently drank himself to death one night. Grimball sadly reported W. Skirving Smith's death "brought on, doubtless by a long course of intemperance – This unfortunate man's life is a melancholy example of misapplied talents – There were few men who were more gifted by nature with the means of distinction – and none who have gone down to the tomb, so perfectly falsifying the hopes of his friends." Dr. J. Marion Sims recalled Captain McKenna, owner of one hundred slaves and half a village in Lancaster District, who went on two- or three-week sprees that ended with delirium tremens.[58]

Political, professional, and social leaders drank heavily. William Campbell grew up in elite political circles, and saw W. C. Rives and Frank Gilmer, among the leading men in Virginia, drink excessively. A disgusted Edmund Ruffin observed the Speaker of the House of Delegates drunk as usual. Tennessee's prominent politicians – among them Andrew Jackson Donelson, William T. Haskell, and Tom Marshall – campaigned and lectured while drunk. Henry S. Foote of Mississippi guessed that a third of his contemporaries shortened their lives by heavy drinking: "Drunken Governors, drunken legislators, and drunken judges, with many other persons of wealth and intelligence there, had so long set an example of intemperance to the multitude, and this example had been so extensively imitated." The prominent public men who drank heavily included George Poindexter and Wiley P. Harris; S. S. Prentiss probably died from alcoholism. In Alabama, Representative Felix G. McConnell, for one, committed suicide, apparently while drunk.[59]

Simms advised Hammond on deportment in the U.S. Senate: "Above all, my dear fellow, drink nothing. That good foolish fellow Keitt, it is reported here currently, got drunk after or during his oration, & was

(Westport, CT, 1970), 74–76, 82; Allan Nevins, ed., *American Social History as Recorded by British Travellers* (New York, 1923), 8. On production for home use, see Francis Wayles Eppes to Thomas Jefferson, Oct. 31, 1822, in Edwin Morris Betts and James Adams Bear, Jr., *The Family Letters of Thomas Jefferson* (Columbia, MO, 1966), 447. Most southern states neither licensed nor taxed liquor.

58 Henry Howe, *Historical Collections of Virginia* (Charleston, SC, 1845), 155; Michael Tuomey to Sarah E. Tuomey, Apr. 23, 1846, in Lewis S. Dean, ed., *The Papers of Michael Tuomey* (Spartanburg, SC, 2001), 83. Carson, *Life, Letters and Speeches of Petigru*, 221; J. B. Grimball Diary, Aug. 21, 1832; Sims, *Story of My Life*, 146. The temperance movement curbed drinking in Presbyterian Lexington, Virginia: Ollinger Crenshaw, *General Lee's College: the Rise and Growth of Washington and Lee University* (New York, 1969), 77.

59 Minnie Clare Yarbrough, ed., *The Reminiscences of William C. Preston* (Chapel Hill, NC, 1933), 10; Jan. 5, 1860, *ERD*, 1:389; "Political Journal," Sept. 4, 1856, Feb. 25, 1859, in Herschel Gower et al., eds., *Pen and Sword: The Life and Journals of Randal*

with difficulty carried from the stand & into the Citadel." The gifted Chancellor William Harper recognized his alcoholism but did not control it. At the Confederate inauguration in Montgomery, Thomas R. R. Cobb of Georgia complained to his wife, Marion, that Texas politicians were famous for hard drinking. Senator Louis Wigfall "promises to be as troublesome to us, as he was to the Congress in Washington. He is half drunk all the time and bullies and blusters about everywhere."[60]

Drunken parishioners beset conscientious pastors. Cornish reported on Mr. Horry, a thirty-eight-year-old bachelor worth $80,000 to $100,000. A drunk since age ten, Horry spent his life eating and getting drunk. James Heriot was "his own worst enemy – loving strong drink more than a good name or the health of his soul." And Mr. Stewart, "a confirmed drunkard," caused his son's death in a drunken rage. Drunken husbands abused wives and children, mothers and sisters. White women suffered; black women suffered worse. Slaves frequently complained about mean-drunk masters who hurt people around them and did not take care of business. Masters might have to sell slaves to cover debts or, worse, lose their plantation and sell them all.[61]

Drunkenness became a problem in the Confederate army, apparently worse among officers and surgeons than among troops, who themselves drank a good deal. An upcountry South Carolina yeoman found Texans the most dissipated infantrymen in the Confederate army and simultaneously the bravest of the brave. They reminded him of high-spirited horses, so hard to manage that riders submitted to their reins. The army cashiered General Earl Van Doren and a number of other officers for drunkenness at the front. Van Doren's mischief ended on the eve of the

W. McGavock, Colonel, C. S. A. (Nashville, TN, 1959), 382–383, 509; Henry S. Foote, *Casket of Reminiscences* (New York,1874), 270–271; Rowland, ed. *Mississippi*, 35, 43, 269–270; Dickey, *Seargent S. Prentiss*, 389; Garrett, *Public Men in Alabama*, 161–163, 180–181, 285, 594.
60 Simms to Hammond, July 16, 1858, in Oliphant, et al., eds., *Letters of Simms*, 4:80; T. R. R. Cobb to Marion Cobb, April 30, 1861, in A. L. Hull, ed., "The Correspondence of Thomas Reade Roots Cobb, 1860–1862," *Publications of the Southern Historical Association*, 11 1907), 312–313.
61 Cornish Diary, July 25, 1843, Dec. 8, 1846, July 6, 1847, Dec. 8, 1846. For women's reports see Henderson Journal, Aug. 20, 1855; Hutchinson Journal, Feb. 15, 16, 1838; Serena R. Lea to Martha Jackson, July 5, 1840, in Jackson-Prince Papers; Fletcher Autobiography (ms.), Winter 1841–1842; Jeff Hamilton, *My Master: The Inside Story of Sam Houston and His Times, as Told to Lenoir Hunt* (Austin, TX, 1992), 4. For those who drank themselves to death or were ruined by dissipation, see, e.g., J. Walker Diary, Dec. 21, 1833; Baker Diary, Dec., 1858; Annie Hopkins, *AS: Okla.*, 7 (pt. 1), 132.

siege of Vicksburg when an irate husband shot him for dallying with his wife.[62]

Although men drank more than women, the United States had some 100,000 female drunkards. Women consumed an estimated sixth to a quarter of America's enormous alcohol intake, a portion of which they took in alcohol-based medicines and cordials. Southern newspapers reported drunkenness among men but little among women – except for reports of arrests of lower-class women. Gossip, private letters, and diaries told a fuller story. Ingraham remarked on ladies whose servants brought them a mint julep to get them up in the morning. Susan Dabney Smedes of Mississippi discreetly suggested that mistresses taught female slaves and, presumably, their own daughters to drink whiskey "properly" (mixed with sugar and water). The churches, especially on the frontier, often disciplined women as well as men for intemperance. In the early Southwest, drunkenness accounted for probably half the dismissals from the Presbyterian and Baptist churches. Baptist and Methodist clergymen cooperated in temperance campaigns, and some southern Old and New School Presbyterian synods supported legislation to curb alcohol consumption.[63]

---

[62] Milton Barrett to Jesse and Caroline McMahan, March 28, 1862, in J. Roderick Heller and Carolyn Ayres Heller, eds., *The Confederacy Is on Her Way Up the Spout: Letters to South Carolina, 1861–1864* (Athens, GA, 1992), 55; Richard N. Current, ed., *Encyclopedia of the Confederacy*, 4 vols. (New York, 1993), 4:1498; J. William Jones, *Christ in the Camp: Religion in Lee's Army* (Richmond, VA, 1888), 268–271; William C. Davis, *Jefferson Davis: The Man and His Hour* (New York, 1991), 445–446 (Van Doren), 496, 501; C. C. Jones, Jr. to C. C. Jones, March 7, 1862, in Robert Manson Myers, ed., *The Children of Pride: A True Story of the Children of the Civil War* (New Haven, CT, 1972), 857.

[63] Rorabaugh, *Alcoholic Republic*, 11–13; J. H. Ingraham, *Sunny South; Or, The Southerner at Home* (New York, 1968 [1860], 52; Smedes, *Memorials of a Southern Planter*, 19. For intemperance among women, see also Smyth, *Autobiographical Notes, Letters*, 480–481; Hutchinson Journal, Aug. 30, 1829; Haralson Diary, Jan. 31, 1837; Currie, *Enclave*, 24–25. On church disciplining of women, see William Warren Sweet, *Religion on the Frontier: The Baptists, 1783–1830: A Collection of Source Material* (New York, 1931), 49–53; Jean E. Friedman, *The Enclosed Garden: Women and the Community in the Evangelical South, 1830–1900* (Chapel Hill, NC, 1985), 15. For the southwestern churches, see Walter Brownlow Posey, *Frontier Mission: A History of Religion West of the Southern Appalachians to 1861* (Lexington, KY, 1966), 301; July 20, 1854, in Richard L. Troutman, ed., *The Heavens Are Weeping: The Diaries of Richard Browder, 1852–1856* (Grand Rapids, MI, 1987), 82; Wade Crawford Barclay, *History of Methodist Missions: Early American Methodism, 1769–1844*, 2 vols. (New York, 1949), 2:26–38; Ernest Trice Thompson, *Presbyterians in the South*, 3 vols. (Richmond, VA, 1963), 1: 311–312; Groene, *Ante-Bellum Tallahassee*, 128.

No opprobrium attached to rural Virginians' being drunk at home. But from Virginia to Texas, no gentleman wanted to be found drunk in public, if only because the code required that he be able to drink liberally without showing the effects. David Outlaw of North Carolina complained in 1849 that responsible people excluded liquor at their parties because many guests drank too much. Southern young ladies tolerated hard-drinking men but not those who got drunk in their presence.[64]

Temperance reformers ran afoul of agricultural reformers who sought to develop a native wine industry. Agricultural societies and periodicals vigorously promoted the production of local wines, giving prizes for the best grapes and wines. At least they did not have to confront abolitionists for whom temperance was good for the import business. André Rebouças of Brazil, outstanding entrepreneur, economic reformer, and mulatto abolitionist, praised American women for their efforts to thwart the degradation of the Anglo-Saxon race and lessen the demand for liquor, thereby increasing the demand for Brazilian coffee. Meanwhile, shopkeepers in Arkansas complained bitterly that the Sons of Temperance were driving them out of the lucrative liquor trade and compelling them to sell dry goods and the like. By the 1850s, demands for legislation noticeably receded. The churches worried about the radical political tendencies of the temperance movement and veered toward an emphasis on moral suasion. In Georgia, for example, temperance advocates, led by churchmen, mounted an impressive campaign until it became entwined with abolitionism in the public mind. When the religiously grounded temperance movement swept the "Burned-Over District" in New York, its links to abolitionism appeared for all to see. The temperance movement coated northern agitators and abolitionists with respectability, helping lay the foundation for the Republican Party.[65]

[64] William E. Hatcher, *Life of J. B. Jeter, D. D.* (Baltimore, 1887), 32–33; Elizabeth Silverthorne, *Plantation Life in Texas* (College Station, TX, 1986), 184; Aug. 23, 30, 1865, in Daniel E. Sutherland, ed., *The Civil War Diary of Ellen Renshaw House* (Knoxville, TN, 1996), 182–184; David to Emily Outlaw, Dec. 16, 1849; Mary D. Robertson, ed., *A Confederate Lady Comes of Age: The Journal of Pauline DeCaradeuc Heyward, 1863–1888* (Columbia, SC, 1992), Apr. 22, 1865 (73).

[65] Planters' Club Letters: Hancock County, GA (ms); *Transactions of the State Agricultural Society of North Carolina,1857* (Raleigh, NC, 1858), 103 and address by J. L. Bridges; T. L. Clingman, *Annual Address to the State Agricultural Society of North Carolina, 1858* (Raleigh, NC, 1859), U. S. Commissioner of Patents, *Report on Agriculture for 1858* (Washington, DC, 1859), 383; *SA*, 1 (1828), 7, 18, 50, 98, 145, 193, 242, 289; 4 (1831), 57, 108, 130, 525; André Rebouças, *Agricultura nacional: estudos econômicos* (Rio de Janeiro, 1883), 38; for Arkansas shopkeepers, see J. O. Andrew, "Travels in the West," *Miscellanies: Comprising Letters, Essays, and Addresses* (Louisville, KY, 1854),

Fear of radicalism emerged in the ambivalence of whites toward recruitment of blacks to temperance. Whites applauded such efforts so long as they promised more docile slaves, much as Bostonians appreciated efforts to tame the Irish. Thus planters near Tuscaloosa, Alabama, threw a huge barbecue for their slaves in 1851 to celebrate the twelfth anniversary of the Colored Total Abstinence Society. But many had second thoughts. They approved of their slaves staying off the bottle, but they did not want to hear about whites who agitated among them. An arresting case: Tom Holcombe of Lynchburg, Virginia, a respectable lawyer and temperance man, devoted himself to getting blacks to take the pledge. Whites erroneously smelled a closet abolitionist, and Holcombe's friends had to rescue him from a mob intent on tarring-and-feathering him. That chapter of his career ended well, the sequel badly. William Reid Holcombe, his son, married an unbearable harpy, and in the words of a relative, "the Son of Virginia's greatest temperance advocate died of the effects of alcohol."[66]

LAUDANUM AND OTHER PLEASANTRIES

Opium and other addictive drugs struck hard at the affluent in Britain and America. Southerners cried out in horror at Britain's opium trade and its atrocious "Opium War" in China, but opium at home proved more controversial. In the 1830s, southern medical journals discussed opium poisoning as a common occurrence. In the 1850s, respectable publications like De Bow's Review printed advertisements for opium and other drugs and ran articles on the properties of poppies and conditions for their cultivation. It concluded that America could drastically reduce its dependence on Asian sources by cultivating poppies

184–185; H. A. Scomp, King Alcohol in the Realm of King Cotton, 2 vols. (Chicago, 1888), 1:5–6, 210, 2:447–450; Whitney R. Cross, The Burned-Over District: The Social and Intellectual History of Enthusiastic Religion in Western New York, 1800–1860 (New York, 1965), ch. 13; Louis Filler, The Crusade against Slavery, 1830–1860 (New York, 1960), 39–40, 239; Chester Forrester Dunham, The Attitude of the Northern Clergy toward the South, 1860–1865 (Toledo, OH, 1942), 12; Parsons, Inside View of Slavery, 213–216. For plantation recipes for beer, wine, and brandy, see Weymouth T. Jordan, ed., Herbs, Hoecakes and Husbandry: The Daybook of a Planter of the Old South (Tallahassee, FL, 1960), 39–46, 51–52. The temperance movement's great strength was in the Northeast: Ian R. Tyrrell, Sobering Up: From Temperance to Prohibition in Antebellum America, 1800–1860 (Westport, CT, 1979).

[66] James Benson Sellers, Slavery in Alabama (University, AL, 1964), 94–95; Holcombe "Autobiography" (ms.), 1:25–27.

in California. Wounded Confederate troops commonly resorted to opium.[67]

Leading physicians in Dublin and Glasgow approved the free use of opium, while those in London thought it dangerous. British apothecaries sold opium over the counter until curbed by law in 1868. In the first half of the nineteenth century, most Britons, especially professionals, were believed to have taken opium at some point in their lives. From early colonial times, southern country stores sold pure opium and especially laudanum (tincture of opium mixed with alcohol). In either form it sold throughout Britain and America in bottles and pills, and American imports rose to more than $400,000. When used in moderation, opium and morphine served as effective painkillers. In 1834, Dr. Richard D. Arnold of Savannah, secretary of the American Medical Association, reported the widespread use of opium in the wake of cholera epidemics. In ordinary matters, Southerners took morphine to stop coughing, and found that opium and laudanum silenced crying babies. At the University of North Carolina, Professor William Hooper declared the use of opium and alcohol serious problems on American campuses, including his own.[68]

Southerners appreciated the narcotic properties of poppy, which grew easily in their backyards and carried no moral censure. In the 1820s, Joseph Vallance Bevan of Georgia, state legislator and pioneer state historian, advocated its cultivation in a committee report in favor of crop diversification. The Associate Presbyterian Reverend Samuel Agnew, eminently respectable if a bit stiff, grew poppies on his plantation in Mississippi and wondered "whether opium making will pay." His sick wife took it. Men on hunts took laudanum to ease their digestion.[69]

[67] J. Newton Smith, "A Case of Poisoning by Opium," *Transylvania Journal of Medicine and the Associated Sciences*, 9 (1836), 722–723; Emanuel Weiss, "Opium-Can We Compete with the Indies in Its Production," *DBR*, 20 (1856), 60–66; for Confederate soldiers, see Gary D. Joiner et al., eds., *No Pardons to Ask, No Apologies to Make: The Journal of William Henry King, Gray's 28th Louisiana Infantry Regiment* (Knoxville, TN, 2006), 33, 106, 180. For southern condemnation of the Opium War, see Fox-Genovese and Genovese, *Mind of the Master Class*, 217–218.

[68] Johnson, *Birth of the Modern*, 761–770; Lewis E. Atherton, *The Southern Country Store, 1800–1860* (Baton Rouge, LA, 1949), 77; Damon L. Fowler, "Historical Commentary" to Annabella P. Hill, *Mrs. Hill's Southern Practical Cookery and Receipt Book* (Columbia, SC, 1995 [1867, 1872]), xlii; William Hooper, *The Force of Habit: A Discourse Delivered before the Students of the University of North Carolina*, 2nd. ed. (Raleigh, NC, 1851 [1833]), 7, 14–18. For the medicinal use of opium in "large doses," see Steven M. Stowe, *Doctoring the South: Southern Physicians and Everyday Medicine in the Mid-Nineteenth Century* (Chapel Hill, NC, 2004), 161 and *passim*. On imports, see Murray, *This Our Land*, 117; R. D. Arnold to Thomas Spaulding, Sept. 14, 1834, in Shryock, ed., *Letters of Richard D. Arnold*, 11–12.

[69] E. Merton Coulter, *Joseph Vallance Bevan: Georgia's First Official Historian* (Athens, GA, 1964), 96–97; Agnew Diary, June 1, Sept. 4, 1865; West, *Methodism in Alabama*,

Horror stories, nonetheless, appeared everywhere. Robert Carter II, from one of Virginia's first families, died from an overdose of opium at age twenty-nine. Only opium relieved the pain, cough, and diarrhea of old and sickly John Randolph of Roanoke. "I am," he wrote his friend Dr. John Brockenbaugh, "fast sinking into an opium-eating sot." He then switched to morphine or added it to the opium. Everyone knew that James Ogilvie, a celebrated schoolmaster, who taught Thomas Ritchie, Winfield Scott, W. C. Rives, William C. Archer, and F. W. Gilmer, took laudanum when he prepared his lectures. He might have avoided notice if he had not also been addicted to William Godwin's radical political views. Richard Dabney, a talented poet and accomplished linguist, took opium to ease the pain from bad burns. Addicted, he graduated to alcoholism, and died at age forty-eight.[70]

Anson Jones of Texas, a physician and politician, charged that Sam Houston, whom he hated, mismanaged the San Jacinto campaign because he was incapacitated by laudanum. James Knox Polk's father sometimes functioned under the influence of laudanum. The death of the Episcopal Reverend Mr. DuPont saddened Aiken, South Carolina. As reported by Cornish, he died "by laudanum, in a fit of insanity." Cornish also reported heavy use of drugs by sick parishioners. He took for granted that they used drugs for medication but grew impatient for the effects to wear off so that he might visit and comfort them. Ebenezer Pettigrew of North Carolina had better luck: Under doctor's advice he used opium to relieve his pain and sustain him through his illnesses. The northern-born mother of Henry Hitchcock of Mobile – prominent jurist, politician, and businessman – became a drug addict. Occasionally, a gentleman attempted or committed suicide with an overdose of laudanum.[71]

Addiction seems especially to have gripped the ladies. James M. Legaré, Charleston's poet, accused the elite girls' schools of turning their pupils into opium addicts. Mary Boykin Chesnut provided the best-known case of women who freely used opium as a painkiller and sedative. Jane

---

15; on hunts, see I. Jenkins Mikell, *Rumbling of the Chariot Wheels* (Charleston, SC, 1923), 271.

[70] Andrew Levy, *The First Emancipator: The Forgotten Story of Robert Carter, the Founding Father Who Freed His Slaves* (New York, 2005), 10. In Kenneth Shorey, ed., *Collected Letters of John Randolph of Roanoke to Dr. John Brockenbrough, 1812–1833* (New Brunswick, NJ, 1988), see Randolph to Brockenbrough, May 30, 1828 (105), June 16, 1831, Dec. 16 (144), 1832 (144); Richard Beale Davis, *Intellectual Life in Jefferson's Virginia, 1790–1830* (Chapel Hill, NC, 1964), 37–42 (Ogilvie); *SBN*, 11:249 (Dabney).

[71] Herbert Gambrell, *Anson Jones: The Last President of Texas*, 2nd ed. (Austin, TX, 1964), 424; Jane Polk to James K. Polk and Sarah Polk, January 5, 1828 in Herbert Weaver et. al., eds., *Correspondence of James K. Polk*, 9 vols. (Nashville, TN, 1969), 1:123; Cornish Diary, June 24, 1848, Aug. 30, 1858; W. H. Brantley, Jr., "Henry Hitchcock of Mobile,

Amelia Petigru, wife of J. L. Petigru, became addicted to the morphine prescribed to ease her way through a painful miscarriage and assorted ailments. Fannie Page Hume of Virginia found that morphine "had a marvellous effect – relieved pain &, tho' it did not put me to sleep, produced the most delightful feelings – and I TALKED & repeated poetry the whole night – alarmed as well as amused the girls. But – oh, the nausea this morning. Could not retain a particle of food or drink, nor lift MY HEAD." She suffered through a long day. Octavia Bryant Stephens of Florida, a young plantation mistress, tried laudanum but only got sick.

Susan Dabney Smedes noted the popularity of opium as medicine and the problems it frequently caused. Those who, like Clara Solomon, suffered from headaches could buy "Cocaine," a legal medicine. Promoters recommended that passengers carry a bit of opium and a flask of brandy as antidotes to stagecoach sickness. Dr. Elijah Millington Walker of rural Mississippi applied opium to treat a woman for pains from "excessive menstrual discharge." The English-born Amelia Barr of Texas expressed a common notion when she maintained that laudanum was the only available effective painkiller for women. Parents quieted children with laudanum. Thomas G. Clemson and Anna Maria (Calhoun) Clemson almost killed their daughter Nina with an overdose.[72]

Southern journals of opinion discussed the work of Thomas de Quincy, including his writings on political economy. *Confessions of an Opium Eater* circulated widely through the elite circles in the South and was especially popular in the libraries of college student societies. *Confessions* had a ready audience, since Southerners who read it were likely to have at least dipped into his other works and found much to praise in, say, *Avenger, de Profundis*, and his essay on Pope. Mrs. Henry Schoolcraft praised *Confessions* for its exposure of the effects of opium. The Reverend Dr. James Henley Thornwell followed the lead of James McCosh in citing de Quincy's opium adventures to demonstrate the power of conscience and to draw some useful moral lesson. Yet, although Benjamin Johnson Barbour and others admired the

1816–1839, *Alabama Review*, 5 (1952), 21; Amelia E. H. Barr, *All the Days of My Life: An Autobiography. The Red Leaves of a Human Heart* (New York, 1980 [1913]), 217. On suicides: James Graham to W. A. Graham, June 18, 1832, in Hamilton, ed., *Graham Papers*, 1:238–239; Emma Holmes, June 29, 1863, in John F. Marszalek, ed., *The Diary of Miss Emma Holmes* (Baton Rouge, LA, 1979), 271–272.

72 Curtis Carroll Davis, *That Ambitious Mr. Legaré: The Life of James M. Legaré of South Carolina, Including a Collected Edition of His Poems* (Columbia, SC, 1971), 100–101. In Sarah McCulloh Lemmon, ed., *The Pettigrew Papers*, 2 vols. (Raleigh, NC, 1971,1988), 2:42, 45, 128: Ann Blount Pettigrew to Mary Williams Bryan, May 27, 1824, July, 1824, Ann Blount Pettigrew to Ebenezer Pettigrew, Dec. 31, 1829; Hume Diary, April 5, 1860; Lynette Boney Wrenn, ed., *A Bachelor's Life in Antebellum Mississippi: The Diary of*

moral instruction of *Confessions,* Edmund Ruffin and the editors of *Russell's Magazine* feared that de Quincy encouraged rather than fought opium addiction.[73]

Tobacco was not considered a drug, but its popularity among southern women raised eyebrows. Union troops expressed shock at seeing southern women of all classes smoking, chewing, and "dipping." They neither exaggerated nor slandered. Rough frontier countrywomen, including wives and daughters of well-to-do planters, indulged. David Hunter Strother ("Porte Crayon") depicted pipe-smoking backcountry women of the North Carolina in the 1850s. Ann Bona Johnston of Davidson, a well-read, upper-class Presbyterian, might have served Strothers as an example. In rural Alabama, white women smoked pipes before and after church services. Pipe smoking proved a pleasant pastime, especially for those who had slaves to keep the pipes lit.[74]

Drugs became a dangerous weapon in the hands of slaves. Public opinion in Christian County, Kentucky, divided sharply over the hanging of a slave girl for poisoning a white child. Many thought she had accidentally overdosed the child with laudanum to keep her quiet. In other cases no one thought of an accident, as when a slave woman in Virginia in 1857 fatally overdosed a white baby she did not wish to nurse.[75]

Dr. Elijah Millington Walker, 1849–1852 (Knoxville, TN, 2004), July 4, 1850 (61); Lander, *Calhoun Family and Clemson,* 159.

[73] *Plantation Life: The Narratives of Mrs. Henry Schoolcraft* (New York, 1969 [1860], 497, and "Letters on the Condition of the African Race," appendix, 19; *JHTW,* 1:417; Benjamin Johnson Barbour, "Address Delivered before the Literary Societies of the Virginia Military Institute," *SLM,* 20 (1854), 520–521; Dec. 2, 1862, Ruffin, *Diary,* 2:500–501; Editor's Table, *Russell's Magazine,* 2 (1857–1858), 382. See Fox-Genovese and Genovese, *Mind of the Master Class,* 142–143.

[74] Bell I. Wiley, *The Life of Billy Yank: The Common Soldier of the Union* (Baton Rouge, LA, 1978), 102; Thomas Perkins Abernethy, *From Frontier to Plantation in Tennessee: A Study in Frontier Democracy* (Memphis, TN, 1955), 162; Cecil D. Eby, Jr., *"Porte Crayon": The Life of David Hunter Strother* (Chapel Hill, NC, 1960), 90; on Johnston, see Chalmers Gaston Davidson, *The Plantation World Around Davidson: The Story of North Mecklenberg "Before the War,"* 2nd ed. (Davidson, NC, 1973), 21; Jasper Rastus Nall, *Freeborn Slave: Diary of a Black Man in the South* (Birmingham, AL, 1996), 31. On the Northwest, see R. Carlyle Buley, *The Old Northwest: Pioneer Period, 1815–1840,* 2 vols. (Bloomington, IN, 1950), 1:364. Texas women took snuff in their mouths ("dipped") rather than in their noses.

[75] Marion B. Lucas, *A History of Blacks in Kentucky,* 2 vols. (Frankfort, KY, 1992), 1:6; Philip J. Schwarz, *Twice Condemned: Slaves and the Criminal Law of Virginia, 1705–1865* (Baton Rouge, LA, 1988), 297.

Editor's Epilogue

Good historians, even those who favor theory, know how important contingency can be in their reconstructions of the past. Gene Genovese understood the difference between explanation and dogma. Born in 1930 in Brooklyn in a rather apolitical working-class home, headed by a hard-nosed dockworker, he became close during his early teens to an uncle, a left-wing labor activist. Inspired by his uncle's passion and commitment, Gene at fifteen moved into the Communist youth movement and envisioned a life dedicated to organizing workers and building a socialist society.[1] "As a young Communist militant in the late 1940s," he later wrote, he aspired to be fully engaged in "political action."[2] But being a member of an organized and disciplined movement meant that his aspirations had to be subordinated to the Party's determination of how to best utilize his talents. With the Party's encouragement he enrolled in Brooklyn College, but he resented having to spend time and energy with his studies rather than on what he considered the far more valuable work of political organizing. In a 1978 interview, Gene described himself during those undergraduate days at Brooklyn College as "very anti-intellectual. I was an activist and not at all interested in either Marxist theory or intellectual work in general ... I hated the intellectual. I was very contemptuous of the whole business and very single-minded in

---

[1] Betsey appreciated the contingent nature of Gene's encounter with his uncle even more than Gene did. Imagine, she mused, how much Gene's life might have been different had that uncle been, say, a Catholic priest.

[2] Eugene D. Genovese, *In Red and Black: Marxian Explorations in Southern and Afro-American History* (Knoxville, TN, 1984 [1970]), viii.

my activist commitment."[3] But being a young Communist at Brooklyn College in those days, especially in Professor Hans Rosenberg's history classes, meant having to become well versed in Marxist theory – if only to defend oneself from the attacks of political and ideological enemies within the classroom, which Gene lovingly described as a "war zone."[4] By 1950 the eager organizer decided rather grudgingly "to leave, what had amounted to full-time political work for scholarship." Even after his expulsion from the Communist Party ("I zigged when I was supposed to zag"), his service in the army during the Korean War, and his graduate work at Columbia, Gene remained "rent by his decision" to become an academic, which he "considered a dismal settling for second best and a waste of what appeared to be my primary talent." But he eventually "learned to enjoy the work,"[5] and in the process came to understand how liberating it was, how peculiarly suited he was for the task, and how engaging the past as a professional historian to the best of his ability fulfilled both his personal desire for a meaningful life and his political, indeed moral, commitment to contributing to a better world. Gene ended up where he was meant to be; his vocation answered the bell.

For the rest of his life, he never doubted that he had made the right decision, especially as he proceeded more deeply into what he always referred to as his "life's work," the history of the slaveholders of the Old South. He not only made peace with academic work, but came to champion the notion that scholarship could be ennobling, regardless of the subject one studied. What he said as a socialist in 1970 remained true to him long after he abandoned socialism: "[S]ocialists (and all decent human beings) have a duty to contribute through their particular callings to the dignity of human life, a part of which is the preservation of the record of all human existence."[6] Gene never labored as a historian to win accolades nor even remotely to secure tenure or promotion or to pay the bills. An iron self-discipline prohibited any lapses into self-congratulation or self-indulgence. Gene wrote to be read, by literate laypersons as well as scholars. He sought, above all, to contribute to the collective project of

---

[3] See Eugene Genovese and Ronald Radosh, "An Interview with Eugene Genovese: The Rise of a Marxist Historian," *Change*, Vol. 10, No. 10 (November, 1978), 34.

[4] Genovese, "Hans Rosenberg at Brooklyn College: A Communist Student's Recollections of the Classroom as War Zone," *Central European History*, Vol. 24, No. 1 (1991), 51. The article is included in Eugene D. Genovese, *The Southern Front: History and Politics in the Cultural War* (Columbia, MO, 1995).

[5] Genovese and Radosh, "An Interview," 34.

[6] Genovese, "On Being a Socialist and a Historian," in *In Red and Black*, 5.

historical understanding, convinced that such understanding enriched us as human beings, contributed to the common good, and helped the best of political people avoid the grossest of errors.

II

The Sweetness of Life provides a fitting coda to Gene's "life's work," which spanned five decades and shaped more than a generation of scholarship on the subjects of slavery and the Old South. "With *The Political Economy of Slavery*," he wrote in 1989, "I began to try to tell the story of a great historical tragedy." In large part *The Sweetness of Life* stands as an attempt to complete the story during the last years of his life. Largely but not necessarily fully, for the hard drive I received back in 2014 contains several unfinished but intriguing manuscripts that testify to Gene's seemingly inexhaustible curiosity for and knowledge of the world the slaveholders made. Like *The Sweetness of Life*, these incomplete projects – on the southern oratorical tradition, on crime and justice, on education, and on democracy and hierarchy in southern political culture – reflect the years Gene spent sifting through mountains of evidence – private papers, pamphlets, sermons, published reminiscences, journals, books – years of work that made him intimately familiar with and constantly intrigued by his subjects. And the unfinished manuscripts contain the penetrating insight and analytical flair that made him one of the great historians and prose stylists of the past half-century. Most of all, they reflect the passion he had for all aspects of a society that elicited both admiration and condemnation from him, that reflected both the noble and ignoble aspects of the human beings – both black and white, slave and free – who inhabited it. He never tired of his subjects, never seriously considered changing his scholarly focus on the masters. For him, the slaveholders, like any group of people who build a civilization, proved to be anything but one- or two-dimensional. The more he studied them, the more they revealed the complexities of themselves, their world, and the human condition. The complexity of his subjects and their world and his own understanding of his profession demanded that he explore indefatigably the entirety of their internal and external worlds.

Gene grappled throughout his professional life with the tensions that resulted from the historian's search for "truth" and the inherently subjective nature of the historian. While labeling as "illusion" the notion that "a historian could proceed without a worldview and attendant political bias and somehow arrive at an objectivity that one might have thought only God capable of," he nonetheless emphatically insisted that "the inevitability of ideological bias does not free us from the responsibility to struggle for maximum objectivity"; "we must rein in our prejudices if we wish to do honest scientific work" and strive "to approximate [objectivity] as closely as possible."[7] His professional commitment to his vocation as a historian compelled him to mine evidence in the deepest caverns and then to sift through it and assay it with the greatest of care to provide the interpretation that best captured the reality of the antebellum South's slave society. His personal beliefs, his political convictions, even his religious faith, although never silent in the undertaking, were never allowed to predominate, never allowed to impose a telos or ideological abridgement that distorted what his sources were telling him about his subjects. For Gene, and for any honest historian, ensuring the integrity of the approach proved challenging, especially for a man who had such passionate beliefs and convictions. "My biggest problem as a historian," he said in a 1998 interview, "has always been, I suppose, the conscious effort to rein in that hatred [of the bourgeoisie] and not let it distort my reading of the historical record."[8] No one reading any of Gene's work can miss his presence; he did not write as a dispassionate scientist. But he believed that his work had value not because it advanced a political cause or an ideological objective. True to his calling, as he understood it, he saw the value of his work primarily in its contribution "to the dignity of human life, a part of which is the preservation of the record of all human existence." The record he believed he was called to preserve was that of the human beings who inhabited the Old South, and he pursued that calling with a passion that reflected a dynamic heat that resulted from the disciplining of his political passions by the high authority of his professional standards.

The Sweetness of Life does reflect, as Gene makes explicit in his introductory remarks, his fondness for the slaveholders and his appreciation of the "many admirable qualities" of their way of life. But his fondness for them and his appreciation of the "admirable qualities" of both themselves and the world they made did not blind him either to their "brutal oppression of black people" or to the "tragedy with which their finest qualities proceeded *pari passu* with their worst in defense of a historical

---

[7] Eugene D. Genovese, "Marxism, Christianity, and Bias in the Study of Southern Slave Society," in Genovese, *The Southern Front*, 3, 6.

[8] "Eugene D. Genovese and History: An Interview," in Robert Louis Paquette and Louis A. Ferleger, *Slavery, Secession, and Southern History* (Charlottesville, VA, 2000), 201.

enormity."[9] He did, indeed, "like them." But liking or disliking them was never, for Gene, the point of devoting his life to studying them. He wanted to grasp their essence, their collective mind(s), who they actually were, for only by doing so could one understand the complex patterns of southern life, the classes that wove them, and the South's collision course with the North. "I remain convinced," he wrote in 1987, "that those who are unwilling or unable to understand the history of the ruling classes will never understand any history at all and certainly not the history of the classes ruled."[10]

What mattered to Gene most, through all the political battles, academic arguments, and personal attacks, was whether he had fulfilled his calling, whether he had read the historical record correctly, whether his "considered judgment" had done justice to his subjects. "One way or the other," he remarked upon reflecting on his career, "the only thing I have ever cared about is the extent to which my interpretation of the slave society of the Old South will prove as accurate and useful as one can reasonably hope for."[11] He cared – passionately – about his profession, and *The Sweetness of Life* affords us an additional chapter of his "life's work" to "preserve the record" of the world antebellum Southerners made. He died hoping that it, like all his scholarship, might provide an "accurate and useful" contribution to "the dignity of human life."

---

[9] Genovese, *Sweetness of Life*, ***.
[10] Eugene D. Genovese, *The World the Slaveholders Made: Two Essays in Interpretation* (Middletown, CT 1988 [1969]), xxii.
[11] "Genovese: An Interview," in Paquette and Ferleger, eds., *Slavery, Secession, and Southern History*, 210.

Index